Albert Vathapally.

Global History and Geography

Steven Goldberg / Judith Clark DuPré

Ordering Information

Send orders to:
  Pearson
  PO Box 6820
  Chandler, AZ 85246

or call toll free:
  1-800-848-9500
  (8:00 A.M.-6:00 P.M. EST)

or order online:
  k12oasis.pearson.com

School orders:
  k12.oasis.pearson.com

Individual orders:
  pearsonschool.com/nybriefreviews

 **Pearson**

13-digit ISBN 978-0-328-98337-7
10-digit ISBN 0-328-98337-3

2 18

Table of Contents

About This Book vi
The Social Studies Standards viii
Key Themes and Concepts ix
Preparing for the Regents xii
Unit Pre-Tests xxxvii

New York Standards

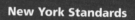

Standard   Key Idea

4.2

Unit 1 — An Age of Revolutions (1750–1914)   1

Section 1	Scientific Revolution and Enlightenment	2
Section 2	Political Revolutions	6
Section 3	Reaction Against Revolutionary Ideals	14
Section 4	Global Nationalism	20
Section 5	Economic and Social Revolutions	25
Section 6	Japan and the Meiji Restoration	32
Section 7	Imperialism	35

Questions for Regents Practice	41
Thematic Essay Question	43
Document-Based Question	44

Unit 1 Standards

1.1   2.1   3.1   4.1   5.1
       2.2
       2.3
       2.4

Unit 2 — Crises and Achievements (1900–1945)   47

Section 1	Scientific and Technological Achievements	48
Section 2	World War I	52
Section 3	Revolution in Russia: Causes and Impacts	58
Section 4	Between the Wars	64
Section 5	World War II	72

Questions for Regents Practice	78
Thematic Essay Question	81
Document-Based Question	82

Unit 2 Standards

1.1   2.1   3.1   4.1   5.1
       2.2
       2.3
       2.4

Table of Contents

New York Standards

Unit 3 **The Twentieth Century and Beyond (1945–The Present)**   **87**

Section 1	Cold War Balance of Power	88
Section 2	Economic Issues	95
Section 3	Chinese Communist Revolution	100
Section 4	Collapse of European Imperialism	104
Section 5	Conflicts and Change in the Middle East	111
Section 6	Collapse of Communism and the Soviet Union	117
Section 7	Political and Economic Change in Latin America	122

Questions for Regents Practice	126
Thematic Essay Question	129
Document-Based Question	130

Unit 3 Standards

1.1	2.1	3.1	4.1	5.1
1.2	2.2			
1.3	2.3			
1.4	2.4			

Unit 4 **The World Today: Connections and Interactions (1980–The Present)**   **135**

Section 1	Economic Trends	136
Section 2	Conflicts and Peace Efforts	144
Section 3	Social Patterns and Political Change	155
Section 4	Science and Technology	163
Section 5	The Environment	168

Questions for Regents Practice	174
Thematic Essay Question	176
Document-Based Question	177

Unit 4 Standards

1.1	2.1	3.1	4.1	5.1
1.2	2.2		4.2	
	2.3			
	2.4			

Thematic Review	TR-1
Glossary	G-1
Index	I-1
Acknowledgments	C-1
Regents Examination – January 2017	
Regents Examination – August 2016	
Regents Examination – June 2016	
Regents Examination – January 2016	
Regents Examination – August 2015	
Regents Examination – June 2015	
Regents Examination Draft – April 2016	

About This Book

This book has been written to help you, the student, review the tenth-grade global history and geography course. Its purposes are to:

- Help you focus on the key facts, themes, and concepts that you need to know to succeed on the Regents Examination in global history and geography.
- Allow you to become familiar with the format of the new transition Regents Examination.
- Provide you with the test-taking skills you will need to apply your social studies knowledge to the Regents Examination.

In This Book

The ninth-grade global history and geography curriculum introduced you to many of the events that happened during the earliest periods of global history. Although this book covers only the tenth-grade curriculum, it builds on what you learned in grade nine. It presents the tenth-grade curriculum chronologically. In other words, it is presented in time order starting about 1750 and continuing to the present. Within this organization, there has been a careful attempt to group the material in meaningful eras, or periods of time, in which certain types of activities were going on all over the world. For example, Unit 1 covers the period from 1750 through 1914. During this period of more than 160 years, revolutions were occurring all over the world, and nations formed and grew strong.

In the ninth-grade curriculum, you were introduced to key themes and concepts. This book highlights how these key themes and concepts continue to be woven through modern history. Concentrating on themes and concepts will help you organize the global history and geography that you have studied. It will also start you thinking about history in ways that will help you excel on the Regents Examination.

Four Overall Themes

Four overall themes—history; geography; economics; and civics, citizenship, and government—draw these units together. As you review and study, these themes will help you make connections between different times and places. In the side column, several types of help are available.

- **The Big Idea** notes at the beginning of each section organize the section content at a glance. This feature highlights key content in list form.
- **Preparing for the Regents** notes provide questions, explanations, and activities that will give you practice in applying your knowledge to Regents-type questions.
- **Key Themes and Concepts** notes summarize important content and link it to key themes and concepts.

Other sections of this book are also important.

- **Preparing for the Regents** provides instructions and hints for Regents success, using questions like those you will see on the test.
- **Questions for Regents Practice**, found at the end of each unit, will help you figure out your strengths and weaknesses as you practice taking the test.
- **Sample Regents Examinations** also appear at the back of the book.
- **Thematic Review** reviews key content within those themes that the Regents Examination may focus on.

Transition to the new Social Studies Framework

Pearson is committed to supporting the Common Core Standards and the New York State K12 Social Studies Framework. With that in mind, this Brief Review includes new Unit Opener activities for understanding and applying good Social Studies practices. Updated skills notes reinforce Social Studies Practices from the new framework and Common Core skills.

The goal of this book is to help you attain success on the Regents Examination. It will focus your efforts and give you the tools to master the material and present it effectively. Best of luck on exam day!

About the Consulting Authors

Steven Goldberg

Steven Goldberg is the District Chairperson of Social Studies for the City School District of New Rochelle. He received his bachelor's degree in history from the University of Rochester, a master's degree in East Asian Studies from Yale University, and an administrative certificate from Teachers' College, Columbia University. He was a Fulbright Fellow to the Netherlands and studied at Sophia University in Tokyo. He is past president of both the New York State Council for the Social Studies and the New York State Social Studies Supervisory Association and has served on the executive board of the Westchester Council of the Social Studies and the National Council for the Social Studies. A consultant to the State Education Department, he has been on numerous Regents Examination committees, as well as the design team for Global History and Geography.

Judith Clark DuPré

Judith Clark DuPré is a retired social studies teacher from the Fairport School District and current College Supervisor for student teachers at the Ralph C. Wilson School of Education at St. John Fisher College. She received her bachelor's and master's degrees from the State University of New York, Brockport. She is past-president of the Rochester Area Council for the Social Studies, is a member of the New York State Council for the Social Studies, and served on the Advisory Council of the International Studies Program at St. John Fisher College. She has received numerous local, state, and national teaching awards. She was a Fulbright Fellow in China and has studied in Germany and Japan. As a consultant to the State Education Department, she has served on numerous Regents Examination Committees and contributed to several curriculum projects in Global Studies and Global History and Geography.

The Social Studies Standards

Standard 1:
History of the United States and New York

Students will use a variety of intellectual skills to demonstrate their understanding of major ideas, eras, themes, developments, and turning points in the history of the United States and New York.

Standard 2:
World History

Students will use a variety of intellectual skills to demonstrate their understanding of major ideas, eras, themes, developments, and turning points in world history from a variety of perspectives.

Standard 3:
Geography

Students will use a variety of intellectual skills to demonstrate their understanding of the geography of the interdependent world in which we live—local, national, and global—including the distribution of people, places, and environments over Earth's surface.

Standard 4:
Economics

Students will use a variety of intellectual skills to demonstrate their understanding of how the United States and other societies develop economic systems and associated institutions to allocate scarce resources, how major decision-making units function in the United States and other national economies, and how an economy solves the scarcity problem through market and nonmarket economies.

Standard 5:
Civics, Citizenship, and Government

Students will use a variety of intellectual skills to demonstrate their understanding of the necessity for establishing governments; the governmental system of the United States and other nations; the U.S. Constitution; the basic civic values of American constitutional democracy; and the roles, rights, and responsibilities of citizenship, including avenues of participation.

Key Themes and Concepts

Global history and geography can be best understood if it is organized by studying key themes and key concepts that recur in many times and places. Themes and concepts are mental images and classifications that help you to:

- understand important ideas.
- recognize global connections and linkages.
- see similarities and differences among events.
- determine the causes that lead up to events and the effects that result from events.

The Regents Examination uses a number of themes and concepts in constructing questions for the test. They are listed and explained below in four categories: history; geography; economics; and civics, citizenship, and government.

History: Some Key Themes and Concepts

- **Belief Systems** means the established, orderly ways in which groups or individuals look at religious faith or philosophical tenets.
- **Change** is a basic alteration in things, events, and ideas.
- **Choice** means the right or power to select from a range of alternatives.
- **Conflict** is disagreement or opposition between ideas or groups, which may lead to an armed struggle.
- **Culture and Intellectual Life** means the patterns of human behavior that include ideas, beliefs, values, artifacts, and ways of making a living that any society transmits to succeeding generations to meet its fundamental needs. It also includes ways of thinking, studying, and reflecting on ideas and life.
- **Diversity** means understanding and respecting others and oneself, including any similarities or differences in language, gender, socioeconomic class, religion, and other human characteristics and traits.
- **Empathy** means the ability to understand others through identifying in oneself responses similar to the experiences, behaviors, and responses of others.
- **Identity** means awareness of one's own values, attitudes, and capabilities as an individual and as a member of various groups.
- **Imperialism** means the domination by one country of the political and/or economic life of another country or region.
- **Interdependence** means reliance upon others in mutually beneficial interactions and exchanges.
- **Movement of People and Goods** is the exchange of people, ideas, products, technologies, and institutions from one region or civilization to another, a process that has existed throughout history.
- **Nationalism** means a feeling of pride in and devotion to one's country or the desire of a people to control their own government, free from foreign interference or rule.
- **Urbanization** means the movement of people from rural to urban (city) areas.

Key Themes and Concepts

Geography: Some Key Themes and Concepts

The six essential elements of geography follow.

- **The World in Spatial Terms**—Geography studies the relationships among people, places, and environments by mapping information about them in a spatial context.
- **Places and Regions**—The identities and lives of individuals and peoples are rooted in particular places and in those human constructs called regions.
- **Physical Systems**—Physical processes, such as erosion and flooding, shape Earth's surface and interact with plant and animal life to create, sustain, and modify ecosystems.
- **Human Systems**—People are central to geography in that human activities help shape Earth's surface, human settlements and structures are part of Earth's surface, and humans compete for control of Earth's surface.
- **Environment and Society**—Environment means surroundings, including natural elements and elements created by humans. The physical environment is modified by human activities, largely as a consequence of the ways in which human societies value and use Earth's natural resources, and human activities are also influenced by Earth's physical features and processes.
- **The Uses of Geography**—Knowledge of geography enables people to develop an understanding of the relationships between people, places, and environments over time—that is, of Earth as it was, is, and might be.

Economics: Some Key Themes and Concepts

- **Economic Systems** include traditional, command, market, and mixed systems. Each must answer the three basic economic questions: What goods and services are to be produced and in what quantities? How shall these goods and services be produced? For whom shall goods and services be produced?
- **Factors of Production** are human, natural, and capital resources that, when combined, can be converted to various goods and services (for example, land, labor, and capital are used to produce food).
- **Needs and Wants** means those goods and services that are essential, such as food, clothing, and shelter (needs), and those goods and services that people would like to have to improve the quality of their lives, such as education, security, health care, and entertainment (wants).
- **Scarcity** means the conflict between unlimited needs and wants and limited natural and human resources.
- **Science and Technology** means the tools and methods used by people to get what they need and want.

Civics, Citizenship, and Government:
Some Key Themes and Concepts

- **Citizenship** means membership in a community (neighborhood, school, region, state, nation, world) with its accompanying rights, responsibilities, and dispositions.

- **Civic Values** are those important principles that serve as the foundation for our democratic form of government. These values include justice; honesty; self-discipline; due process of law; equality; majority rule with respect for minority rights; and respect of self, others, and property.

- **Decision Making** means the process through which people monitor and influence public and civil life by working with others, clearly articulating ideals and interests, building coalition, seeking consensus, negotiating compromise, and managing conflict.

- **Government** means the formal institutions and processes of a politically organized society with authority to make, enforce, and interpret laws and other binding rules about matters of common interest and concern. Government also refers to the group of people—acting in formal political institutions at national, state, and local levels—who exercise decision-making power or enforce laws and regulations.

- **Human Rights** are those basic political, economic, and social rights to which all human beings are entitled, such as the right to life, liberty, security of person, and a standard of living adequate for the health and well-being of oneself and one's family. Human rights are inalienable and are expressed in various United Nations documents, including the United Nations Charter and the *Universal Declaration of Human Rights.*

- **Justice** means fair, equal, proportional, or appropriate treatment rendered to individuals in interpersonal, societal, or government interactions.

- **Nation-State** means a geographic/political organization that unites people through a common government.

- **Political Systems** include monarchies, dictatorships, and democracies and address certain basic questions of government, such as: What should a government have the power to do? What should a government not have the power to do? A political system also provides for ways in which parts of that system interrelate and combine to perform specific functions of government.

- **Power** is the ability of people to compel or influence the actions of others. Legitimate, or rightful, power is called authority.

This section of the book provides you with strategies for success on the Regents Examination in Global History and Geography. Because you will need to pass the examination in order to graduate from high school, these strategies are important for you to learn and master. They will also help you to succeed in other types of academic work.

Understanding Social Studies

To do well in your study of global history and geography and to pass the Regents Examination, you need to understand three related elements of social studies. On the Regents Examination, you will be asked to demonstrate your mastery of the *factual content* of the global history and geography course, the *concepts* that recur over time, and the *skills* you have mastered.

Specific Factual Content

In a social studies course, you learn about specific historical events and figures. For example, you learn that the French Revolution occurred in 1789 and that Napoleon carried its ideals throughout much of Europe. This is part of the specific content of the global history and geography course you are taking.

Concepts

In social studies courses, you also learn about themes and concepts such as *change and nationalism*. (See "Key Themes and Concepts," which begins on page ix of this book.) You learn how the French Revolution brought change to France and other lands. You also examine the role that this revolution played in developing and spreading nationalism. In addition, you link developments in France to developments in other places and at different times. You may discuss the similarities and differences in other revolutions, or the types of factors that lead to revolutionary movements. Understanding these connections across place and time is as important as knowing facts about the events themselves.

Skills

In a social studies course, you acquire skills. These skills help you to gather, organize, use, and present information. For example, you learn to interpret various types of documents. Historical documents include maps, graphs, and political cartoons. When you read a circle graph that illustrates class structure and land ownership in France, or when you interpret a political cartoon about Napoleon, you are using social studies skills.

A Glossary of Skill Words

The following is a glossary of skill words that you will see often on the Regents Examination and in other social studies materials. Comprehending these words will help you do well on the Regents Examination.

Analyze to break an idea or concept into parts in order to determine their nature and relationships

Assess to determine the importance, significance, size, or value of

Categorize to place in a class or group; to classify

Classify to arrange in classes or to place in a group according to a system

Compare to state the similarities between two or more examples

Contrast to differentiate; to state the differences between two or more examples

Define to explain what something is or means

Describe to illustrate in words; to tell about

Develop to explain more clearly; to reveal bit by bit

Differentiate to state the difference or differences among two or more examples

Discuss to make observations using facts, reasoning, and argument; to present in some detail

Evaluate to examine and judge the significance, worth, or condition of; to determine the value of

Explain to make plain or understandable; to give reasons for

Generalize to reach a broad conclusion, avoiding specifics, or to base an overall law on particular examples

Hypothesize to present an explanation or an assumption that remains to be proved

Identify to establish the essential character of

Illustrate to make clear or obvious by using examples or comparisons

Incorporate to introduce into or include as a part of something

Infer to conclude or judge from evidence; to draw a conclusion through reasoning

Investigate to research; to inquire into and examine with care

Organize to arrange in a systematic way

Recognize to identify by appearance or characteristics

Restate to say again in a slightly different way

Scrutinize to investigate closely; to examine or inquire into critically

Show to point out; to set forth clearly a position or idea by stating it and giving data that support it

Structure of the Regents Examination

You will have three hours to complete the Regents Examination. The test will include three types of questions.

Multiple-Choice Questions

Together, the multiple-choice questions will account for 55 percent of the points to be earned. There will be 30 multiple-choice questions on the transition Regents Examination in Global History and Geography. Four possible choices will be provided for each question, only one of which is correct.

Preparing for the Regents

Thematic Essay Question

There will be one question of this type on the test. You will be asked to write a thematic essay on a particular topic. Clear and definite directions will be provided to guide you in writing your essay.

Document-Based Question

There will be one multisection document-based question. This question has two major parts. Part A requires that you look at several historical documents and answer one or more questions about each one. Part B requires that you write a clear essay, using evidence from these documents and your knowledge of global history and geography.

You will find examples of all of these types of questions at the end of every unit, in the sample tests, and in the part of the book you are now reading. By working with these examples, you will become familiar with the Regents Examination and build skills for approaching these types of questions. This work will help you get the highest score possible.

Part I: Multiple Choice	50 questions	Approximately 55% of exam grade
Part II: Thematic Essay	1 question based on a specific theme	Approximately 15% of exam grade
Part III: Document-Based Question	Part A: Scaffolding (documents) Part B: Essay	Approximately 15% of exam grade Approximately 15% of exam grade

Strategies for the Regents Examination

The Regents Examination will cover material that you studied in your Global History and Geography course. Some subjects are more likely to appear on the test than others, however. This book will help you review these topics thoroughly.

This book will also teach you how to approach the topics in ways that will help you succeed on all parts of the Regents Examination. Several concepts are especially important.

Understanding the Themes

The test will be built around major themes that recur throughout history. Many themes are listed and defined for you in the Key Themes and Concepts portion of this book. The most common Regents themes are reviewed with examples in the Thematic Review section of this book. As you prepare for the Regents Examination, keep in mind the themes that are most likely to appear on the test. Make sure that you understand these themes and can provide examples of each. Some of the most important themes are listed below.

Belief Systems

Change

Conflict

Culture and Intellectual Life

Diversity

Economic Systems

Geography and the Environment

Imperialism

Interdependence

Justice and Human Rights

Movement of People and Goods (Cultural Diffusion)

Nationalism

Political Systems

Science and Technology

Urbanization

Making Connections Across Place and Time

You will do well on the test if you can make connections among events and developments in different parts of the world and in different time periods. As you study various regions and eras, try to see similarities and differences in events that took place. For example, revolutions occurred in many parts of the world in the 1700s and 1800s. How were these revolutions similar? How were they different? How did earlier revolutions have an impact on later ones? As you review global history and geography, look for patterns and generalizations that hold true across place and time.

Understanding Causes and Impacts

The Regents Examination will also require that you understand the cause-and-effect links between events. As you review major events and turning points, make sure that you understand the factors and conditions that caused them. Then make sure that you can explain the impacts that these events had on later developments.

Practice in Analyzing Documents

This review book provides you with many historical documents, including written documents, maps, tables, charts, graphs, and political cartoons. The multiple-choice and document-based parts of the test will require you to analyze many types of documents. You will be expected to take into account both the source of each document and the author's point of view.

Developing Your Writing Skills

You will earn a higher score on the test if you practice and improve your ability to communicate through writing. Essay-writing skills are required for both the thematic essay and the document-based question. It is most important to write essays that demonstrate a logical plan of organization and include a strong introduction and conclusion.

Multiple-Choice Questions

More than half of the points to be earned on the Regents Examination (55 percent) are earned by answering multiple-choice questions. You will therefore want to get the highest possible score in this section.

Preparing for the Regents

Strategies for Multiple-Choice Questions

Keep several points in mind when you are answering the multiple-choice questions on the Regents Examination.

1. Read the entire question carefully. Read all the choices before you make a decision.
2. Eliminate any choices that you are sure are not true, crossing them out in the test booklet.
3. Remember that in the Regents Examination, there is no penalty for guessing. (This is *not* true of all multiple-choice tests.) Therefore, you should make your best guess at an answer to *every* question.
4. See if there is a key phrase that signals what you should be looking for in the question. Not all questions have such phrases. However, you should be aware of certain signal words and phrases.

Signals for Questions About Cause and Effect: *one effect, one result, is most directly influenced by, have led directly to, have resulted in, a major cause of, are a direct result of*

Signals for Questions That Require an Example: *best illustrates, best reflects, are all examples of, best explains, is an example of*

Signals for Questions That Ask for a Main Idea: *main idea, primarily characterized by, formed the basis for*

Signals for Questions That Ask About Similarities or Differences: *are similar, one similarity, one difference between*

Types of Multiple-Choice Questions

Although you will see many types of multiple-choice questions on the Regents Examination, all fall into one or more of the following general categories.

Unit Content Questions The test will include multiple-choice questions that cover material from each of the four units in this book.

Cross-Unit Questions Questions that ask you to respond to historical situations or people discussed in several different units will also appear on the test. These questions often ask you to make a deduction that is *valid* (true) about the situations or people, find a *similarity* between them, or identify a *characteristic* that is common to all.

Thematic Questions Some questions will address general social studies themes such as nationalism, imperialism, political systems, or economic systems. These questions often ask you to provide *the best example of* something, explain *how it developed,* or describe *characteristics of* a particular concept or system. The themes that these questions may deal with are listed in the Key Themes and Concepts section of this book and highlighted in the Thematic Review.

Questions Based on Documents Some multiple-choice questions are based on documents. Types of documents that may appear include:

- A short passage
- A map
- A graph
- A table or chart
- A political cartoon

Such document-based questions often ask for the *main idea* of a passage or cartoon. Sometimes they ask you to identify an *accurate statement* or the statement *best supported by the data*. They may also ask you to choose the *valid conclusion* drawn from the document. These types of questions often require both skills in interpreting documents and factual knowledge of global history and geography.

Sample Unit Content Questions

Each of the next two questions tests your knowledge of content from a specific unit of the Global History and Geography course.

1   A negative effect of the partitioning of India in 1947 was that
     (1) foreign rule was reestablished in India
     (2) Hinduism became the only religion practiced in India
     (3) the government policy of nonalignment further divided Indian society
     (4) civil unrest, territorial disputes, and religious conflict continued
          throughout the region

You know from the question that the answer must be an *effect* and that it must be *negative*. Choice 1 cannot be the answer, since British rule ended in 1947. Choice 2 is incorrect because Islam, Sikhism, and other religions besides Hinduism are practiced in India. Choice 3 cannot be correct, since nonalignment was a reaction to the Cold War, not to partition. Choice 4 is the correct answer because the creation of Pakistan and India increased tensions and conflicts between Hindus and Muslims in the region.

2   As a result of the Russo-Japanese War, Japan came to be seen by Europeans as
     (1) a likely area for colonization
     (2) the strongest of the imperialist countries
     (3) a leader in the movement for nonalignment
     (4) an emerging global threat

Japan was never an area of colonization (Choice 1). The Western powers did not seize land from Japan as they did in other areas of Asia (Choice 2). Great Britain was considered the strongest of the imperialist countries ("the sun never sets on the British Empire") (Choice 3). The nonalignment movement refers to a policy followed by some Third World nations (e.g., Egypt, India) during the Cold War. It was a policy of not supporting either the United States or the Soviet Union. Choice 4 is the correct answer. As a result of Japan's defeat of Russia in the Russo-Japanese War, Japan came to be seen by the Europeans as an emerging global threat. It was the first time that an Asian nation had defeated a European nation.

Sample Thematic Questions

Each of the next two multiple-choice questions deals with a specific theme or concept.

3   Which aspect of a nation's culture is most directly influenced by the physical
     geography of that nation?
     (1) form of government
     (2) population distribution
     (3) religious beliefs
     (4) social class system

The question involves physical geography and its influence on a nation. The key phrase in the question is *is most directly influenced*. If you understand physical geography, you know that it has a great influence on where people live. For example,

Preparing for the Regents

people tend to live near sources of water. Large populations live where the geography easily allows settlement. The answer to this question would therefore be Choice 2. Geography sometimes influences forms of government (Choice 1), as in the Greek city-states, but it has a more direct influence on population distribution. It has even less influence on religious beliefs (Choice 3) and the social class system (Choice 4).

4   Which quotation best reflects a feeling of nationalism?
     (1) "An eye for an eye and a tooth for a tooth."
     (2) "A person's greatest social obligation is loyalty to the family."
     (3) "For God, King, and Country."
     (4) "Opposition to evil is as much a duty as is cooperation with good."

This question is about nationalism, a theme you need to understand to prepare for the Regents Examination. First, you must know what nationalism is: a feeling of pride in and devotion to one's country. Then you must decide which of the possible answers best expresses that idea. Choice 1 has to do with justice, not nationalism. Choice 2 has to do with social behavior and Choice 4 with moral behavior. Only Choice 3 expresses the idea of devotion to one's nation, so Choice 3 is the correct answer.

Sample Cross-Unit Questions
Each of the next two questions deals with content from two or more units of the Global History and Geography course.

5   One similarity found in the leadership of Peter the Great of Russia, Kemal Atatürk of Turkey, and Jawaharlal Nehru of India is that each leader
     (1) expanded his territory by invading Greece
     (2) borrowed ideas and technology from Western Europe
     (3) supported equal rights for women
     (4) increased the power of religious groups in his nation

Each of these leaders appears in a different unit of this book. Note that this question asks for *one similarity*. This means that the answer must be true for all three leaders. Therefore, if you know that a choice is not true of even one leader, it cannot be the right answer. Choice 1 is not correct because none of the three leaders invaded Greece. Although each of these leaders supported some reforms or societal changes that involved women, none called for equal rights for women, so Choice 3 is incorrect. Peter the Great and Kemal Atatürk actually decreased the power of religious groups in their nations, so Choice 4 cannot be correct. All of these leaders did, however, borrow ideas and technology from the West, making Choice 2 the correct answer.

6   "Liberty, Equality, Fraternity" and "Peace, Land, and Bread" are slogans used by revolutionaries to represent
     (1) frameworks for economic stability
     (2) political and economic ideals
     (3) plans for maintaining the social hierarchy
     (4) methods of political reform

"Liberty, Equality, Fraternity" became popular during the French Revolution in the 1790's and today is the French national motto. "Peace, Land, and Bread" was used by Lenin, the leader of the Bolshevik Party, to gain support of the peasants

during the Russian Revolution of 1917 in an effort to win popular support to overthrow the provisional Russian government after the czar was removed. Choice 1 is incorrect, because neither of these slogans had an outline to provide for economic stability. They were slogans to promote revolutionary ideals. Choice 3 is not correct because the goals of these slogans was to end the social hierarchy, not preserve it. These slogans also did not outline methods of political reform. They were designed to gain popular support and did not provide specific methods of political reform, so Choice 4 cannot be correct. "Liberty, Equality, Fraternity" and "Peace, Land, and Bread" are political slogans used by revolutionaries to represent political and economic ideas. (Choice 2 is correct).

Sample Document-Based Questions

The remaining sample questions are based on historical documents.

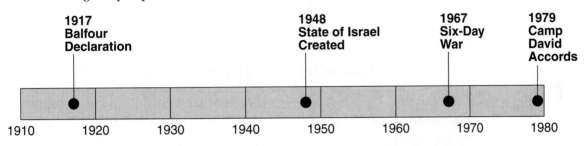

7   Which region is directly associated with the events shown on this time line?
   (1) Latin America
   (2) Middle East
   (3) Central Africa
   (4) Southeast Asia

Choices 1, 3, and 4 are incorrect. None of these regions are associated with the events shown on the time line. Choice 2 is correct. The Middle East is directly associated with the events shown on the time line. In 1917, the British government issued the Balfour Declaration, which promised to support a Jewish homeland in Palestine. The civil and religious rights of Arabs who were Muslim were guaranteed. After the Holocaust, the Jewish population in Palestine increased. In 1947, the United Nations drew up a plan to divide Palestine, which was under British rule, into an Arab and a Jewish state. In 1948, Israel proclaimed its independence. However, the Arabs refused to recognize the partition and invaded Israel. Israel won the war; additional wars ensued, including the Six-Day War in 1967. This resulted in significant territorial gains: the Golan Heights, the Gaza Strip, East Jerusalem, the Sinai Peninsula, and the West Bank. Israel refused to give up these territories until the Arab nations recognized Israel's right to exist. In 1979, Israel and Egypt signed the Camp David Accord, an agreement to end the state of war between the two countries. Egypt recognized the sovereignty of Israel and Israel returned the Sinai Peninsula to Egypt.

Base your answer to question 8 on the poem below and on your knowledge of social studies.

> May our country
> Taking what is good
> And rejecting what is bad
> Be not inferior
> to any other
> —Mutsuhito

8   According to this Japanese poem, Mutsuhito believed that Japan should modernize by
    (1) completely changing Japanese society
    (2) borrowing selectively from other societies
    (3) controlling other cultures that were superior
    (4) rejecting foreign influence

Here, you are asked to demonstrate understanding of Mutsuhito's poem. Choice 1 is not appropriate because the poem does not indicate whether Mutsuhito favored just a little change or massive change. Choice 3 is incorrect because the poem talks about borrowing from other cultures, not controlling them. Choice 4 is wrong because the poem advises rejection only of "what is bad." Choice 2 correctly summarizes the meaning of the poem.

Base your answer to questions 9 and 10 on the table below and on your knowledge of social studies.

Statistics for Selected Nations of South Asia

Nations	Bangladesh	Malaysia	Myanmar	Pakistan	Thailand
Population Density (per sq mi)	2,294	164	181	440	303
Per Capita Income (dollars)	1,260	10,750	1,120	2,300	7,700
Percentage of Labor Force in Agriculture	65	21	67	47	43
Literacy Rate (percentage)	38	83	83	38	94

9   Which nations have more than half of the labor force engaged in agriculture?
    (1) Bangladesh and Myanmar
    (2) Pakistan and Bangladesh
    (3) Thailand and Malaysia
    (4) Myanmar and Thailand

Question 9 asks you to examine one column of the table. Choices 2 and 3 are incorrect because none of those nations have more than 50 percent of the labor force engaged in agriculture. Choice 4 is incorrect because only Myanmar has the appropriate percentage. Choice 1 is correct, listing the two nations with more than half of the labor force in agriculture.

10   Which is a valid conclusion, based on the information in the table?
    (1) Bangladesh has the highest per capita income.
    (2) Myanmar has the smallest percentage of workers involved in farming.
    (3) Malaysia has the highest population density.
    (4) Thailand has the highest percentage of children enrolled in school.

For question 10, the correct answer is Choice 4. A high literacy rate (94 percent) indicates that a high percentage of children are learning to read in school. Choice 1 is not true: Bangladesh has nearly the lowest per capita income of the nations shown. Choice 2 is incorrect, since Myanmar has the highest percentage of workers involved in farming. Choice 3 is incorrect because Malaysia actually has the lowest population density, not the highest.

Base your answer to question 11 on the graph below and on your knowledge of social studies.

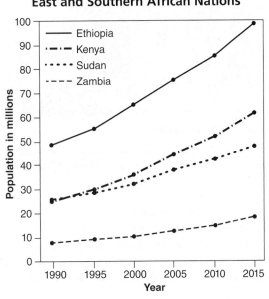

Population Projections for Selected East and Southern African Nations

Source: *The World Bank*

11 Based on the information in the graph, which is a valid conclusion about the populations of East and Southern African nations?
(1) The nation with the largest population in 1990 will have the lowest population in 2015.
(2) Population will rise in all countries, but it will rise fastest in Ethiopia.
(3) Populations will level off in all of these nations after the year 2005.
(4) In 1995, the population of Zambia was approximately 28 million people.

You can rule out Choice 1 because the ranks of the nations changed very little if at all. You can eliminate Choice 3 because one glance at the lines shows all four populations continuing to rise more steeply after 1995. You can rule out Choice 4 by reading the graph and seeing that Zambia's population in 1995 was about 10 million. Choice 2, however, is a valid conclusion to draw from this graph.

Base your answer to question 12 on the cartoon below and on your knowledge of social studies.

THE OLD MAN AND THE SEA

By permission of Rex Babin, *Times Union*, Albany, NY.

12   What is the main idea of the cartoon?
   (1) Cuba's fishing industry is suffering a decline.
   (2) Castro rode the wave of world communism to a successful conclusion.
   (3) Cuba is isolated without Soviet economic support.
   (4) Castro bears responsibility for the failure of communism in Eastern Europe.

Questions on political cartoons require skill in interpreting such cartoons as well as knowledge of global history. When you look at a political cartoon, make sure that you can identify its elements. Many are symbolic. For example, the small boat marked *Cuba* represents the country of Cuba. The figure in it is a caricature of Fidel Castro, the president of Cuba. The carcass of the fish has a hammer and sickle, the national symbol of the former Soviet Union. The image communicates the idea that the Soviet Union is dead.

Choice 1 is incorrect because the cartoon is clearly about political issues, not about the Cuban fishing industry. You can rule out Choice 2 because the figure in the boat does not look happy. Also, you have read that Cuba has experienced difficulty since the fall of communism. Choice 4 is not correct because Castro is feeling the *effects* of change; he was not the *cause*. That leaves only Choice 3, which you know to be true: Cuba has had difficulties without Soviet support.

Base your answer to question 13 on the cartoon below and on your knowledge of social studies.

13 Which conclusion is best supported by the cartoon?
(1) Imprisonment of political dissidents rarely ends opposition to the government.
(2) The United Nations supports punishment of acts of civil disobedience.
(3) Better media coverage would prevent the imprisonment of protesters.
(4) Mistreatment of political prisoners often results in their acceptance of government policies.

Again, you must first examine the cartoon and analyze its elements. The name *Mandela* and your knowledge of global history tell you that this cartoon shows the time when Nelson Mandela was in prison in South Africa. You notice that Mandela is of normal size when he enters prison in 1962 but has grown greatly by the time he emerges in 1990. His increased size represents his increased world stature during the time of his imprisonment. You can eliminate Choice 2 because it is untrue and because the United Nations is not featured in this cartoon. Choice 3 can be ruled out because media coverage is not shown by the cartoon. Choice 4 is also not supported by the cartoon, since there is no indication that Mandela accepted government policies. Instead, Mandela's changed size indicates that Choice 1 is the answer. Instead of stopping opposition by imprisoning Mandela, the South African government only succeeded in furthering his cause of opposition to apartheid.

Thematic Essay Question

There will be one thematic essay question on the Regents Examination. It will count for approximately 15 percent of the total points you may receive. This section of the exam requires you to understand, interpret, and explain a key social studies theme or concept. In your essay, you should be able to:

- State a main idea in a thesis statement.
- Develop it and add supporting details.
- Summarize it with an effective conclusion.

Basic Characteristics
The directions for thematic essay questions always consist of three parts: a theme, a task, and suggestions.

The Theme This part of the question identifies a broad social studies theme that will be the general topic of your essay. The theme is given more focus by a brief explanatory statement that follows the statement of the theme. (To review the most common themes tested in Regents Examinations, see the Thematic Review section at the end of this book.)

The Task The second part of a thematic essay question is the task. The task section usually has three parts and presents the instructions you will need to write your essay. Generally, you will be asked to define or describe a theme or concept, to give a specific number of examples or results, and then to evaluate the theme or concept in some way. Typical forms of evaluation include describing causes or effects and evaluating positive or negative aspects.

Suggestions The final part of a thematic essay question is the suggestions section. This part lists specific areas that you might choose to discuss in your essay. The suggestions might name people, nations, or civilizations, depending on the topic of the question. These are, of course, only suggestions, and you may choose to write about other examples that are relevant to the essay topic. Often, the suggestions will caution you not to choose the United States as your topic. If this warning is present, pay attention to it. You will not receive full credit for an answer that does not follow the directions.

Strategy for the Thematic Essay Question
Keep the following strategies in mind as you approach a thematic essay question.

1. Read the entire question through first.
2. After you have read the question, begin jotting down any ideas you have.
3. After you have jotted down your initial ideas, begin to make a brief outline. Organization is important in writing a good essay. The outline does not need to be very detailed, but it should include enough information to help you remember all the points that you want to use in the essay. It should also help you to see whether your essay has a logical organization.
4. Use the suggestions to help you recall the importance of the theme in different places and times.
5. Develop your essay logically.
6. Do not merely list facts. Analyze and evaluate the information, and compare or contrast various aspects.
7. Make sure that you provide examples to support your ideas.

8. Make sure that you have completed each of the items listed in the task section.
9. Make sure that your essay has both a strong introduction and a strong conclusion. You cannot get full credit for your essay if either of these elements is missing or weak.

Sample Thematic Essay Questions

The thematic essay questions included throughout this book will provide you with insight into the types of questions you will see on the actual Regents Examination. Below are two sample thematic essay questions. They follow the same format as those that will appear on the actual Regents Examination.

Sample One
Directions
Write a well-organized essay that includes an introduction, several paragraphs addressing the task below, and a conclusion.

Theme: Geography

> Geographic features can positively or negatively affect the development of a nation or region.

Task:

> Select *one* geographic feature from your study of global history.
>
> • Explain how this geographic feature has had an effect on the historical development of *two* nations or regions. Be sure to include specific historical examples in your essay.

You may use any geographic features from your study of global history. Some suggestions you might wish to consider include: river valley, mountain, desert, island, rain forest, and climate. Do not use the United States in your answer.

Sample Two
Directions
Write a well-organized essay that includes an introduction, several paragraphs addressing the task below, and a conclusion.

Theme: Revolution

> Throughout history, revolutions have developed in response to a variety of conditions. These revolutions have often resulted in significant political, economic, and social change.

Task:

> Select two revolutions and for each
>
> • Describe the historical circumstances leading to the revolution
> • Discuss the political, economic, and/or social effects of this revolution

You may use any revolution from your study of global history and geography. Some suggestions that you might wish to consider include the French Revolution, Haitian Revolution, Industrial Revolution, Russian Revolution, Cuban Revolution, Iranian Revolution, Green Revolution in Agriculture.

Thematic Essay Scoring

Knowing how your essay will be scored will help you write it effectively. Essays are scored with point values from 0 to 5. An essay receiving a score of 5 answers the question in a complete, comprehensive manner. You would receive a score of 0 only if you failed to address the theme at all, wrote an essay that was completely illegible, or turned in a blank paper.

The scoring rubric that follows represents the generic criteria on which your essay will be scored.

Generic Scoring Rubric

Thematic Essay
Score of 5:
- Thoroughly develops all aspects of the task evenly and in depth
- Is more analytical than descriptive (analyzes, evaluates, and/or creates information)
- Richly supports the theme with many relevant facts, examples, and details
- Demonstrates a logical and clear plan of organization; includes an introduction and a conclusion that are beyond a restatement of the theme

Score of 4:
- Develops all aspects of the task but may do so somewhat unevenly
- Is both descriptive and analytical (applies, analyzes, evaluates, and/or creates information)
- Supports the theme with relevant facts, examples, and details
- Demonstrates a logical and clear plan of organization; includes an introduction and a conclusion that are beyond a restatement of the theme

Score of 3:
- Develops all aspects of the task with little depth or develops most aspects of the task in some depth
- Is more descriptive than analytical (applies, may analyze, and/or evaluate information)
- Includes some relevant facts, examples, and details; may include some minor inaccuracies
- Demonstrates a satisfactory plan of organization; includes an introduction and a conclusion that may be a restatement of the theme

Score of 2:
- Minimally develops all aspects of the task or develops some aspects of the task in some depth
- Is primarily descriptive; may include faulty, weak, or isolated application or analysis
- Includes few relevant facts, examples, and details; may include some inaccuracies
- Demonstrates a general plan of organization; may lack focus; may contain digressions; may not clearly identify which aspect of the task is being addressed; may lack an introduction and/or a conclusion

Score of 1:
- Minimally develops some aspects of the task
- Is descriptive; may lack understanding, application, or analysis
- Includes few relevant facts, examples, or details; may include inaccuracies
- May demonstrate a weakness in organization; may lack focus; may contain digressions; may not clearly identify which aspect of the task is being addressed; may lack an introduction and/or a conclusion

Score of 0:
- Fails to develop the task or may only refer to the theme in a general way; *OR* includes no relevant facts, examples, or details; *OR* includes only the theme, task, or suggestions as copied from the test booklet; *OR* is illegible; *OR* is a blank paper

Document-Based Question

This type of question presents you with up to eight historical documents on a single subject. The documents may be letters, speeches, or other written records; maps; charts; political cartoons; graphs; or tables.

Basic Characteristics

Questions based on historical documents have several characteristics. The documents provided give information or express viewpoints about a common theme. For space reasons, the samples you will see here and at the end of each unit will include only a few documents. Those on the test, however, may include up to eight documents.

A document-based question always has two parts. Part A requires short answers to specific questions about the documents. Part B requires you to write an essay. The themes for these essays are based on the same social studies themes and concepts as are used for thematic essays. Refer to the sample shown on the following pages as you read this information about document-based questions.

General Directions The question will begin with a set of directions. These directions will tell you what to do for each part of the question.

Historical Context Each question will contain a short statement that defines the historical context for the question. Read this statement carefully. It will help you understand the main topic to be discussed.

Task This statement defines the overall task that you will perform as you examine the documents provided.

Part A: Short Answer In this part of the question, you will be presented with the documents themselves. Documents that are quotations will be enclosed within boxes. The author of the quotation will be clearly identified. Documents may also be maps, charts, or political cartoons. Each document will be followed by one or possibly more questions. The questions will ask you to consider the viewpoint and source of the document. This is important because the author of a document may have a bias or a special motive that makes it difficult to accept his or her words as the whole truth. For example, a person who is trying to persuade soldiers to go into battle will not present the point of view of the opposing side very completely. Skills in interpreting the information in documents are very important.

Part B: Essay The essay portion of the question includes a set of general instructions and repeats the historical context. Pay very close attention to the instructions. Note that they call for a well-organized essay with both an introduction and a conclusion. They require you to use evidence from the documents to support your response. You should not, however, merely repeat the contents of the documents. Be sure also to include specific, related information from your knowledge of global history and geography. You must use additional relevant information that is not found in the documents. Otherwise you will not receive full credit for your essay. For the highest possible score, refer to all of the documents provided in the question, and include additional information from your knowledge of global history.

Strategy for the Document-Based Question

Answering Part A Your first task is to answer each of the questions about the documents. Examine each passage carefully, and look closely at each image. Read the question or questions and then reexamine the documents. Keep in mind the historical context. Recognize the various viewpoints that are being expressed. Finally, write a clear answer to each question.

Answering Part B You can approach this part much as you would a thematic essay, except that you need to consider how to incorporate evidence from the documents provided as well as knowledge from your Global History and Geography course.

You will find it useful to make a brief outline as you did for the thematic essay, showing what you plan to use as a thesis statement, what your supporting facts will be, where you will use various documents for support, and what your conclusion will be.

Take a look at the scoring rubric that follows the sample document-based question. A rubric like this one will be used to score Part B of the document-based question.

To get a high score on the essay portion of the test, do the following:

- Complete all parts of the task thoroughly.
- Provide analysis and interpretation of all or most of the documents supplied in the question. Information from the documents must be included within the body of your essay.
- Include as much related outside information as you can. Relevant outside information is crucial to a high score. Support your essay with related facts, examples, and details.
- Write an essay that is organized clearly and logically. Outlining your essay will help you maintain a clear organization.
- After you have finished writing, check to be sure that you have included a strong introduction and a strong conclusion.

Sample Document-Based Question

The following sample of a document-based question includes three documents. As already noted, a document-based question on the Regents Examination could show up to eight documents. Otherwise, the short-answer questions and essay question in this sample are similar to what you will see on the Regents Examination. For additional practice with questions based on documents, see the Questions for Regents Practice at the end of each unit as well as the sample tests.

Historical Context:

Throughout history, leaders have had vastly differing viewpoints on whether violence or war is ever justified. Some leaders, for example, have felt that violence is justified for certain purposes. Others have believed that violence against others is never the right choice. These viewpoints have had powerful effects on historical events.

Task: Using information from the documents and your knowledge of global history, answer the questions that follow each document in Part A. Your answers to the questions will help you write the Part B essay, in which you will be asked to

> • Evaluate several viewpoints on whether violence or war is ever justified in order to achieve a desired goal

Part A: Short-Answer

Directions: Analyze the documents and answer the question or questions that follow each document, using the space provided.

Document #1

> *What difference does it make to the dead, the orphans and the homeless, whether the mad destruction is wrought under the name of totalitarianism or the holy name of democracy and liberty?*
>
> — **Mohandas Gandhi, 1948**

1 Does Gandhi think that violence may be justified if the cause is a good one? Explain your answer, referring to the quotation.

_____

_____

_____

_____

_____

_____

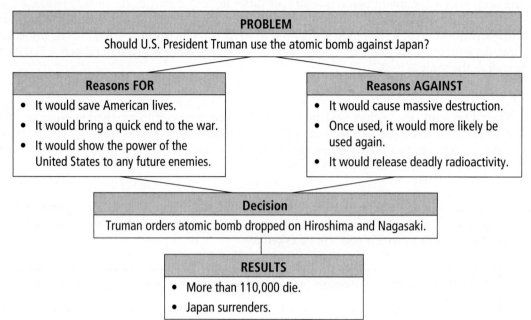

Document #2
The Atomic Bomb

PROBLEM

Should U.S. President Truman use the atomic bomb against Japan?

Reasons FOR

- It would save American lives.
- It would bring a quick end to the war.
- It would show the power of the United States to any future enemies.

Reasons AGAINST

- It would cause massive destruction.
- Once used, it would more likely be used again.
- It would release deadly radioactivity.

Decision

Truman orders atomic bomb dropped on Hiroshima and Nagasaki.

RESULTS

- More than 110,000 die.
- Japan surrenders.

2   List two reasons why President Truman decided to use atomic bombs against Japan.

_____

_____

_____

_____

_____

_____

3   Describe two reasons why some Americans disagreed with President Truman's decision.

_____

_____

_____

_____

_____

_____

Document #3

Brutality is respected. Brutality and physical strength. The plain man in the street respects nothing but brutal strength and ruthlessness—women, too, for that matter, women and children. The people need wholesome fear.

— **Adolf Hitler, 1936**

4   How did Adolf Hitler justify his inhumanity? Explain your answer, referring to the quotation.

_____

_____

_____

_____

_____

Document #4

A government should not mobilize an army out of anger, military leaders should not provoke a war out of wrath. Act when it is beneficial, desist when it is not. Anger can revert to joy, wrath can revert to delight, but a nation destroyed cannot be restored to existence, and the dead cannot be restored to life.

— **Sun Tzu, *The Art of War*, c. 300 B.C.**

5   Why did Sun Tzu say it is bad to start a war out of anger? Explain your answer, referring to the quotation.

_____

_____

_____

_____

_____

Document #5

A revolution is not a dinner party, or writing an essay, or painting a picture or doing embroidery; it cannot be so refined, so leisurely and gentle, so kind, courteous, restrained, and generous. A revolution is an insurrection, an act of violence by which one class overthrows another.

— **Mao Zedong, leader of the Communist Revolution in China**

6   According to Mao, what means are necessary in order for a revolution to succeed? Explain your answer, referring to the quotation.

_____

_____

_____

_____

_____

_____

Part B

Essay

Directions: Write a well-organized essay that includes an introduction, several paragraphs, and a conclusion. Use evidence from *at least **three*** documents in your essay. Support your response with relevant facts, examples, and details. Include additional outside information.

Historical Context:

Throughout history, leaders have had vastly differing viewpoints on whether violence or war is ever justified. Some leaders, for example, have felt that violence is justified for certain purposes. Others have believed that violence against others is never the right choice. These viewpoints have had powerful effects on historical events.

Task: Using information from the documents and your knowledge of global history and geography, write an essay in which you

- Evaluate whether violence or war is ever justified in order to achieve a desired goal

Guidelines:

In your essay, be sure to
- Develop all aspects of the task
- Incorporate information from *at least **three*** documents
- Incorporate relevant outside information
- Support the theme with relevant facts, examples, and details
- Use a logical and clear plan of organization, including an introduction and a conclusion that are beyond a restatement of the theme

Document-Based Question Scoring

Knowing how your document-based essay will be scored will help you write it effectively. Like thematic essays, document-based essays are scored with point values from 0 to 5. An essay receiving a score of 5 answers the question in a complete, comprehensive manner. You would receive a score of 0 only if you failed to address the theme at all, wrote an essay that was completely illegible, or turned in a blank paper.

The scoring rubric that follows represents the generic criteria on which your document-based essay will be scored.

Generic Scoring Rubric

Document-Based Question

Score of 5:
- Thoroughly develops all aspects of the task evenly and in depth
- Is more analytical than descriptive (analyzes, evaluates, and/or creates information)
- Incorporates relevant information from *at least* one more than half of the documents
- Incorporates substantial relevant outside information
- Richly supports the theme with many relevant facts, examples, and details
- Demonstrates a logical and clear plan of organization; includes an introduction and a conclusion that are beyond a restatement of the theme

Score of 4:
- Develops all aspects of the task but may do so somewhat unevenly
- Is both descriptive and analytical (applies, analyzes, evaluates, and/or creates information)
- Incorporates relevant information from *at least* half of the documents
- Incorporates relevant outside information
- Supports the theme with relevant facts, examples, and details
- Demonstrates a logical and clear plan of organization; includes an introduction and a conclusion that are beyond a restatement of the theme

Score of 3:
- Develops all aspects of the task with little depth *or* develops most aspects of the task in some depth
- Is more descriptive than analytical (applies, may analyze, and/or evaluates information)
- Incorporates some relevant information from some of the documents
- Incorporates limited relevant outside information
- Includes some relevant facts, examples, and details; may include some minor inaccuracies
- Demonstrates a satisfactory plan of organization; includes an introduction and a conclusion that may be a restatement of the theme

Score of 2:

- Minimally develops all aspects of the task *or* develops some aspects of the task in some depth
- Is primarily descriptive; may include faulty, weak, or isolated application or analysis
- Incorporates limited relevant information from the documents *or* consists primarily of relevant information copied from the documents
- Presents little or no relevant outside information
- Includes few relevant facts, examples, and details; may include some inaccuracies
- Demonstrates a general plan of organization; may lack focus; may contain digressions; may not clearly identify which aspect of the task is being addressed; may lack an introduction and/or a conclusion

Score of 1:

- Minimally develops some aspects of the task
- Is descriptive; may lack understanding, application, or analysis
- Makes vague, unclear references to the documents or consists primarily of relevant and irrelevant information copied from the documents
- Presents no relevant outside information
- Includes few relevant facts, examples, or details; may include inaccuracies
- May demonstrate a weakness in organization; may lack focus; may contain digressions; may not clearly identify which aspect of the task is being addressed; may lack an introduction and/or a conclusion

Score of 0:

- Fails to develop the task or may only refer to the theme in a general way; *OR* includes no relevant facts, examples, or details; *OR* includes only the historical context and/or task as copied from the test booklet; *OR* includes only entire documents copied from the test booklet; *OR* is illegible; *OR* is a blank paper

A Few Final Words

You have learned a number of strategies to help you prepare for the multiple-choice, thematic essay, and document-based questions on the Regents Examination in Global History and Geography. Try out these strategies on the practice tests included in the book and on the questions at the end of each unit. This practice will help you find out what works best for you and will allow you to become comfortable with the various types of questions found in the Regents Examination. As you practice more, you will also become confident of your ability to do well on the test.

Make sure you are well rested on the day of the examination. If you have devoted serious effort to your study of global history and geography, reviewed the material in this book, and used the many test items provided here for practice, you will be thoroughly prepared for the exam.

Unit 1 Pre-Test

Name _____ **Date** _____

Directions Review the Preparing for the Regents section of this book. Then answer the following questions, drawn from actual Regents examinations. For each statement or question, choose the *number* of the word or expression that, of those given, best completes the statement or answers the question.

1. Which statement best describes the effects of the works of Nicolaus Copernicus, Galileo Galilei, Sir Isaac Newton, and Rene Descartes?
   (1) The acceptance of traditional authority was strengthened.
   (2) The scientific method was used to solve problems.
   (3) Funding for education was increased by the English government.
   (4) Interest in Greek and Roman drama was renewed.

2. The Enlightenment philosophers believed that the power of government is derived from
   (1) divine right rulers
   (2) the middle class
   (3) a strong military
   (4) those who are governed

3. "Estates General Meet for First Time in 175 Years"; "National Assembly Issues Declarations of the Rights of Man"; "Reign of Terror Ends; Robespierre Dies"

   Which event in European history is most closely associated with these headlines?
   (1) Puritan Revolution
   (2) Hundred Years' War
   (3) French Revolution
   (4) signing of the Magna Carta

4. Simón Bolívar, José de San Martín, and Toussaint l'Ouverture are important in Latin American history because they were
   (1) twentieth-century caudillos
   (2) leaders of liberation movements
   (3) members of the Organization of American States (OAS)
   (4) winners of the Nobel Peace Prize

5. One of the main purposes of the Congress of Vienna (1814–1815) was to
   (1) promote the unification of Italy
   (2) preserve the German territories gained by Otto von Bismarck
   (3) restore the power of the Holy Roman Empire
   (4) establish a balance of power in Europe after the defeat of Napoleon

6. Which nineteenth-century ideology led to the unification of Germany and of Italy and to the eventual breakup of Austria-Hungary and of the Ottoman Empire?
   (1) imperialism   (3) liberalism
   (2) nationalism   (4) socialism

7. The main cause of the mass starvation in Ireland during the nineteenth century was the
   (1) British blockade of Irish ports
   (2) failure of the potato crop
   (3) war between Protestants and Catholics in northern Ireland
   (4) environmental damage caused by coal mining

8. During the nineteenth century, industrialization in Great Britain differed from industrialization in Japan mainly because Great Britain
   (1) had greater deposits of natural resources
   (2) encountered government resistance to economic growth
   (3) used isolationism to increase its economic power
   (4) duplicated the factory systems used in China

9. Laissez-faire capitalism as attributed to Adam Smith called for
   (1) heavy taxation of manufacturers
   (2) strict government control of the economy
   (3) minimal government involvement in the economy
   (4) government investments in major industries

Name _____ **Date** _____

10. Karl Marx and Friedrich Engels encouraged workers to improve their lives by
    (1) electing union representatives
    (2) participating in local government
    (3) overthrowing the capitalist system
    (4) demanding pensions and disability insurance

11. The needs of the Industrial Revolution in nineteenth-century Europe greatly contributed to the
    (1) growth of overseas empires
    (2) beginning of the triangular trade
    (3) development of international peacekeeping organizations
    (4) promotion of political and economic equality in Asia and Africa

12. The theory of Social Darwinism was sometimes used to justify
    (1) the establishment of communist governments in Asia
    (2) Latin American revolutions in the early nineteenth century
    (3) the independence movement in India
    (4) European imperialism in the late nineteenth century

13. "Take up the White Man's Burden -
    Send forth the best ye breed -
    Go, bind your sons to exile
    To serve your captives' need. . . ."
    —Rudyard Kipling, *The Five Nations* (1903)

    The words of this poem have been used to support the practice of
    (1) imperialism   (3) cultural borrowing
    (2) isolationism   (4) self-determination

14. The Sepoy Rebellion in India and the Boxer Rebellion in China were similar in that both were
    (1) attempts to improve foreign trade
    (2) nonviolent resistance efforts
    (3) revolts against foreign influence
    (4) revolutions against traditional monarchs

15. During the Meiji Restoration, Japan's leaders focused on
    (1) isolating Japan from the influence of foreign ideas
    (2) existing peacefully with their Asian neighbors
    (3) increasing the emperor's power by returning Japan to a feudal political system
    (4) modernizing Japan's economy to compete with western nations

Unit 2 Pre-Test

Name _____ **Date** _____

Directions Review the Preparing for the Regents section of this book. Then answer the following questions, drawn from actual Regents examinations. For each statement or question, choose the *number* of the word or expression that, of those given, best completes the statement or answers the question.

1. The Balkans were referred to as the "Powder Keg of Europe" in the period before World War I because of their
   (1) manufacturing ability
   (2) stockpiles of weapons
   (3) nationalistic rivalries
   (4) economic strength

2. Growing nationalism and militarism in Europe and the creation of secret alliances were
   (1) reasons for the rise of democracy
   (2) causes of World War I
   (3) requirements for economic development
   (4) reasons for the collapse of communism

3. The harsh terms included in the treaties ending World War I have been used to explain the
   (1) Fascist Revolution in Spain
   (2) Bolshevik Revolution in Russia
   (3) rise of Nazism in Germany
   (4) Armenian massacre in Turkey

4. In the 1920s and 1930s, Mustafa Kemal Atatürk changed the Turkish government by
   (1) introducing democratic reforms
   (2) increasing the power of the sultan
   (3) supporting absolutism
   (4) incorporating religious teachings into civil law

5. During the Russian Revolution of 1917, the slogan "peace, bread, and land" appealed to many Russian peasants because this slogan
   (1) called for continued Russian expansion in East Asia
   (2) supported an increase in the power of the Russian czar
   (3) addressed the needs and concerns of the peasants
   (4) promised to return all peasants to serfdom

6. What was the major goal of Joseph Stalin's five-year plans in the Soviet Union?
   (1) encouraging rapid industrialization
   (2) supporting capitalism
   (3) improving literacy rates
   (4) including peasants in the decision-making process

7. Which statement describes one major aspect of a command economy?
   (1) Supply and demand determines what is produced.
   (2) Most economic decisions are made by the government.
   (3) The means of production are controlled by labor unions.
   (4) The economy is mainly agricultural.

8. Which type of political system did V. I. Lenin, Adolf Hitler, and Benito Mussolini establish in their countries?
   (1) constitutional monarchy
   (2) totalitarianism
   (3) representative democracy
   (4) theocracy

9. One characteristic of a totalitarian state is that
   (1) minority groups are granted many civil liberties
   (2) several political parties run the economic system
   (3) citizens are encouraged to criticize the government
   (4) the government controls and censors the media

Name _____ **Date** _____

10. Which global event caused the overall reduction of unemployment between 1914 and 1918?

    (1) the Great Depression
    (2) completion of the Panama Canal
    (3) World War I
    (4) World War II

11. What was a major reason for Adolf Hitler's rise to power?

    (1) provisions of the Treaty of Versailles
    (2) Germany's military support of Poland and France
    (3) strong German economy
    (4) refusal by the League of Nations to admit Germany as a member

12. In Europe during the 1930s, several national leaders, in order to preserve peace at any cost, agreed to the demands of an aggressor. This policy is referred to as

    (1) militarism   (3) reparation
    (2) nonalignment   (4) appeasement

13. What was a major reason for Japan's invasion of Manchuria in 1931?

    (1) The province of Manchuria was originally a Japanese territory.
    (2) The government of Japan admired Manchurian technical progress.
    (3) The people of Manchuria favored Japanese control.
    (4) Japan needed the natural resources available in Manchuria.

14. During World War II, which geographic features contributed most to the Soviet Union's defense against the German invasion?

    (1) deposits of many natural resources
    (2) size and climate
    (3) Atlantic ports and rivers
    (4) mountainous territory and desert areas

15. The Holocaust is an example of

    (1) conflict between political parties
    (2) violations of human rights
    (3) limited technological development
    (4) geography's influence on culture

Name _____ **Date** _____

Directions Review the Preparing for the Regents section of this book. Then answer the following questions, drawn from actual Regents examinations. For each statement or question, choose the *number* of the word or expression that, of those given, best completes the statement or answers the question.

1. The formation of the North Atlantic Treaty Organization (NATO), the division of Germany into East Germany and West Germany, and the Korean War were immediate reactions to

   (1) Japanese military aggression in the 1930s
   (2) the rise of German nationalism after World War I
   (3) ethnic conflict and civil war in Africa in the 1950s
   (4) communist expansion after World War II

2. One similarity between the Korean War and the Vietnam War is that both wars were

   (1) resolved through the diplomatic efforts of the United Nations
   (2) fought as a result of differing political ideologies during the Cold War
   (3) fought without foreign influence or assistance
   (4) caused by religious conflicts

3. Which statement best describes India's foreign policy between 1947 and 1990?

   (1) It imitated Great Britain's policies.
   (2) It usually reflected the policies of China.
   (3) It rejected all assistance from communist dictatorships.
   (4) It generally followed a policy of nonalignment.

4. One reason the Chinese Communists were able to gain control of China was primarily due to the support of the

   (1) peasants   (3) foreigners
   (2) landed elite   (4) warlords

5. Which development took place in China under Mao Zedong?

   (1) The family became the dominant force in society.
   (2) The Four Modernizations became the basis for economic reform.
   (3) The people adopted the practice of ancestral worship.
   (4) Communist teachings became required learning in all schools and universities.

6. Since the 1980s, Chinese leaders have tried to improve China's economy by implementing a policy of

   (1) isolationism
   (2) collectivization
   (3) limited free enterprise
   (4) representative government

7. What was one reason that India was divided into two nations in 1947?

   (1) Indian leaders disagreed about India's role in the United Nations.
   (2) Great Britain feared a unified India would be a military threat.
   (3) The Soviet Union insisted that India should have a communist government.
   (4) Differences between the Hindus and the Muslims created religious conflict.

8. One similarity in the actions of Ho Chi Minh and Jomo Kenyatta was that both leaders

   (1) introduced Western ideas to their societies
   (2) established democratic forms of government
   (3) led nationalist movements
   (4) supported separation of church and state

Name _____   **Date** _____

9. Which situation existed under the policy of apartheid in South Africa?
   (1) All people were guaranteed suffrage.
   (2) The black majority held the most political power.
   (3) Society was controlled by the white minority.
   (4) Social inequality was eliminated.

10. What was one factor that contributed to the downfall of apartheid in the Republic of South Africa?
    (1) The African National Congress was outlawed.
    (2) Afrikaners demanded that only they should have ruling power.
    (3) Many foreign countries boycotted South African products.
    (4) President de Klerk and Desmond Tutu were imprisoned.

11. A major source of the dispute between the Israelis and the Palestinians is that each side
    (1) wants to control oil resources in the area
    (2) has historic ties to the same land
    (3) believes in different interpretations of the same religion
    (4) has close military alliances with neighboring countries

12. Since the creation of the Organization of Petroleum Exporting Countries (OPEC), member nations have joined together to
    (1) determine the supply of oil on the world market
    (2) establish a policy of independence in trade
    (3) maintain a low price of oil per barrel
    (4) isolate themselves from the rest of the world

13. Mikhail Gorbachev instituted the policies of glasnost and perestroika to
    (1) reinforce the basic economic principles of communism
    (2) bring the Soviet Union into the European Economic Community
    (3) reform the Soviet Union politically and economically
    (4) gain acceptance for free political elections

14. One way in which Lech Walesa, Mikhail Gorbachev, and Nelson Mandela are similar is that each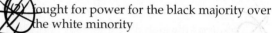
    (1) led the people of his nation toward a more democratic government
    (2) fought for power for the black majority over the white minority
    (3) worked to end communism in his country
    (4) refused to participate in the United Nations

15. In Iran, both the Revolution of 1979 and the rise of Islamic fundamentalism have caused
    (1) an increase in women's rights
    (2) tension between traditionalism and modernization to continue
    (3) foreign control of natural resources to expand
    (4) the introduction of a communist form of government

Unit 4 Pre-Test

Name _____ **Date** _____

Directions Review the Preparing for the Regents section of this book. Then answer the following questions, drawn from actual Regents examinations. For each statement or question, choose the *number* of the word or expression that, of those given, best completes the statement or answers the question.

1. What is a major reason for the differences in economic prosperity in various areas of the world today?
   (1) an unequal distribution of resources
   (2) the success of nationalist movements
   (3) religious unity between nations
   (4) membership in the United Nations

2. In many of the world's developing nations, improvements in life expectancy and health care have contributed to
   (1) population pressures that limit economic development
   (2) an increased number of epidemics
   (3) a reduction in the need for land reform
   (4) a steady rise in income for all citizens

3. As a society becomes more urbanized and industrialized, it tends to
   (1) develop a more rigid class system
   (2) modify traditional beliefs and customs
   (3) resist cultural diffusion
   (4) depend more on the extended family structure

4. The Green Revolution of the 1960s resulted in
   (1) the destruction of large industrial enterprises
   (2) an increase of food output in many developing nations
   (3) a decrease in world agricultural output
   (4) improvements in human genetic engineering

5. An example of economic interdependence is
   (1) South Africans mining their gold and diamond resources
   (2) the government of France issuing new currency
   (3) Japan selling technological goods to buy Middle Eastern oil
   (4) an Indian subsistence farmer waiting for the rains to water his crops

6. The main purpose of the European Union (EU) and the North American Free Trade Agreement (NAFTA) is to
   (1) reduce the spread of nuclear weapons
   (2) address the problem of international political corruption
   (3) increase educational opportunities for underdeveloped nations
   (4) stimulate economic growth for participating countries

7. Which issue continues to raise concern from the world community regarding the nations of India, Iraq, Pakistan, and North Korea?
   (1) overpopulation
   (2) ethnic cleansing
   (3) desertification
   (4) nuclear proliferation

8. Which environmental issue most concerns Central Africa, the Amazon River Basin, and the Malay Peninsula?
   (1) nuclear contamination
   (2) desertification
   (3) overpopulation
   (4) deforestation

9. • Chernobyl experiences nuclear disaster.
   • Chlorofluorocarbons (CFCs) deplete the ozone layer.
   • Rivers and seas are polluted throughout the world.

   Which conclusion can best be drawn from these statements?

   (1) Modern technology can have serious negative effects.
   (2) Today's environment renews itself.
   (3) Only developing nations have environmental problems.
   (4) Most environmental problems originate in Europe.

Name _____ **Date** _____

10. The late-twentieth-century conflicts in Rwanda, Yugoslavia, and India were similar in that each was caused by the

(1) deforestation conducted by multinational companies

(2) collapse of communism

(3) intervention of United Nations peacekeeping forces

(4) rivalries between ethnic groups

11. Which statement best describes the impact of the computer on the global economy?

(1) Countries can increase tariffs on imports.

(2) Companies now market more products worldwide.

(3) Wages have risen dramatically for most people in developing nations.

(4) Prices of oil and other resources have declined worldwide.

12. The reason that the Organization of Petroleum Exporting Countries (OPEC) greatly influences the world today is that it

(1) commands the loyalty of the worldwide Islamic community

(2) develops and exports important technology

(3) controls access to trade routes between the East and West

(4) manages the oil supply that affects the global economy

An Age of Revolutions (1750–1914)

Section 1: **Scientific Revolution and Enlightenment**

Section 2: **Political Revolutions**

Section 3: **Reaction Against Revolutionary Ideals**

Section 4: **Global Nationalism**

Section 5: **Economic and Social Revolutions**

Section 6: **Japan and the Meiji Restoration**

Section 7: **Imperialism**

Unit Overview

The years between 1750 and 1914 were years of enormous change. The Scientific Revolution and the Enlightenment brought a completely new way of looking at the world. Monarchies were overthrown, and representative forms of government emerged. In some areas, people tried to return to previous ways. In other areas, however, feelings of nationalism arose that led to the growth of nations. During this same time, enormous changes were occurring in Europe and Japan. The Industrial Revolution brought changes in social structure and created new ways of living and working. Industrialization also spurred nations to build empires in Africa and Asia, creating an economy that spanned the globe.

Using Good Social Studies Practices

Comparison and Contextualization

Some of the many themes developed in Unit 1 are:

change	political systems	science and technology
nationalism	conflict	culture and intellectual life
power	imperialism	

Choose one of the themes listed above. As you review Unit 1, identify, describe, and compare people's perspectives on historical developments, economic changes, and social movements having to do with your theme.

Scientific Revolution and Enlightenment

The
Big Idea

From the 1500s through the 1700s, Europeans:

• experienced the Scientific Revolution, which caused people to change their views about the universe.

• entered the Enlightenment, in which philosophers applied reason to society and government.

• developed ideas about basic human rights and proper government.

• began to consider democratic ideas and the concept of nationalism.

Section Overview

In the 1500s and 1600s, the Scientific Revolution changed the way Europeans looked at the world. People began to make conclusions based on experimentation and observation instead of merely accepting traditional ideas. During the 1600s and 1700s, belief in the power of reason grew. Writers of the time sought to reform government and bring about a more just society. Despite opposition from government and church leaders, Enlightenment ideas spread. Some absolute rulers used their power to reform society. Over time, concepts of democracy and of nationhood developed from Enlightenment ideas and contributed to revolutions.

Key Themes and Concepts

As you review this section, take special note of the following key themes and concepts:

Science and Technology How did the Scientific Revolution change the way Europeans looked at the world?

Culture and Intellectual Life How did the Scientific Revolution lead to the ideas of the Enlightenment?

Government What reforms did Enlightenment thinkers want to bring to government in the 1600s and 1700s?

Change What impact did the Enlightenment have on Europe?

Key People and Terms

Key People and Terms

• What do many of the key people and terms have in common? Explain.

As you review this section, be sure you understand the significance of these key people and terms:

Scientific Revolution	natural laws
Nicolaus Copernicus	John Locke
heliocentric	natural rights
Galileo Galilei	Baron de Montesquieu
Isaac Newton	Voltaire
scientific method	Jean-Jacques Rousseau
René Descartes	enlightened despots
Enlightenment	Joseph II

New Ideas About the Universe

Throughout the Middle Ages, European scholars believed that Earth was the center of the universe. This idea was based on Greco-Roman theories and the teachings of the Church. However, European scientists began to think differently in the 1500s. Influenced by the critical spirit of the Renaissance, they questioned the old ideas about the world. This period of change was called the **Scientific Revolution.**

Copernicus

In the mid-1500s, Polish scholar **Nicolaus Copernicus** challenged the belief that Earth was at the center of the universe. Using mathematical formulas, Copernicus suggested that the universe was **heliocentric,** or sun-centered. He said that the planets revolved around the sun. Most scholars rejected Copernicus's theory.

Galileo

In the early 1600s, an Italian astronomer, **Galileo Galilei,** provided further evidence to support the heliocentric theory. He did this by observing the skies with a telescope he had constructed. Galileo's conclusions caused an uproar because they contradicted Church teachings about the world. Church leaders put Galileo on trial. Threatened with death, Galileo was forced to take back his ideas publicly.

Newton

English scholar **Isaac Newton** built on the knowledge of Copernicus and Galileo. He used mathematics to prove the existence of a force that kept planets in their orbits around the sun. Newton called the force gravity, the same force that made objects fall toward Earth. Newton eventually theorized that nature follows uniform laws.

New Ways of Thinking

The Scientific Method

A new approach to science had emerged by the 1600s. It relied on experimentation and observation rather than on past authorities. This new way of thinking was called the **scientific method.**

The Scientific Method

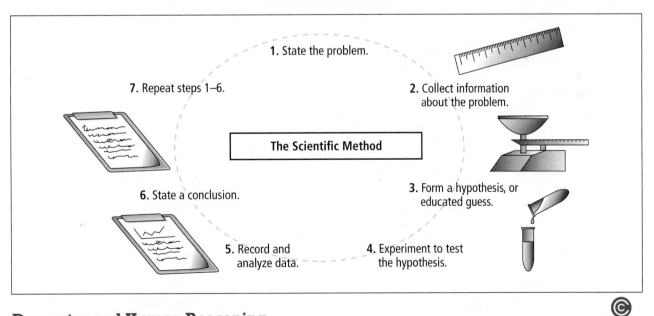

1. State the problem.
2. Collect information about the problem.
3. Form a hypothesis, or educated guess.
4. Experiment to test the hypothesis.
5. Record and analyze data.
6. State a conclusion.
7. Repeat steps 1–6.

The Scientific Method

Descartes and Human Reasoning

Frenchman **René Descartes** challenged the idea that new knowledge should be made to fit existing traditional ideas. Descartes emphasized the power of human reason. He believed that reason, rather than tradition, should be the way to discover truth. The ideas of Descartes and other thinkers of the Scientific Revolution paved the way for other changes that would occur in Europe in the 1700s.

• How did the Scientific Revolution prepare the way for the Enlightenment?

• Thomas Hobbes was an Enlightenment thinker, even though his philosophy favored absolutism. Contrast Locke's theory of natural rights with the thinking of Thomas Hobbes and the theory of divine right.

Science and the Enlightenment

During the Scientific Revolution, scientists used reason to explain why things happened in the physical universe. This success inspired great confidence in the power of reason. By the early 1700s, writers sought to use reason to discover **natural laws,** or laws that govern human behavior. By applying the scientific method of investigation and observation, scholars thought that they could solve the problems of society.

This way of thinking led to the Enlightenment, the period in the 1700s in which people rejected traditional ideas and supported a belief in human reason. The belief that logical thought can lead to truth is called rationalism. The Enlightenment introduced new ways of viewing authority, power, government, and law.

Leading Thinkers of the Enlightenment

Four of the most influential Enlightenment philosophers were John Locke, Baron de Montesquieu, Voltaire, and Jean-Jacques Rousseau.

Locke

John Locke, an English thinker of the late 1600s, believed that all people possess **natural rights.** These rights, he said, include the rights to life, liberty, and property. According to Locke, people form governments to protect their rights. If a government does not protect these rights, people have the right to overthrow it.

Montesquieu

In the 1700s, French thinker **Baron de Montesquieu** wrote that the powers of government should be separated into three branches: legislative, executive, and judicial. This separation of powers would prevent tyranny by creating what is called a system of checks and balances. Each branch could keep the other two from gaining too much power.

Voltaire

Voltaire was a French thinker of the 1700s who believed in free speech. He used his sharp wit to criticize the French government and the Catholic Church for their failure to permit religious toleration and intellectual freedom.

Rousseau

Jean-Jacques Rousseau, another French philosopher of the 1700s, put forth his ideas in a book titled *The Social Contract.* He believed that people are naturally good but are corrupted by the evils of society, such as the unequal distribution of property. He felt that in agreeing to form a government, people choose to give up their own interests for the common good. Rousseau believed in the will of the majority, which he called the general will. He believed that the majority should always work for the common good.

Key Themes and Concepts

Government
Locke's ideas about natural rights and the obligations of government later influenced both Thomas Jefferson's writing of the Declaration of Independence and the French revolutionaries.

Thinkers of the Enlightenment

Thomas Hobbes	John Locke
People are greedy and selfish. Only a powerful government can create a peaceful, orderly society.	People have natural rights. It is the job of government to protect these natural rights. If government does not protect these rights, the people have the right to overthrow it.
Baron de Montesquieu	**Jean-Jacques Rousseau**
The powers of government should be separated into three branches. Each branch will keep the other branches from becoming too powerful.	In a perfect society, people both make and obey the laws. What is good for everyone is more important than what is good for one person.

Impact of the Enlightenment

The ideas proposed by Enlightenment thinkers had a great impact throughout Europe in the 1700s. Greater numbers of people began to question established beliefs and customs. Enlightenment beliefs affected leaders and the development of nations.

Government Censorship

As Enlightenment ideas gained in popularity, government and Church leaders worked to defend the established systems. They started a campaign of censorship to suppress Enlightenment ideas. Many writers, including Voltaire, were thrown into prison, and their books were banned and burned.

Enlightened Despots

Some monarchs accepted Enlightenment ideas. They were known as **enlightened despots,** absolute rulers who used their power to reform society.

Maria Theresa Austrian ruler Maria Theresa implemented several reforms during her reign in the 1700s. She improved the tax system by forcing nobles and the clergy to pay taxes. This measure eased the tax burden on peasants. Maria Theresa also absorbed Enlightenment ideas on education and made primary education available to children in her kingdom.

Joseph II Maria Theresa's son, Joseph II, continued and expanded many of his mother's reforms. The most radical of the enlightened despots, Joseph modernized Austria's government, chose officials for their talents rather than because of their status, and implemented legal reforms. He also practiced religious toleration, ended censorship, and abolished serfdom. However, many of Joseph's reforms were later overturned.

Catherine the Great Catherine II, who became empress of Russia in 1762, read Enlightenment works and even corresponded with Voltaire and Montesquieu. As a result of her exposure to Enlightenment ideas, Catherine asked for the advice of nobles, free peasants, and townspeople. Never before had Russian citizens been allowed to advise the government. Catherine also built schools and hospitals, promoted the education of women, and extended religious tolerance. Unfortunately, many of Catherine's reforms were short-lived. Later in her reign, Catherine grew more repressive after a peasant uprising.

Democracy and Nationalism

Enlightenment ideas inspired a sense of individualism, a belief in personal freedom, and a sense of the basic equality of human beings. These concepts, along with challenges to traditional authority, became important in the growth of democracy. Nationalism also grew. As people in a country drew together to fight for a democratic government, strong feelings of nationalism arose. In the late 1700s, Enlightenment ideas would contribute to an age of revolution.

Summary

Beginning in the 1500s, the Scientific Revolution introduced a way of thinking based on observation and experimentation instead of acceptance of traditional authority. These changes inspired intellectuals to apply reason to the study not only of science but also of human society. The thinkers of the Enlightenment used this emphasis on reason to suggest reforms in government and society. Many Europeans, including several monarchs, were influenced by these ideas and sought to change the old order. These changes had an impact on all of Europe as democratic and nationalistic ideas grew and contributed to revolutions.

Vocabulary Builder

censorship—(SEN sur ship) *n.* the practice of examining books, films, letters, etc., to remove anything that is considered offensive, morally harmful, or politically dangerous, etc.

Key Themes and Concepts

Change
The term *enlightened despot* almost seems like a contradiction. These rulers believed in absolute power but also saw the value of reforms in government.

Nationalism
In both the American and French Revolutions, Enlightenment ideas contributed to democratic movements as well as strong nationalistic feelings. To learn more about the American and French Revolutions, see Section 2 of this unit.

Government
Enlightenment thinkers sought to use reason to improve government and society. Although they were able to influence only a few leaders of their day, they created a whole new set of assumptions about the proper use of power, who had authority, and what made up a good and lawful government.

Preparing for the Regents

- What policies did enlightened despots have in common?

Political Revolutions

The
Big Idea

Revolution brought change to Europe and the Americas in the 1700s and 1800s.

• People in Great Britain's 13 colonies applied Enlightenment ideas to the fight for independence from Great Britain.

• French revolutionaries rebelled against absolute monarchy and reformed the French social order.

• Napoleon spread democratic ideals and nationalism across Europe.

• The revolutionary spirit brought independence to Latin American nations.

Section Overview

In the late 1700s and early 1800s, revolutions shook Europe and the Americas. In North America in 1776, Great Britain's 13 colonies, inspired by Enlightenment ideals, declared their independence. They then fought the American Revolution to throw off British rule. In France, economic misery and social discontent led to a revolt against the absolute monarchy in 1789. Periods of chaos and reform were followed by the rise of Napoleon Bonaparte. Napoleon built an empire that was short-lived, but his military victories fanned French nationalistic feelings and spread the revolution's ideals. Inspired by the American and French Revolutions, revolutionaries in Latin America threw off Spanish rule.

Key Themes and Concepts

As you review this section, take special note of the following key themes and concepts:

Culture and Intellectual Life What role did Enlightenment ideas play in the major revolutions of the late 1700s and early 1800s?

Conflict Why did the French people rebel against King Louis XVI?

Change What short-term and long-term effects did the revolutions of the late 1700s and early 1800s have on Europe and the Americas?

Key People and Terms

As you review this section, be sure you understand the significance of these key people and terms:

Key People and Terms

• Place each of the key people and terms into these three categories: leader, government body, political document.

Declaration of Independence

Estates General

National Assembly

Declaration of the Rights of Man and of the Citizen

Maximilien Robespierre

Napoleon Bonaparte

coup d'état

Napoleonic Code

Toussaint L'Ouverture

Simón Bolívar

José de San Martín

The American Revolution

By 1750, the British empire included 13 colonies along the eastern coast of North America. In 1776, the colonies declared their independence from Great Britain. Great Britain sent troops to crush the rebellion. However, with the aid of the French as well as the Dutch and Spanish, American forces defeated the British army and gained their independence. In their struggle, the colonists were inspired by Enlightenment ideals and by the traditions of British government. They established a new nation based on representative government and a guarantee of rights and freedoms.

Influence of British Traditions

Magna Carta and Parliament The Magna Carta had limited the power of English monarchs. For example, it stated that the king could not raise new taxes without consulting the body that would later become Parliament. The American colonists interpreted this idea to mean that any taxation without representation was unjust. Because colonists had no representative in Great Britain's Parliament, they felt that Parliament had no right to tax them. They protested by using the slogan "No taxation without representation."

English Bill of Rights The English Bill of Rights inspired colonists to fight for the creation of their own bill of rights.

Influence of the Enlightenment

The theories of thinkers such as Locke, Montesquieu, and Rousseau helped inspire the colonists' opposition to British policies after 1763.

Paine's Common Sense Influenced by Enlightenment ideas about a limited, representative government, Thomas Paine wrote in his pamphlet *Common Sense* that the colonists should no longer be the subjects of a distant monarch. Paine appealed to reason and natural law in his arguments for breaking away from Great Britain. His ideas were widely read in the colonies in 1776.

The Declaration of Independence Influenced by Locke and other Enlightenment thinkers, Thomas Jefferson drafted the Declaration of Independence. Jefferson wrote that governments rule only with the consent of the governed and that they should protect the unalienable rights of their citizens. The declaration also stated that people have a right to throw off governments that are unjust and that do not protect their citizens. After listing specific grievances against the British monarch, Jefferson wrote that the colonists were justified in forming their own government, independent of Great Britain.

The Constitution Like the Declaration of Independence, this document reflected the influence of Enlightenment ideas.

- **Social Contract** The Constitution of the United States set up a government by social contract. The government was established by the consent of the governed. The Constitution begins with these words: "We the People of the United States . . ."

- **Separation of Powers** Influenced by the ideas of Montesquieu, the Constitution created a republic in which power was to be divided between the federal government and the states. In addition, the writers of the Constitution established a government that divided powers among an executive, a legislative, and a judicial branch. Each branch could provide checks and balances on the other branches.

- **Protection of Rights** The Bill of Rights was added to the Constitution to protect the basic rights of American citizens, including freedom of speech and freedom of religion. The Constitution stated that it was the duty of the government to protect these rights.

Impact of the American Revolution

The American Revolution had a great impact around the world.

- The American republic stood as a symbol of freedom to both Europe and Latin America.

- The United States Constitution created the most liberal government of its time. Other nations would copy the ideas in this document.

- The success of the American Revolution would soon inspire major global changes as other peoples challenged the power of absolute monarchs.

Note Taking

Reading Skill:
Identify Main Ideas
As you read, fill in a table with main ideas about these political documents.

Common Sense	Declaration of Independence	Constitution

Key Themes and Concepts

Human Rights
The Declaration of Independence reflects many of Locke's Enlightenment ideas. These ideas include people's natural rights to life and liberty, the role of the government in protecting those rights, and the right of people to overthrow unjust governments.

Government and Change
The United States Constitution contributed to change in other parts of the world. It was a model for many other nations that formed new governments in the years that followed.

Preparing for the Regents

- Describe some Enlightenment ideas that inspired the American Revolution and influenced the founders of the United States of America.

- Why was the American Revolution an important turning point in global history?

Stages of Political Revolutions

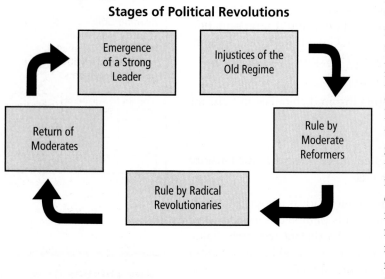

The French Revolution

Soon after the American Revolution, a major revolution broke out in France. Starting in 1789, the French Revolution had a deep and lasting impact on France, Europe, and other areas of the world. The French Revolution followed a pattern common to many political revolutions. In this pattern, revolutions pass through different stages, caused by changes in leadership and shifts in power. Problems begin to appear in a country, and revolutionary groups form, hoping to correct the injustices. At the beginning of the revolution, moderate reformers come to power and as their compromise reforms fail, power passes to a more radical group of revolutionaries. The revolution grows more violent and extreme. A reaction to the violence follows, bringing moderates back to power. Often, at that point, there is a return to the old order as the people turn to a leader who promises order along with reform.

Causes of the Revolution

Many injustices existed in prerevolutionary France. Political, social, economic, and intellectual factors combined to bring about the French Revolution.

Absolute Monarchy On the eve of revolution, France was an absolute monarchy. Under absolutism, most people in France were denied basic rights and any say in government.

Social Inequality Since the Middle Ages, everyone in France had belonged to one of three social classes called estates. The clergy were the First Estate; the titled nobility composed the Second Estate. These two classes held enormous wealth, did not have to pay taxes, and enjoyed other special rights and privileges. The Third Estate made up most of French society and included a bourgeoisie (middle class), poor city workers, and rural peasants, the largest group. The Third Estate, which resented its heavy tax burden and lack of rights, grew increasingly discontented.

Population and Land Ownership in France, 1789

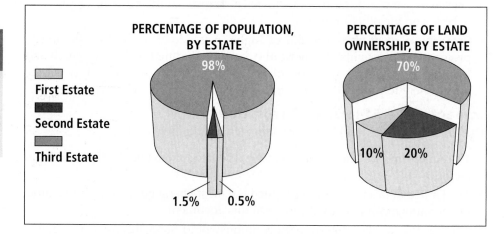

PERCENTAGE OF POPULATION, BY ESTATE

PERCENTAGE OF LAND OWNERSHIP, BY ESTATE

First Estate
Second Estate
Third Estate

98%
1.5%   0.5%

70%
10%   20%

Economic Injustices The situation in France became worse because of economic conditions in the late 1780s. The government, with its lavish court and expensive wars, spent more money than it earned. This debt added to the tax burden of the Third Estate. Bad harvests in 1789 caused food prices to rise. Peasants and city dwellers often did not have enough to eat and began to riot, demanding bread.

Enlightenment Through the 1600s and 1700s, Enlightenment thinkers were critical of France's absolute monarchy and called for democratic reforms. Enlightenment ideas led many French to question the traditional way of ordering society. It was not reasonable, they felt, for the First and Second Estates to have privileges at the expense of the Third Estate.

English and American Examples England's Glorious Revolution provided an example of how existing authority could be challenged. In addition, the French were inspired by the American colonies' successful fight for liberty and equality in the American Revolution.

Stages of the Revolution

The Revolution Begins As conditions grew worse in France, demands for reform increased. In 1789, King Louis XVI finally called the **Estates General,** a body made up of representatives of all three estates, into session. After this, change came swiftly.

- **National Assembly** The Third Estate, the only elected group in the Estates General, declared itself the National Assembly. The National Assembly vowed to write a new constitution for France.
- **Seizure of the Bastille** Working-class people, already rioting over the price of bread, stormed a prison called the Bastille on July 14, 1789. Fighting broke out through city and countryside. In a period known as the Great Fear, peasants attacked nobles and destroyed their homes.
- **Moderates in Power** The king, frightened by the increasing turmoil, agreed to allow the National Assembly to begin reforms.
- **Declaration of the Rights of Man and of the Citizen** The National Assembly abolished the privileges of the First and Second Estates and adopted the Declaration of the Rights of Man and of the Citizen. Based partly on the Declaration of Independence, it contained many Enlightenment ideas.
- **A Limited Monarchy** By 1791, the Assembly had written a constitution. The Constitution of 1791 defined the role and purpose of a new government.
  - It set up a limited monarchy and a representative assembly.
  - It declared that people had natural rights and that it was the job of the government to protect those rights.
  - It put the Church under state control.

News about the French Revolution quickly spread across Europe. Many European rulers and nobles feared that revolutionary ideas would spread to their own countries. They threatened to intervene—with military force, if necessary—to save the French monarchy. In 1792, to fight tyranny and spread the revolution, France declared war on Austria, Prussia, Great Britain, and several other states.

Preparing for the Regents

- List three factors that led to the French Revolution.

1.

2.

3.

Key Themes and Concepts

Individual Cultural Identity As you study the French Revolution, take note of the roles played by individual citizens. Members of the Third Estate formed the National Assembly. Working-class people stormed the Bastille, and peasants attacked the homes of nobles.

Preparing for the Regents

- What influences from the Enlightenment and the American Revolution can you see in the Declaration of the Rights of Man and the Citizen?

The French Declaration of Rights

DECLARATION OF THE RIGHTS OF MAN AND OF THE CITIZEN

- Written in 1789
- Uses American Declaration of Independence as model
- States that all men have natural rights
- Declares the job of government to protect the natural rights of the people
- Guarantees all male citizens equality under the law
- States that people are free to practice any religion they choose
- Promises to tax people according to how much they can afford

Key Themes and Concepts

Change
During the course of the revolution, the people in power changed, and ideas of those in power changed. At first, moderates were in power, and the constitution called for a limited monarchy. By 1793, the radicals were in control, and the king had been executed.

Radicals in Power The war with the other European nations went badly for France. In 1792, radicals took control of the Assembly, ended the monarchy, and declared France a republic. Their slogan was "Liberty, Equality, Fraternity." In 1793, the king was executed for treason. This event was followed by a period in France called the Reign of Terror, led in part by **Maximilien Robespierre,** a radical revolutionary. During this time, tens of thousands of people were executed. Thousands more were put into prison. Within a year, however, the violence turned back on itself. Robespierre himself was executed, and the Reign of Terror ended.

Moderates Return Beginning in 1795, a five-man "Directory" supported by a legislature held power in France. This government was weak and inefficient. Rising bread prices brought the threat of riots. Into this chaotic situation stepped an ambitious military leader, Napoleon Bonaparte.

Napoleon in Power

His Rise to Power When the revolution started, **Napoleon Bonaparte** was a low-level military officer with dreams of glory. Bonaparte rose in the ranks and won important victories against the British and Austrians. A popular general by 1799, Napoleon helped overthrow the weak Directory in a **coup d'état,** or revolt by military leaders to overthrow a government. He organized a new government and put himself in charge. Three years later, he took the title "Emperor of the French." Napoleon now had absolute power. The French people, hoping for stability, supported Napoleon at each step in his rise.

Napoleon in Europe, 1812

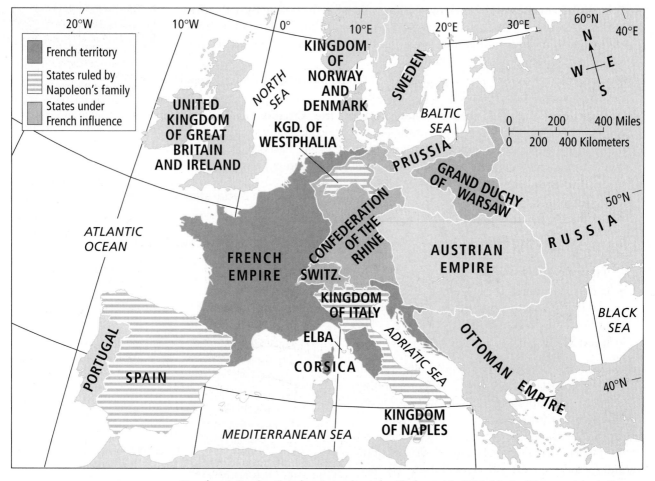

Napoleon's Empire *Napoleon's empire was at its largest in 1812. Most of the countries in Europe today have different names and borders.*

His Achievements Much of Napoleon's popularity came from his effective policies.

- **Economy** Napoleon controlled prices, supported new industry, and built roads and canals.
- **Education** Napoleon established a government-supervised public school system.
- **Napoleonic Code** The Napoleonic Code was a legal code that included many Enlightenment ideas, such as the legal equality of citizens and religious toleration.

Napoleon's Empire From 1804 to 1814, Napoleon ruled an empire. He conquered much of Europe. Napoleon often replaced the monarchs of defeated nations with his friends and relatives.

Of the European powers, only Great Britain and Russia remained beyond Napoleon's reach. Great Britain was shielded from French troops by a powerful navy and the English Channel.

Napoleon's Fall Napoleon's empire began to crumble for several reasons. First, most people in conquered states looked on Napoleon's armies as foreign oppressors. Inspired by nationalism, people across Europe revolted against French rule.

Another factor was Napoleon's invasion of Russia in 1812. As Napoleon's armies invaded from the west, the Russians retreated eastward. The "scorched earth" policy of the Russians, in which they burned crops and villages as they retreated, left the French troops hungry and cold. Most of Napoleon's army was lost during the long Russian winter.

The following year, an alliance of Russia, Great Britain, Austria, and Prussia defeated Napoleon, forcing him to step down in 1814. Napoleon returned to power in 1815, but the British and Prussians defeated him at the decisive Battle of Waterloo. This battle ended Napoleon's reign, and he lived the rest of his life in exile.

Key Themes and Concepts

Power
Despite Napoleon's reforms, order and authority were still higher priorities for him than individual rights. The Napoleonic Code included many Enlightenment ideas, such as the equality of citizens under the law. However, it also undid some reforms of the revolution, such as rights that had been granted to women.

Preparing for the Regents

- How did nationalism help Napoleon to build his empire? How did nationalism lead to Napoleon's defeat?

Preparing for the Regents

Practice interpreting political cartoons by answering these questions.

1. What does the large plum pudding represent? How do the slices represent Napoleon's quest for power?

2. Based on your knowledge of Napoleon's relationship with Great Britain, would this dinner be a cordial one? Explain.

British Prime Minister William Pitt and Napoleon carve a large plum pudding

Preparing for the Regents

- Create a chart that outlines the causes and lasting effects of the French Revolution.

- In what way was the French Revolution a turning point in global history?

Effects of the French Revolution

The French Revolution and the reign of Napoleon transformed both France and Europe in many ways.

Democratic Ideals Napoleon's conquests spread the ideals of democracy throughout Europe. Groups struggled to achieve the goals of the French republic: "Liberty, Equality, Fraternity." People wanted liberty from absolute monarchs and unjust governments. They pursued equality by opposing social inequality and injustice. They expressed fraternity, or brotherhood, by working together for a common cause.

Nationalism Among the French, the revolution and the conquests of Napoleon inspired feelings of national pride. This pride and sense of national identity replaced earlier loyalty to local authority and the person of the monarch.

The conquests of Napoleon also increased nationalistic feeling across Europe and around the world. His conquests had a part in the eventual unification of both Italy and Germany. His weakening of Spain led to the Latin American independence movements.

Key Themes and Concepts

Nationalism
Feelings of nationalism often develop when a group of people is under the control of a foreign power. List other examples of people embracing nationalism and working together to drive out foreign rulers.

Latin American Independence Movements

In the late 1700s, Enlightenment and revolutionary ideas spread from Europe and the United States to Latin America. Educated Latin Americans read works by Enlightenment writers. They debated about political and social reform. Thomas Jefferson's Declaration of Independence and the Constitution were eagerly read. The success of the American Revolution showed that foreign rule could be thrown off. Latin Americans also were inspired by what the French Revolution had accomplished. Beginning in the 1790s, they struggled to gain independence as well as other rights and freedoms.

Toussaint L'Ouverture

The French colony of Haiti was the first Latin American colony to revolt against European rule. In Haiti, French planters owned large sugar plantations. Here nearly half a million enslaved Africans lived and worked in terrible conditions. Moreover, the French gave few rights to free mulattoes (persons of mixed ancestry) living on the island.

In 1791, a self-educated former slave named **Toussaint L'Ouverture** led a revolt. Toussaint was familiar with the works of the Enlightenment thinkers and wanted to lead his people to liberty. Toussaint proved to be an effective military leader and gained control of much of the island. Haitian slaves won their freedom in 1798.

Preparing for the Regents

- Explain the role of imperialism as a cause of the revolution in Haiti. Why would you expect other revolutions to occur in Latin America?

In 1802, Napoleon sent an army to Haiti to reestablish French dominance. Toussaint led a guerrilla war to gain Haitian independence. The French captured Toussaint, but yellow fever took a heavy toll on their forces. In 1804, Haitians declared their independence. Napoleon then abandoned the island. Haiti became a republic in 1820.

Simón Bolívar

In South America in the early 1800s, an educated creole named **Simón Bolívar** led resistance movements against the Spanish. Bolívar had become an admirer of Enlightenment ideas and the French Revolution during a stay in Europe. He was also inspired by the American Revolution. He vowed to fight Spanish rule in South America. Called "the Liberator," Bolívar became one of the greatest Latin American nationalist leaders of this period.

Struggle For Independence In 1810, Bolívar started his long struggle against the Spanish. Over the next 12 years, he led a series of military campaigns that won independence for Venezuela, New Granada (present-day Colombia), Ecuador, Peru, and Bolivia. He then joined forces with **José de San Martín,** who had defeated the Spanish in Argentina and Chile in the 1810s.

Difficulties Ahead Despite his victories against the Spanish, Bolívar failed in his attempt to create a large, united Latin American state. Spain's former empire thus became divided into a number of separate independent states. These nations faced a long struggle to gain stability, achieve social equality, and eliminate poverty.

Summarize

- Who were the key revolutionaries for independence in Latin America?

- What were their accomplishments?

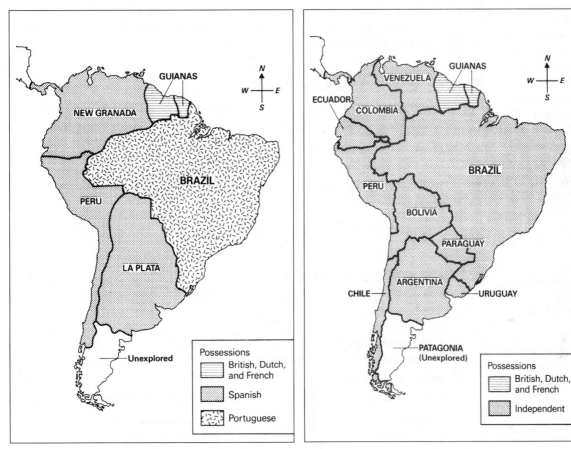

South America, 1790

South America, 1828

Summary

Enlightenment ideas about natural rights and rejection of absolutist authority inspired major revolutions in the late 1700s and early 1800s. Colonists in America declared independence from Great Britain in 1776 and created a government based on the ideas of Locke and Montesquieu. Influenced by the American Revolution, revolutionaries in France overturned the monarchy and created a new social order. Napoleon helped spread revolutionary ideals across Europe. Both the American and French Revolutions contributed to revolutions in Latin America in the early 1800s. Leaders such as Toussaint L'Ouverture and Simón Bolívar led popular movements to overthrow European rule.

Key Themes and Concepts

Change
The revolutions of the late 1700s and early 1800s had several lasting effects. These included the creation of the United States, the spread of nationalism and democratic ideals, and the establishment of independent republics in Latin America.

Reaction Against Revolutionary Ideals

After the French Revolution, there was a reaction against revolutionary ideals.

• Conservative leaders at the Congress of Vienna opposed such ideals.

• New uprisings across Europe were largely unsuccessful.

• Russian czars remained absolute rulers.

• Reform movements faced difficult obstacles in Latin America.

Section Overview

After the French Revolution, there was a reaction against revolutionary ideals. In 1815 at the Congress of Vienna, the leaders of the nations of Europe restored the old monarchies. In the following decades, conflicts between revolutionary ideals and the desire to maintain the old order would cause uprisings and repression. Although some reforms slowly took hold in Western Europe, absolutism remained strong in Russia. In Latin America, democratic reforms were slow to develop. In the early 1900s, however, Mexico experienced a political and social revolution accompanied by the growth of nationalistic feelings.

Key Themes and Concepts

As you review this section, take special note of the following key themes and concepts:

Power How did leaders react to revolutionary ideals in Europe after the French Revolution and the reign of Napoleon?

Political Systems What barriers to reform existed in Russia and Latin America in the 1800s?

Change What reforms occurred in Mexico in the early 1800s?

Key People and Terms

• What do three of the key people and terms have in common? Explain.

Key People and Terms

As you review this section, be sure you understand the significance of these key people and terms:

Congress of Vienna	pogroms
Prince Clemens von Metternich	oligarchy
balance of power	caudillos
conservatism	cash crop economy
liberalism	Porfirio Díaz
nationalism	Emiliano Zapata
Russification	Francisco "Pancho" Villa

Key Themes and Concepts

Power
The leaders at the Congress of Vienna wanted to keep France from dominating the continent. They also wanted to restore monarchs to power.

The Congress of Vienna

After Napoleon's defeat, European diplomats met at the Congress of Vienna in 1815 to devise a peace settlement. The meeting was dominated by **Prince Clemens von Metternich** of Austria, who wanted to restore Europe to the way it was before the French Revolution. The decisions made at this meeting were designed to bring stability and order to Europe by repressing the feelings of nationalism and preventing liberal political change unleashed by the French Revolution and Napoleon.

The Congress of Vienna

GOAL	ACTION
To prevent France from going to war again	Strengthen countries around France • Add Belgium and Luxembourg to Holland to create the kingdom of the Netherlands • Give Prussia lands along the Rhine River • Allow Austria to take control of Italy again
To return Europe to the way it was in 1792, before Napoleon	Give power back to the monarchs of Europe
To protect the new system and maintain peace	Create the Concert of Europe, an organization to maintain peace in Europe

Preparing for the Regents

• Explain how the Congress of Vienna was a reaction against revolutionary ideals.

Balance of Power and Restored Monarchs

Despite their sometimes different goals, the leaders at the Congress of Vienna accomplished a great deal. Much of what the leaders did at the Congress of Vienna occurred for two reasons. First, they wanted to establish a **balance of power,** or a distribution of military and economic power that prevents any one nation from becoming too strong. They also wanted to restore power to monarchs. The Congress of Vienna was the first of many reactions in Europe against the revolutionary ideals of the 1700s and 1800s. It was also a victory for conservatives. **Conservatism** was a set of beliefs held by those who wanted to preserve traditional ways. As conservatism clashed with the ideals of the French Revolution, revolutions would occur throughout Europe and Latin America.

Vocabulary Builder

clash—(klash) v. if two people or groups clash, they argue because they have very different beliefs and opinions

New Revolutions in Europe

The Vienna settlement helped to maintain peace among nations in Europe for almost 100 years. Revolutions did occur within nations, however. Revolutionaries were not happy with the results of the Congress of Vienna. They opposed the Congress's policy of trying to restore Europe to the way it had been before the French Revolution.

Preparing for the Regents

• How do the events of 1848 reflect the long-term impact of the French Revolution?

Causes

Revolts occurred in many places across Europe from the time of the Congress through about 1850. There were two main causes of these revolutions.

• **Liberalism** People opposed the power of monarchs and sought democratic reforms.

• **Nationalism** People wanted independent nation-states that were free from foreign rule.

Key Themes and Concepts

Civic Ideals
Note that nationalism has its roots in the Enlightenment and the French Revolution.

Revolutions of 1830

In 1830, the French, alarmed by their monarch's attempt to restore absolutism, successfully revolted and created a constitutional monarchy. Attempts to gain independence in Greece and Belgium were successful while similar attempts in Italy, Germany, and Poland were defeated.

Revolutions of 1848

Additional revolutions occurred in 1848, led by the events in France.

• **France** King Louis Philippe's government was denounced as corrupt, prompting another revolution in 1848. Louis Philippe stepped down, and a republic was established. Within months of the uprising, upper- and middle-class interests gained control of the government and violently put down a

Key Themes and Concepts

Interdependence
As had occurred in 1789, a revolution in 1830 in France affected the other nations of Europe.

Revolutions in Europe, 1830 and 1848

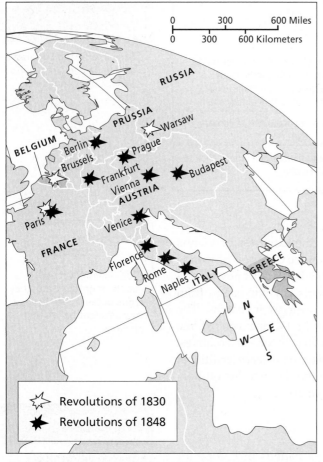

Revolutions in Europe *In 1830 and 1848, revolutions in Europe took place in many cities and countries. Most failed. However, Europe was changed by reforms that resulted from the revolts.*

workers' rebellion in Paris. The fighting left bitter feelings between the working class and the middle class.

- **Austrian Empire** When students revolted in Vienna in 1848, Metternich tried to suppress them. He resigned when workers rose up to support the students. As revolution quickly spread to other areas of the empire, the Austrian government agreed to certain reforms. However, the Austrian army soon regained control, and many revolutionaries were imprisoned, executed, or sent into exile.

- **Italy and Germany** Rebellions in Italy were successful just for short periods of time. In Germany, student protesters who were backed by peasants and workers demanded reforms. Although an assembly was formed, it was later dissolved as the revolutionaries turned on each other.

Impact of the Revolutions

The revolutions that occurred in 1830 and 1848 frightened many of Europe's rulers. As a result, some agreed to reforms. For the most part, however, the revolts of 1830 and 1848 failed. There were several reasons for these failures.

- Most revolutionaries did not have widespread support.
- Sometimes the revolutionaries themselves were divided.
- Powerful government forces often crushed the revolts.

Preparing for the Regents

- Use your map skills to tell which areas were the most affected by the revolutions between 1830 and 1850.

Absolutism in Czarist Russia

Impact of the French Revolution

While the countries of Western Europe were profoundly changed by the French Revolution, Russian czars strove to keep the ideals of the French Revolution—liberty, equality, and fraternity—from reaching their people. Unlike the countries of Western Europe, Russia changed very little throughout the 1800s.

Political Conditions

Russian czars resisted reforms, fearing that change would weaken their control. Czars refused to introduce elements of democracy into their societies, although democratic ideals were gaining strength in Western European countries at that time.

Social Conditions

A Feudal Society Russia had a rigid feudal social structure. Landowning nobles were powerful and resisted any change that would weaken their position. The middle class was too small to have any influence. Although serfdom had gradually disappeared in Western Europe by the 1700s, it had continued in Russia. Serfs were bound to the land, and the owner of the land had almost total power over the serfs who worked it.

Freeing of the Serfs Russia became involved in the Crimean War after trying to seize Ottoman lands along the Danube. Russia suffered a defeat in this war, making its leaders aware of the country's need to modernize and industrialize. Demands for reform, including freedom for the serfs, followed.

In 1861, during the reign of Alexander II, the serfs were freed. Freeing the serfs brought problems, however. Former serfs had to buy the land they had worked, and many were too poor to do so. Even those who could buy land often did not have enough to support their families. Discontent continued.

Many freed serfs moved off their land and into the cities, where they took jobs in industries. These freed serfs were sometimes part of the pressure for reform in Russia.

Russification Russia, as a vast empire, contained many ethnic minorities. The czars aimed to maintain tight control over these people as well as to encourage feelings of Russian unity. This policy of Russification was an attempt to make all groups think, act, and believe as Russians.

For example, Russian czar Alexander III persecuted non-Russians, including Poles, Ukrainians, and Armenians. He insisted on one language, Russian, and one church, the Russian Orthodox Church. Alexander also persecuted Jews, restricting the jobs they could have and even where they could live. These policies encouraged violent attacks on Jews, called **pogroms**. The authorities stood by and watched as the homes of Jews were burned and their businesses looted.

Imperialism in Asia

In the 1700s, Russia had expanded to the Baltic Sea, to the Black Sea, and into Eastern Europe, occupying much of Poland. The Russians also expanded eastward across Siberia and beyond the Bering Strait, into Alaska. During the early 1800s, the Russians began their practice of exiling convicts to Siberia.

Czars in the 1800s added lands in central Asia. This territory gave Russia the largest and most diverse empire in Europe and Asia. The construction of the Trans-Siberian Railway, begun in the 1890s, extended Russian economic and political control over the region.

Instability in Latin America

As you have learned, revolutionaries in Latin America had thrown off Spanish rule in the early 1800s. Life, however, did not improve for most people after they achieved independence. Revolts and civil wars broke out while poverty and prejudice continued. Many factors made it difficult for Latin American nations to benefit from the revolutions that had occurred.

Geographic Barriers

The Latin American nations that gained independence in the 1800s covered a vast area, from Mexico to the southern tip of South America. This area included numerous geographic barriers, such as the Andes Mountains, that hindered attempts at creating a unified Latin America. Fights between various leaders and nationalistic feelings within different groups also kept Latin Americans from uniting.

Social Injustice

Despite the establishment of Latin American republics with constitutions, democracy did not follow. One problem was that the colonial class structure remained largely intact. Creoles replaced peninsulares as the ruling class, and

Key Themes and Concepts

Change
Despite the problems faced by freed serfs, their emancipation in 1861 marked a major turning point in Russian history. A similar development occurred in the United States a few years later, when the enslaved African Americans were freed.

Diversity
Russian czars fought diversity in their nation. They tried to force minorities to abandon their own cultures and adopt Russian culture.

Preparing for the Regents

• How did conditions in Russia in the late 1800s contribute to the revolutions that occurred in the early 1900s?

Key Themes and Concepts

Political Systems
Three centuries of strong Spanish rule left most Latin Americans with little practical knowledge of how to establish a representative democracy.

land and wealth remained in their hands. This kind of system, in which ruling power belongs to a small, powerful elite, is known as an **oligarchy.** Mestizos, mulattoes, Indians, and Africans gained few rights and still faced racial prejudice. Most had to work as peasants on the large estates of the landowners.

Military Rulers

Because of the strong rule that colonial empires had exerted in Latin America, people of these countries had little experience with self-government. Local military strongmen called **caudillos** put together their own armies and challenged central governments. Some caudillos were strong enough to gain control of governments. These dictators were repressive, usually ignoring existing constitutions. Their policies usually favored the upper class.

Power of the Church

The Roman Catholic Church had acted as a stabilizing influence in Latin America. It also promoted education. But the Church had an interest in preserving the old order in Latin America. As in colonial days, the Church still owned large amounts of land. Liberals in Latin America hoped to end the Church's power over education and reduce its vast landholdings.

Economic Problems

Cash Crop Economies Under colonial rule, Latin American economies had become dependent on trade with Spain and Portugal. Latin Americans relied on a cash crop economy. The colonies sent raw materials such as sugar, cotton, and coffee to Europe and had to import manufactured goods. Dependence on just one crop or even a few crops makes a nation's economy very unstable. If a drought or crop failure occurs, or if prices for the products fall, the economy can be devastated.

Economic Imperialism In the mid-1800s, some Latin American economies began to grow. Foreign investment allowed them to develop mining and agriculture. Foreigners also invested in transportation improvement, such as the development of ports and the building of railroads. Even so, there were few benefits for the majority of Latin Americans. The rigid class structure limited economic gains to the few at the top of the social structure. In general, only the upper classes and the foreign investors profited.

The Mexican Revolution (1910–1930)

Causes

General **Porfirio Díaz** ruled Mexico as a dictator in the late 1800s and early 1900s. Díaz brought economic advances to Mexico. Railroads were built and industry grew. However, the wealth went to a small upper class as well as to foreign investors. The rule of Díaz, who brutally suppressed opposition, left most Mexicans uneducated, landless, and poor. In 1910, the discontent boiled over into a revolution that forced Díaz from power.

Key Figures

No one person led the revolution. Several local leaders gathered their own armies, destroying railroads and estates.

- **Emiliano Zapata,** an Indian, was one of the most famous leaders. He led a large peasant revolt in the south, calling for land reform.
- **Francisco "Pancho" Villa,** a rebel leader in the north, won the loyalty of a large number of peasants. When the United States supported the Mexican government against Villa, conflict erupted across the border between Villa and the United States government in 1916.

Preparing for the Regents

- In both Russia and Latin America, there were obstacles to reform. Which obstacles were shared by Russia and Latin America? Which obstacles were unique to Latin America?

- What economic problems can result from dependence on a cash crop economy?

Preparing for the Regents

- Compare the causes of the Mexican Revolution to those of the French Revolution.

- Venustiano Carranza was elected president of Mexico in 1917. He approved a new constitution that, with amendments, is still in force today.

Effects of the Revolution

The Constitution of 1917 The new constitution agreed to by Carranza in 1917 called for land reform, gave the government control of Church estates, and guaranteed more rights to workers and to women.

Social Reforms Reforms were eventually carried out in the 1920s, making Mexico the first Latin American nation to achieve social and economic reform for the majority of its people. For example, the government set up libraries and schools. Some Indian communities were given the opportunity to regain land that had been taken from them in the past.

Economic Nationalism Mexico, along with other countries of Latin America, experienced strong feelings of nationalism in the early 1900s. Much of the nationalistic spirit was aimed at ending economic dependence on industrial powers. Mexico became determined to develop its own economy. The Mexican government brought industries under government control or took over foreign-owned industries.

Cultural Nationalism In the 1920s and 1930s, nationalistic feeling caused writers in Mexico and other parts of Latin America to reject the influences of Europe. They began to take pride in Latin American culture, which displayed a mixture of Western European and Indian traditions. In Mexico, mural painting, which had been a common art form in the Aztec empire, was revived. Muralists such as Diego Rivera and José Clemente Orozco created works of great beauty. Many showed the struggles of the Mexican people for freedom.

Summary

After the defeat of Napoleon, conservative leaders sought to suppress the ideals of the French Revolution and restore monarchy. In 1830 and 1848, uprisings against the old order occurred all across Europe. Although these revolts were mostly unsuccessful, the ideals behind them continued to have an impact on Europe. In Russia and in Latin America, numerous barriers to reform existed. In Mexico, however, reforms took place that benefited the majority of the population.

Note

Reading
Identify
chart. A
the effects of the Mexican Revolution. Include the main idea and at least one supporting detail.

Effects of the Mexican Revolution

Key Themes and Concepts

Nationalism
In Mexico, nationalism had economic and cultural aspects. Mexicans wanted to end their economic dependence on foreign powers. They also wanted to show their pride in Latin American culture.

Preparing for the Regents

- Compare the reactions against revolutionary ideals in Europe, in Russia, and in Latin America in the 1800s.

The Cold War

Arab States
- Years involved - 1952-1970 (or 1991)
- Conflict begun following the Egyptian Revolution and the rise to power of Nasser.
- Some countries that fought in the area are- Egypt, Syria, Iraq, North and South Yemen, and most other arab states.
- Results of the conflict include
   - Decline of Pan-Arabism and Nasserism after the death of Gamal Abdel Nasser.

Global Nationalism

The
Big
Idea

The force of nationalism:

• inspired revolutions in Europe and Latin America.

• led to a united Italy and a united Germany in the late 1800s.

• arose among Indians, Turks, and Jews.

• created conflict in the Balkans by the early 1900s.

Section Overview

During the French Revolution, people in France expressed great pride in their nation. Nationalism later spread to other peoples, inspiring uprisings across Europe and in Latin America. In the 1860s, nationalism led to the unification of Italy. By 1871, Germany had also united. Outside Europe, nationalist movements took root in India, Turkey, and elsewhere. Among Jews, a movement arose to create a separate Jewish state in Palestine. As the 1800s drew to a close, nationalistic forces created tensions in the Balkans that set the stage for a world war.

Key Themes and Concepts

As you review this section, take special note of the following key themes and concepts:

Nationalism How did nationalism cause revolutions?

Nation-State How did nationalism lead to the creation of nation-states in Italy and Germany?

Change How did nationalism affect Indians, Turks, and Jews?

Diversity How did nationalism cause conflict in the Balkans?

Key People and Terms

Key People and Terms

• Place each of the key people and terms into these two categories: person or movement/political group.

As you review this section, be sure you understand the significance of these key people and terms:

Giuseppe Mazzini	Zionism
Count Camillo Cavour	Indian National Congress
Giuseppe Garibaldi	Muslim League
Otto von Bismarck	Young Turks
kaiser	Pan-Slavism

Nationalism and Revolution

Key Themes and Concepts

Nationalism
Nationalism is a feeling of pride in and devotion to one's nation. It is a feeling that develops among people who may share a common language, history, set of traditions, or goal. Nationalism often causes people to join together to choose their own form of government, without outside interference.

As you have learned, nationalism is a feeling of strong devotion to one's country. This feeling often develops among people who share a common language and heritage. Nationalism played an important role in political revolutions of the 1800s.

Revolution and war in the 1790s created a strong sense of national unity in France. This feeling inspired French armies to battlefield success as they sought to spread the ideals of their revolution. Napoleon also inspired nationalism among the nations he conquered. However, nationalistic feelings encouraged conquered peoples to rise up against Napoleon. In the years following the French Revolution, nationalism led to upheaval in Europe and elsewhere.

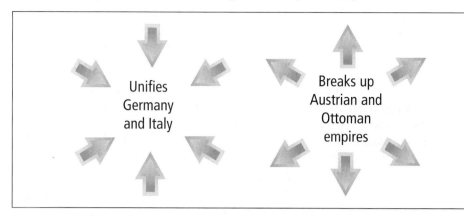

Unifies
Germany
and Italy

Breaks up
Austrian and
Ottoman
empires

Unifying Germany and Italy
Before unification, the areas that became Germany and Italy were divided into small-sized states.

Unification Movements in Europe

Nationalistic feeling became an increasingly significant force for self-determination and unification in Europe.

Italy

Ever since the Roman empire had fallen in the 400s, Italy had been divided into many small states. After Napoleon invaded Italy, he united some of the Italian states into the Kingdom of Italy. The Congress of Vienna, however, redivided Italy and put much of it under Austrian or Spanish control.

The three great leaders of Italian nationalism were Giuseppe Mazzini, Count Camillo Cavour, and Giuseppe Garibaldi.

- **Giuseppe Mazzini** formed the Young Italy national movement in 1831, but he was exiled for his views. His writings and speeches provided inspiration to the nationalist movement.
- **Count Camillo Cavour,** prime minister of the Italian state of Sardinia, shrewdly formed alliances with France and later with Prussia. He used diplomacy and war to drive Austrian power from Italy.
- **Giuseppe Garibaldi** was a soldier who led the forces that won control of southern Italy and helped it to unite with the north.

By 1861, Victor Emmanuel of Sardinia was crowned king of a united Italy. Rome and Venetia, at first not part of Italy, were included by 1870. With no tradition of unity, the new nation faced conflicts. The urban north quarreled with the rural south. Also, the Catholic Church resisted the new government. Despite economic growth, unrest grew in the late 1800s.

Germany

Another national unification movement occurred in Germany. In the early 1800s, most German-speaking people lived in small states, to which they felt loyalty. During Napoleon's conquests, feelings of nationalism stirred in those Germans who wanted to be free of French rule. After Napoleon's defeat in 1815, some nationalists called for a united Germany. Metternich, however, blocked this idea at the Congress of Vienna.

The Rise of Prussia In the 1830s, Prussia set up a trade union among German states called the Zollverein. This agreement ended trade barriers between the states and was a step toward unity. More important, it established Prussia as a leader among the states.

In 1862, **Otto von Bismarck** was appointed chancellor of Prussia. Over the next decade, Bismarck, a strong and practical leader, guided German unification. Bismarck was not driven by a feeling of German nationalism, however. His loyalty was to the Prussian king. Unification was merely a means for him to make the Prussian king the ruler of a strong and united German state.

Preparing for the Regents

• What role did Prussia and Bismarck play in German unification?

Vocabulary Builder

prestige—(prehs TEEZH) *n.* the respect and admiration that someone or something gets because of their success or important position

"Blood and Iron" Bismarck believed that the only way to unify Germany was through a policy he called "blood and iron." Bismarck had no faith in speeches and representative government. He believed that the only way to unite the German states was through war. In seven years, Bismarck led Prussia into three wars. Each war increased Prussia's prestige and moved the German states closer to unity.

• **Danish War** In 1864, Prussia allied with Austria to seize land from Denmark.
• **Austro-Prussian War** In 1866, Prussia turned against Austria to gain more land. Prussia overwhelmed Austria in just seven weeks. Several German states were united with Prussia in the North German Confederation.
• **Franco-Prussian War** In 1870, Bismarck used nationalism and the bitter memories of Napoleon's conquests to stir up support for a war against France. Prussia and its German allies easily defeated France. During the war, southern German states agreed to unite with Prussia.

In 1871, the German states united under the Prussian king, William I. As their ruler, William called himself the **kaiser,** a title that was derived from the name *Caesar* and meant "emperor."

Zionism

The rise of nationalism in Europe had led to an intensification of anti-Semitism in the late 1800s. As citizens grew more patriotic about their own nations, they often grew more intolerant of those whom they saw as outsiders, including Jews. The pogroms that occurred in Eastern Europe and Russia are one example of this trend.

As anti-Semitism grew in Europe, some Jews moved to Palestine, the ancient Jewish homeland, buying land that they organized into farming communities. A Jewish journalist named Theodor Herzl became alarmed by the strong anti-Semitism he witnessed in France. In 1896, Herzl called for Jews to establish their own state. Herzl's writings helped to build Zionism, the movement devoted to building a Jewish state in Palestine. In 1897, he organized the first world congress of Zionists, which met in Switzerland. Herzl's dream of an independent Israel was realized a little more than 50 years later.

Preparing for the Regents

• The anti-Semitism that grew in Europe during the 1800s is an example of the negative effects of a group's nationalism on other peoples. Can you think of other examples of nationalism causing discrimination and violence against religious or ethnic minorities?

Nationalism in Asia

National movements were also at work outside of Europe.

India

Since the 1700s, the British had maintained control of the Indian subcontinent. Under British rule, nationalistic feelings began to stir among Indians, especially those who had been educated in the West. As Indian students learned about democracy and natural rights, they called increasingly for self-rule.

Indian National Congress In 1885, nationalist leaders in India formed the Indian National Congress, which became known as the Congress party. This group was made up mainly of Hindu professionals and business leaders. At first, the Congress party called merely for equal opportunity to serve in the government

Key Themes and Concepts

Change
Western education introduced Indians to the ideals of democracy, nationalism, and basic human rights. This kind of thinking led eventually to self-rule for India. Western education brought change to other nations as well.

of India. They called for greater democracy and Western-style modernization, looking ahead to self-rule.

Muslim League Initially, Muslims and Hindus cooperated in their campaign for self-rule. However, Muslims grew distrustful of the Indian National Congress because the organization was mostly Hindu. The increasing strength of Hindu nationalism alarmed Muslims. In 1906, Muslim leaders formed the Muslim League to protect their own rights and interests. They even talked about setting up a separate Muslim state. After World War I, calls for Indian self-rule increased, followed by demands for independence. This goal would finally be achieved in 1947.

Turkey

In the 1800s, the multinational Ottoman empire faced challenges from the various ethnic groups in the empire.

Young Turks A group of liberals in the 1890s established a movement called the Young Turks. This group wanted to strengthen the Ottoman empire and end the threat of Western imperialism. In 1908, they overthrew the sultan and took control of the government.

The Armenian Massacre The Young Turks supported Turkish nationalism. They abandoned traditional Ottoman tolerance of diverse cultures and religions. Muslim Turks turned against Christian Armenians who were living in the Ottoman empire. Accusing the Armenians of plotting with Russia against the Ottoman empire, the Turks unleashed a massacre that resulted in the death of over a million Armenians over the next 25 years.

Key Themes and Concepts

Diversity
Religion and cultural differences made it difficult for Hindus and Muslims to unite in a single national movement. Eventually, two nations—predominantly Muslim Pakistan and predominantly Hindu India—were created. Conflicts between the two groups still exist today.

Nationalities in Eastern Europe Around 1870

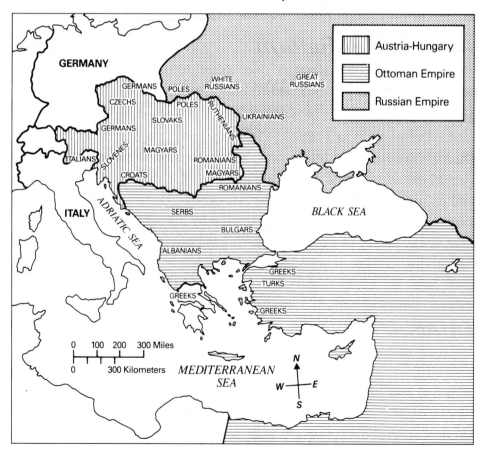

Preparing for the Regents

• Practice your map skills by listing the nationalities that existed in the Ottoman empire in 1870.

• Romanians
• Serbs
• Bulgars
• Albanians
• Greeks
• Turks

The Balkans The peninsula in southeastern Europe is called the Balkans. In the late 1800s, this area was a center of conflict. The various peoples and empires competed for power.

Preparing for the Regents

- How has nationalism been a force that divides as well as unifies? Give examples to support your answer.

- By the 1800s, the Ottoman empire was becoming weaker. How did European nations react to the decreasing power of the Ottomans?

- Choose one of the regions discussed in this section. Explain how nationalism remains a force in that region today.

Russia- They still have their own Space scientists who want to beat Americans.

Note Taking

Reading Skill: **Summarize** Make a chart. Summarize the main ideas about nationalism in the three areas listed in the chart.

Nationalism	
Europe	• •
Asia	• •
Balkans	• •

Nationalism and Conflict in the Balkans

Nationalism was a source of conflict in the Balkan peninsula of southeastern Europe. In the 1800s, the Ottoman empire still ruled much of the area, which was home to many groups. Among these were Serbs, Greeks, Bulgarians, and Romanians. During the 1800s, nationalist groups in the Balkans rebelled against foreign rule. From 1829 to 1908, Greece, Montenegro, Serbia, Romania, and Bulgaria all gained their independence.

The nations of Europe viewed the Ottoman empire as "the sick man of Europe." They hoped to gain land from the Ottoman empire. Russia, Austria-Hungary, Great Britain, and France all entered into alliances and wars that were designed to gain territory from the Ottoman empire.

Russia sponsored a nationalistic movement called **Pan-Slavism,** based on the idea that all Slavic peoples shared a common nationality. Serbia had a large Slavic population and was supported by Russia. Austria-Hungary, however, feared Serbian nationalism and angered Serbia by taking control in 1908 of two provinces that would have given Serbia access to the Adriatic Sea.

In the early years of 1900, crisis after crisis broke out on the Balkan peninsula. By 1914, the Balkans were the "powder keg of Europe." Tensions soon exploded into a full-scale global conflict: World War I.

Summary

Starting in the late 1700s, nationalism became a major force that helped inspire uprisings across Europe and Latin America. In the mid-1800s, nationalism led to the creation of two strong, united nations: Italy and Germany. Nationalistic sentiments also spread among Indians, Turks, Jews, and other peoples. Nationalism did not always draw people together, however. In the early 1900s, nationalism created conflicts in southeastern Europe that drove the continent to the brink of war.

Economic and Social Revolutions

Section Overview

Starting around 1750, Europe experienced a series of major changes. They began with improvements in farming that led to an increase in population. These changes contributed to the Industrial Revolution. With the Industrial Revolution, social classes, people's roles, working conditions, and city life changed greatly. When the new conditions led to problems, differing thinkers wanted to solve them in different ways. Some groups emphasized the rights of individuals. Socialists and others stressed the needs of society as a whole. A period of reforms followed. By the early 1900s, the world had changed even more: Global migration occurred and movement toward a global economy accelerated.

Key Themes and Concepts

As you review this section, take special note of the following key themes and concepts:

Change What changes occurred during the Agrarian Revolution?

Science and Technology What role did technology play in the Industrial Revolution?

Economic Systems What economic and social developments occurred as part of the Industrial Revolution?

Political Systems What parliamentary reforms came about as a result of the Industrial Revolution?

The
Big Idea

In the 1700s and 1800s in Europe:

- the Agrarian Revolution led to population growth.

- the Industrial Revolution eventually transformed economic systems and social conditions around the world.

- people proposed different ways to deal with the problems created by industrialization.

- economic life became more global, and mass migrations of people occurred.

Key People and Terms

As you review this section, be sure you understand the significance of these key people and terms:

Agrarian Revolution	Adam Smith	Robert Owen
enclosure	capitalism	socialism
Industrial Revolution	supply and demand	Karl Marx
factories	Thomas Malthus	suffrage
laissez faire	Social Darwinism	

Key People and Terms

- Place each of the key people and terms into these three categories: science and technology, economic system, political system.

The Agrarian Revolution

In 1750, most people still lived in small villages and made their own clothing and tools. In the century that followed, dramatic changes took place in the ways people lived and worked.

Increased Food Production

The movement away from rural life began with the Agrarian Revolution, a change in methods of farming.

Vocabulary
Builder

dike—(dyk) *n.* a wall
or bank built to keep
back water and
prevent flooding

Technology The Dutch led the way by building dikes to protect their farmland from the sea and using fertilizer to improve the soil. The British discovered ways to produce more food. Jethro Tull invented the seed drill, which planted seeds in rows.

Enclosure Movement Landowners found a new purpose for enclosure, taking over and fencing off land that once had been shared by peasant farmers. The purpose of the enclosure movement was to replace the many small strip farms with larger fields. This practice made farming more efficient, improving agricultural production.

Population Explosion

The Agrarian Revolution led to rapid population growth. With a better diet, women had healthier and stronger babies. In addition, improved medical care and sanitation helped people live longer. During the 1700s, Europe's population increased from 120 million to about 190 million.

The Industrial Revolution

The Industrial Revolution was the period, beginning around 1750, in which the means of production of goods shifted from hand tools to complex machines and from human and animal power to steam power. During this period, technology developed rapidly and production increased. The Industrial Revolution brought great changes into people's lives.

Causes of the Industrial Revolution

Industrialization began in Great Britain. Belgium, France, Germany, the United States, and Japan would all industrialize by the end of the 1800s. In time, the Industrial Revolution would spread throughout the world. It happened first in Great Britain for several reasons.

Key Themes
and Concepts

Change
As larger areas were
enclosed, farm yields
rose. Profits grew
because fewer people
were needed to work
the farms. Unemployed
farmers moved to cities.

**Preparing for
the Regents**

• How did the Agrarian
Revolution of the 1700s
contribute to the
Industrial Revolution?

**Preparing for
the Regents**

• Explain three reasons for
the start of the Industrial
Revolution.

1. Food
2. Geography
3. Technology.

The Industrial Revolution Begins in Great Britain

Geography	Population Growth and Change
Great Britain had plenty of iron ore and coal needed for industrialization. As an island, Great Britain had many natural harbors for trade and was protected from invasion. Rivers served both as a means of transportation and as sources of power for factories.	Growth in population due to the Agrarian Revolution led to more available workers. Because of the enclosure movement, fewer farm laborers were needed. People moved to the cities where they could work in factories.
Capital for Investment	**Energy and Technology**
The British overseas empire had made the economy strong. As a result, the middle class had the capital to invest in mines, railroads, and factories and the commercial and financial skills to manage investment.	Great Britain had experienced an energy revolution. In the 1700s, giant water wheels were used to power new machines. Soon coal was used to power steam engines, which would become an important power source for machines.

Factory System and Mass Production

The textile industry was the first to use the inventions of the Industrial Revolution. Before the Industrial Revolution, families spun cotton into thread and then wove cloth at home. By the 1700s, new machines were too large and expensive to be operated at home. Spinners and weavers began to work in long sheds that were owned by the manufacturers. These sheds, which brought workers and machines together in one place, became the first **factories.** At first, these factories were located near rapidly moving streams, which provided water power. Later, machines were powered by steam engines, fueled by coal. The factory system promoted mass production, meaning that goods were produced in huge quantities at lower cost.

Effects of the Industrial Revolution

The Industrial Revolution brought about many economic and social changes.

Laissez Faire Economics Before the Industrial Revolution, European nations had followed a policy of mercantilism, which called for government regulations, such as tariffs, to achieve a favorable balance of trade. However, during the Enlightenment, a theory called laissez faire emerged, which argued that businesses should be allowed to operate free of government regulation. In 1776, **Adam Smith** wrote *The Wealth of Nations* which promoted laissez-faire ideas. These ideas became the basis of the prevailing economic system during the Industrial Revolution. This system, known as **capitalism,** said that the economy should be governed by the natural forces of **supply and demand** and competition among businesses.

Rise of Big Business With new technology came the need for the investment of large amounts of money in businesses. To acquire this money, business owners sold stocks, or shares in their companies, to investors. Each stockholder therefore owned a part of the company. Stockholders allowed businesses to form corporations and expand into many areas.

New Class Structure In the Middle Ages, the two main classes in Europe had been nobles and peasants. During the 1600s, a middle class had emerged. The Industrial Revolution added more complexity.

- The upper class consisted of very rich industrial and business families. Members of these families often married into noble families.
- A growing upper middle class of business people and professionals—such as lawyers and doctors—emerged. Their standard of living was high. Below them a lower middle class of teachers, office workers, shopowners, and clerks existed.
- At the bottom of this social structure were factory workers and peasants. They benefited least from the Industrial Revolution. People in this class faced harsh living and working conditions in overcrowded cities.

Urbanization People moved from small villages to the towns and cities where factories were located. At first, conditions were very bad. Working-class people lived in crowded buildings. Without a sewage or sanitation system, garbage rotted in the streets. Disease spread.

Working Conditions Factory work hours were long. Men, women, and even children worked 12 to 16 hours a day. Mass production methods led to work that was boring. Many machines were dangerous.

Preparing for the Regents

- How did the Industrial Revolution contribute to changing the roles of men and women?

Changing Social Roles The roles of men, women, and children changed in the new industrial society. Farming families had all worked the land together. Artisans had worked in their homes. Now the workplace became separated from the home.

The roles of middle-class men and women were redefined. Men worked in the public world of business and government. Women worked at home, where they were responsible for maintaining the dwelling and raising the children, including their moral instruction. Social class had an impact on family life. Middle-class children had a high standard of living and a better chance at education. Among the working class, on the other hand, children had to work long hours to help support their families. Working-class women also worked long hours, although they were paid less than men. Family life sometimes suffered as women worked 12 hours or more in a factory and then came home to care for their families.

Improved Transportation The growth of industry led to improvements in transportation.

- Roads and canals were built and improved.
- The steam locomotive was invented. Railroads grew.
- Steam engines powered ships at sea.

Rising Standards of Living Settlement patterns shifted over time. The rich lived in pleasant neighborhoods on the edges of the cities. The poor were crowded into slums in city centers, near factories. Over time, conditions in cities improved, however. In addition, people ate more varied diets and were healthier, thanks to advances in medicine.

Competing Philosophies

The hardships and changes brought by the Industrial Revolution inspired many varying solutions. Several different ways of thinking competed against each other.

Laissez-Faire Capitalism

Many economic thinkers supported Adam Smith's idea that natural laws governed economic life. **Thomas Malthus** published his *Essay on the Principle of Population* in 1798. He argued that because population tended to increase more rapidly than the food supply, the poor would continue to suffer. However, because he believed in laissez faire, he did not urge the government to step in to help the poor. He urged the poor to have fewer children.

Social Darwinism

Other new ideas of the 1800s challenged long-held beliefs. In 1859, British naturalist Charles Darwin caused an uproar by saying that humans had evolved over millions of years. This theory of evolution, as it was called, stirred conflicts between religion and science.

Part of Darwin's theory involved the idea of natural selection. Using the ideas of Thomas Malthus, Darwin said that species naturally produced more offspring than the food supply could support. Members of each species had to compete to survive. Thus, natural forces selected the most able members, producing an improved species.

Later thinkers used Darwin's ideas to develop a theory known as **Social Darwinism.** According to Social Darwinism, successful businesspeople were successful because they were naturally more "fit" to succeed than others. War allowed

Note Taking

Reading Skill:
Identify Main Ideas and Supporting Details
As you read Competing Philosophies, complete an outline with the main ideas and supporting details. An outline has been started for you.

Competing Philosophies
I. Laissez-faire capitalism
  A. Adam Smith
    1. natural laws govern economic life
  B.
II.

stronger nations to weed out weaker ones. Social Darwinism played a part in racism, the belief that one race is superior to another. It also contributed to the rise in imperialism.

Social Reformism

In contrast to laissez-faire philosophy, which advised governments to leave business alone, other theorists believed government should intervene to improve people's lives. Many different types of social reformism arose. Socialists hoped to replace the capitalist economic system. Reform movements attempted to correct the abuses of child labor. Labor unions attempted to improve the dangerous working conditions in the factories.

Socialism

Socialism concentrated less on the interests and rights of individuals and more on the interests of society. Industrial capitalism, the socialists claimed, had created a large gap between rich and poor. Under socialism, farms and businesses would belong to all the people, not to individuals. Different types of socialism emerged.

Utopian Socialism Early socialists, called Utopians, sought to create self-sufficient communities, where all property and work would be shared. Since all would have equal wealth, Utopians believed that fighting would end. In Scotland, **Robert Owen** set up a Utopian factory community.

Marxist Socialism German philosopher **Karl Marx** promoted a more radical theory, "scientific socialism." In 1848, Marx and German economist Friedrich Engels explained their ideas, listed here, in *The Communist Manifesto*.

- History was a class struggle between wealthy capitalists and the working class, or proletariat.
- In order to make profits, the capitalists took advantage of the proletariat.
- The proletariat would eventually rise up and overthrow the capitalist system, creating its own society.
- The proletariat society would take control of the means of production and establish a classless, communist society, in which wealth and power would be equally shared.

In the Soviet Union in the 1900s, Marx's ideas would lead to a communist dictatorship and a command economy, in which government officials made all economic decisions.

Labor Unions and Reform Legislation

Throughout the 1800s, reform movements sought to address the negative impact of the Industrial Revolution. The actions of workers and reformers forced governments to examine and reform many of the worst abuses.

Labor Unions By the 1800s, workers in the same occupation began to join together to form organizations to press for reforms. These unions engaged in collective bargaining with their employers, negotiating for higher pay and better working conditions. Workers would strike, or refuse to work, if employers refused their demands. From 1799 to 1824, labor unions were illegal in Great Britain. Eventually, however, labor unions contributed to improved wages, hours, and conditions for workers.

Preparing for the Regents

- Create a chart listing and briefly explaining the competing philosophies that emerged during and after the Industrial Revolution.

Vocabulary Builder

abuse—(uh BYOOS) *n.* the use of something in a way that it should not be used

Preparing for the Regents

- Compare and contrast Utopian socialism with Marxist socialism.

Note Taking

Reading Skill:
Identify Effects Complete a concept web with the effects of labor unions. Add more circles if needed.

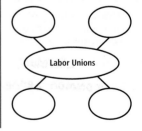

British Reform Laws

British Reform Laws Throughout the 1800s, the British Parliament passed many important laws. These laws improved conditions for women, children, and the working class.

DIRECTION OF REFORM	LAWS ENACTED
Toward greater human rights	1884: Slavery is outlawed in all British colonies.
Toward more representative government	1832: Reform Act of 1832 gave representation to new industrial towns. 1858: Law ended property qualifications for members of Parliament. 1911: Law restricted powers of House of Lords; elected House of Commons became supreme.
Toward universal **suffrage** (the right to vote)	1829: Parliament gave Catholics the right to vote and to hold most public offices. 1867: Reform Act gave vote to many working-class men. 1884: Law extended voting rights to most farmers and other men. 1918: Women won the right to vote.
Toward more rights for workers	1825: Trade unions were legalized. 1840s to 1910s: Parliament passed laws • limiting child labor. • regulating work hours for women and children. • regulating safety conditions in factories and mines. • setting minimum wages. • providing for accident and unemployment insurance.
Toward improved education	1870: Education Act set up local elementary schools run by elected school boards. 1902: Law created a system of state-aided secondary schools. Industrial cities, such as London and Manchester, set up public universities.

Preparing for the Regents

1. Describe a reform law that helped women.

2. Describe a law that helped children.

1.) Toward universal suffrage.

2.) Toward improved education.

Reform Legislation In the early 1830s, British lawmaker Michael Sadler persuaded Parliament to investigate the horrible conditions faced by child laborers in factories. **The Sadler Report** led to the Factories Regulations Act of 1833. This act prohibited children under the age of 9 from being employed in textile mills, and it limited the working hours of children under 18. This is just one of many types of reforms introduced in Great Britain in the 1800s. France and Germany enacted labor reforms as well.

Education and the Arts

Artists, musicians, and writers also took new directions during the Industrial Revolution.

Advances in Education

Governments had begun to set up public schools and require basic education for all children by the late 1800s. Schools not only taught subjects such as reading, writing, and mathematics but encouraged obedience to authority and punctuality as well.

Romanticism

From about 1750 to 1850, a movement known as romanticism thrived. The romantics appealed to emotion rather than to reason. In this way romanticism

Preparing for the Regents

• Discuss one important characteristic of each of these artistic movements.

Romanticism: Literature

Realism: common sense.

was a rebellion against the ideas of the Enlightenment. It was also a reaction against the impersonal nature of industrial society.

Realism

The mid-1800s brought an artistic movement known as realism to the West. Realists sought to show the world as it was. They often looked at the harsh side of life, showing poverty and cruel working conditions. Many writers, such as Charles Dickens, were critical of the abuses of industrial society and hoped to contribute to ending them.

Global Impact of Industrialization

Global Migrations

A Wave of Migrations Improvements in transportation, population growth, and social and political conditions led to a wave of global migrations from about 1845 through the early 1900s.

- Polish nationalists fled Poland for Western Europe and the United States after the Russian army crushed the revolt of 1830.
- Several thousand Germans moved to cities in the United States after the failed revolutions of 1848.
- Russian Jews, escaping pogroms, left Eastern Europe.
- Italian farmers, seeing economic opportunity, also traveled to the Americas.

Mass Starvation in Ireland Another migration occurred from Ireland. Under British rule, the majority of Irish farmland had been used to grow crops, such as wheat and oats, which were sent to England. The Irish themselves used the potato as their main food crop. This system supported the Irish population until 1845, when a disease destroyed the potato crop. Other crops were not affected. Still, the British continued to ship the other products out of Ireland. Four years later, one million Irish had died of starvation or disease. Millions of others moved to the United States and Canada.

Movement Toward a Global Economy

By the mid-1800s, the Industrial Revolution had moved beyond Great Britain. New powers were emerging. As they became strong industrially, they competed for a share of the wealth in markets around the world. In addition, manufacturers traded with other countries for resources they needed. Steamships and railroads, and then automobiles and airplanes, made global trade easier and quicker. As markets expanded around the world and global trade increased, a new imperialism developed.

Summary

In the mid-1700s, the Agrarian Revolution in Europe contributed to an increase in population. The Agrarian Revolution led to the Industrial Revolution, which began in Great Britain and then spread to other countries. Economic and social conditions around the world changed dramatically as a result of the Industrial Revolution. Many new ideas about how to deal with the problems of industrialization developed, and reforms were enacted. Eventually, industrialization led to mass migration and increased global trade.

Preparing for the Regents

- How did British policy contribute to starvation in Ireland and mass migration from Ireland?

Note Taking

Reading Skill:
Recognize Sequence
List the important events of the Economic and Social Revolutions. Record them in the order they occurred. Add boxes as needed.

Date	Event

Preparing for the Regents

- Compare the ways in which the Neolithic Revolution, the Industrial Revolution, and the Computer Revolution changed human life.

Japan and the Meiji Restoration

Section Overview

In 1853, an American fleet sailed to Japan and ended over 200 years of isolation by opening Japan to trade. Soon afterward, Japan's ruling shogun was overthrown, and the Meiji Restoration began. During this period, Japan underwent a rapid period of modernization and industrialization. Changes took place within government, the economy, and social life. Within decades Japan became a modern industrial power and began to build an overseas empire.

Key Themes and Concepts

As you review this section, take special note of the following key themes and concepts:

Change What political, social, and economic changes occurred in Japan in the late 1800s?

Interdependence How did Japan use Western ideas to modernize and industrialize?

Power How did Japan become a global power by the early 1900s?

Key People and Terms

As you review this section, be sure you understand the significance of these key people and terms:

Matthew Perry
Treaty of Kanagawa
Meiji Restoration

zaibatsu
Sino-Japanese War
Russo-Japanese War

The Opening of Japan

In 1853, United States ships sailed into Edo (now Tokyo) Bay, ending more than 200 years of Japanese isolation. This contact led to changes that had a great impact on Japan.

Tokugawa Isolation

European traders had first arrived in Japan in the 1500s. In the 1600s, the Tokugawa shoguns had gained control of Japan. They brought stability to Japan but also banned almost all contact with the outside world. Limited trade was allowed only with the Dutch at Nagasaki.

Commodore Matthew Perry

In 1854, American warships commanded by Commodore **Matthew Perry** sailed to Japan. Perry presented a letter to the Japanese from the United States president, asking that Japan open its ports to trade. Europeans and Americans were not only offended by the Tokugawa isolation but resentful at not being able to use Japanese ports to resupply or repair their ships.

Impressed by the American show of strength, the shogun agreed to the Treaty of Kanagawa, ending his country's long period of isolation. It was the first of many treaties Japan would sign with foreign powers.

The Treaty of Kanagawa

In the **Treaty of Kanagawa,** the shogun agreed to open two Japanese ports to American ships. The United States soon won other trading rights with Japan. In time, Great Britain, France, and Russia gained similar trading rights.

The Treaty of Kanagawa had a powerful impact on Japan.

- Some Japanese felt that the shogun had shown weakness in front of the foreigners by agreeing to the treaty.
- Some Japanese felt that Japan needed to modernize in order to compete with the industrialized West.
- A rebellion overthrew the shogun, restored the emperor to power, and launched Japan on the road to modernization and industrialization.

Modernization and Industrialization

In 1867, daimyo and samurai led a rebellion that removed the Tokugawa shogun from power. In 1868, the emperor was established as the leader of Japan. The period from 1868 to 1912 is known as the **Meiji Restoration.** *Meiji* means "enlightened rule." During this time, the emperor and his advisors implemented a series of reforms that changed Japan forever.

Borrowing From the West

The Meiji reformers were determined to strengthen Japan against the West. Members of the government traveled abroad to learn about Western government, economics, technology, and customs. In addition, foreign experts were invited to Japan.

Economic Development

The Meiji government used Western methods and machinery to develop an industrial economy in Japan. The government built factories and then sold them to wealthy families. These families became powerful in banking and industry and were known as **zaibatsu.**

The government supported the economy by developing a banking system and a postal system. It also built railroads and improved ports. By the 1890s, the economy was flourishing. The population grew, and peasants migrated to the cities in search of jobs.

Strong Central Government

Meiji reformers wanted to create a strong central government. They chose the government of Germany as their model. A constitution gave the emperor autocratic power and created a two-house legislature. Only one of the houses was elected, and suffrage was limited.

Military Power

By the 1890s, Japan had a modern army and a strong navy. No longer were the samurai the only warriors—all men had to enter military service. When Japan and China fought over Korea in 1894, Japan won easily. Later, Japanese troops defeated Russian troops in Manchuria. This victory marked the first time in modern history that an Asian power defeated a European nation.

Preparing for the Regents

- What effects did the visit of Commodore Perry and the Treaty of Kanagawa have on Japan's development?

Preparing for the Regents

- Why did the Industrial Revolution occur earlier in Japan than in African and other Asian nations?

Key Themes and Concepts

Choice
The reformers chose the German government as their model. Their choice influenced how Japan developed over the next 50 years.

Japanese Exports and Imports
Meiji leaders made the economy a major priority. Imports and exports grew at an amazing speed.

Social Change

Meiji reforms established a system of public education and set up universities with Western instructors to teach modern technology. Despite social reforms, however, class distinctions still existed. Also, Japanese women faced continuing inequality. Meiji reformers took away some political and legal rights that women had previously won.

Japanese Exports and Imports

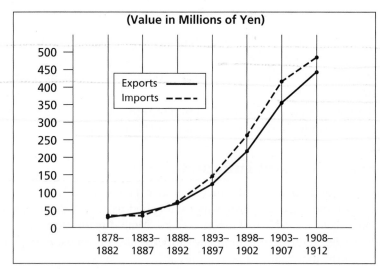

(Value in Millions of Yen)

Japan as a Global Power

Soon, like Western powers, Japan used its industrial and military strength to begin a policy of imperialism. It sought colonies as sources of raw materials and as markets for finished products. Colonies were gained through war.

Sino-Japanese War

In 1894, Japan's territorial ambitions in Korea led to war with China. The conflict, which lasted from 1894 to 1895, was called the **Sino-Japanese War.** Japan quickly won, gaining Formosa (later Taiwan) and treaty ports in China from the Chinese. Japan later made Korea a Japanese protectorate.

Russo-Japanese War

From 1904 to 1905, Japan fought the **Russo-Japanese War** with Russia after the interests of the two nations conflicted in Korea. Japan's modern military defeated Russian troops and crushed Russia's navy. By 1910, Japan had complete control of Korea as well as parts of Manchuria.

Dependence on a World Market

Japan's industrialization drew it increasingly into the global market. Its economy therefore became dependent on trade. An island empire with few natural resources, Japan relied on raw materials from outside the country. It needed foreign markets for its manufactured products. In the years ahead, Japan would continue to compete with other industrialized nations. It would also continue its policy of imperialism.

Summary

In the mid-1800s, Japan ended its long policy of isolation. The Meiji government that took power in 1868 used Western ideas to begin a program of modernization that quickly turned Japan into a major industrial power. In the 1890s and 1900s, Japan used its modern military to become a global imperial power.

Imperialism

Section Overview

From the mid-1800s through the first decades of the 1900s, Western nations pursued an aggressive policy of expansion. European powers were motivated by economic, political, and social factors as well as by a strong sense of nationalism. During this time, Great Britain took control of India. In Africa, several European nations engaged in a scramble for colonies. Meanwhile, imperialistic nations forced unequal trade agreements on China. Imperialism had many immediate and long-term effects on the colonial nations and also had an impact on Europe and the rest of the world. Imperialism led to increased competition and conflict.

Key Themes and Concepts

As you review this section, take special note of the following key themes and concepts:

Imperialism What factors led to the new imperialism of the 1800s?

Power How did imperialistic countries gain power over the peoples of Africa and Asia?

Change What were the effects of imperialism?

Nationalism How did imperialism lead to nationalistic feelings in China and other nations of Asia and Africa?

Key People and Terms

As you review this section, be sure you understand the significance of these key people and terms:

imperialism	Opium War	Taiping Rebellion
"White Man's Burden"	Treaty of Nanjing	Boxer Rebellion
Sepoy Mutiny	spheres of influence	Sun Yixian
Boer War		

The New Imperialism

Imperialism is the domination by one country of the political, economic, or cultural life of another country. Historians often divide imperialism into two periods.

- **The Old Imperialism** Between about 1500 and 1800, European nations established colonies in the Americas, India, and Southeast Asia and gained territory on the coasts of Africa and China. Still, European power in these regions of the world was limited.
- **The New Imperialism** Between 1870 and 1914, nationalism had produced strong, centrally governed nation-states. The Industrial Revolution had made economies stronger as well. During this time, Japan, the United States, and the industrialized nations of Europe became more aggressive in expanding into other lands. The new imperialism was focused mainly on Asia and Africa, where declining empires and local wars left many states vulnerable. In Africa, many states had been weakened by the legacy of the slave trade.

The
Big Idea

The imperialism that emerged in the mid-1800s had a lasting impact on the world.

- Powerful industrialized nations sought to gain power and economic might by building empires.
- Through economic and military power, Great Britain colonized and dominated India.
- European nations divided up the continent of Africa.
- Western powers and Japan established spheres of influence in China.
- Imperialism has had short-term and long-term effects on various regions of the world.

Key People and Terms

- What do most of the key people and terms have in common? Explain.

Key Themes and Concepts

Imperialism
The strong central governments and thriving economies of industrialized nations gave them the confidence to expand through imperialism.

Causes of Imperialism

Several important factors combined to lead to the development of the new imperialism.

Causes of the New Imperialism

Economy	Politics and the Military	Society	Science and Invention
• Need for natural resources • Need for new markets • Place for growing populations to settle • Place to invest profits	• Bases for trade and navy ships • Power and security of global empire • Spirit of nationalism	• Wish to spread Christianity • Wish to share Western civilization • Belief that Western ways are best	• New weapons • New medicines • Improved ships

The New Imperialism
From 1870 to 1914, European countries, the United States, and Japan gained control over much of the world.

Nationalism and Social Darwinism

A spirit of nationalism was one cause of the new imperialism. Because nationalism promotes the idea of national superiority, imperialists felt that they had a right to take control of countries they viewed as weaker. Social Darwinism also encouraged imperialism. This idea applied Darwin's theory of survival of the fittest to competition between nations. Social Darwinists argued that it was natural for stronger nations to dominate weaker ones.

Military Motives

Military motives were linked to nationalism, since military power was a way to promote a nation's goals. Colonies were important as bases for resupply of ships. A nation with many colonies had power and security.

Economic Motives

Imperialists needed raw materials to supply their factories. They needed foreign markets in which to sell their finished products. They needed places to invest their profits. Colonies could provide all these things.

"White Man's Burden"

Rudyard Kipling's poem **"White Man's Burden"** offered a justification for imperialism. Kipling expressed the idea that white imperialists had a moral duty to educate people in nations they considered less developed. Missionaries spread Western ideas, customs, and religions to people in Africa and Asia.

Preparing for the Regents

• How did the Industrial Revolution lead to imperialism?

British in India

British East India Company

The British East India Company had established trading rights in India in the early 1600s. By the mid-1800s, with the decline of the Mughal empire and the defeat of French rivals, this company controlled three fifths of India. The company employed Indian soldiers, called sepoys.

The Sepoy Mutiny

In 1857, tensions rose. The British had angered the sepoys by demanding that soldiers follow rules that were against their religious beliefs. The **Sepoy Mutiny,** or the Sepoy Rebellion, called for Hindus and Muslims to unite against the British. The British, however, crushed the revolt.

The Sepoy Mutiny left bitter feelings. It also caused the British to change their policies. In 1858, Parliament ended the rule of the East India Company. The British government took direct command of India.

The Effects of British Rule in India

GOOD EFFECTS	BAD EFFECTS
• New roads and railroads link parts of India. • Telegraph and postal systems unite people. • Irrigation systems improve farming. • New laws mean justice for all classes. • British schools offer education. • Customs that threaten human rights are ended.	• Indian resources go to Great Britain. • British-made goods replace local goods. • Farms grow cash crops rather than food crops; Indians go hungry. • Top jobs go to the British. • Indians are treated as inferiors. • Great Britain tries to replace Indian culture with Western ways.

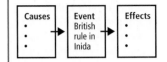
The Scramble for Africa

In the 1870s, King Leopold of Belgium sent a mission to the interior of Africa to establish trade agreements with leaders in the Congo River basin. The Belgian presence in the Congo set off a scramble among other European powers to establish their presence on the continent.

The Berlin Conference

In 1884, to avoid conflict among themselves, European leaders met in Berlin, Germany, to set up rules for colonizing Africa. European powers divided Africa with little regard for the people who lived there. The new imperialism affected Africa strongly. In 1850, most of Africa had been free. Seventy years later, most of the continent was under European rule.

Battle for Southern Africa

The Zulu Empire In the early 1800s in southern Africa, an African leader named Shaka organized Zulu warriors into a fighting force. He used his power against European slave traders and ivory hunters. Through conquest of other African groups, he united the Zulu nation.

Arrival of Europeans Dutch farmers, called Boers, had settled in southern Africa in the mid-1600s. They had built Cape Town as a supply station. In the 1700s, Dutch herders and ivory hunters began to move north. They fought African groups, such as the Zulus. In the early 1800s, the British acquired the Cape Colony from the Dutch.

Zulu Resistance Large numbers of Boers, resenting British rule, migrated north during the 1830s, coming into conflict with Zulus. Fighting between the Boers and the Zulus continued until late in the century.

The Zulus eventually came into conflict with the British as well. The Zulus experienced victory in 1879. Soon afterward, however, the superior weaponry of the British crushed the Zulu resistance. Others in Africa also resisted imperialism, including groups in Ethiopia and West Africa.

The Boer War Cecil Rhodes became prime minister of the Cape Colony in 1890. Under his leadership, Great Britain expanded its control of southern Africa.

In the late 1800s, Great Britain decided to annex the Boer republics. The Boers resisted and the Boer War began, lasting from 1899 to 1902. After heavy losses, the British won. In 1910, the British combined the Boer republics with the Cape Colony to form the Union of South Africa. The bitter struggles left a legacy of distrust and hatred.

Anti-Slave Trade Legislation Most European powers had abolished the slave trade before the scramble for African colonies began. For example, Denmark passed anti-slave trade legislation in 1803, followed by Great Britain in 1807, and France in 1818. Illegal slave trading, however, continued throughout the 1800s.

The Scramble for Africa, 1880–1914

The Scramble for Africa
During the late 1800s, European countries started to take over Africa. By 1914, they controlled nearly the entire continent.

Preparing for the Regents

- Practice your map skills by identifying the colonial power that occupied each of the following areas: Algeria in 1830, Togo in 1884, and the Union of South Africa in 1910.

Algeria- French
Togo- German
USA - British

Map:

SPANISH MOROCCO 1912
MOROCCO 1912
TUNIS 1881
ALGERIA 1830
LIBYA 1912
EGYPT 1882
RIO DE ORO 1885
ERITREA 1890
GAMBIA 1888
FRENCH WEST AFRICA 1874
ANGLO-EGYPTIAN SUDAN 1889
FRENCH SOMALILAND 1884
BRITISH SOMALILAND 1884
NIGERIA 1884
ETHIOPIA Independent
PORTUGUESE GUINEA 1901
SIERRA LEONE 1808
LIBERIA Independent
GOLD COAST 1874
TOGO 1884
RIO MUNI 1901
CAMEROONS 1884
UGANDA 1895
ITALIAN SOMALILAND 1889
FRENCH EQUATORIAL AFRICA 1910
BELGIAN CONGO 1908
GERMAN EAST AFRICA 1885
BRITISH EAST AFRICA 1886
ANGOLA 1891
NYASALAND 1891
N. RHODESIA 1891
S. RHODESIA 1890
MOZAMBIQUE 1500
GERMAN SOUTH WEST AFRICA 1884
BECHU-ANALAND 1885
MADAGASCAR 1895
SWAZILAND 1907
UNION OF SOUTH AFRICA 1910
BASUTOLAND 1871

Legend:
- British
- French
- German
- Italian
- Other Europeans

Dates indicate year of colonization

Imperialism in China

Since 1644, rulers of the Qing dynasty had refused to adopt Western ways. As a result, the economic, political, and military strength of European imperialists was able to challenge China's Middle Kingdom.

The Opium War and the Treaty of Nanjing

British merchants began to trade opium in China in the late 1700s. China tried to halt imports of the addictive drug. In 1839, to keep trade open, the British fought with China in a conflict called the **Opium War.** Great Britain's superior military and industrial strength led to a quick victory.

Recognize Cause and Effect

- What were the causes of the Opium War?

- What were the effects of the Opium War?

In 1842, Great Britain forced China to agree to the harsh terms of the **Treaty of Nanjing.** China had to pay for Great Britain's war costs, open ports to British trade, and give Great Britain the island of Hong Kong. China also had to grant British citizens extraterritoriality, the right to live under their own laws and be tried in their own courts. In the years that followed, other Western powers forced China to sign unequal treaties. The Western powers carved out **spheres of influence,** areas in which an outside power claimed exclusive trade privileges.

Chinese Reactions to Imperialism

Foreign imperialism led to further clashes between the imperialist powers and China—and among the Chinese themselves.

The Taiping Rebellion From 1850 to 1864, Chinese peasants, angry at their poverty and at corrupt Qing officials, rose up in revolt. The Taiping Rebellion resulted in millions of Chinese deaths and weakened China.

The Boxer Rebellion In 1900, a group known to Westerners as the Boxers assaulted foreign communities across China in a conflict known as the Boxer Rebellion. Armies from Japan and the West, however, soon crushed the uprising and forced China to grant more concessions to foreign powers. After this defeat, greater numbers of Chinese called for Western-style reforms.

Sun Yixian and the Chinese Revolution In the first decade of the 1900s, Chinese nationalism blossomed. Many reformers called for a new government. Sun Yixian, also called Sun Yat-sen, led the movement to replace the Qing dynasty. He had three goals:

- To end foreign domination
- To form a representative government
- To create economic security for the Chinese people

Preparing for the Regents

- How did imperialism contribute to the rise of nationalistic feelings in China?

- Compare Japanese and Chinese responses to Western industrial power and Western imperialism.

Vocabulary Builder

concession—(kun SESH un) *n.* something that you allow someone to have in order to end an argument or a disagreement

Spheres of Influence in China Until 1914

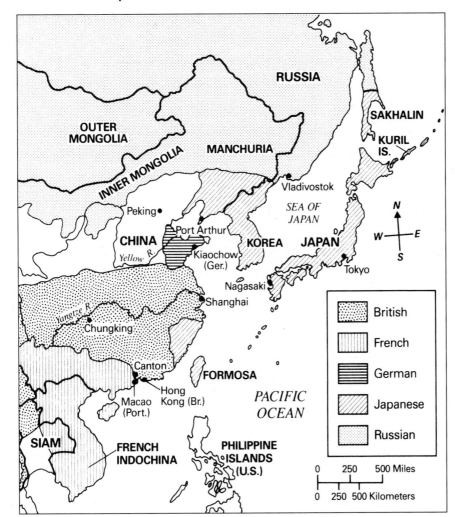

Preparing for the Regents

- Practice your map skills by describing Japan's sphere of influence in Asia in 1914. How do you think this influence benefited Japan?

- Showing them what they needed to improve on.

Spheres of Influence in China The Western countries used diplomacy and war to gain power in China. They divided the country into special trade areas.

- List three arguments that were used by imperialist powers to justify imperialism.

1. Foreign Rule
2. Industrialised Powers
3. European Domination

- List three motives people of Africa and Asia had to oppose imperialism.

1. Western Culture
2. Resistance
3. Dependance on cash crops.

In 1911, workers, peasants, students, and warlords toppled the monarchy. Sun Yixian was named president of the Chinese Republic.

Impact of Imperialism: Multiple Perspectives

The new imperialism had a major impact on the European nations and on their colonies.

Effects on the Colonies

Imperialism had a number of short-term and long-term effects on the colonies themselves. Some were negative; others were positive.

Short-Term Effects Some effects were immediate.

- Large numbers of Asians and Africans came under foreign rule.
- Local economies became dependent on industrialized powers.
- Some nations introduced changes to meet imperialist challenges.
- Individuals and groups resisted European domination.
- Western culture spread to new regions.
- Traditional political units were disrupted or destroyed.
- Famines occurred in lands where farmers grew export crops for imperialist nations in place of food for local use.

Long-Term Effects Other effects took longer to emerge.

- Western culture continued to influence much of the world.
- Transportation, education, and medical care were improved.
- Resistance to imperial rule evolved into nationalist movements.
- Many economies became dependent on single cash crops grown for export.

Effects on Europe and the World

The West also changed because of imperialism.

- The West discovered new crops, foods, and other products.
- Westerners were introduced to new cultural influences.
- Competition for empires created and increased conflict between imperial powers. These conflicts sometimes led to war.
- The industrial nations controlled a new global economy.

Summary

In the 1800s, industrialized powers greatly expanded their empires. Great Britain took control of India, and European nations occupied much of Africa. Imperial powers also forced China to grant trading concessions. This led to the growth of nationalism in China. Other effects of imperialism included the emergence of a global economy, the spread of Western culture, and conflict between imperial powers.

Key Themes and Concepts

Nationalism
Nationalist movements in Asia and Africa often grew out of resistance to imperial rule.

Questions for Regents Practice

Multiple Choice

Directions: Review the Test-Taking Strategies section of this book. Then answer the following questions, drawn from actual Regents examinations. For each statement or question, choose the *number* of the word or expression that, of those given, best completes the statement or answers the question.

1 John Locke and Jean-Jacques Rousseau would be most likely to support

    (1) a return to feudalism in Europe

    (2) a government ruled by a divine monarchy

    (3) a society ruled by the Catholic Church

    (4) the right of citizens to decide the best form of government

2 The writers and philosophers of the Enlightenment believed that government decisions should be based on

    (1) fundamental religious beliefs

    (2) the concept of the divine right of kings

    (3) laws of nature and reason

    (4) traditional values

3 A primary cause of the French Revolution in 1789 was the

    (1) increasing dissatisfaction of the Third Estate

    (2) rise to power of Napoleon Bonaparte

    (3) actions of Prince Metternich

    (4) execution of Louis XVI

4 In a number of European countries in the 1800s, which situation occurred as a result of the influence of the French Revolution?

    (1) increase in religious conflict

    (2) rise of nationalistic movements

    (3) decentralization of governmental power

    (4) economic depression

5 During the early 1800s, which was a major influence on the struggles for political independence in Latin America?

    (1) poor conditions in urban centers in Latin America

    (2) the American and French Revolutions

    (3) the desire of the Roman Catholic Church in Latin America to escape European control

    (4) demands by Latin American workers to own their own factories

6 Nationalism is most likely to develop in an area that has

    (1) land suited to agriculture

    (2) adequate industry to supply consumer demands

    (3) a moderate climate with rivers for irrigation

    (4) common customs, language, and history

7 Which statement about nationalism is most accurate?

    (1) It becomes a unifying force among a people.

    (2) It encourages diversity within nation-states.

    (3) It prevents the rise of militarism.

    (4) It eliminates the ethnic identities of different groups.

8 Which term refers to the Jewish movement to establish a homeland in Palestine?

    (1) Zionism

    (2) Marxism

    (3) animism

    (4) secularism

Questions for Regents Practice

9 The theory of laissez-faire capitalism advocates

   (1) government control of the economy
   (2) noninvolvement of the government in the economy
   (3) government regulation of big business
   (4) government sponsorship of labor unions

10 An important result of the Industrial Revolution was the

   (1) concentration of workers in urban areas
   (2) increased desire of the wealthy class to share its power
   (3) formation of powerful craft guilds
   (4) control of agricultural production by governments

11 The arrival of Commodore Matthew Perry in Japan in 1853 signaled the end of Japanese

   (1) cultural contacts with the West
   (2) policies of isolationism
   (3) militarism in Southeast Asia
   (4) trade relations with the United States

12 In Japan, the period of the Meiji Restoration was primarily characterized by

   (1) strict isolation
   (2) feudal government
   (3) religious revival
   (4) reform and modernization

13 Russia in the 1700s and Japan in the 1800s were similar in that both countries

   (1) began the process of modernization after a long period of isolation
   (2) developed democratic governments after years under absolute monarchies
   (3) refused to accept Western technological ideas
   (4) adopted socialist economic systems after capitalism had failed

14 "All great nations . . . have desired to set their mark upon barbarian lands, and those who fail to participate in this great rivalry will play a pitiable role in time to come."

   This quotation supports the concept of

   (1) socialism
   (2) human rights
   (3) revolution
   (4) imperialism

15 One way in which the Sepoy Rebellion in India and the Boxer Rebellion in China are similar is that both attempted to

   (1) remove foreign influences
   (2) restore democracy
   (3) modernize their economy
   (4) end religious conflict

16 The Boxer Rebellion of the early twentieth century was an attempt to

   (1) eliminate poverty among Chinese peasants
   (2) bring Western-style democracy to China
   (3) restore trade between China and European nations
   (4) remove foreign influences from China

In developing your answer, be sure to keep these general definitions in mind:

   (a) <u>describe</u> means "to illustrate something in words or tell about it"
   (b) <u>explain</u> means "to make plain or understandable; to give reasons for or causes of; to show the logical development or relationships of"

Directions: Write a well-organized essay that includes an introduction, several paragraphs addressing the task below, and a conclusion.

Theme: Revolution

> Throughout global history, there have been major political, economic, social, and cultural revolutions. These revolutions have had complex causes and left lasting impacts on people's lives.

Task:

> - Define the term *revolution.*
> - Select a specific revolution that you have studied, and describe three of the factors that helped to bring about that particular revolution.
> - Identify and explain at least one immediate effect and at least one long-term effect of this revolution on people's lives.

   You may discuss any revolution from your study of global history, except the American Revolution. Some suggestions you may wish to consider are the Commercial Revolution, the Reformation, the Enlightenment, the French Revolution, the Industrial Revolution, the Mexican Revolution, and the Russian Revolution.

You are *not* limited to these suggestions.
Do not use the United States in your answer.

Guidelines:

   In your essay, be sure to
   - Develop all aspects of the task
   - Support the theme with relevant facts, examples, and details
   - Use a logical and clear plan of organization, including an introduction and a conclusion that are beyond a simple restatement of the theme

Document-Based Question

This question is based on the accompanying documents. The question is designed to test your ability to work with historical documents. Some of these documents have been edited for the purposes of this question. As you analyze the documents, take into account the source of each document and any point of view that may be presented in the document.

Historical Context:

Throughout history, imperialism has been interpreted from multiple perspectives. Some have seen it as a beneficial influence, while others have seen it as a harmful influence.

Task: Using the information from the documents and your knowledge of global history, answer the questions that follow each document in Part A. Your answers to the questions will help you write the Part B essay in which you will be asked to

> • Evaluate both the positive and the negative effects of imperialism

In developing your answers, be sure to keep this general definition in mind:

> **evaluate** means "to examine and judge the significance, worth, or condition of; to determine the value of"

Part A: Short Answer

Directions: Analyze the documents and answer the question or questions that follow each document, using the space provided.

Document #1

> *Modern progressive nations lying in the temperate zone seek to control "garden spots" in the tropics, [mainly in Africa, Latin America, and Asia]. Under [the progressive nations'] direction, these places can yield tropical produce. In return, the progressive nations bring to the people of those garden spots the foodstuffs and manufactures they need. [Progressive nations] develop the territory by building roads, canals, railways, and telegraphs. They can establish schools and newspapers for the colonies [and] give these people the benefit of the blessings of civilization which they have not the means of creating themselves.*
>
> **—O.P. Austin, "Does Colonization Pay?"** *The Forum,* **1900**

1. What nations does the author probably consider to be the "modern progressive nations"? Explain the reason for your answer.

_____

_____

Document #2

When the whites came to our country, we had the land and they had the Bible. Now we have the Bible and they have the land.

—**African proverb**

2. Does this proverb express a positive or negative viewpoint toward the white missionaries? Explain.

_____

_____

Document #3
"The Devilfish in Egyptian Waters"

3. What view of English imperialism is expressed in this cartoon? Explain.

_____

_____

Document #4

To begin with, there are the exporters and manufacturers of certain goods used in the colonies. The makers of cotton and iron goods have been very much interested in imperialism. Their business interests demand that colonial markets should be opened and developed and that foreign competitors should be shut out. Such aims require political control and imperialism.

Finally, the most powerful of all business groups are the bankers. Banks make loans to colonies and backward countries for building railways and steamship lines. They also make loans to colonial plantation owners, importers, and exporters.
—**Parker T. Moon,** *Imperialism and World Politics,* **1926**

4. Based on this passage, explain two ways in which European businesspeople hoped to profit from imperialism.

_____

_____

Part B
Essay

Directions: Write a well-organized essay that includes an introduction, several paragraphs, and a conclusion. Use evidence from *at least* **three** of the documents in your essay. Support your response with relevant facts, examples, and details. Include additional outside information.

Historical Context:

Throughout history, imperialism has been interpreted from multiple perspectives. Some have seen it as a beneficial influence, while others have seen it as a harmful influence.

Task: Using the information from the documents and your knowledge of global history, write an essay in which you

- Evaluate the positive and negative impacts of imperialism, developing a position either in favor of or against imperialism

Guidelines:

In your essay, be sure to
- Develop all aspects of the task
- Incorporate information from *at least* **three** documents
- Incorporate relevant outside information
- Support the theme with relevant facts, examples, and details
- Use a logical and clear plan of organization, including an introduction and a conclusion that are beyond a restatement of the theme

Crises and Achievements
(1900–1945)

Section 1: **Scientific and Technological Achievements**

Section 2: **World War I**

Section 3: **Revolution in Russia: Causes and Impacts**

Section 4: **Between the Wars**

Section 5: **World War II**

Unit Overview

Science and technology brought many benefits to society in the late 1800s and early 1900s. In most industrialized countries, life expectancy increased and standards of living rose. People became hopeful, for they had experienced peace for many years. However, the forces of nationalism, militarism, and imperialism were moving the world toward war. By the time World War I was over, people understood how science and technology could change their lives in negative ways. The war caused new social and economic problems. In Russia, a communist revolution produced a totalitarian state. Perhaps worst of all, the problems that had led to World War I remained unresolved. A second global conflict erupted in 1939, resulting in even greater destruction than the first.

Using Good Social Studies Practices

Chronology and Causation

Some of the many themes developed in Unit 2 are:

change	nationalism	human rights
science and technology	political systems	economic systems
culture and intellectual life	power	

Choose one of the themes listed above. As you review Unit 2, create a timeline based on the theme you have chosen. Your timeline should emphasize your theme and stretch from 1900 to 1945. It should include major developments, key turning points, and their causes.

Scientific and Technological Achievements

Section Overview

In the late 1800s and early 1900s, advances in science and technology led to dramatic changes in daily life. Medical discoveries and better sanitation allowed people to live longer, contributing to a population explosion. New inventions revolutionized energy production, communications, and transportation. Scientific discoveries led to new knowledge about the universe and the workings of the human mind.

Key Themes and Concepts

As you review this section, take special note of the following key themes and concepts:

Change How did medical advances in the late 1800s affect life expectancy and population growth?

Science and Technology How did the scientific discoveries of the late 1800s and early 1900s change the way people lived?

Culture and Intellectual Life How did new theories affect the ways in which people thought about their world?

Key People and Terms

As you review this section, be sure you understand the significance of these key people and terms:

Louis Pasteur	dynamo	radioactivity
germ theory	Thomas Edison	Albert Einstein
antibiotics	Marie Curie	Sigmund Freud

Advances in Medicine

A series of discoveries revolutionized the field of medicine at the turn of the twentieth century. These medical advances greatly improved health care and increased human life expectancy.

The Germ Theory and Disease

Before the mid-1800s, the cause of disease was not clear, even to physicians. However, by the late 1800s, scientists were making great progress in this area.

Louis Pasteur In the 1600s, a Dutch scientist named Anton van Leeuwenhoek had discovered the existence of microbes, or germs, by using a microscope. He did not, however, recognize the role of these tiny organisms in causing disease.

In 1870, French scientist **Louis Pasteur** made two very important discoveries. He showed clearly the link between germs and disease. He also proved that killing certain germs stops the spread of certain diseases.

Robert Koch In the 1880s, the German physician Robert Koch discovered the bacteria that caused tuberculosis. His discovery started the long process of developing a cure for this deadly disease. The work of Pasteur and Koch established the **germ theory** of disease, the idea that many diseases are caused by the action of microorganisms. After people learned about the germ theory, they washed more often and made other lifestyle changes to limit the spread of disease.

Joseph Lister and Antiseptics

Before the mid-1800s, even a very minor surgical operation might be followed by infection and even death. An English surgeon named Joseph Lister became convinced that germs caused these infections. Lister insisted that doctors use antiseptics—substances that destroy or inhibit the growth of germs—on their hands, on their instruments, and on wounds. Lister's discoveries were a turning point in medicine, and they greatly reduced the number of deaths from infection in hospitals.

Antibiotics

In 1928, another turning point in medicine occurred. English scientist Alexander Fleming discovered that a mold called *Penicillium* killed germs. This discovery paved the way for the development of a class of drugs called **antibiotics** that attacked or weakened the bacteria that cause many diseases. Antibiotics were not widely developed and used, however, until the 1940s.

Improved Standard of Living

The advances of the late 1800s and early 1900s extended beyond the field of medicine. The standard of living of most Europeans began to rise.

Better Wages and Working Conditions

In the early years of the Industrial Revolution, workers had found it difficult to improve their harsh job conditions. By the late 1800s, however, labor unions became legal in many countries of Europe. Unions, reformers, and working-class voters pushed for better working conditions and higher wages. Over time, wages improved. People ate more varied diets and lived in cleaner, safer homes. Reform laws regulated working conditions and provided social benefits to the elderly and the unemployed.

Better Housing

Urban conditions were improving in the late 1800s and early 1900s. City governments paved their streets, making cities better places to live. Housing improved. Architects began to use steel to construct stronger, taller buildings.

Improved Sanitation

Underground sewage systems, introduced first in London and Paris, made cities healthier places to live. With underground systems, waste no longer ran through the streets, spreading disease and polluting sources of drinking water. A supply of clean water was necessary to combat diseases such as tuberculosis and cholera. Death rates were dramatically cut after the introduction of the new sewer systems.

Preparing for the Regents

Describe an effect on daily life of each of these inventions.

Electricity: Light bulbs

Telephone: Communication

Radio: Broadcasting

Automobile: Transportation

Draw Conclusions

How did the new inventions help business and industry?

New Inventions

A tremendous number of new inventions appeared in the late 1800s and early 1900s. These inventions improved daily life in many ways.

Use of Electricity Early in the 1800s, Alessandro Volta and Michael Faraday had discovered how to produce small amounts of electricity. The later development of the **dynamo** enabled the generation of large amounts of electricity and made electricity a useful source of power. In 1879, an American inventor named **Thomas Edison** developed the first practical light bulb. Soon cities had electric street lights. By the 1890s, factories were powered by electricity. In homes, people used electricity to run appliances that made their lives more comfortable.

The Telephone In 1876, Alexander Graham Bell patented the telephone. His machine changed the human voice into electrical impulses, sent them through a wire, and then changed them back into sounds at the other end. The invention of the telephone transformed long-distance communication.

The Radio The telephone was an important means of communication, but it depended on wires. Guglielmo Marconi, in 1895, sent radio signals directly through the air. The first radios transmitted Morse code signals. The year 1906 marked the first voice broadcast over radio.

The Automobile Inventions also transformed transportation in the last half of the 1800s. In the 1870s, Nikolaus Otto developed a gasoline-powered internal combustion engine. In the 1880s, Gottlieb Daimler used Otto's engine to power the first automobile. By 1900, thousands of automobiles were on the roads of Europe and North America. Henry Ford's development of the assembly line for the mass production of automobiles made the United States a strong leader in the auto industry.

The Airplane The internal combustion engine also allowed humans to fly. In 1903, Orville and Wilbur Wright made the first powered flight.

Technology of the Industrial Age

INVENTOR OR DEVELOPER	NATION	INVENTION OR DEVELOPMENT	YEAR
Henry Bessemer	Great Britain	Process to turn iron ore into steel	1856
Alexander Graham Bell	United States	Telephone	1876
Thomas Edison	United States	Electric light bulb	1879
Gottlieb Daimler	Germany	Automobile	1887
Henry Ford	United States	Mass-produced automobile	1903
Orville & Wilbur Wright	United States	Airplane	1903

Population Explosion

In many ways, new technology made life healthier, safer, and easier. As a result, fewer children died, and the average life expectancy increased. In other words, people lived longer. Because of these changes, populations grew dramatically.

Western Populations in the Late 1800s

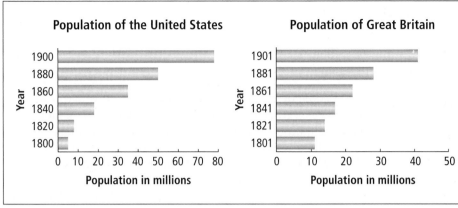

Source: *The World Almanac*

New Scientific Theories

While some scientists were developing knowledge and inventions that improved the quality of daily life, others were exploring the universe and the workings of the human mind.

The Curies and Radioactivity

Just before the turn of the century, French scientist **Marie Curie** was experimenting with **radioactivity,** a powerful form of energy released by certain substances. Working with her husband, Pierre, Marie Curie discovered two new radioactive elements that the Curies called radium and polonium. The discoveries of these scientists had enormous effects on fields such as energy production, medicine, and military technology.

Einstein and Relativity

In 1905, the German-born physicist **Albert Einstein** announced his theory of relativity. This theory revolutionized scientific thought. It proposed that space and time measurements are not absolute but are determined by many factors, some of which are not known. Einstein's work caused many people to question the common view of the universe as a machine that worked by easily understood laws.

Freud and the Human Mind

During the same period, an Austrian physician named **Sigmund Freud** was questioning basic ideas about the human mind. He believed that a part of the mind, which he called the unconscious, drives much of human behavior. Freud felt that the tension between the drives of the unconscious mind and the demands of civilized society caused psychological and physical illness. Freud pioneered psychoanalysis, a new way of thinking about and treating mental illness.

Summary

Scientific and technological advances brought many changes in the late 1800s and early 1900s. Improvements in medicine and sanitation led to a higher life expectancy, which caused an increase in population. People's lives were made easier by inventions such as electrical appliances, the telephone, and automobiles. In other areas of science, theories about the universe and the human mind shook ideas that had once been commonly accepted.

Preparing for the Regents

Practice your graph skills by answering the following questions.

1. About how many people lived in Great Britain in 1801? *12 million*

2. What was the approximate population of Great Britain in 1901? *40 million*

3. What developments could explain the population growth shown in these two graphs? *Industrial Revolution.*

Vocabulary Builder

element—(EL uh munt) *n.* a simple chemical substance such as carbon or oxygen that consists of atoms of only one kind

Key Themes and Concepts

Science and Innovation
The theories of both Einstein and Freud had an unsettling effect on many people of the time. The idea of a powerful unconscious mind or a universe without absolute laws disturbed many.

Preparing for the Regents

• What benefits have resulted from the use of radioactive elements? What problems have resulted?

• Write a short paragraph about whether you think that science and technology bring more problems or more benefits into people's lives.

World War I

The
Big Idea

World War I:

• was caused by nationalism, militarism, imperialism, and alliance systems.

• was sparked in the Balkans and blossomed into a global war.

• was fought with highly destructive weapons, made possible by modern technology.

• resulted in enormous human and economic losses.

Section Overview

As the 1900s began, the people of Europe had enjoyed nearly a century of relative peace. At the same time, forces were pushing the continent toward war. Nationalistic feeling, a glorification of the military, imperial rivalries, and tangled alliances led to unrest. War was sparked in the Balkans, where the Ottoman empire had once maintained control. Soon all of Europe was at war. Industrialization and technology had allowed nations to develop more destructive weapons that resulted in millions of deaths. As Russia left the war and the United States entered, the Allies gained control and an armistice was signed. The costs of World War I were enormous.

Key Themes and Concepts

As you review this section, take special note of the following key themes and concepts:

Nationalism and Imperialism What role did nationalism and imperialism play in causing World War I?

Diversity How did ethnic diversity in the Balkans contribute to starting the war?

Science and Technology What impact did innovations in science and technology have on World War I?

Key People and Terms

What do three of the key people and terms have in common? Explain.

As you review this section, be sure you understand the significance of these key people and terms:

militarism	total war
Bosnia	propaganda
Archduke Francis Ferdinand	neutral
Central Powers	armistice
Allied Powers	reparations
trench warfare	

Causes

Although the world seemed at peace in the early 1900s, powerful forces were pushing Europe toward war. These forces included nationalism, militarism, imperial rivalries, alliance systems, and the decline of the Ottoman empire.

Nationalism

As you have learned, nationalism can bring people together. It can also, however, be a source of conflict. In Europe in the early 1900s, aggressive nationalism was a source of tension.

Germany and France Nationalism was strong in both Germany and France. Germany, now unified, was proud of its growing military and industrial strength. France, meanwhile, wanted to regain its position as a leading European power. It had lost the Franco-Prussian War in 1871. Besides having to pay money to Germany, France lost the provinces of Alsace and Lorraine. Many of the French people wanted revenge on Germany.

Pan-Slavism Russia had encouraged a form of nationalism in Eastern Europe called Pan-Slavism. The movement tried to draw together all Slavic peoples. Russia was the largest Slavic country, and it was ready to defend Serbia, a young Slavic nation in the Balkans. Throughout the Balkans, in fact, small Slavic populations looked to Russia for leadership in their desire for unity. The multinational empire of Austria-Hungary opposed Slavic national movements.

Militarism

During the late 1800s, **militarism,** the glorification of military power, arose in many nations of Europe. This development led to fear and suspicion as nations became more willing to use military force to attain their national goals. There was an arms race, in which the great powers competed with each other to expand their armies and navies. One of the fiercest rivalries was between Great Britain and Germany.

Imperialism and Economic Rivalry

Great Britain, France, Germany, and other nations competed for colonies and economic power. France and Germany competed especially for colonial gains in Africa. Great Britain and Germany competed industrially. Germany had industrialized rapidly, and the British felt threatened by this. Because of their mutual competition with Germany, Great Britain and France began to form close ties with each other.

Alliance Systems

Increased tensions and suspicions led nations to form alliances. Nations agreed to defend each other in case of attack. By 1914, there were several alliances. The two most important were the Triple Alliance and the Triple Entente. The triple Alliance consisted of Germany, Austria-Hungary, and Italy. The Triple Entente consisted of Great Britain, France, and Russia.

Decline of the Ottoman Empire

Other situations also set the stage for war. The Ottoman empire had become weak. British relations with the empire became strained after Great Britain signed an agreement with Russia. Germany, on the other hand, had taken an interest in establishing good relations with the Ottoman empire.

The Armenian Massacres Nationalistic feelings had caused periodic waves of violence against Armenians since the 1890s. New violence was a brutal result of the rivalry between Turkey, which ruled the Ottoman empire, and Russia. The Muslim Turks distrusted the Christian Armenians, believing that they supported Russia against the Ottoman empire. When Armenians protested oppressive Ottoman policies, the Turks unleashed a massacre on the Armenians. Additional massacres leading to the deaths of a million or more Armenians occurred over the next 25 years.

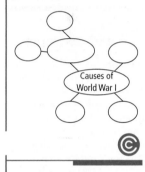

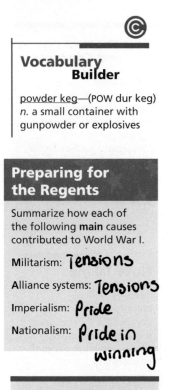

Preparing for the Regents

Summarize how each of the following **main** causes contributed to World War I.

Militarism: *Tensions*

Alliance systems: *Tensions*

Imperialism: *Pride*

Nationalism: *Pride in winning*

Key Themes and Concepts

Diversity
Serb nationalism led to the assassination of Archduke Francis Ferdinand. Slavic groups in the Ottoman empire hoped to unite and throw off the rule of Austria-Hungary.

Recognize Effects

How did Austria-Hungary react to the murder of the archduke?

The Balkan Powder Keg The Ottoman empire's control over the Balkans had weakened over time. Serbia declared its independence in 1878, hoping to build a Slavic state in alliance with Russia. Serbia wanted control of **Bosnia** and Herzegovina, two provinces that would give landlocked Serbia an outlet to the Adriatic Sea. These provinces, however, were Ottoman provinces administered by Austria-Hungary. Austria opposed Serbian ambitions, fearing that the same kind of nationalism would spread to its own multinational empire. Also, Austria-Hungary feared Russian expansion.

Tensions grew, and in 1912, Serbia and its allies attacked the Ottoman empire. The great European powers were all interested in gaining lands from the crumbling empire. By 1914, the Balkans were known as the "powder keg of Europe." Any small spark was likely to lead to an explosion.

The War Begins

The Balkan Crisis

Not surprisingly, World War I began in the Balkans. Although many Serbs lived in Bosnia, it was still ruled by Austria-Hungary. Serb nationalists felt that Bosnia belonged to Serbia.

Archduke Francis Ferdinand was the heir to the Austrian throne. On June 28, 1914, the duke and his wife were traveling through Sarajevo, the capital of Bosnia. Gavrilo Princip, a member of a radical Slavic nationalist group that opposed Austrian rule, shot and killed the archduke and his wife.

A Chain Reaction

After the assassination, the major nations of Europe responded. Each hostile action led to another hostile action.

The Outbreak of War

1. Austria-Hungary blamed Serbia for the murders of the archduke and his wife and made harsh demands in Serbia.
2. Serbia refused to comply with any of the demands.
3. Austria-Hungary declared war on Serbia on July 28.
4. Russia, a Slavic nation and a friend of Serbia, mobilized its forces in preparation for war.
5. Germany, an ally of Austria-Hungary, declared war on Russia.
6. Germany declared war on France, an ally of Russia.
7. Germany invaded Belgium on August 3, 1914, so that German forces could enter France more easily.
8. Great Britain declared war on Germany.

World War I: Who Was to Blame?

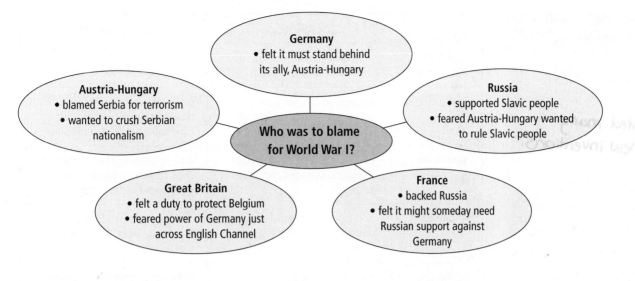

Central Powers and Allied Powers

The two opposing sides in World War I were the Central Powers and the Allied Powers. The **Central Powers** were Germany, Austria-Hungary, and the Ottoman empire (later joined by Bulgaria). On the other side were the **Allied Powers:** Great Britain, France, and Russia. Italy at first remained neutral, but it eventually joined the Allies. Other nations, including the United States, also joined the Allies later.

There were three major fronts in Europe where fighting occurred. The Western Front extended across Belgium and northeastern France to the border of Switzerland. The Eastern Front ran from the Baltic Sea to the Black Sea. The Southern Front ran between Italy and Austria-Hungary. Fighting also took place in Africa and the Middle East.

An Industrialized War

World War I was a war between groups of major industrial powers. New technology made this war an enormously destructive one. For example, Swedish chemist Alfred Nobel had invented dynamite in 1867. Used in mining and construction, it also became important in weaponry. Many of the other recent inventions of the time—the internal combustion engine, the airplane, and communications devices—were also put to military use.

Trench Warfare

Heavy fighting took place along the Western Front, a 600-mile stretch from the English Channel to Switzerland. The Germans hoped to win an early victory there, but French and British troops stopped them. For four years, neither side could make any significant gains.

Trench warfare began, so called because the troops dug trenches along the front. Very little ground was gained by either side in this way, and many soldiers were killed.

New Air and Sea Weapons

World War I was the first war to make full use of modern technology and machinery. Technology changed methods of warfare greatly.

Preparing for the Regents

• Study the graphic organizer and review the chain of events that occurred in 1914. Which nation or group do you think was to blame for World War I? Explain.

France – building military power.

Preparing for the Regents

List the members of the Central Powers and the Allied Powers.

Central Powers: *Germany, Austria, Ottoman Empire*

Allied Powers: *U.S. Britain, France Russia.*

Summarize

What made World War I extremely destructive? Explain.

Technology Changes Warfare

Preparing for the Regents

• What role did technology play in World War I?

Created many new inventions.

Invention	Description	Use in World War I
Automatic machine gun	mounted gun that fires a rapid, continuous stream of bullets	made it possible for a few gunners to mow down waves of soldiers
Tank	armored vehicle that travels on a track and can cross many kinds of land	protected advancing troops as they broke through enemy defenses; Early tanks were slow and clumsy
Submarine	underwater ship that can launch torpedoes, or guided underwater bombs	used by Germany to destroy Allied ships; submarine attacks helped bring United States into war
Airplane	one- or two-seat propeller plane equipped with machine gun or bombs	at first, mainly used for observation; later, flying "aces" engaged in air combat
Poison gas; gas mask	gases that cause choking, blinding, or severe skin blisters; gas masks can protect soldiers from poison gas	lobbed into enemy trenches, killing or disabling troops; gas masks lessened the importance of poison gas

Vocabulary Builder

draft—(draft) v. to order someone to join the army, navy, etc., especially during a war

Civilian Life and Total War

The war was fought at home as well as on the battlefield. A war fought in this way is called a **total war.** In a total war, all of a nation's resources go into the war effort.

• Governments drafted men to fight in the war.

• Governments raised taxes and borrowed money to pay for the war.

• Governments rationed, or limited the supply of, goods at home so that the military could be provided for.

• Governments used the press to print **propaganda,** the spreading of ideas to promote a cause or to damage an opposing cause.

• Women at home took jobs that the soldiers had left behind. Some women joined the armed services. Other women went to the fronts as nurses.

Major Turning Points of the War

Several events that took place during World War I are seen as major turning points. They include the withdrawal of Russia from the war and the entry of the United States into the war.

Entry of the United States

Although the United States had allowed American ships to carry supplies to the Allies, the country had tried to remain **neutral** (not supporting either side) in the war. In 1917, however, Germany used unrestricted submarine warfare, meaning that it attacked any ships on the Atlantic, even if they were carrying American passengers. This policy brought the United States into the war in April 1917. The entry of the Americans helped the Allies win the war.

Preparing for the Regents

• Analyze how interdependence caused the United States to enter World War I.

• How was the entry of the United States a turning point?

Russian Withdrawal

In Russia, low morale contributed to a revolution in 1917. Early in 1918, Russia's new leader signed a treaty with Germany that took Russia out of the war.

Costs of the War

On November 11, 1918, an **armistice,** or an agreement to end the fighting, was declared. The costs of World War I were enormous. It would take many years for people and nations to recover.

Human Casualties

The costs of the war in terms of human lives were staggering.

- More than 8.5 million people had died.
- More than 17 million had been wounded.
- Famine threatened many regions.
- Disease was widespread in many regions.

Economic Losses

All over the world, there were also economic and political losses.

- Factories, farms, and homes had been destroyed.
- Nations had huge war debts to repay.
- The Allies, bitter at the destruction, insisted that the Central Powers make **reparations,** payments for war damage they had caused.

Percentage of Money Spent by Allies

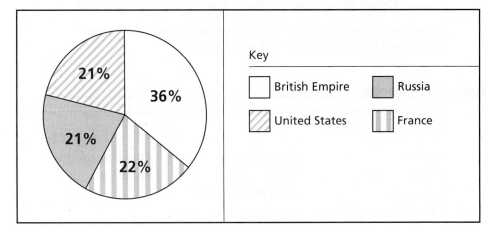

Key

- British Empire
- United States
- Russia
- France

21%
36%
21%
22%

Summary

Nationalism, militarism, imperialism, and political rivalries led to World War I. In the Balkans, what began as a local incident blossomed into a global war. Industrialization and new technology made the weapons of World War I much more destructive than any that had been used before. The war caused great human and economic losses.

Money Spent by Allies
World War I cost an enormous amount of money. The Allies spent about 160 billion dollars.

Revolution in Russia: Causes and Impacts

Section Overview

Factors such as dissatisfaction with czarist rule, peasant unrest, and economic difficulties created long-term discontent in Russia. After a revolution in 1905, Czar Nicholas II agreed to reforms, but they failed to solve underlying problems. Hardships caused by World War I sparked a revolution that ended Nicholas's reign. Promises of peace, land, and bread allowed Vladimir Lenin and his Bolsheviks, later called Communists, to gain control of the country. After Lenin's death, Joseph Stalin created a communist dictatorship that controlled every aspect of people's lives. He brought the economy completely under government control. Stalin industrialized the country, focusing on heavy industry. Stalin also brought agriculture under state control, causing mass starvation in the process.

Key Themes and Concepts

As you review this section, take special note of the following key themes and concepts:

Change Why did the Russian people demand change in 1917?

Power How did the Bolsheviks take control of the Russian government from the czar?

Human Rights What was life like in Stalin's totalitarian state?

Economic System How did Stalin's command economy affect the Soviet Union's industry and agriculture?

Key People and Terms

As you review this section, be sure you understand the significance of these key people and terms:

soviets	Joseph Stalin	five-year plans
Vladimir Lenin	Great Purge	collectives
Bolsheviks	totalitarian state	
New Economic Policy	command economy	

Long-Term Causes of Revolution

A variety of factors had been leading up to revolution in Russia for a long time. Through the 1800s and early 1900s, discontent grew as Russian czars resisted needed reforms.

Czarist Rule

In the late 1800s, Alexander III and his son, Nicholas II, sought to industrialize the country and build Russia's economic strength. Although these czars wanted to import western industrialization, they hoped to block the ideals of the French Revolution. Still, Russian liberals called for a constitution and reforms that would eliminate corruption in government. Both Alexander and Nicholas used harsh tactics, such as the use of secret police, to suppress reform.

Peasant Unrest

A rigid system of social classes still existed in Russia at the beginning of World War I. Landowning nobles, priests, and an autocratic czar dominated society. A small middle class was prevented from gaining power.

Peasants faced many difficulties. Most were too poor to buy the land they worked. Even those who owned land often did not have enough to feed their families. Even though industrialization had proceeded slowly, it had angered some peasants. Some opposed it because they feared the changes it brought and preferred the old ways.

Problems of Urban Workers

Some peasants had moved to cities and found jobs in new industries. They worked long hours, and their pay was low. Most lived in slums that were nests of poverty and disease. It was among these workers that socialists spread ideas about revolution and reform.

Diversity and Nationalism

Russia ruled a vast and diverse empire. It included many ethnic minorities. The czars maintained strict control over these groups. Under the policy of Russification, czars attempted to make all people in their empire think, act, and believe as Russians. However, ethnic minorities did not want their native cultures destroyed. Pockets of nationalism remained.

Revolution of 1905

Russia's defeat in the Russo-Japanese War of 1904 triggered a crisis in Russia. On Sunday, January 22, 1905, peaceful marchers carrying a petition for reform were shot down by the czar's troops. "Bloody Sunday," as it was called, destroyed the people's faith and trust in the czar, and strikes and revolts exploded across the country.

In the face of this chaos, Nicholas made some changes. He agreed to reforms and promised to grant more rights, such as freedom of speech. He agreed to set up an elected national legislature, the Duma. However, the Duma had limited powers and did little to relieve peasant and worker discontent.

The Russian Revolution of 1905

The Russian Revolution of 1905
The "Bloody Sunday" killings were a turning point for the Russian people. It destroyed their faith and trust in the czar.

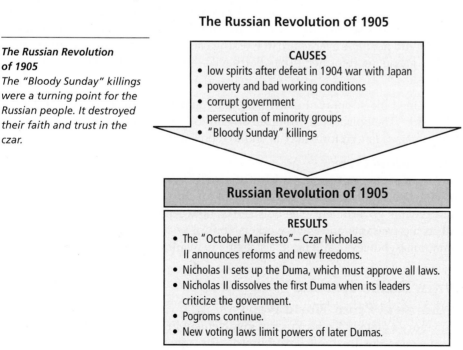

CAUSES
- low spirits after defeat in 1904 war with Japan
- poverty and bad working conditions
- corrupt government
- persecution of minority groups
- "Bloody Sunday" killings

Russian Revolution of 1905

RESULTS
- The "October Manifesto"– Czar Nicholas II announces reforms and new freedoms.
- Nicholas II sets up the Duma, which must approve all laws.
- Nicholas II dissolves the first Duma when its leaders criticize the government.
- Pogroms continue.
- New voting laws limit powers of later Dumas.

World War I and the End of Czarist Rule

A Nation in Chaos

As you have learned, Russia was one of the Allied Powers in World War I. With little industry, however, Russia was not ready to fight a modern war. Russian soldiers lacked adequate weapons and supplies, and Russia suffered a series of battlefield defeats. Food was scarce. Many soldiers lost confidence in Russia's military leadership and deserted.

The March Revolution

In March 1917, military defeats and shortages of food, fuel, and housing in Russia sparked a revolt. In the capital city, St. Petersburg, rioters in the streets demanded bread. The czar's soldiers sympathized with the demonstrators and refused to fire on them. With no control over his troops and with the country nearing anarchy, Czar Nicholas II abdicated, or gave up his rule, in March 1917.

Failure of the Provisional Government

After the removal of the czar, Duma officials set up a provisional, or temporary, government. Middle-class liberals in the government planned to write a constitution and promised democratic reforms. However, the provisional government continued the war against Germany, an unpopular decision that drained away men and resources. The new government implemented only moderate reforms that did little to end unrest among peasants and workers.

The Bolshevik Revolution

The provisional government's slowness to bring about meaningful change led revolutionary socialists to plot further actions. They set up **soviets,** or councils of workers and soldiers, in Russian cities. At first, these soviets worked within the system set up by the government. Soon, however, they were taken over by a radical Socialist Party.

Lenin Gains Support

Following the March Revolution, an exiled Russian revolutionary named **Vladimir Lenin** returned home. Lenin and Leon Trotsky headed a revolutionary Socialist Party, the **Bolsheviks.** Lenin and Trotsky followed the ideas of Karl Marx, but they adapted them to the Russian situation. For example, Marx had said that the urban workers would rise on their own to overthrow the capitalist system. Russia, however, did not have a large urban working class. Lenin therefore suggested that an elite group of reformers—the Bolsheviks—would guide the revolution in Russia.

Lenin gained the support of many people by making promises of "Peace, Land, and Bread." The Bolsheviks promised an end to Russia's involvement in the war. They promised land reform and an end to food shortages.

Lenin Takes Over

The provisional government had lost the support of the people. In November 1917, the Bolsheviks led soldiers, sailors, and factory workers in an uprising that overthrew the government. The Bolsheviks, now called Communists, distributed land to the peasants and gave workers control of the factories and mines. The Communists, however, still faced a struggle to maintain control over Russia.

Lenin Rules Russia

Withdrawal From World War I

Lenin moved quickly to end Russian involvement in World War I. In March 1918, Russia signed the Treaty of Brest-Litovsk. The agreement was costly for Russia, giving Germany a large amount of Russian territory. Lenin, however, believed that he needed to make peace with Germany at any price so that he could deal with his enemies at home.

Russia's Civil War

From 1918 to 1921, Lenin's Red Army battled against forces loyal to the czar, called the Whites. Nationalist groups in the Russian empire also rose up against the Red Army at this time, winning independence for Estonia, Latvia, Lithuania, and Poland.

Both sides used brutal tactics during the war. To eliminate a potential rallying symbol for the Whites, Communists executed Czar Nicholas II and his entire family.

Great Britain, France, and the United States sent troops to help the Whites. This foreign intervention, however, stirred Russian nationalism. An inspired Red Army, under Trotsky's leadership, defeated its enemies by 1921.

Тов. Ленин ОЧИЩАЕТ землю от нечисти.

Vladimir Lenin
Lenin (1870–1924) believed that only revolution could bring needed changes to Russia.

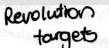

Preparing for the Regents

• Lenin is the figure with the broom at the top of this poster. What is the point of the poster? Whom do the other figures represent?

Revolution targets

Preparing for the Regents

How is a communist government different from a democratic government?

Communist – Govt controls profits in busn
Democratic – Owner controls entire business.

One-Party Government

Lenin's government had a constitution and an elected legislature. However, the Communist Party, not the people themselves, had the real power. The Communist Party was the only legal party, and only its members could run for office. The Party enforced its will through the military and a secret police force.

New Economic Policy

During Russia's civil war, Bolshevik leaders had taken over banks, mines, factories, and railroads. This takeover had resulted in economic disaster. In 1921, Lenin adopted the **New Economic Policy.** Under this plan, also called the NEP, the government still controlled banks, large industry, and foreign trade. Some privately owned businesses were allowed, however. These helped the economy to recover.

Key Themes and Concepts

Economic Systems
The private ownership allowed by the New Economic Policy helped the Soviet economy to recover. Even in the early years, socialist economic policies met with limited success in the Soviet Union.

The Soviet Union

By 1922, Lenin and the Communists had gained control over much of the old Russian empire. The Communist government then created the Union of Soviet Socialist Republics, also called the Soviet Union. It was made up of diverse European and Asian peoples. Russia, the largest republic, controlled the other states in the Soviet Union.

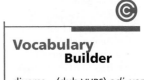

Vocabulary Builder

diverse—(duh VURS) *adj.* very different from each other

Stalin and Communist Dictatorship

Lenin died in 1924, ending the reign of Russia's first Communist leader. A new Soviet leader, **Joseph Stalin,** emerged. Stalin ruled through terror and brutality. In the 1930s, for example, out of fear that other Communist Party members were plotting against him, Stalin launched the **Great Purge.** During the Great Purge,

Describe five specific ways in which Stalin failed to respect the human rights of Russians and minority national groups in the Soviet Union.

1. Promoting Russian first
2. Appointing Russians to key posts
3. Drew boundaries of republics
4. Forbidding culture
5. Secret police

Summarize

Write a sentence explaining the term "Russification."

Stalin accused thousands of people of crimes against the government. Many of the accused were executed; others were exiled or sent to prison camps. For the next 20 years, he pursued ruthless policies that created a totalitarian state in the Soviet Union.

Totalitarian Rule

Stalin turned the Soviet Union into a **totalitarian state.** In this form of government, a one-party dictatorship attempts to regulate every aspect of the lives of its citizens.

Russification

Early in his rule, Stalin promoted individual local cultures. By the end of the 1920s, however, he had changed this policy. Stalin became a strong Russian nationalist. He began to create a Russian ruling elite throughout the Soviet Union. Like the czars before him, Stalin pursued a policy of Russification.

- He promoted Russian history, language, and culture, sometimes forbidding the cultural practices of native peoples.
- He appointed Russians to key posts in the government and secret police.
- He redrew the boundaries of many republics to ensure that non-Russians would not gain a majority.

Life in a Communist Totalitarian State

Economics	Politics	Arts	Religion	Society
• Growth of industry • Growth of military • Low standard of living • Shortage of foods and consumer goods	• One-party dictatorship • Total government control of citizens • Total government control of industry and agriculture • Use of propaganda to win government support	• Censorship of books, music, art • Purpose of all art to praise communism • Observation of artists, writers, and musicians by secret police	• Government war on religion • Takeover of houses of worship • Secret police control religious worship • Communist ideals replace religious ideals	• Fear of secret police • An upper class of Communist Party members • Free education and health care • Public transportation and recreation • Jobs for women

Economic Systems
In a command economy, the state controls all factories and businesses and makes all economic decisions. In a capitalist economy, businesses are privately owned and operated for a profit. The free market controls economic decisions.

Power
When peasants resisted Stalin's plan of collectivization, he ruthlessly eliminated them through starvation.

A Command Economy

Stalin established a **command economy,** in which government officials made all basic economic decisions. Under Stalin, the government controlled all factories, businesses, and farms.

Industrialization One of Stalin's chief goals was to make the Soviet Union strong by turning it into a modern industrial power. In 1928, Stalin launched the first of a series of **five-year plans** to build industry and increase farm output. Emphasis was placed on heavy industry, while consumer goods were neglected. In the 1930s, Soviet production in oil, coal, steel, mining, and military goods increased. Across the nation, factories, hydroelectric power stations, and railroads were built.

Despite this progress, however, most Russians remained poor and endured a low standard of living. Soviet central planning created shortages in consumer goods. Also, to meet high production quotas, many factories mass-produced goods of low quality.

Collectivization Stalin forced peasants to give up their small farms and live on state-owned farms or on **collectives,** which were large farms owned and operated by peasants as a group. The collective owned all farm animals and equipment. The government controlled prices and farm supplies and set production quotas. Stalin's plan was for the collectives to grow enough grain for the workers in the cities and to produce surplus grain to sell abroad.

Many peasants resisted collectivization. They killed farm animals, destroyed tools, and burned crops. Stalin responded with a ruthless policy aimed at crushing all who opposed him. The government seized the land of those who resisted and sent the farmers to prison labor camps. There, many died from overwork or were executed.

Forced Famine The results of Stalin's policies were devastating. Some peasants continued to resist by growing just enough grain to feed themselves. The government then seized all the grain from some of those communities. Mass starvation resulted. In the Ukraine, where opposition to collectivization was especially strong, more than five million people died from starvation. Millions more died in other parts of the Soviet Union.

Vocabulary Builder

devastating—(DEV uh stayt ing) *adj.* badly damaging or destroying something

First Leaders of the Soviet Union

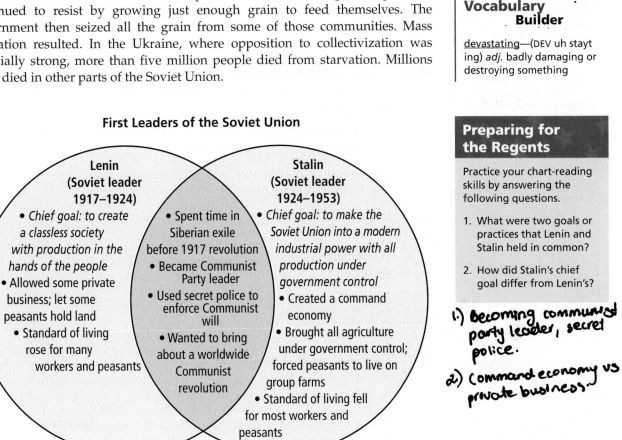

Lenin (Soviet leader 1917–1924)
- *Chief goal: to create a classless society with production in the hands of the people*
- Allowed some private business; let some peasants hold land
- Standard of living rose for many workers and peasants

(shared)
- Spent time in Siberian exile before 1917 revolution
- Became Communist Party leader
- Used secret police to enforce Communist will
- Wanted to bring about a worldwide Communist revolution

Stalin (Soviet leader 1924–1953)
- *Chief goal: to make the Soviet Union into a modern industrial power with all production under government control*
- Created a command economy
- Brought all agriculture under government control; forced peasants to live on group farms
- Standard of living fell for most workers and peasants

Preparing for the Regents

Practice your chart-reading skills by answering the following questions.

1. What were two goals or practices that Lenin and Stalin held in common?

2. How did Stalin's chief goal differ from Lenin's?

1.) becoming communist party leader, secret police.

2) command economy vs private business.

Summary

In the late 1800s and early 1900s, autocratic rule and poor economic conditions caused many Russians to demand political and social reforms. In 1917, this discontent led to a revolution that ended czarist rule in Russia. Bolshevik leader Vladimir Lenin gained power by promising better economic conditions and an end to Russian involvement in World War I. He then set up a Communist government. After Lenin's death, Joseph Stalin took over and established a totalitarian state, in which every aspect of life was controlled. Stalin's five-year plans boosted industry but did little to improve the life of the average worker. His collectivization of agriculture angered peasants, whose resistance resulted in mass starvation.

Preparing for the Regents

- To what extent was the Russian Revolution a turning point in global history?

Between the Wars

The
Big Idea

After World War I:

- the Treaty of Versailles severely punished Germany.

- new nations formed and old empires collapsed.

- nationalist movements struggled to throw off foreign domination.

- women gained the right to vote in many countries.

- the global economy experienced a severe downturn.

- fascist powers took control in Italy and Germany.

- militarists took power in Japan.

Key People and Terms

Make a list of the people in the Key People and Terms. Also write each person's country.

Key Themes and Concepts

Global Connections
The Treaty of Versailles did not resolve the issues that had led to World War I. Nationalism continued to be a cause of conflict. German discontent with the Treaty of Versailles would help lead to World War II.

Section Overview

After World War I, global problems remained. The Treaty of Versailles punished Germany. The League of Nations had little power. Old empires had collapsed, and new nations had come into being. Nationalism continued to cause conflict. World War I had disillusioned many, altered society, and prompted new forms of expression. In Europe and the United States, women struggled to gain the right to vote. Then, in 1929, the global economy crashed, leading to a worldwide depression. During this time, fascism, a new kind of dictatorship, rose in Italy and Germany. In Japan, aggressive military leaders gained power.

Key Themes and Concepts

As you review this section, take special note of the following key themes and concepts:

Interdependence How did the major powers try to resolve troublesome issues after World War I?

Nationalism What factors led to the nationalist movements of the 1920s and 1930s?

Human Rights What rights did women gain after World War I?

Economic Systems What were the causes and effects of the world economic crisis of the 1930s?

Political Systems What are the major characteristics of fascism?

Key People and Terms

As you review this section, be sure you understand the significance of these key people and terms:

Treaty of Versailles	**Pan-Arabism**	**fascism**
League of Nations	**Mohandas Gandhi**	**Benito Mussolini**
Kemal Atatürk	**civil disobedience**	**Adolf Hitler**
Reza Khan	**Kuomintang**	**Third Reich**
mandates	**Great Depression**	

Treaty of Versailles

World War I had a lasting impact on international politics. In January 1919, the victorious Allies gathered at the palace of Versailles, outside Paris, to work out the terms of peace. United States President Woodrow Wilson and Prime Minister David Lloyd George of Great Britain joined French leader Georges Clemenceau. They were known as the "Big Three" of the meeting that would be called the Paris Peace Conference. These men had differing goals. Wilson stressed self-determination, by which people would choose their own government.

He also hoped to create a world organization that would guarantee peace in the future. Great Britain and France wanted to punish Germany and be sure that it would never again become a threat.

Harsh Provisions for Germany

In the end, Great Britain's and France's ideas guided the **Treaty of Versailles.**

Territorial Losses Land was taken from Germany. Some of it was used to help create the new country of Poland. Alsace and Lorraine were returned to France. Germany also lost many of its overseas colonies.

Military Restrictions Germany's army and navy were limited. Germany had to remove its troops from the Rhineland, an industrial area along the French border.

War Guilt Germany had to accept full responsibility for the war and pay huge reparations, or large sums of money to help undo war damage. Accepting the blame and paying the reparations caused bitterness in Germany.

The League of Nations

The Treaty of Versailles also formed the **League of Nations,** a group of more than 40 countries that hoped to settle problems through negotiation, not war. The countries that joined the League of Nations promised to take cooperative economic and military action against any aggressor state. Although the league had been Woodrow Wilson's concept, the United States never joined. Many Americans were afraid that participation in it would drag the United States into future European wars. In refusing to join, the United States weakened the League of Nations.

Preparing for the Regents

- How did the League of Nations plan to deal with future international conflicts?

Preparing for the Regents

Practice your map skills by listing five nations that were created as a result of World War I.

1. Finland
2. Poland
3. Hungary
4. Latvia
5. Estonia

Europe After World War I
The peace treaties that ended World War I changed the map of Europe.

Europe After World War I

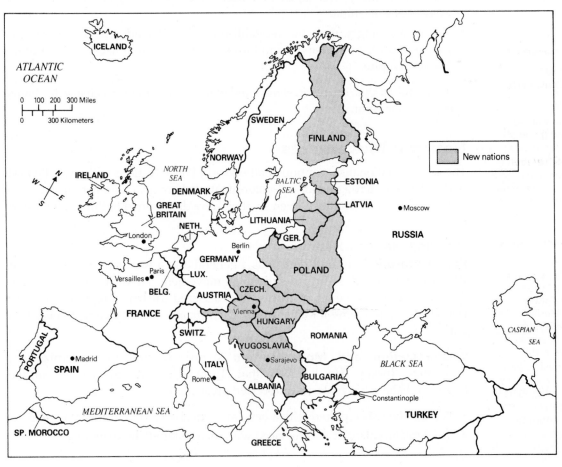

Vocabulary
Builder

carve out—(kahrv owt) v.
to divide land into smaller
parts and share it between
people

Collapse of Empires

World War I caused the collapse of the Austro-Hungarian and Ottoman empires. New nations were carved out of their former territories.

Breakup of Austria-Hungary

As a result of the war, the government in Austria-Hungary had collapsed. Several new nations were created out of the former empire. Austria and Hungary became independent nations. Czechoslovakia and Yugoslavia, two multinational states, were formed. Italy and Romania each gained land.

Breakup of the Ottoman Empire

The Ottoman empire, one of the defeated Central Powers, collapsed in 1918. Most of the Arab lands of the Ottoman empire were placed under the control of Great Britain and France. In theory these countries were being prepared for self-determination. In practice, however, the Allies added to their own overseas empires by creating a system of territories administered by western powers. The remainder of the empire became the country of Turkey.

Unfulfilled National Goals

Many nations were dissatisfied with the results of World War I. Various groups felt that their goals had not been achieved.

- Germany was horrified by the terms of the Treaty of Versailles.
- Italy had hoped to gain more land than it received. It had made a secret treaty with the Allies that was not fulfilled.
- Japan was angry because the Allies did not recognize its claims in China.
- China was angry that Japan had been given control over former German possessions in China.
- Russia was angry over the reestablishment of Poland and the creation of independent Estonia, Latvia, and Lithuania on lands that had been part of the Russian empire.

Nations and groups, however, waited and watched, hoping for a chance to change events in their favor.

National Movements

The spirit of nationalism continued after World War I. Nations in the Middle East, Africa, and Asia struggled for self-determination. In many cases, nationalists were influenced by western ideas. Even so, they were determined to throw off western rule.

Turkish Nationalism

Kemal Atatürk Mustafa Kemal was a general and a war hero in Turkey. After World War I, he led a Turkish nationalist movement. He overthrew the sultan, defeated western occupation forces, and declared Turkey a republic. Mustafa Kemal later called himself **Kemal Atatürk**. The name *Atatürk* meant "father of the Turks."

Westernization and Modernization Atatürk wanted to modernize and westernize Turkey. He believed that Turkey had to change to survive. In accomplishing his goals, he introduced great changes.

- Islamic law was replaced with a new law code, based on European models.
- The Muslim calendar was replaced with the western (Christian) one.

Key Themes
and Concepts

Nationalism
Mustafa Kemal wanted to unite Turks and throw off European domination. At the same time, he felt that Turkey must modernize and westernize to survive in the twentieth century.

Key Themes
and Concepts

Interaction of Cultures
Some Turkish Muslims rejected westernization, believing that it was a betrayal of Islam. This conflict continues today. The government of Turkey remains secular, but some Islamic groups work strongly for a return to traditional ways.

- People were required to wear western dress.
- State schools were set up. Arabic script was replaced with the western (Latin) alphabet.
- Women no longer had to wear veils and were allowed to vote. They could work outside their homes.
- Turkey was industrialized. Atatürk built roads, railroads, and factories.

Iranian Nationalism

Nationalists in Iran followed Turkey's lead. In Iran, the British and the Russians had carved out spheres of influence. In 1925, **Reza Khan,** an army officer, overthrew the ruler of Iran, called the shah. He set up his own dynasty and proclaimed himself shah. Reza Khan quickly tried to modernize and westernize Iran and make it fully independent. Factories, roads, and railroads were built. The army was strengthened. The western alphabet and western dress were adopted, and secular schools were set up. Islamic law was replaced by secular law, and women were encouraged to take part in public life. Reza Khan had the support of wealthy urban Iranians but not of Muslim religious leaders.

Arab Nationalism

During World War I, many Arabs had helped the Allies. In return they had been promised independence. After the war, however, Great Britain and France divided up the Ottoman lands between themselves. They set up **mandates,** territories administered by European powers. France had mandates in Syria and Lebanon. Great Britain had mandates in Palestine and Iraq.

In the 1920s and 1930s, Arab nationalists sought to be free of foreign control. Arab nationalism gave rise to **Pan-Arabism.** This movement sought a unity of all Arab peoples based on their shared heritage.

Zionism

Zionism, as you have learned, had arisen during the 1890s in Europe and the Middle East. Jewish people wanted to establish a Jewish state in Palestine. The situation was complex, however, since Arab peoples were already living there. The Allies had made conflicting promises during World War I. They had promised Arabs land that included Palestine. They had also pledged to set up a Jewish nation in the same region. As more Jews moved to Palestine to escape persecution in the 1930s, tensions grew.

Indian Nationalism

Nearly 1 million Indians had served the Allied cause in Europe during World War I, and many had died. At home, however, Indians had few rights. During World War I, Great Britain had promised India greater self-government. After the war was over, Great Britain failed to fulfill these promises.

The Amritsar Massacre A turning point came in 1919. There were riots and attacks on British citizens in the city of Amritsar. In response, public meetings were banned. When a large group of Indians assembled on April 13, British troops fired on them without warning, killing about 400 people and wounding about 1,200 more. The incident convinced many Indians that British rule must be ended.

Gandhi In the 1920s and 1930s, a leader named **Mohandas Gandhi** headed the Indian nationalist movement. He taught that nonviolent resistance and **civil disobedience** (the refusal to obey unjust laws), rather than bloodshed, were the way to win rights. He used tactics such as boycotting, or refusing to buy, British goods and peaceful demonstrations such as the "Salt March." Gandhi embraced

Key Themes and Concepts

Change
In Iran—unlike Turkey—modernization eventually led, in 1979, to an Islamic revolution in which the government turned from secularism.

Preparing for the Regents

- What are the similarities among Pan-Slavism, Pan-Arabism, and Zionism? What are some differences?

Mohandas Gandhi
Gandhi's philosophy reflected Western and Indian influences. His ideas inspired Indians of all religious and ethnic backgrounds.

Preparing for the Regents

Write a brief statement about the historical importance of each of these figures.

Kemal Atatürk:

Reza Khan:

Mohandas Gandhi: *Indian Freedom Fighter*

western ideas of democracy and nationalism. He rejected the caste system and urged equal rights for all, including women. India, however, did not achieve independence until 1947, one year before Gandhi's death.

Chinese Nationalism

Chinese civilization was in great disorder during and after World War I. After Sun Yixian (also known as Sun Yat-sen), founder of the Chinese Republic, stepped down, rival warlords fought for power. The economy collapsed, and peasants faced great economic hardship. During this time, foreign powers—especially Japan—increased their influence in China.

Rival Groups in China After the death of Sun Yixian in 1925, an army officer named Jiang Jieshi (also known as Chiang Kai-shek) took over the **Kuomintang**. Jiang's government, supported by middle class businessmen, did little to help the peasants. As a result the peasants were attracted to Mao Zedong and his Communist Party.

Civil War At first, the Nationalists and the Communists had worked together to unite China. Over time, however, Jiang Jieshi began to see the Communists as a threat. A civil war began between the Nationalists and the Communists that would last for 22 years.

Preparing for the Regents

• How did World War I affect the literature and arts of the 1920s and 1930s?

Literature and Arts: The Lost Generation

World War I had produced disquiet in social as well as political arenas. The war had shaken many people's long-held beliefs. Scientific discoveries—such as those of the Curies, Einstein, and Freud—had brought new understanding, but they had also cast doubt on the ideas of the past.

The war itself had left scars on those who survived it. Writers, artists, and musicians throughout the 1920s and 1930s expressed a loss of hope, rejecting former rules and moral values. They became known as the "Lost Generation."

Writers such as Ernest Hemingway expressed a loss of faith in western civilization. Poet T. S. Eliot portrayed the modern world as spiritually empty and barren. Some painters stopped trying to reproduce the real world. In an attempt to express their feelings of loss of meaning, they experimented with color and distorted shapes.

Key Themes and Concepts

Justice and Human Rights World War I brought great progress for women. Women kept the economy going at home by taking on jobs left vacant by men who became soldiers. Some joined the armed forces. This independence gave them a new sense of pride and confidence. After the war, women in various western democracies gained the right to vote.

Women's Suffrage Movement

In the mid-1800s in western democracies, women had begun to demand greater rights. These included property rights and suffrage, or the right to vote. The first country in which women won the right to vote was New Zealand in 1893. In Great Britain, Parliament finally granted women over 30 the right to vote in 1918. By 1928, Great Britain had granted suffrage to all women over the age of 21. In the United States, President Wilson proposed the Nineteenth Amendment in 1918. This amendment gave American citizens over the age of 21 the right to vote, regardless of gender. Congress adopted the amendment two years later in 1920. Women also gained the right to vote in Canada, Finland, Germany, and Sweden in the early 1900s.

Worldwide Depression

After World War I, economic problems emerged in Europe. Soldiers, returning from the war, needed jobs. Nations had war debts to pay and cities to rebuild. In the decade following the war, the economies of many European countries began a shaky recovery. Middle-class families enjoyed a rising standard of living.

The United States, on the other hand, experienced an economic boom after the war. It became the world's leading economic power and made investments in Europe to promote recovery. These came to an end, however, with the crash of the American stock market in 1929. This event triggered the **Great Depression** of the 1930s, a time of global economic collapse.

Causes of the Depression

Weaknesses in the economies of the United States and other nations around the world led to the Great Depression.

Impact of the Depression

The collapse of the American economy had a ripple effect around the world. American investors pulled their money out of Europe, and placed high tariffs on imported goods. Nations that depended on American loans and investments or on exporting their goods to the United States, saw their economies collapse. Unemployment soared in many countries.

As the Great Depression continued, some people lost faith in democracy and capitalism. Extreme ideas of many types arose. Communists celebrated what they saw as the failure of capitalism. Strong leaders supported intense nationalism, militarism, and a return to authoritarian rule.

The Rise of Fascism

Widespread economic despair paved the way for the rise of dictators. Strong leaders in Italy and Germany promised solutions.

Key Themes and Concepts

Economics and Interdependence
Global economic interdependence was an important factor in the Great Depression. Because the United States economy was part of a network of trade and finance, the American stock market crash of 1929 had a world-wide effect.

Note Taking

Reading Skill:
Identify Causes and Effects
Make a flowchart. Show the causes and the effects of the Great Depression.

Causes	Event	Effects
•	The Great Depression	•
•		•
•		•

Preparing for the Regents

• Identify specific examples of how Hitler and Mussolini carried out the fascist policies shown on this chart.

Censorship, state control of army nationalism

The Fascist State

- strong military
- censorship and government control of news
- extreme nationalism
- use of violence and terror
- **FASCISM**
- state control of economy
- blind loyalty to leader
- rule by dictator
- strict discipline

Common Ideals of Fascism

Fascism is the rule of a people by dictatorial government that is nationalistic and imperialistic. Fascist governments are also anticommunist. Fascism emerged in both Italy and Germany after World War I.

Democracy is more freedom.

Preparing for the Regents

• Describe several ways in which fascism differs from democracy.

Mussolini in Italy

Italy was troubled after World War I. Treaties had given away land that the Italians had expected to control. In addition, many war veterans could not find jobs. Trade was slow and taxes were high. Furthermore, workers went on strike.

Benito Mussolini took advantage of the unrest, gathering a following of war veterans and other unhappy Italians. He called his group the Fascist Party and pledged to solve the nation's problems and strengthen Italy. Mussolini promised to end unemployment and gain more land for Italy. He also vowed to outlaw rebellion among workers and stamp out all threats of communism.

In 1922, the Fascists used force and terror to gain control of Italy. They ended free elections, free speech, and the free press. They killed or jailed their enemies. Grasping desperately for order, Italians put the goals of the state above their individual rights.

Hitler in Germany

The Weimar Republic After World War I, the kaiser stepped down. Germany was in chaos. The new democratic government, called the Weimar Republic, was blamed for agreeing to the harsh terms of the Versailles Treaty. Inflation created major economic problems. The troubles of the time led to the Nazi rise to power.

Adolf Hitler promised to provide jobs and rebuild German pride. He stated that the Germans were a superior race who were destined to build a new empire. In 1920, he headed the National Socialist German Workers, or Nazi, Party. His Party grew. In 1933, Hitler was appointed chancellor.

Hitler as Dictator Hitler's Germany, called the **Third Reich,** was a totalitarian state. He built a one-party government, ended civil rights, silenced his enemies with force, put businesses under government control, and employed many people in large public works programs. Germany's standard of living rose. Hitler rearmed Germany and rebuilt its military, which violated the Treaty of Versailles.

Preparing for the Regents

• Practice your graph skills by identifying the years during which the cost of living in Germany was the highest. What impact do you think this had on Hitler's rise to power?

1920–1925

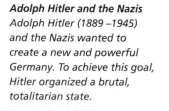

Germany: Cost of Living

Adolph Hitler and the Nazis
Adolph Hitler (1889–1945)
and the Nazis wanted to
create a new and powerful
Germany. To achieve this goal,
Hitler organized a brutal,
totalitarian state.

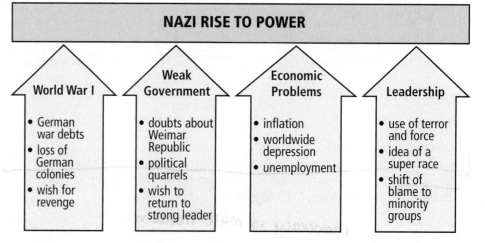

NAZI RISE TO POWER

World War I
• German war debts
• loss of German colonies
• wish for revenge

Weak Government
• doubts about Weimar Republic
• political quarrels
• wish to return to strong leader

Economic Problems
• inflation
• worldwide depression
• unemployment

Leadership
• use of terror and force
• idea of a super race
• shift of blame to minority groups

Hitler used the Jews as a scapegoat for Germany's problems. He instituted anti-Semitic policies. He used education and the arts as propaganda tools to push these policies. At first, Nazis organized boycotts of Jewish businesses, but by 1938 they were seizing the property and businesses of Jews and selling them to non-Jews. The Nuremberg Laws of 1935 took away the political rights and German citizenship of Jews. Few German citizens worried about Hitler's policies. Most were pleased at the growth of German pride and Germany's increased military and economic power.

Totalitarianism in Nazi Germany

Propaganda	Lack of Civil Liberties
The government controlled all sources of information–newspapers, radio, movies, and books. Schools taught Nazi ideas, and children joined the Hitler Youth. Forbidden books were burned.	Only the Nazi Party was allowed, and rival political parties were outlawed. The Gestapo (secret police) arrested and executed people without a trial.
Anti-Semitism	**Economic Controls**
Jews lost their property and citizenship. Their shops and synagogues were destroyed. They were forced to wear the yellow Star of David on their clothing. They were moved to ghettoes and concentration camps.	Agricultural and industrial production was controlled. Labor unions and strikes were outlawed. Germans were put to work building highways and weapons factories and drafted into the military.

Japan: Militarism and Expansion

Japan had moved toward greater democracy during the 1920s. However, there were underlying problems in Japanese society. The Great Depression that began in 1929 made these problems more apparent. Militarists and extreme nationalists gained power.

Japanese Militarists of the 1930s

CAUSES

- unhappiness over loss of traditions
- loss of foreign markets due to Great Depression
- unemployment
- poverty among peasants
- feelings of nationalism
- demand for expansion of Japanese empire

Rise of Militarists in Japan

EFFECTS

- 1931 attack on Chinese province of Manchuria
- withdrawal from League of Nations
- anti-western feelings
- end of many democratic freedoms
- renewed practice of traditions
- increased honor for emperor
- renewed expansion and efforts to control China

Summary

After World War I, conflict and turmoil continued. The Treaty of Versailles gave some nations self-determination, punished Germany severely, and created the League of Nations. New nations formed and old empires collapsed. Change occurred as nationalist groups struggled to overthrow foreign domination. Society and culture changed after the war, and people lost faith in old ideas. In 1929, the global economy plunged into a terrible depression. Fascism in Italy and Germany threatened the peace in Europe, while aggressive militarism by Japan caused tension in Asia.

Vocabulary Builder

scapegoat—(SKAYP goht) *n.* someone who is blamed for something bad that happens, even if it is not their fault

Preparing for the Regents

- How did war and economic depression lead to the rise of fascism?

Key Themes and Concepts

Power and Human Rights Both Mussolini in Italy and Hitler in Germany improved the economies of their nations and brought order. The price of order, however, was loss of personal freedoms and human rights.

Because of unrest in Japan in the 1930s, the government accepted military domination. It revived ancient warrior values.

Preparing for the Regents

The militarists in Japan were determined to restore Japan to greatness, rid themselves of western influence, and gain foreign territories.

1. What economic problems led to the rise of militarism in Japan?

2. What were the political effects of the rise of militarism in Japan?

World War II

The
Big Idea

World War II:

• began when aggressive empire building by Germany, Italy, and Japan was opposed by Great Britain and France.

• was very destructive because of the technological power of new weaponry.

• was a total war that involved civilians as well as the military.

• created political and geographical divisions within Europe.

• affected global politics and culture for many years.

Section Overview

During the 1930s, Italy, Germany, and Japan sought to build new empires. At first, the democratic powers did not stop them. When German aggression became impossible to ignore, in 1939, World War II began. With advanced technology, the war covered a larger area and was more destructive than any before. Civilians became involved on a larger scale as well. At first, the Axis powers—Germany, Italy, and Japan—won major victories. After the entry of the United States and the Soviet Union into the war on the Allied side, however, the tide began to turn. The war finally ended in 1945. It had many lasting effects. There were enormous losses of life and property. The United Nations was formed to try to maintain peace. Europe became divided, with communist governments in Eastern Europe and democratic governments in Western Europe.

Key Themes and Concepts

As you review this section, take special note of the following key themes and concepts:

Power What events led up to World War II?

Science and Technology How did new weapons technology affect the course of the war?

Citizenship How were the lives of individuals affected by the war?

Change What were the major turning points of the war that helped determine its outcome?

Key People and Terms

What do three of the key people and terms have in common? Explain.

Key People and Terms

As you review this section, be sure you understand the significance of these key people and terms:

appeasement	D-Day	concentration camps
Munich Conference	Hiroshima	Holocaust
Franklin Roosevelt	blitz	Bataan Death March
Pearl Harbor	Winston Churchill	United Nations
Stalingrad	genocide	

Key Themes and Concepts

Power
Militarists had gained great power in Japan. Japan's successful aggression increased their political power.

The Road to War

In the 1930s, Italy, Germany, and Japan aggressively sought to build new empires. The League of Nations was weak. Western countries were recovering from the Great Depression and did not want any more war. As a result, acts of aggression occurred and were allowed to go unchecked.

Japan Invades China

The militaristic leaders of Japan wanted to build a Japanese empire. In 1931, Japan seized the Chinese territory of Manchuria. When the League of Nations condemned the action, Japan merely withdrew its membership from the League.

This incident strengthened militarism in Japan. In 1937, the Japanese army invaded the Chinese mainland. They established a puppet government in the former Chinese Nationalist capital of Nanjing. Their invasion of this city was so brutal that it became known as the "rape of Nanjing." Japan continued to gain territory during the period of war with China.

Italy Attacks Ethiopia

In 1935, the Italian army invaded the African country of Ethiopia. The Ethiopians resisted the attack, but their weapons were no match for the armored vehicles, aircraft, and poison gas of the Italians. The Ethiopian king appealed to the League of Nations. The league agreed to stop the sale of weapons and other war materials to Italy. However, the agreement was not honored by all nations.

German Aggression in Europe

Hitler glorified war as a means of restoring German national pride. This philosophy led to a policy of expansion.

- Hitler rebuilt the German army, in violation of the Treaty of Versailles.
- In 1936, Hitler sent troops into the Rhineland. This was an area located on Germany's border with France. The Treaty of Versailles had required that Germany remove its troops from this border region.
- In 1938, Hitler made Austria part of the German empire. In the same year, he also forced Czechoslovakia to give Germany a border area called the Sudetenland, where many Germans lived.

Appeasement

Western democracies adopted a policy of **appeasement.** Under this policy, nations gave in to aggressive demands to maintain peace. The western democracies responded weakly to German aggression. At the **Munich Conference** in 1938, western democracies agreed that Germany would seize control of the Sudetenland from Czechoslovakia.

Military Aggression Leading to World War II

1930	1932	1934	1936	1938	1940

1935 Italy attacks Ethiopia

1937 Japan invades China

1939 Germany invades Poland / Germany takes Czechoslovakia

1931 Japan invades Manchuria

1936 Germany occupies Rhineland

1938 Germany invades Austria / Germany seizes Sudetenland

World War II Begins

In the face of this weakness, Japan, Italy, and Germany formed the Rome-Berlin-Tokyo Axis. These nations agreed to fight Soviet communism and not to stop each other from making foreign conquests.

It began to be clear that appeasement had failed. Several events led to a declaration of war. In March 1939, Hitler took over the rest of Czechoslovakia. In August 1939, he made a pact with Joseph Stalin, the leader of the Soviet Union. In the

Vocabulary Builder

puppet—(PUP ut) *n.* a person or organization that allows other people to control them and make their decisions

Key Themes and Concepts

Political Systems
Leaders of Great Britain, France, and the United States knew that their citizens were reluctant to get involved in another costly war. This factor and others kept them from responding immediately to the aggression of Germany, Italy, and Japan.

Preparing for the Regents

List five acts of aggression that led to World War II.

1.

2.

3.

4.

5.

Nazi-Soviet Pact, the two enemies agreed not to fight each other. In September 1939, Germany invaded Poland. Finally, Great Britain and France responded by declaring war on Germany. World War II had begun.

The Axis Powers Advance

The war was fought between the Axis powers (Germany, Italy, and Japan) and the Allied powers (France and Great Britain). The Allies were later joined by the Soviet Union, China, and the United States. At first, Germany and its allies prevailed. Nazi forces conquered Poland in a swift, massive attack known as blitzkrieg, or lightning warfare. In April 1940, Hitler overran Norway, Denmark, the Netherlands, and Belgium. By June 1940, the Germans had entered Paris. Charles de Gaulle formed a French government in exile, calling on French forces to continue fighting Germany. These "Free French" worked from England to liberate their homeland.

The Axis war machine extended across the world. It reached its height in Europe in 1942.

The World at War: World War II

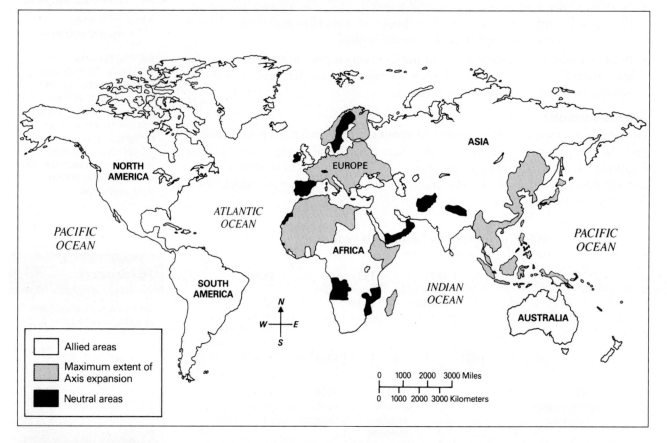

Allied areas

Maximum extent of Axis expansion

Neutral areas

Preparing for the Regents

Describe the importance of each of the following turning points of the war.

Entry of the United States:

Battle of Stalingrad:

Invasion of Normandy:

Turning Points of the War

The Axis powers won quick victories in the first several years of the war. Several events after 1940, however, are seen as turning points for the Allies.

The Entry of the United States (1941)

Although the United States had declared its neutrality in the war, President **Franklin Roosevelt** met with England's prime minister, Winston Churchill, in August 1941, and they declared their common desire to end Nazi tyranny.

Roosevelt continued to supply arms to the Allies. To stop Japanese aggression, the United States banned the sale of war materials to Japan. Angered by the ban, Japan launched a surprise attack on American military bases at **Pearl Harbor,** Hawaii, on December 7, 1941. More than 2,400 people were killed, and many ships and planes were destroyed. In response, Franklin Roosevelt asked Congress to declare war on Japan. The entry of the United States into the war gave the Allies added strength.

Battle of Stalingrad (1942–1943)

The Germans invaded the Soviet Union in 1941. After steadily advancing, they became stalled outside Moscow and Leningrad. Hitler turned south in 1942 to try to take **Stalingrad.** Russian troops and a freezing winter caused the German invaders to surrender in 1943. The Red Army drove the Germans out of the Soviet Union. Soon Soviet troops were advancing toward Germany.

Invasion of Normandy (1944)

The Allies invaded France on June 6, 1944, also known as **D-Day.** Allied troops were ferried across the English Channel, landing on the beaches of Normandy. They broke through German defenses to advance toward Paris and freed France from German control. The Allies then moved from France into Germany.

The War Ends

The war in Europe ended on May 7, 1945, with the Germans' surrender. Fighting in the Pacific would continue until the Japanese surrendered in August 1945.

Yalta Conference

In February 1945, Roosevelt, Churchill, and Stalin met at a Soviet resort called Yalta. They knew then that the war was close to an end. The three leaders decided that at war's end, they would divide Germany temporarily. British, French, American, and Soviet forces would each control a zone of Germany. They agreed that Stalin would oversee the creation of new governments in Eastern Europe.

Victory in the Pacific

Japan was greatly weakened, and the United States took the offensive after two Japanese fleets were severely damaged by Americans in 1942. Gradually, American forces recaptured Japanese-held islands south of Japan and advanced north. By 1944, the Americans had begun to bomb Japanese cities. The Japanese, however, refused to surrender.

Hiroshima and Nagasaki

With no war in Europe, the Allies poured resources into the Pacific. By mid-1945, most of the Japanese navy and air force had been destroyed. Japan's army was still strong, however. On August 6, 1945, an American plane dropped an atomic bomb on the Japanese city of **Hiroshima.** The bomb flattened 4 square miles of the city and killed 70,000 people. They dropped another bomb on Nagasaki, killing 40,000 people. Some militarists wanted to hold out, but on August 10, Japanese emperor Hirohito forced his government to surrender. Japan signed a peace treaty on September 2, 1945.

Technology and World War II

Throughout the war, advanced technology led to more power, greater speed, and better communications. Technological innovation resulted in more widespread destruction than ever before.

Preparing for the Regents

Describe the significance of each of the following leaders.

Hitler:

Mussolini:

Stalin:

Churchill:

Roosevelt:

Identify Effects

Japan refused to surrender to the United States. What were the two main effects?

Preparing for the Regents

- How did World War II affect civilian life? How did civilians contribute to the war effort?

Civilian Life and Total War

Both the Allied powers and the Axis powers had engaged in total war. Cities became targets of bombing. In 1940, Germany began a **blitz,** or massive bombing, of London using warplanes. **Winston Churchill,** prime minister of Great Britain, rallied his people.

Democratic governments increased their power during the war. They ordered factories to produce war materials instead of civilian products. Prices and wages were fixed, and consumer goods were rationed.

Democratic governments sometimes limited the rights of individuals. In the United States and Canada, some people of Japanese descent were forced into internment camps. The British took similar action with those of German ancestry.

As men joined the war, women worked in the factories. They helped produce planes, ships, and ammunition. British and American women served in the armed forces by driving trucks and ambulances, decoding messages, and serving as nurses at field hospitals.

Key Themes and Concepts

Human Rights
The Holocaust as well as other atrocities committed during World War II were extreme violations of human rights.

The Holocaust

One of Hitler's goals was to create "living space" for Germans who he considered racially superior. He planned to destroy people he found inferior. Jews were the main target, but he also wanted to destroy or enslave others, including Slavs, Gypsies, and the mentally or physically disabled.

The attempt to destroy an entire ethnic or religious group is called **genocide.** Hitler committed genocide against the Jews. He began by limiting the rights and encouraging violence against Jews. On November 8, 1938, called Kristallnacht, organized violence began. Thousands of Jewish synagogues, businesses, cemeteries, schools, and homes were destroyed. The next day, 30,000 Jews were arrested for being Jewish and more restrictive laws on Jews and Jewish businesses began. Jews were forced to live in separate areas. Then, Hitler set up **concentration camps.** At death camps, like Auschwitz, Jews were starved, shot, or gassed to death. By 1945, more than six million Jews had died in what became known as the **Holocaust.**

Vocabulary Builder

atrocity—(uh TRAHS uh tee) *n.* an extremely cruel and violent action, especially during a war

Other Wartime Atrocities

The Holocaust stands as the starkest example of wartime inhumanity. Several other incidents, however, also stand out as especially brutal aspects of World War II.

- The Japanese invasion of Nanjing in 1937 involved mass shootings and terrible brutality. As many as 250,000 Chinese were killed.
- In the Philippines, Japanese soldiers forced American and Filipino prisoners of war on a march up the Bataan peninsula. Along the way, prisoners were beaten, stabbed, and shot. This event became known as the **Bataan Death March.**
- In Poland, Soviet troops subjected thousands of Poles to imprisonment, torture, and execution.

Impact of World War II

Human Losses

World War II had killed as many as 75 million people. In European countries alone, about 38 million people died. The Soviets, however, had suffered the heaviest losses, with more than 22 million dead. The Holocaust had inflicted death and misery on millions of Jews and others in the Nazi concentration camps.

Economic Losses

Throughout Europe and parts of Asia, cities were in ruins. Aerial bombardment had been very destructive. Coventry in England; Hamburg and Dresden in Germany; and Tokyo, Hiroshima, and Nagasaki in Japan were some of the hardest-hit cities. The European countryside was devastated as well. The economies of war-torn countries took many years to recover.

War Crime Trials

At meetings during the war, Allied leaders had agreed to punish those responsible for "crimes against humanity." Trials were held in Nuremberg, Germany, from November 1945 through September 1946. Hitler was already dead, but 22 surviving Nazi leaders were tried at the Nuremberg trials. Some received the death penalty; others were imprisoned. Additional trials were held in Italy and Japan. The trials demonstrated that leaders could be held accountable for their actions during war.

Occupied Nations

In order to prevent another world war and to promote democracy, western nations occupied West Germany and Japan. They built new governments with democratic constitutions, which protected individual rights and liberties.

However, Soviet forces occupied East Germany and most of Eastern Europe. They established communist governments in these nations, backed by the power of the Soviet Union. Thus, Europe was divided in two—between democracy in the West and communism in the East.

The United Nations

World War II resulted in the formation of a new international body. In April 1945, representatives from nations around the world met in San Francisco to establish the **United Nations.** The purpose of the United Nations is to provide a place to discuss world problems and develop solutions. The two main bodies of the United Nations are:

- the General Assembly, which includes representatives from all member nations; each representative has one vote.
- the Security Council, with 15 member nations, 5 of which are permanent: the United States, Russia, France, Great Britain, and China.

Summary

Germany, Italy, and Japan tried in the 1930s to build world empires. When Germany invaded Poland in 1939, World War II began, and the world faced the most devastating conflict in human history. During World War II, new weapons with massive power caused the loss of millions of lives. Civilians were greatly affected by the war, facing rationing, military attacks, and sometimes severe repression. The conflict continued until 1945. World War II resulted in millions of deaths, heavy economic losses, and brutality on a scale such as the world had not seen before. After 1945, the world became divided between communist and democratic forms of government.

Compare and Contrast

Compare and contrast the United Nations and the League of Nations.

Questions for Regents Practice

Multiple Choice

Directions: Review the Test-Taking Strategies section of this book. Then answer the following questions, drawn from actual Regents examinations. For each statement or question, choose the *number* of the word or expression that, of those given, best completes the statement or answers the question.

Base your answer to question 1 on the graph below and on your knowledge of social studies.

World Population 1800–1900

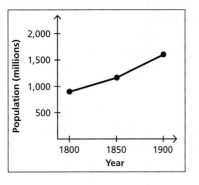

1   What factors would best account for the rise in population shown on this graph after 1850?

   (1) lack of public sewer systems

   (2) the end of World War I

   (3) medical advances and improved diets

   (4) the decline of feudalism

2   A major cause of World War I was

   (1) a decline in the policy of imperialism

   (2) the existence of opposing alliances

   (3) an increase in acts of aggression by England

   (4) the spread of communism throughout Europe

3   In Eastern Europe after World War I, the greatest obstacle to national unity in many nation-states was the

   (1) great ethnic diversity found in the region

   (2) economic dependence of Eastern Europe on Japan

   (3) acceptance of democratic traditions by most Eastern Europeans

   (4) expansion of United States influence in the region

4   The Russian peasants supported the Bolsheviks in the 1917 revolutions mainly because the Bolsheviks promised to

   (1) establish collective farms

   (2) maintain the agricultural price-support system

   (3) bring modern technology to Russian farms

   (4) redistribute the land owned by the nobility

5   The French Revolution of 1789, the Chinese Revolution of 1911, and the Bolshevik Revolution of 1917 were similar in that these revolutions

   (1) were led by ruthless dictators

   (2) were motivated by a desire to overthrow a monarch

   (3) led directly to the establishment of communism

   (4) established a higher standard of living for the middle class

6   Which statement best describes the political situation that existed in the Soviet Union immediately after the death of Lenin in 1924?

   (1) The nation adopted a constitutional monarchy.

   (2) Trotsky and his followers assumed full control of the Communist Party.

   (3) Popular elections were held to choose a new general secretary.

   (4) A power struggle developed among Communist Party leaders.

7 "... The organizations of the revolutionaries must consist first, foremost, and mainly of people who make revolutionary activity their profession. . . . Such an organization must of necessity be not too extensive and as secret as possible. . . ."

—V. I. Lenin, 1917

This quotation refers to Lenin's plan to

(1) defeat Germany in World War I

(2) establish representative democracy in Russia

(3) maintain Communist power in Western Europe

(4) overthrow the Russian government

8 Under Joseph Stalin, the Soviet Union emphasized centralized economic planning and five-year plans primarily to

(1) produce more consumer goods

(2) expand exports

(3) create an increased demand for high-quality imports

(4) develop heavy industry

9 A significant effect of Joseph Stalin's policy of collectivization on Soviet agriculture was

(1) a widespread food shortage

(2) an increase in the export of agricultural products

(3) a surplus of agricultural products

(4) the immediate creation of many small private farms

10 One similarity between Russia under the czars and the Soviet Union under Joseph Stalin is that in both types of government, these leaders

(1) tried to reduce their nation's influence in world affairs

(2) developed policies to limit industrial growth

(3) supported the creation of a national church

(4) established an authoritarian form of government

11 A study of the causes of the American, French, and Russian Revolutions indicates that revolutions usually occur because the

(1) society has become dependent on commerce and trade

(2) society has a lower standard of living than the societies around it

(3) existing government has been resistant to change

(4) lower classes have strong leaders

12 The harsh conditions imposed by the Treaty of Versailles after World War I helped lay the foundation for the

(1) rise of fascism in Germany

(2) uprisings during the French Revolution

(3) division of Korea along the 38th parallel

(4) Bolshevik Revolution in Russia

13 Mohandas Gandhi is best known for his

(1) use of passive resistance to achieve Indian independence

(2) desire to establish an Islamic nation

(3) opposition to Hindus holding public office

(4) encouragement of violence to end British rule

14 Which situation contributed to Adolf Hitler's rise to power in Germany after World War I?

(1) support of Hitler's radical policies by the Social Democrats in the Reichstag

(2) strong feelings of resentment and nationalism built up by economic and political crises

(3) refusal by the League of Nations to admit Germany as a member

(4) violence and terrorism promoted by Germany's former enemies

15 Which was characteristic of France under Napoleon's rule and Germany under Hitler's rule?

(1) Democratic ideas and diversity were encouraged.

(2) Authoritarian control and a strong sense of nationalism prevailed.

(3) Peaceful relations with neighboring countries were fostered.

(4) Artistic and literary freedom flourished.

16 Which policy best demonstrates appeasement?

(1) British policy toward Germany during the 1930s

(2) Japanese policy toward China in the 1930s

(3) Spanish policy toward Native Americans in the 1500s

(4) German policy toward the French during World War I

17 Which series of events is arranged in the correct chronological order?

(1) The Treaty of Versailles is signed. Adolf Hitler becomes chancellor of Germany. German troops invade Poland.

(2) German troops invade Poland. The Treaty of Versailles is signed. Adolf Hitler becomes chancellor of Germany.

(3) Adolf Hitler becomes chancellor of Germany. The Treaty of Versailles is signed. German troops invade Poland.

(4) The Treaty of Versailles is signed. German troops invade Poland. Adolf Hitler becomes chancellor of Germany.

18 The treatment of the Jews in Europe during World War II and of the Armenians in the Ottoman empire are examples of

(1) cultural diffusion

(2) fundamentalism

(3) modernization

(4) genocide

19 Which was a major result of the Nuremberg trials?

(1) National leaders were held personally responsible for war crimes against humanity.

(2) The State of Israel was created as a home for victims of the war.

(3) Soldiers were required to pay for the property damages they caused during the war.

(4) Prisoners from all countries were immediately released from captivity.

In developing your answer, be sure to keep these general definitions in mind:

      (a) <u>describe</u> means "to illustrate something in words or tell about it"

      (b) <u>explain</u> means "to make plain or understandable; to give reasons for or causes of; to show the logical development or relationships of"

Directions: Write a well-organized essay that includes an introduction, several paragraphs addressing the task below, and a conclusion.

Theme: **Nationalism**

> Throughout global history, nationalism has had positive and negative effects.

Tasks:

- Define the term *nationalism*
- Select one country or region you have studied
- Describe two specific examples of nationalism within that country or region
- Explain how each of the two examples had either a positive or negative impact on the future development of the country or region

    You may use any nation or region from your study of global history, except the United States. Some suggestions you may wish to consider are: Latin America (1800s), Italy (1800s and 1900s), China (1900s), India (1900s), Kenya (post-World War II), and the Balkans (1900s).

You are *not* limited to these suggestions.
Do *not* use the United States in your answer.

Guidelines:

In your essay, be sure to
- Develop all aspects of the task
- Support the theme with relevant facts, examples, and details
- Use a logical and clear plan of organization, including an introduction and a conclusion that are beyond a simple restatement of the theme

Document-Based Question

This question is based on the accompanying documents. The question is designed to test your ability to work with historical documents. Some of these documents have been edited for the purposes of this question. As you analyze the documents, take into account the source of each document and any point of view that may be presented in the document.

Historical Context:

> Throughout history, leaders have viewed power in many different ways. There have been a variety of viewpoints on the acquisition and use of power.

Task: Using the information from the documents and your knowledge of global history, answer the questions that follow each document in Part A. Your answers to the questions will help you write the Part B essay in which you will be asked to

---

- Discuss several viewpoints on the attainment and use of power
- Evaluate positive and negative effects that the various viewpoints have had on people in different countries

---

In developing your answers, be sure to keep these general definitions in mind:

(a) <u>discuss</u> means "to make observations about something using facts, reasoning, and argument; to present in some detail"
(b) <u>evaluate</u> means "to examine and judge the significance, worth, or condition of; to determine the value of"

Part A: Short Answer

Directions: Analyze the documents and answer the question or questions that follow each document, using the space provided.

Document #1

> *Under the leadership of the working class and the Communist party, these classes [the working class, the peasantry, the petty bourgeoisie, and the national bourgeoisie] unite to create their own state . . . so as to enforce their . . . dictatorship over the henchmen of imperialism—the landlord class and bureaucratic capitalist class. . . . The people's government will suppress such persons.*
>
> **– Mao Zedong, speech on the anniversary of the founding of the Communist party, 1949**

1 According to Mao Zedong, do all classes share power in a communist state? Explain.

_____

_____

2 Describe one goal that Mao thought a communist government should strive to achieve.

_____

_____

Document #2
The Fascist State

3 According to this chart, what methods have fascist leaders used to acquire and maintain power?

_____

_____

Document #3

> *Passive resistance is a method of securing rights by personal suffering; it is the reverse of resistance by arms. When I refuse to do a thing that is repugnant to my conscience, I use soul-force.*
>
> **– Mohandas Gandhi, *Hind Swaraj*, 1938**

4 What did Gandhi mean by the term *passive resistance*?

_____

_____

Document #4

> *The nation has placed its destiny in the hands and heads and hearts of its millions of free men and women; and its faith in freedom. . . . Freedom means the supremacy of human rights everywhere. Our support goes to those who struggle to gain those rights or keep them.*
>
> **– Franklin D. Roosevelt, address to Congress in January 1941**

5 According to President Roosevelt, who or what is the ultimate source of power in the United States?

_____

_____

6 For what purpose did Roosevelt promise to use the power of the United States?

_____

_____

Part B

Essay

Directions: Write a well-organized essay that includes an introduction, several paragraphs, and a conclusion. Use evidence from *at least* **three** documents in your essay. Support your response with relevant facts, examples, and details. Include additional outside information.

Historical Context:

Throughout history, leaders have viewed power in many different ways. There have been a variety of viewpoints on the acquisition and use of power.

Task: Using the information from the documents and your knowledge of global history, write an essay in which you

- Evaluate the differing views that leaders have had on the attainment and use of power
- Discuss how the views of at least two leaders have affected people of their own nations and people of other nations

Guidelines:

In your essay, be sure to
- Develop all aspects of the task
- Incorporate information from *at least* **three** documents
- Incorporate relevant outside information
- Support the theme with relevant facts, examples, and details
- Use a logical and clear plan of organization, including an introduction and a conclusion that are beyond a restatement of the theme

UNIT 3

The Twentieth Century and Beyond (1945–The Present)

Section 1: Cold War Balance of Power

Section 2: Economic Issues

Section 3: Chinese Communist Revolution

Section 4: Collapse of European Imperialism

Section 5: Conflicts and Change in the Middle East

Section 6: Collapse of Communism and the Soviet Union

Section 7: Political and Economic Change in Latin America

Unit Overview

After World War II, many nations participated in a struggle called the Cold War. On one side were communist states led by the Soviet Union and China. On the other side were noncommunist nations led by the United States. The Cold War finally ended in the 1980s with the collapse of the Soviet Union and the end of communism in Eastern Europe.

During the Cold War, imperialism ended and new nations were born. In the Middle East, there were many conflicts. Elsewhere, newly independent nations had to establish workable economic and political systems. In Latin America, there was political unrest.

Using Good Social Studies Practices
Civic Participation

Some of the many themes developed in Unit 3 are:

change	economic systems	diversity
political systems	conflict	belief systems
human rights	nationalism	

Choose one of the themes listed above. As you review Unit 3, identify how individuals participated in some way to initiate change locally, within their country, or on a global level. Include events from 1945 to the present, major developments, and key turning points having to do with your theme.

Cold War Balance of Power

The
Big Idea

After World War II:

- **West Germany and Japan developed democratic governments.**

- **the United States and the Soviet Union emerged as superpowers with differing political and economic systems.**

- **the Cold War developed, and the superpowers confronted one another throughout the world.**

- **the United Nations tried to maintain peace.**

Section Overview

After World War II, Japan and West Germany adopted constitutions that built democratic governments. Two major powers emerged from the war: the United States and the Soviet Union. Political and economic differences between the two led to a division of Europe that would last more than 40 years. The conflict between democracy and communism also spread around the globe, resulting in a buildup of arms as well as a race to explore space. The United Nations experienced both failure and success in its quest to maintain peace in the years after 1945.

Key Themes and Concepts

As you review this section, take special note of the following key themes and concepts:

Change What impact did World War II have on the development of democracy in Germany and Japan?

Political Systems How did differing political systems help cause the Cold War between the United States and the Soviet Union?

Conflict How did the rivalry between the United States and the Soviet Union involve other nations around the world?

Justice and Human Rights What role does the United Nations play in the struggle for justice and human rights?

Key People and Terms

Key People and Terms

Place each of the key people and terms into one of these two categories: political or military.

As you review this section, be sure you understand the significance of these key people and terms:

iron curtain	Truman Doctrine	surrogate
asylum	containment	Fidel Castro
superpowers	Marshall Plan	Cuban Missile Crisis
Cold War	NATO	nonaligned nations
satellites	Warsaw Pact	

A Divided Europe

Preparing for the Regents

- How were conditions in Europe after World War II similar to the conditions that existed after World War I? How were the two postwar periods different?

After World War II, with help from the United States and Great Britain, democracy and free enterprise were restored to the nations of Western Europe. Eastern Europe, however, was occupied by armies of the Soviet Union. Joseph Stalin, the leader of the Soviet Union, wanted to spread communism throughout the area. He hoped to create a buffer zone of friendly governments to prevent possible attacks from Germany and other Western nations.

Although Stalin had promised free elections for Eastern Europe, he instead supported the establishment of procommunist governments throughout the region. Soon Europe was divided by an imaginary line known as the **iron curtain.** In the East were the Soviet-dominated communist countries. In the West were the Western democracies, led by the United States.

Germany and Japan Transformed

Both Germany and Japan had been physically and socially devastated by the war. The victorious Allied powers occupied the two countries.

Germany was divided into four zones of occupation. Great Britain, France, and the United States occupied the three zones in western Germany. The Soviet Union controlled eastern Germany. The United States alone occupied Japan.

Democracy in West Germany

Germany's armed forces were disbanded, and the Nazi party was outlawed. Nazi war criminals were tried in the Nuremberg trials, and some were executed. In western Germany, the Allies helped set up political parties. Germans wrote a federal constitution. This constitution set up a democratic government and was approved in 1949. In that year, West Germany also regained self-government as the Federal Republic of Germany.

Germany's constitution included an article that guaranteed political asylum for people who were persecuted for political reasons. **Asylum** is protection from arrest or from the possibility of being returned to a dangerous political situation. For many years, Germany's asylum policy was the most liberal in Europe. Germany's recognition of its role in the persecution of Jews and other groups probably led to this constitutional guarantee. In the late 1990s, Germany began to restrict this right after large numbers of asylum seekers came to Germany for economic rather than political reasons.

The Lessons of the Holocaust Germany was deeply shaken by the experience of the Holocaust. Germans wanted to be sure that such a thing could not happen again. Today, Germany's relationship with the nation of Israel is very friendly. Germany and Israel have strong diplomatic, economic, and cultural ties. There has also been an attempt to financially compensate some of the victims of the Holocaust.

Democracy in Japan

Like Germany, Japan was occupied after World War II by Allied troops, most of whom were American. Japan's armed forces were disbanded. Trials were held to punish people who had been responsible for wartime atrocities, and some of these people were executed. General Douglas MacArthur was the supreme commander of the American military government that ruled postwar Japan. The American government wanted to end militarism and ensure democratic government in Japan.

Japan's New Constitution In Germany, a German council had written the new constitution. Japan's constitution, on the other hand, was drafted by MacArthur and his advisors.

- It created a constitutional monarchy that limited the power of the emperor.
- It promised that Japan would not use war as a political weapon.
- It set up a democratic government. Representatives were elected to the Diet, the Japanese parliament.
- Women gained the right to vote.
- Basic rights, such as freedom of the press and of assembly, were guaranteed.

The Japanese government accepted this new constitution and signed a treaty that took away Japan's overseas empire. In 1952, the Allied occupation officially ended.

Preparing for the Regents

- Why do you think Germany developed one of Europe's most liberal asylum laws?

Key Themes and Concepts

Change
Germany's experiences in the Holocaust had many lasting effects on the nation's development.

Preparing for the Regents

- How were the political conditions in Germany and Japan similar after World War II? How were they different?

- How was the Japanese government after World War II different from the Japanese government that had existed before and during the war?

Two Superpowers

After World War II, several powerful nations of the past were in decline. Germany was defeated and divided. France and Britain were economically drained and needed to concentrate on rebuilding. The United States and the Soviet Union emerged from World War II as the two world superpowers. The word *superpower* has been used to describe each of the rivals that came to dominate global politics in the period after World War II. Many other states in the world came under the domination or influence of these powers.

Europe After World War II

Europe After World War II In 1949, the United States, Canada, and ten other countries formed the NATO military alliance. In 1955, the Soviet Union formed the Warsaw Pact military alliance with its seven satellites.

Preparing for the Regents

• Practice your map skills by listing the nations that were members of NATO and the nations that were members of the Warsaw Pact in 1955.

Nato
· West Germany
· Italy
· France
· Turkey

Warsaw
· Hungary
· Romania
· East Germany
· Bulgaria

Key Themes and Concepts

Political and Economic Systems
The Cold War was much more than just a military rivalry. It was a struggle between two very different political and economic systems.

Preparing for the Regents

• What factors led to the breakup of the alliance between Britain, France, the United States, and the Soviet Union?

The Cold War Begins

The United States and the Soviet Union had cooperated to win World War II. Soon, however, conflicts in ways of thinking and mutual distrust led to the Cold War—a continuing state of tension and hostility between the superpowers. This tension was a result of differences in political and economic thinking between the democratic, capitalistic United States and the communist Soviet Union. It was a "cold" war because armed battle between the superpowers did not occur.

The Western powers feared the spread of communism. Stalin had forced pro-communist governments in Poland, Czechoslovakia, and elsewhere. These countries came to be known as **satellites** of the Soviet Union. When Stalin began to put pressure on Greece and Turkey, the United States took action.

The Truman Doctrine

In March of 1947, President Harry S. Truman established a policy known as the **Truman Doctrine.** This was an economic and military program designed to help other nations resist Soviet aggression. It was based on the theory of **containment,** which involved limiting communism to areas already under Soviet control. The United States pledged to resist Soviet expansion anywhere in the world. Truman sent military and economic aid to Greece and Turkey so that they could resist the threat of communism.

The Marshall Plan

The **Marshall Plan,** also proposed in 1947, was a massive economic aid package designed to strengthen democratic governments and lessen the appeal of communism. Billions of American dollars helped Western European countries recover from World War II. Although the United States also offered this aid to Eastern Europe, Stalin forbade these countries to accept it.

Crisis in Germany

The division of Germany into four zones after World War II was supposed to be temporary. Soon Great Britain, France, and the United States had combined their democratically ruled zones. Tension grew between democratic western Germany and Soviet-controlled eastern Germany. Germany became a major focus of Cold War tension. The Allies were trying to rebuild the German economy, but Stalin feared a strong, united Germany. Berlin, the divided capital, was located in East Germany.

The Berlin Airlift In 1948, Stalin hoped to force the Allies out of Berlin by closing all land routes for bringing essential supplies to West Berlin. In response to the crisis, the Western powers mounted a successful airlift. For almost a year, food and supplies were flown into West Berlin. Finally, the Soviets ended the blockade.

A Divided Germany This incident, however, led to the creation of the Federal Republic of Germany (West Germany) in 1949. Germany, like the rest of Europe, remained divided. In 1961, the East German government built a wall that separated East Berlin from West Berlin. East German soldiers shot anyone who tried to escape from East Germany.

Opposing Military Alliances

The NATO Alliance After the Berlin airlift and the division of West Germany from East Germany, Western European countries formed a military alliance. It was called the North Atlantic Treaty Organization, or NATO. Members of NATO pledged to support each other if any member nation was ever attacked.

The Warsaw Pact In 1955, the Soviet Union formed the Warsaw Pact. It included the Soviet Union and seven of its satellites in Eastern Europe. This was also a defensive alliance, promising mutual military cooperation.

The Cold War Heats Up

Repression in Eastern Europe

The Soviet Union kept a tight grip on its Eastern European satellites. Tensions arose in both East Germany and Poland in the 1950s. In East Germany, a revolt was put down with Soviet tanks. In Poland, some reforms were made, yet the country remained under the domination of the Soviet Union. Though Stalin died in 1953, his successors continued his policy of repression.

The Hungarian Revolt In 1956, a revolution began in Hungary. It was led by Imre Nagy, who was a Hungarian nationalist and communist. Nagy ended one-party rule, got rid of Soviet troops, and withdrew Hungary from the Warsaw Pact. In response, the Soviet Union quickly sent in troops and tanks. Thousands of Hungarians died, and the revolt against Soviet domination was suppressed.

The Invasion of Czechoslovakia Another rebellion against Soviet domination occurred in Czechoslovakia in the spring of 1968, when Alexander Dubçek called for liberal reforms and the easing of communist controls. The government of Czechoslovakia eased censorship and began to plan for a new constitution. The

Preparing for the Regents

- Briefly describe each of the terms listed below.

Truman Doctrine: Policy established by President Truman
Marshall Plan: Massive Aid package
NATO: Alliance between companies.
Warsaw Pact: Defense alliance
Berlin Airlift: Supply drop

Preparing for the Regents

- Why were NATO and the Warsaw Pact formed?

Vocabulary Builder

repression—(rih PRESH un) *n.* cruel and severe control of a large group of people

Key Themes and Concepts

Conflict
The revolts and repression in Hungary and Czechoslovakia were signals to the West that the Soviet Union planned to use military force to ensure the survival of communism in Eastern Europe.

Soviet Union, however, sent troops to overturn the government and restore a communist dictatorship. Through these incidents, it became clear that the Soviet Union would use force whenever necessary to ensure the survival of communism and Soviet domination in Eastern Europe.

The Arms Race

Both the United States and the Soviet Union armed themselves, each preparing to withstand an attack from the other. The United States had developed the atomic bomb during World War II; Soviet scientists developed their own in 1949.

For 40 years, the two superpowers spent great amounts of money to develop more and more powerful weapons. The arms race raised the level of tension between the two superpowers. It also raised fears among many people that the superpowers might become involved in a conflict that would destroy the world.

The Space Race

The superpowers also competed in space. In 1957, the Soviet Union launched *Sputnik,* a satellite, into orbit around the Earth. Congress soon established NASA, the National Aeronautics and Space Administration, to improve American space technology.

The race was on. In 1958, the United States launched its own first satellite. In 1961, the Soviets sent the first man into space. Then, in 1969, the United States was the first nation to put a man on the moon. Both the Soviet Union and the United States explored the military use of space with spy satellites. Many people were concerned about the high cost of space exploration and the extension of the Cold War into space.

Conflicts Around the World

Although the United States and the Soviet Union did not engage in a war with each other, they did clash through **surrogate,** or representative, states. This meant that the United States and Soviet Union supported opposing forces in many nations throughout the world. These conflicts occurred in East Asia, the Middle East, Africa, and Latin America.

The Cold War in East Asia

Cold War tensions grew into bitter wars in Korea in the 1950s and in Vietnam in the 1960s. In each case, the superpowers supported opposing sides with economic aid, advisors, and troops.

Korean War (1950–1953) After World War II, Korea, like Germany, was divided into two parts. North Korea was occupied by Soviet forces and South Korea was occupied by American forces. North Korean forces, seeking to unify the country under communist rule, invaded South Korea in 1950. United Nations forces, commanded by General Douglas MacArthur, drove the North Koreans back, invaded North Korea, and approached the Chinese border. Chinese soldiers then entered the war and pushed the UN forces back into the south. In 1953 an armistice was signed, leaving Korea divided at the 38th parallel with a demilitarized zone between the two countries.

Vietnam War In 1954, Vietnam was temporarily divided into a northern half, ruled by communist leader Ho Chi Minh, and a southern half, headed by non-communist Ngo Dinh Diem. Large numbers of American forces were eventually sent to Vietnam to prevent Ho Chi Minh from uniting Vietnam under northern rule. American forces, however, were not able to defeat the communist forces in Vietnam. In 1973, President Richard Nixon ordered a cease-fire and began to pull

American forces out of Vietnam. In 1975, the North Vietnamese captured Saigon, reuniting Vietnam.

The Cold War in the Middle East

Arab States and Israel In the 1950s, Gamal Abdel Nasser emerged as a leader in the Arab state of Egypt. He was determined to end Western power in Egypt. In 1956, he nationalized the Suez Canal, ending British control. He received support from the Soviet Union and used Soviet money to build the Aswan High Dam. Egypt took part in two wars against the Jewish state of Israel. While the Soviet Union supported Egypt, the United States supported Israel.

Iran and Iraq Rivalries over oil resources fueled Cold War tensions in the Middle East. The United States and the Soviet Union both became interested in Iran after vast oil fields were discovered there. An Iranian nationalist leader who had communist support tried to nationalize the oil industry in the early 1950s. The United States helped to keep him from power. The United States then supported the repressive anticommunist shah of Iran with weapons and advisors. An Islamic revolution in 1979 toppled the shah's regime.

The Soviet Union meanwhile supported Iraq, which had become a socialist dictatorship in the 1960s and also had oil reserves. The Soviet Union eventually also supported governments in Syria and Libya.

The Cold War in Africa

Congo The Congo, a Belgian colony in Africa, became independent in 1960. The new premier asked for help in dealing with a revolt. The Soviet Union supported him against the rebels. Five years later, a strongly anti-communist dictator named Mobutu Sese Seko took control of the country, renaming it Zaire. Because of his anti-communist stance, he received the support of the West, allowing him to stay in power until the late 1990s.

Angola In southwestern Africa, the Portuguese colony of Angola gained independence in 1975, during a bloody civil war. After that, rival rebel groups continued their conflict with each other. One group, the MPLA, was supported by the Soviet Union and Cuba. The Soviet Union sent advisors and equipment; Cuba sent troops. The MPLA established a communist dictatorship in Angola, which the United States tried to undermine. South Africa supported the opposition, UNITA. This confrontation continued until 1991.

The Cold War in Latin America

Cuba Cuba had won independence from Spain in 1898. For 60 years, Cuba was strongly influenced by the United States. In 1952, Fulgencio Batista seized power. His government was repressive and corrupt. A young lawyer named **Fidel Castro** organized a guerrilla army and fought against Batista. He gained victory in 1959, and established a communist dictatorship in Cuba.

Castro turned to the Soviet Union for support. Cuba became involved in the rivalry between the United States and the Soviet Union. In 1961, the United States backed a plot by Cuban exiles to invade Cuba at the Bay of Pigs. However, the invading forces were quickly crushed.

Angered by American interference, Castro sought closer ties with the Soviet Union. Castro allowed the Soviets to build nuclear missile sites in Cuba, just 90 miles off the coast of Florida. In 1962, U.S. President Kennedy demanded the removal of these missiles from Cuba and ordered a naval blockade of Cuba. This incident, known as the **Cuban Missile Crisis,** ended when the Soviet leader, Nikita Khrushchev, agreed to remove the missiles in exchange for a pledge by Kennedy that the United

Key Themes and Concepts

Needs and Wants
The superpowers interfered in the governments of Iran and Iraq. One reason for their interest in these nations was the presence of oil reserves. Both superpowers needed oil to boost their economies.

Cause and Effect

For what reason did the Cold War superpowers support opposite sides in Africa?

Preparing for the Regents

• Describe one way in which the Cold War influenced conflicts or events in each of the following regions.

Asia:

Middle East: Finding Oil, Economy

Africa: Independence

Latin America: Independence from Spain

Note Taking

Reading Skill:
Recognize Sequence
List the important events of the Cold War in Cuba. Record them in the order they occurred. Add boxes as needed.

Date	Event
1898	

States would not invade Cuba. Since Cuba was heavily supported by the Soviet Union, the United States established a trade embargo and diplomatic isolation on Cuba. Cuba's economy suffered over the last 50 years. In 2014, US President Obama and Raul Castro announced they would restore diplomatic relations between the two countries. In 2016, President Obama visited Cuba and loosened the economic sanctions, although Congress has not ended them. Castro has made some reforms to Cuba's economic system and personal freedoms, but with the opening of Cuba, Castro's government is anxious about dissent within Cuba.

Causes and Impact of the Cuban Revolution

Causes of the Cuban Revolution	Impact of the Cuban Revolution
Political Conditions • Rule by a repressive dictatorship • Corruption and bribery among government officials	**Political Changes** • Creation of a communist dictatorship • Denial of basic political rights and freedoms
Economic Conditions • Control of Cuba's sugar plantations by the upper class • Unequal distribution of wealth • Foreign control of many businesses • High unemployment despite prosperity	**Economic Changes** • Establishment of collective farms, jointly operated under government supervision • Government control of business and industry • Seizure of foreign property with little or no compensation

The Nonaligned Nations

The nations that chose not to ally with either side in the Cold War were known as nonaligned nations. These nations remained neutral. India, Yugoslavia, and many African nations adopted a policy of nonalignment. Their goals were to make economic progress and to avoid involvement in the Cold War.

Key Themes and Concepts

Choice
Nonaligned nations did not side with either the Soviets or the United States during the Cold War.

The Role of the United Nations

During the Cold War, the United Nations provided a forum for superpowers to air their differences peacefully. During much of the Cold War countries tended to vote in blocs, either as allies of the United States or as allies of the Soviet Union. This practice limited the United Nations' effectiveness.

After the end of the Cold War in 1991, the United Nations expanded several of its traditional roles. Today, it sends international peacekeeping forces to countries in conflict. It continues to provide health services to less developed countries. It also supports the struggle for human rights throughout the world.

Preparing for the Regents

• What role has the United Nations played in the Cold War and post–Cold War world?

Maintain peace among nations

Preparing for the Regents

• Write a brief essay discussing why the Cold War took place and what impacts it has had on the world.

Summary

After World War II, with the help of the United States, democratic governments were established in Japan and West Germany. The United States and the Soviet Union emerged as two rival superpowers with differing political and economic systems. Their rivalry threatened peace around the world in a struggle called the Cold War that went on for more than 45 years. The two superpowers engaged in the buildup of arms, competition in space, and surrogate conflicts in other parts of the world. Despite difficulties, the United Nations remained a force for stability and peace.

No cold war took place between the two worlds superpowers. It wasn't with physical force, but they had many battles such as who built nuclear weapons first, etc. It helped other countries around the world to improve their military and financial status.

Economic Issues

Section Overview

In the years after 1945, developing nations chose to develop either a market economy, a command economy, or a mixed economy. Countries in South Asia, Latin America, and Africa struggled to industrialize, improve agriculture, and curb population growth. In Western Europe and Japan, economies recovered and grew rapidly. West Germany and Japan became economic superpowers. The economies of the Pacific Rim, modeled on Japanese success, grew aggressively through trade and industrialization. After 1945, the economic interdependence of the world became clearer. When Middle Eastern oil suppliers limited oil in the 1970s, the economies of the West were hurt.

Key Themes and Concepts

As you review this section, take special note of the following key themes and concepts:

Economic Systems What are capitalism and communism?

Factors of Production How have developing nations combined human, natural, and capital resources to promote economic development?

Change Why did Western Europe and Japan experience great economic growth after 1945?

Needs and Wants How has the need for petroleum affected international relations?

Key People and Terms

As you review this section, be sure you understand the significance of these key terms:

developed nations	European Community	balance of trade
developing nations	European Union	Pacific Rim
mixed economy	euro	OPEC
Common Market	zaibatsu	

Market Economies and Command Economies

In the years after World War II, some nations were basing their economic development on the ideas of capitalism. Other countries were adopting command economies, such as that which existed under communism. The choices that countries made were often influenced by the Cold War. The United States and its allies supported market economies. The Soviet Union and its allies supported command economies.

The
Big
Idea

In the Cold War and post–Cold War eras:

- countries developed market economies, command economies, or mixed economies.

- developing nations struggled to strengthen their economies.

- Western Europe and Japan experienced rapid economic recovery.

- the nations of the world became increasingly interdependent.

Key People and Terms

- What do all of the key terms have in common? Explain.

Comparison of Market Economies and Command Economies

Market and Command Economies
After World War II, democratic countries had a market economy. Communist countries had a command economy.

	Market Economy	**Command Economy**
Ownership	All property, including the means of production, is privately owned.	The government owns the means of production, distribution, and exchange.
Economic decisions	Private businesses and individuals are free from public control so that they can make basic economic decisions, including what, where, how much, and at what prices goods will be produced.	Government officials make all basic economic decisions, such as what will be produced, when, and where.
Market controls	Prices are determined by supply and demand. Competition promotes high quality and low prices.	The government plans the economy. There is limited production of consumer goods and an emphasis on industrial growth.

Preparing for the Regents

• Compare and contrast market and command economies.

[handwritten notes:]
Command Economies
- Govt owns profits and everything

Contrast Economy
- Everything owned by respective owners

The Economies of Developing Nations

After World War II, the United States, the Soviet Union, Japan, and the countries of Western Europe came to be called **developed nations.** They had modern agriculture and industries, advanced technology, and strong educational systems. Nations with limited resources and without modern industrial economies were called **developing nations.**

Economic obstacles include overpopulation, natural disasters, and indebtedness. After World War II, many developing nations began to build their economies. Some were just emerging from imperialism. Many had to decide which of the two major economic systems they would follow. Some nations took elements of both.

The issues faced by developing nations were unique to each nation. However, several goals were common:

• Building industry
• Improving agriculture
• Controlling population

Case Study: India

After India became independent in 1947, it developed a **mixed economy** that combined elements of market and command economies. Heavy industry was brought under government control, and the nation worked with a series of five-year plans. These plans set economic goals and managed resources. Dams were built to produce hydroelectric power. The government poured resources into heavy industries such as steel production. In addition, crop output was increased with new types of seeds, chemical fertilizers, and improved irrigation.

However, India also faced obstacles. India lacked oil and natural gas, slowing growth. Many government-run businesses were ineffective. Agricultural output was not enough to keep up with population growth. In the 1990s, pressure from lenders forced India to institute reforms. Some industries were privatized, and foreign investment was made easier.

Case Study: Egypt

After Egypt became independent, Gamal Abdel Nasser installed a socialist government and economy. Nasser nationalized banks and businesses and instituted land reform. Peasant farmers were given land.

Key Themes and Concepts

Economic Systems
A mixed economy uses elements of both market and command economies. Developing nations, such as India and some nations of Africa, established mixed economies after 1945.

With the help of the Soviet Union, Egypt built the Aswan Dam. It controlled the flow of the Nile River and provided 2 million acres of additional farmland. However, it also increased the saltiness of the Nile and caused the soil of the Nile Delta to erode.

Nasser's successor, Anwar Sadat, encouraged foreign investment as well as free market practices. Sadat was assassinated in 1981. Sadat's successor, Hosni Mubarak, faced economic problems and a rising population. He also faced criticism from Islamic fundamentalists.

Case Study: Latin America

After World War II, many Latin American nations experienced unrest. Complex difficulties have sometimes hindered development.

Agricultural Reform Many Latin American nations have had to grow more staple crops, such as corn and wheat, in order to feed their growing populations. Because overdependence on any single cash crop is risky, these nations have sought to diversify their agriculture. Some, however, still rely on cash crops. A few countries, believing that uneven distribution of land leads to poverty, have also tried to institute land reform in order to get more land into the hands of a greater number of people.

Debt Crisis Often, Latin American nations had to borrow money to build industries. When a worldwide recession hit, demand for goods fell. However, these nations still had to make high interest payments. Money went toward paying off loans rather than building industry.

Free Market Reforms Some Latin American governments used free market reforms as a way to recover from their economic crises. Government spending was reduced, and private owners were allowed to buy out state-owned industries. Slowly, economic progress was made.

Population Explosion Many Latin Americans see the need to control population. Some cultural and religious beliefs, however, work against population control. As a result, populations are still growing rapidly, creating a severe economic burden.

Economic Recovery and Cooperation in Europe

After the end of World War II, the United States developed the Marshall Plan to encourage the economic development of Western Europe and to prevent the expansion of communism.

West German Economic Miracle

Capital from the Marshall Plan and the leadership of a democratic government helped West Germany to recover. West Germans rebuilt their cities and factories and developed a strong industrial economy. High-quality German exports were in great demand around the world. The recovery in Germany was so dramatic that it was referred to as an "economic miracle." After East and West Germany were reunited in 1990, difficulties emerged as East Germans made the transition to a market economy.

European Economic Unification

With aid from the Marshall Plan, other Western European countries also recovered quickly from World War II. The countries of Europe promoted their own prosperity through cooperation.

European Coal and Steel Community In 1952, France, West Germany, Belgium, Italy, the Netherlands, and Luxembourg set up the European Coal and Steel Community to regulate the coal and steel industries and spur economic growth.

Preparing for the Regents

- Describe three economic problems that developing nations of Latin America face.

1. Debt
2. Population
3. Free Market

Preparing for the Regents

- Why do you think West Germany's economy achieved much greater success than East Germany's?

Key Themes and Concepts

Interdependence Many European countries prospered economically as a result of cooperation after World War II. Six Western European nations drew together in 1952 to form an economic community. Today, the European Union is made up of both Western and Eastern European nations.

The Common Market In 1957, these same six nations formed the **European Community** (EC), or Common Market. This organization expanded free trade by ending tariffs and allowing labor and capital to move freely across borders. Great Britain, Denmark, and Ireland later joined.

European Union In 1993, the EC expanded further and became the European Union with 12 members, although its membership has grown over the years. A new currency, the **euro,** was introduced in 1999 but not all EU members use the euro. The EU aims to bolster Europe's trade position and its political and economic power in the world.

Japan: An Economic Superpower

Economic Reforms

As you have learned, the United States occupation of Japan after World War II helped to establish democracy in that nation. The United States also brought economic reforms to Japan. Japanese workers were given the right to form unions. Land reform divided up large estates among tenant farmers. The United States tried to break up the **zaibatsu,** the powerful family-owned business concerns that dominated Japanese economic life, but the reform effort achieved only limited success.

Close Ties With the West

As the Cold War intensified, the United States and its allies viewed Japan less as a former enemy and more as a future ally. The outbreak of war in Korea in 1950 reinforced this view. Japan served as a staging area for operations in Korea. The American occupation of Japan ended in 1952. As Japanese industry prospered, the nation engaged in increased trade with the United States and other countries.

How the Japanese Economy Succeeded

Japan rebounded rapidly from the economic devastation that followed World War II. Japan sent many manufactured items to other countries, building a favorable balance of trade. A country that has a favorable **balance of trade** exports more goods than it imports. Why was Japan so successful?

- Japan adapted the latest Western technology to its own industries.
- Japan had a well-educated and highly skilled workforce.
- Japanese savings gave banks capital to invest in industry.
- The government, prohibited from spending money on defense, poured funds into the economy.
- The government imposed high tariffs and strict regulations to limit foreign competition.

How the Japanese Economy Faltered

In the late 1980s, Japan was hit by an economic recession which lasted many years. Banks staggered under a mountain of bad debt, companies went bankrupt, and unemployment rose. Japan's government seemed powerless to end the recession. However, in spite of these economic problems, Japan remained one of the world's largest economies with a strong favorable balance of trade. Its economy mostly held steady rather than growing.

Preparing for the Regents

- Answer the following questions.

1. How did the United States play a vital role in the economic recovery of Europe and Japan?

2. Why did the United States want Europe and Japan to enjoy economic recovery?

Key Themes and Concepts

Science and Technology Among the many reasons for the rapid growth of the Japanese economy was the effectiveness with which Japan adapted Western technology.

Economic Development of the Pacific Rim

Southeast Asia and East Asia are part of a region known as the Pacific Rim, a group of nations in Asia and the Americas that border the Pacific Ocean. The Pacific began to be an important highway for trade in the 1500s. In the latter half of the 1900s, activity in this area increased dramatically. The size of the area's population makes it a huge market.

Four economies in the area have become known as the "Asian Tigers": Taiwan, Hong Kong, Singapore, and South Korea. The Asian Tigers are given this name because of their aggressive economic growth. These economies have followed the Japanese model. They experienced rapid industrialization that led to economic expansion and prosperity.

- **Taiwan** at first set up light industries, such as textile factories. In time, heavy industry developed and created a trade boom, the growth of industrial cities, and a higher standard of living.
- **Hong Kong** is a small island. Formerly a British colony, Hong Kong was returned to communist China in 1997 but was allowed to retain a capitalist economy. Hong Kong is a major financial center with many foreign banks and a busy stock market.
- **Singapore** is a city-state, located on a tiny island at the tip of the Malay Peninsula. Singapore includes one of the world's busiest harbors and is a center of trade.
- **South Korea** initially exported textiles and inexpensive goods. By the 1990s, South Korea was an economic powerhouse, exporting such higher-priced goods as automobiles.

Oil, OPEC, and Economic Interdependence

Oil became the most important energy resource after World War II. Global economic interdependence is shown in the crises that have developed over oil. Much of the world's oil comes from the Middle East.

The Formation of OPEC

In 1960, Iran, Iraq, Kuwait, Saudi Arabia, and Venezuela formed **OPEC,** whose initials stand for the Organization of Petroleum Exporting Countries. Other oil producers joined later and, in 2009, there were 12 members. OPEC's goal was to control the oil industry by setting production levels and prices.

OPEC and Oil Crises

In 1973, OPEC nations halted exports of oil to certain countries. Egypt and Israel were at war, and Arab countries declared the embargo against the United States and other countries that supported Israel. Prices skyrocketed, affecting Western economies by slowing growth. In the 1980s and 1990s, a surplus of oil allowed prices to fall.

Summary

In the years after 1945, some countries developed market economies, while others developed command economies. Developing nations struggled to build their economies. Western Europe and Japan, with the help of the United States, achieved economic success. Through international trade, the Pacific Rim became important to the global economy. Interdependence characterized the world economy. Oil crises in the Middle East, for example, slowed Western economic growth.

Chinese Communist Revolution

The Big Idea

Since 1949, a communist government has ruled China.

• Popular support and military power helped the Communists come to power.

• The programs of Mao Zedong hurt China economically and violated human rights.

• Deng Xiaoping brought economic reforms but not political reforms to China.

Key People and Terms

• What do three of the key people and terms have in common? Explain.

Key Themes and Concepts

Geography
China, the largest Asian country and the most populous nation in the world, is located in eastern Asia. Mountains, deserts, and jungles separate China from neighboring lands.

Section Overview

The establishment of the People's Republic of China in 1949 began a new period in Chinese history. Communists had risen to power during the 1930s and 1940s by appealing to a large part of the population and by achieving military superiority. Under the communist dictatorship of Mao Zedong, however, programs such as the Great Leap Forward and the Cultural Revolution had negative economic results and restricted people's rights and freedoms. The next leader, Deng Xiaoping, made economic reforms but not political ones. The communist government continued to maintain strict control over people's lives.

Key Themes and Concepts

As you review this section, take special note of the following key themes and concepts:

Conflict How did the Communists come to power in China by 1949?

Human Rights In what ways did the communist government improve the status of women in China? How has the Chinese government violated people's rights?

Change What changes did Mao Zedong bring to China after 1949?

Economic Systems How did Deng Xiaoping reform the economy, and what were the results?

Key People and Terms

As you review this section, be sure you understand the significance of these key people and terms:

Mao Zedong	communes	Deng Xiaoping
Long March	Cultural Revolution	Tiananmen Square
Great Leap Forward	Red Guards	

Two Chinas

Today, China is the most populous nation in the world. There are two Chinas, however. The People's Republic of China is a communist state on the Asian mainland. It has a vast land area and many natural resources. Taiwan, also called the Republic of China, is a small island that today is one of the Asian Tigers. It has a noncommunist government. The People's Republic of China still considers Taiwan a part of China proper. Efforts to reunite the two Chinas have sometimes led to tension because Taiwan values its independence.

Communist Rise to Power

As you recall, Jiang Jieshi (also called Chiang Kai-shek) had taken over the Guomindang, or Nationalist Party, after the death of Sun Yixian. In the mid-1920s, Jiang began to strike at the Communist Party, which he saw as a threat to his leadership.

Mao Zedong emerged as the leader of the Communists in the 1930s. Along with 100,000 of his followers, Mao fled the Guomindang forces in 1934 in a retreat known as the **Long March.** After traveling more than 6,000 miles, Mao set up a base in northern China with about 20,000 survivors of the march. In the years that followed, the Communists, the Guomindang, and Japanese invaders battled for control of China. After World War II, civil war continued. Finally, in 1949, Mao's Communists were victorious. Jiang and his followers fled to the island of Taiwan.

Reasons for Communist Success

There were several reasons for the victory of Mao and the Communists over Jiang and the Guomindang.

- Mao won the support of the huge peasant population of China by promising to give land to peasants.
- Mao won the support of women by rejecting the inequalities of traditional Confucian society.
- Mao's army made good use of hit-and-run guerrilla warfare.
- Many people opposed the Nationalist government, which they saw as corrupt.
- Some people felt that the Nationalists had allowed foreigners to dominate China.

Communism Under Mao Zedong

The Communists set up the People's Republic of China (PRC) in 1949. They wanted to transform China from an agricultural society into a modern industrial nation. Under communism, literacy increased, old landlord and business classes were eliminated, and rural Chinese were provided with health care. However, Mao set up a one-party dictatorship that denied people basic rights and freedoms.

The Changing Role of Women

Traditionally, in China, women were treated as inferior to men. The only role for a woman recognized by the five Confucian relationships was that of wife. As a wife, a woman was considered inferior to her husband. The Nationalists did not change these policies greatly.

In Communist China, however, women gained some rights. Under the new Chinese constitution, women won equality under the law. They were now expected to work alongside men on farms and in factories.

Although Chinese women made progress, they did not have full equality with men. Only a few women had top jobs in government. Women were not always paid the same wages as men for doing the same work. Even so, the position of women improved under the Communists.

The Great Leap Forward

In 1958, Mao launched a program called the **Great Leap Forward.** He called on the people to increase agricultural and industrial output. To make farms more productive, he created **communes,** groups of people who live and work together and hold property in common. Communes had production quotas, which were set amounts of agricultural or industrial output that they were to produce.

Note Taking

Reading Skill:
Recognize Sequence
Keep track of important dates in Mao Zedong's rule in China. A table has been started for you. Add boxes as needed.

Mao Zedong in China	
Date	Event
1930s	
1934	

Preparing for the Regents

- Why were Mao and the Communists victorious over Jiang and the Nationalists in China's civil war?

Preparing for the Regents

- Describe three similarities between the Chinese Communist Revolution and other revolutions you have studied.

Key Themes and Concepts

Human Rights
Chinese women gained some rights under communism. However, they never gained full equality. Very few women were able to acquire top government jobs, and most women did not get paid as much as men who did the same work.

The Great Leap Forward failed. Commune-based industries turned out poorly made goods. At the same time, agricultural output declined. Bad weather added to the downturn, creating widespread famine.

The Cultural Revolution

In 1966, Mao launched the **Cultural Revolution** to renew people's loyalty to communism and establish a more equitable society. Mao feared that revolutionary peasants and workers were being replaced by intellectuals in running the country. He shut down schools and universities throughout China and urged Chinese students to experience the revolution for themselves. Students formed groups of fighters called the **Red Guards.** They attacked professors, government officials, and factory managers, many of whom were exiled or executed.

Programs of Mao Zedong

Program	The Great Leap Forward	The Cultural Revolution
Goals	• Increase farm and factory output	• Renew communist loyalties
Methods	• Communes • Production quotas	• Red Guards attack professors and other officials
Results	• Program fails • Two years of hunger and low production	• Economy slows • China closes to outside world • People fear arrest • Civil war threatened

United States Recognition

The Cold War was raging in 1949. Consequently, the United States had refused to recognize the People's Republic of China. In the Korean War, Communist China and the United States took opposing sides. By the 1970s, however, this situation was changing. China won admission to the United Nations in 1971, and President Richard Nixon visited Mao Zedong in Beijing in 1972. In 1979, the United States officially recognized the People's Republic of China.

Communism Under Deng Xiaoping

In 1976, Mao Zedong died. **Deng Xiaoping** took control. His leadership brought more economic freedom but little political change.

Economic Reforms: The Four Modernizations

To make China a more modern country, Deng promoted foreign trade and more contact with Western nations. He also introduced the Four Modernizations. These were concentrated in four areas.

- **Farming** methods were modernized and mechanized.
- **Industry** was upgraded and expanded.
- **Science and technology** were promoted and developed.
- **Defense** systems and military forces were improved.

Limited Privatization Deng got rid of Mao's unpopular communes. He allowed land to be leased to individual farmers. After delivering a certain amount of food to the government, farmers could grow anything they wished and sell it for profit. This system increased agricultural output. The government also allowed some private businesses to produce goods and offer services.

Foreign Investment Deng also welcomed foreign technology and capital. The government set up special enterprise zones where foreigners could own and operate businesses.

Preparing for the Regents

- Describe three similarities between communism in China and communism in the Soviet Union.

1. They had racial discrimination
2. Childrens Rights
3. Womens Rights

Programs of Mao Zedong
Mao Zedong built a Communist totalitarian state. His government and programs tried to reshape the economy and society.

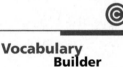

Vocabulary Builder

rage—(rayj) *v.* if something such as a battle, a disagreement, or a storm rages, it continues with great violence or strong emotions

Preparing for the Regents

- Describe two ways in which Deng Xiaoping's methods differed from Mao Zedong's.

1. Command Economy
2. Contrast Economy

Results of Reforms Deng's policies had both positive and negative results. The economy grew, and some Chinese enjoyed a better standard of living. Foreign relations and trade improved. Crime and corruption grew, however, and the gap between rich and poor widened. Deng's economic changes caused some Chinese to demand greater political freedom.

Tiananmen Square

The government was willing to grant economic reforms but not political ones. In May 1989, demonstrators in Beijing occupied **Tiananmen Square,** demanding more rights and freedoms. When they refused to disperse as ordered, the government sent in troops and tanks. Thousands of Chinese were killed or wounded. The incident showed how important it was for China's communist leaders to maintain control. Order was more important than political freedom. During the 1990s, efforts were made to force China to end human rights violations. However, these efforts had limited effects.

LOCKE AND JEFFERSON, PLEASE.

Source: Henry Payne reprinted by permission of United Feature Syndicate, Inc.

Return of Hong Kong

In 1842, Great Britain had gained the island of Hong Kong, off the southern coast of China. During the years that Hong Kong was under British rule, it modernized and became wealthy.

In the 1980s, Britain and China decided that Hong Kong would return to Chinese rule in 1997. China agreed not to change Hong Kong's social or economic system for 50 years and to allow the island a degree of self-rule. The island was turned over to China on July 1, 1997.

Summary

The Communists, under Mao Zedong, rose to power in China after World War II. Their appeal to peasants and to women, their superior army, and lack of support for the Nationalists led to victory for the Communists. The communist government severely restricted the rights and freedoms of most Chinese. Later leaders, such as Deng Xiaoping, allowed free market reforms but little political freedom. Violations of human rights in China have often made relations between China and the United States difficult.

Vocabulary Builder

disperse—(dis PURS) *v.* if a group of people disperse or are dispersed, they go away in different directions

Preparing for the Regents

- Why do you think the leaders of China were willing to accept Western economic reforms but not Western ideas about human rights and political freedom? *They want to maintain ancient cultures*

Preparing for the Regents

- Describe in your own words what this 1989 cartoon says about Chinese leadership and the wishes of the Chinese people. *Treat elders with respect*

Key Themes and Concepts

Economic Systems
Hong Kong was allowed to keep a free market economy, which differed from the rest of China. This created a country with two different economic systems.

Preparing for the Regents

- Create a political cartoon that comments on a major development in China since the 1940s.

Collapse of European Imperialism

The Big Idea

After World War II, European imperialism ended, and nations faced difficult challenges as:

• India struggled with social, ethnic, and religious divisions.

• peoples of Asia and Africa used both peaceful and violent means to achieve independence.

• African nations struggled to overcome the legacy of colonial rule.

• Southeast Asia was ravaged by many years of war.

Key People and Terms

Place each of the key people and terms into these two categories: leader or conflict/cooperation.

Section Overview

The period after World War II marked the final collapse of European imperialism. India gained independence in 1947 but struggled with ethnic and religious conflicts. In Africa, independence was achieved both through peaceful efforts and through bloody conflicts. In South Africa, years of racial separation ended, and black South Africans gained a voice in government. In Southeast Asia, the struggle for independence came to an end only after many years of civil and international war.

Key Themes and Concepts

As you review this section, take special note of the following key themes and concepts:

Imperialism How did European imperialism collapse?

Nationalism How did nationalistic movements in Asia, Africa, and Southeast Asia result in independence?

Political and Economic Systems What kinds of political and economic systems developed in newly independent nations?

Key People and Terms

As you review this section, be sure you understand the significance of these key people and terms:

Mohandas Gandhi	African National Congress
Jawaharlal Nehru	Nelson Mandela
nonalignment	Desmond Tutu
Sikhism	F. W. de Klerk
Pan-Africanism	Ho Chi Minh
Kwame Nkrumah	Ngo Dinh Diem
Organization of African Unity	Khmer Rouge
Jomo Kenyatta	Pol Pot
tribalism	Aung San Suu Kyi
apartheid	

Indian Independence and Partition

Indian nationalists had been demanding independence since the 1800s. Indians were angered when, during World War II, the British put off granting them independence but expected them to support Great Britain in the war. **Mohandas Gandhi,** as you have read, played an important part in the independence movement with his policy of passive resistance. Over time, British control of India was weakened. Finally, in 1947, Britain granted independence to India. **Jawaharlal Nehru,** India's first prime minister, celebrated Independence Day with an impassioned speech, full of hope for India's future. Independence, however, brought some difficult problems.

Muslim and Hindu Conflicts

In India, Hindus were the majority, and Muslims were the minority. The Muslim League had been demanding a Muslim state. Also, there had been fighting between Muslims and Hindus. In 1947, British officials drew borders that created Hindu India and Muslim Pakistan. Pakistan was made up of West Pakistan and East Pakistan, two widely separated areas that had high Muslim populations. East Pakistan later became the nation of Bangladesh.

The partition, or division, of India did not bring peace. Independence set off mass migrations of Muslims fleeing India and Hindus fleeing Pakistan. Millions were killed crossing the borders. Mohandas Gandhi tried to bring peace, but a Hindu fanatic assassinated him.

Although the worst violence began to lessen after Gandhi's death, conflicts continued to occur. In the years ahead, Indian and Pakistani forces would clash repeatedly over border disputes. Tensions between Hindus and Muslims still exist and continue to erupt into violence today.

Indian Government and Foreign Policy

A Democratic Nation India is the world's largest democracy. It has a federal system of government, with powers divided between a strong central government and smaller local governments. For 40 years after independence, India was led by members of the Nehru family. Jawaharlal Nehru was the first prime minister.

Ethnic and religious conflicts have made democracy difficult for India. After Nehru's death, his daughter, **Indira Gandhi,** became prime minister in 1966. She was assassinated in 1984, and her son, Rajiv Gandhi, became prime minister. He too was assassinated, however, in 1991.

Nonalignment During the Cold War, India followed a policy of nonalignment. This policy, instituted by Jawaharlal Nehru, allowed India to accept help from both capitalist and socialist nations.

Obstacles to Progress in India

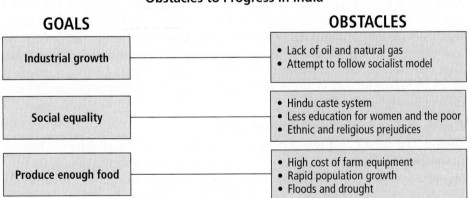

GOALS / **OBSTACLES**

- Industrial growth
  - Lack of oil and natural gas
  - Attempt to follow socialist model
- Social equality
  - Hindu caste system
  - Less education for women and the poor
  - Ethnic and religious prejudices
- Produce enough food
  - High cost of farm equipment
  - Rapid population growth
  - Floods and drought

Social Change in India

The Caste System The caste system, a system of social stratification, has been a part of Indian life for more than 2,000 years. In the 1900s, the system underwent change.

- Mohandas Gandhi campaigned to end the harsh treatment of the caste called Untouchables.
- The Indian constitution of 1950 banned discrimination against Untouchables.
- The government set aside jobs and places in universities for Untouchables.

Caste system was based on jobs, and color.

Key Themes and Concepts

Nationalism
In India, nationalism resulted in freedom from colonial rule. Religious conflict led to the creation of two nations: India and Pakistan.

Note Taking

Reading Skill:
Categorize
Make a table. As you read, fill in the categories for India after independence.

India	
government	
foreign policy	
economy	
religion	
social system	

Key Themes and Concepts

Economic Systems
Nonalignment allowed developing nations to accept help from both communist and capitalist nations. India was a leader among nonaligned nations.

Preparing for the Regents

- How is the caste system that exists in India today different from the caste system of the past?

In spite of improvements in the legal status of Untouchables, discrimination still exists. Although there are movements for caste reform, the system is still a part of Indian society. It has a stronger effect in rural villages than in urban areas.

The Status of Women The Indian constitution of 1950 also granted rights to women. It gave women the right to vote and recognized their right to divorce and inherit property. Indira Gandhi, a woman, became prime minister in 1966. As with the caste system, traditional restrictions on women are more persistent in rural areas.

Sikh Separatism

Sikhism is a religion that began in India in the 1500s by blending elements of Islam and Hinduism. In the 1980s, there was an increased demand for self-rule by Sikhs in the state of Punjab. In the early 1980s, Sikh separatists occupied the Golden Temple in Amritsar to express their demands. Indira Gandhi, still prime minister at the time, sent troops. Many Sikhs died as a result. Not long after that, Gandhi herself was assassinated by two Sikhs who had served as her bodyguards. Continuing tension exists between Sikhs and Hindus.

Dispute Over Kashmir

India and Pakistan have disputed control of the state of Kashmir since the partition of the Indian subcontinent in 1947. Although governed by the secular government of India, the population of Kashmir is predominantly Muslim. The two nations fought wars over Kashmir in 1947–1948 and in 1965 and maintain a fragile truce today. In recent years there have been a number of terrorist attacks by Islamic separatists, which raise the fear of war between these two nuclear powers.

Independent Nations in Africa

A movement called Pan-Africanism had been nourishing nationalist movements in Africa since the 1920s. **Pan-Africanism** emphasized the unity of Africans and people of African descent all over the world.

Although a few African nations had achieved independence before 1945, most gained independence only after World War II. Many Africans had fought in the war. They resented returning home to second-class citizenship. Some Africans had migrated to cities during the war to work in defense industries. There they were exposed to nationalist ideas. In addition, the Atlantic Charter, signed by Franklin Roosevelt and Winston Churchill in 1941, had set forth the goal of self-determination for all nations.

Early Independence Movements

Ghana The Gold Coast was a British colony. American-educated leader **Kwame Nkrumah,** inspired by Pan-Africanism and by the writings of Mohandas Gandhi, organized a political party. Nkrumah used strikes and boycotts to battle the British. In 1957, the British granted the Gold Coast independence, and Nkrumah became its prime minister. Nkrumah renamed the country Ghana, a name that linked the new nation to its African past. In 1963, Nkrumah created the **Organization of African Unity,** or OAU. This group promoted Pan-Africanism and the end of colonialism in Africa.

Kenya In the British colony of Kenya, the independence struggle was led by **Jomo Kenyatta.** He was a spokesman for the Kikuyu people, who had been driven off their land by European settlers. When some Kikuyu turned to violent means to gain liberation, the British jailed Kenyatta. Later, however, Kenyatta was released. In 1963, he became the first prime minister of an independent Kenya.

Obstacles to Progress in Africa

Many of Africa's nations gained independence only after 1945, and more gained independence after 1959. The end of colonialism presented many challenges to the development of the countries of Africa.

Like other developing nations, African countries have focused on building industry and improving agriculture. Although industrial growth has sometimes been successful, many nations remain dependent on imports. Also, money borrowed to build industry created great debts. In some nations, such as Nigeria, people flocked to industrial centers. Food production fell, and rural poverty resulted. Cities could not keep up with population increases.

A continuing reliance on cash crops means that many African nations still need to import food to feed their growing populations. Cash crop economies also have other negative effects. For example, when oil prices fell, the economy of Nigeria—a nation rich in oil—nearly collapsed.

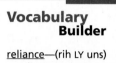

Obstacles to Progress in Africa

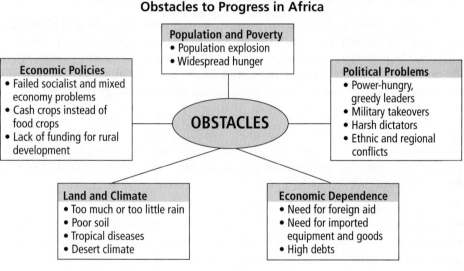

Population and Poverty
- Population explosion
- Widespread hunger

Economic Policies
- Failed socialist and mixed economy problems
- Cash crops instead of food crops
- Lack of funding for rural development

OBSTACLES

Political Problems
- Power-hungry, greedy leaders
- Military takeovers
- Harsh dictators
- Ethnic and regional conflicts

Land and Climate
- Too much or too little rain
- Poor soil
- Tropical diseases
- Desert climate

Economic Dependence
- Need for foreign aid
- Need for imported equipment and goods
- High debts

Even so, Africa shows great potential.

- Many African nations have moved from a socialist model to a free market economy, experiencing growth as a result.
- Other nations have expanded mining and manufacturing and built factories to process agricultural products.
- Some nations have improved transportation and communication.

Economic Links With Europe

Today, much of Africa suffers from trading patterns that were established during the age of imperialism. European nations had created colonial economies that depended on the export of raw materials and cash crops from Africa. Many African nations still rely on the export of just a few products. When the prices of these products fall, the nations' economies can be devastated. Many African countries also rely greatly on manufactured goods imported from Europe. As a result, these countries have trade deficits and rising debts.

Strong economic links have been maintained between many African nations and the colonial powers that once ruled them. Some former French colonies, for example, have adopted the French currency and many give preference to French products. This also occurs in countries that were once British colonies, especially those that are members of the Commonwealth, an association of former British colonies.

Preparing for the Regents

- How did the borders drawn by colonial powers eventually contribute to civil war in Africa?

Ethnic Tensions and Nationalism

Most of the current national boundaries in Africa were established during the colonial period by Europeans. Unfortunately, the boundaries were made without consideration for the traditional territories of tribal and ethnic groups. As a result, some ethnic groups were separated into different nations. Other ethnic groups were united within nations. Today, therefore, the centuries-old loyalty to one's tribe is often stronger than loyalty to one's nation.

Nigeria is one of many nations where **tribalism** has led to civil war. More than 200 ethnic groups live in Nigeria. At independence, several of the larger groups fought for power. Among these groups were the Muslim Hausa and Fulani peoples in the north and the Christian Ibo and Yoruba peoples in the south.

In 1966, when a massacre of 20,000 Ibo took place, Hausa dominated the government. The next year, the Ibo declared their region independent, calling it Biafra. A war raged for several years. Nigeria blockaded Biafra and ended the war, but nearly a million people had been killed or died of starvation.

In Rwanda, ethnic conflict led to genocide. Before 1994, Rwanda was 85 percent Hutu and 14 percent Tutsi. In 1994, Hutu extremists, supported by government officials, launched a murderous campaign against the Tutsis. According to estimates, more than 500,000 people were killed in just a few months. The genocide was stopped when a Tutsi-led rebel army seized control of the government.

In 2002, 53 African countries formed a federation, the African Union (AU). Its goals include solving economic, social, political, and environmental problems in Africa. AU members deal with issues such as desertification, AIDS, and famine. The AU also works to control the conflicts between and within African countries. Eventually it plans to create an economic bloc.

Preparing for the Regents

- Use your knowledge of global history and recent current events to compare the genocide that occurred in Rwanda with another historical example of genocide.

· Humans made groups baised on the color of peoples skin or what they did for a living.

End of Apartheid in South Africa

For nearly 350 years, Europeans ruled South Africa. Although South Africa won independence from Britain in 1910, its white citizens alone held political power. To control the nation's government and economy, whites in 1948 made official a system of **apartheid,** or separation of the races. Apartheid required black Africans and other nonwhites to live in certain zones, segregated public facilities and transportation, and forbade interracial marriage.

The Anti-apartheid Movement In 1912, a political party organized in South Africa. Later called the **African National Congress** (ANC), it used violence, boycotts, and nonviolent civil disobedience to oppose apartheid.

In 1960, the police killed 69 people and wounded 180 at a demonstration in Sharpeville. The South African government reacted by outlawing the ANC. In 1964, **Nelson Mandela,** an important ANC leader, was sentenced to life in prison. He became a powerful symbol of the struggle for freedom.

Desmond Tutu, a black Anglican bishop and civil rights leader, with other activists convinced foreign nations and businesses to limit trade and investment in segregated South Africa. These nonviolent protests had a strong effect.

F. W. de Klerk became president of South Africa in 1989. Knowing reform was necessary, he legalized the ANC, repealed segregation laws, and released Mandela in 1990. In 1994, an election in which people of all races could vote elected Mandela president. After ten years the ANC is still in power, but South Africa still suffers from economic inequality, land redistribution problems, and many HIV cases.

Preparing for the Regents

- Describe the role of each of the following figures in the ending of apartheid.

Nelson Mandela: African Freedom Fighter

Desmond Tutu: Civil Rights leader

F. W. de Klerk: President of South Africa.

Truth and Reconciliation

The South African Truth and Reconciliation Commission (TRC) helped deal with the violence and human rights abuses under apartheid. It revealed past wrongdoing by the government, so to resolve past conflicts.

Difficult Struggles in Southeast Asia

After World War II, growing nationalist feeling spread through Indochina and other parts of Southeast Asia. Southeast Asians fought against foreign imperialist powers to gain their freedom. They also fought bloody civil wars.

Southeast Asia

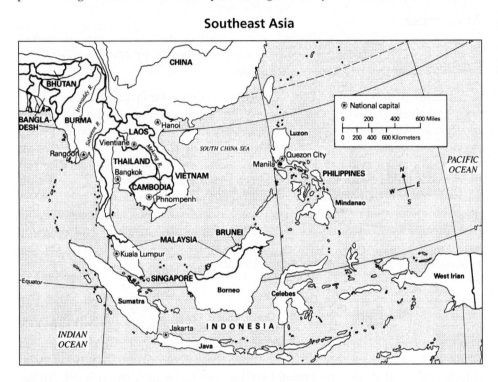

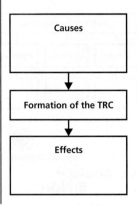

Note Taking

Reading Skill: **Identify Causes and Effects**
Make a flowchart. Show the causes and effects of the formation of the TRC.

Causes

↓

Formation of the TRC

↓

Effects

Southeast Asia
Southeast Asia includes part of the Asian mainland and thousands of islands. By World War II, European countries and the United States had colonized much of the area.

Vietnam

Vietnam had been ruled by the French since the mid-1800s. During World War II, the Vietminh, an alliance of nationalist and communist groups, fought the occupying Japanese. After the war, the French hoped to regain Vietnam. Instead, **Ho Chi Minh,** leader of the Vietminh, declared Vietnam free. Defeated by the Vietminh, the French abandoned Vietnam. A 1954 conference in Geneva led to the division of Vietnam into a communist north and a non-communist south.

The Vietnam War The American-supported South Vietnamese government of **Ngo Dinh Diem** refused to hold the 1956 elections to unite Vietnam because it feared that the Communists would win. Ho Chi Minh, leader of communist North Vietnam, supported the Vietcong, the communist rebels trying to overthrow Diem. The United States sent troops to support Diem's government. The Vietnam War lasted from 1959 to 1975, during which the United States sent hundreds of thousands troops and advisors to support Diem's government. Even with this help, South Vietnam could not defeat the communist forces. Antiwar sentiment in the United States forced President Nixon to withdraw American forces. In 1975, Saigon, the capital of the south, fell. The country was reunited under communist control.

Key Themes and Concepts

Conflict
In Vietnam, a local independence movement became a major Cold War battleground.

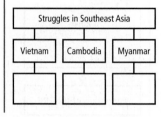

Note Taking

Reading Skill:
Summarize
Make a chart. Summarize the events connected to the struggles in Southeast Asia.

Struggles in Southeast Asia		
Vietnam	Cambodia	Myanmar

Preparing for the Regents

• List three results of the collapse of European imperialism in the years after World War II.

1. Economy
2. Polictical
3. Finanetal

Cambodia

During the Vietnam War, Cambodia was a supply route for the Vietcong and North Vietnamese forces. In 1969, American forces bombed and then invaded Cambodia to destroy that route. After the Americans left, Cambodian communist guerrillas, known as the **Khmer Rouge,** took control of the government. Under the leadership of **Pol Pot,** the Khmer Rouge began a reign of terror to remove all Western influence from Cambodia. More than a million Cambodians were slaughtered in what has become known as the "Killing Fields." In 1979, Vietnamese forces invaded and occupied Cambodia. In the early 1990s, the civil war ended. UN peacekeepers monitored elections, but some fighting continued.

Myanmar

Myanmar, formerly called Burma, was a British possession until it gained independence. It remained a very poor country, plagued by ethnic tensions and after 1962 was ruled by a repressive military.

An opposition party, lead by Nobel Peace Prize winner **Aung San Suu Kyi,** elected representatives in 1991, but the military junta repressed them. Suu Kyi spent 15 years in various forms of detention until 2010 when the government finally freed her. The military junta ended in 2011 and a steady move toward a more democratic government has occurred. This, along with economic reforms, allowed improved relations with various foreign countries. In 2015, Suu Kyi's opposition party won a landslide victory and established a new government by spring 2016. Suu Kyi, who cannot become president, created an expansive role for herself in this new government. However, economic problems, as well as ethnic and religious tensions, continue to affect many refugees who flee the country only to end up as economic slaves in countries such as Thailand.

Summary

European imperialism collapsed throughout the world in the years after World War II. In India, independence was accompanied by conflicts among various ethnic and religious groups. In Africa, nations suffered from the legacy left by colonial rule. Tribal conflicts brought civil war to many nations. In South Africa, the repressive system of apartheid was finally ended. In Southeast Asia, another war erupted between communist North Vietnam and noncommunist South Vietnam. Despite United States intervention, the communist forces were victorious. In Cambodia and Myanmar, hundreds of thousands died or fled their country due to political, military and cultural violence.

Conflicts and Change in the Middle East

Section Overview

Since 1945, the Middle East has been an area of tension and change. The state of Israel was created in 1948. After years of conflict between Israel and its Arab neighbors, the quest for peace began to achieve some success. In Lebanon, years of civil war ravaged the country. In Iran, an Islamic republic was born. Several international conflicts centered on Iraq, largely because of its dictator, Saddam Hussein. Throughout the Middle East, many Muslims have called for a return to a life based on Islamic law.

Key Themes and Concepts

As you review this section, take special note of the following key themes and concepts:

Diversity How has the diversity of the Middle East affected its recent history?

Conflict What efforts have been made to end conflict between Israel and its Arab neighbors?

Interdependence Why did the Persian Gulf War involve many nations from around the world?

Belief Systems How is Islamic fundamentalism affecting life in the Middle East today?

Key People and Terms

As you review this section, be sure you understand the significance of these key people and terms:

Palestine Liberation Organization (PLO)

Yasir Arafat

intifada

Camp David Accords

Yitzhak Rabin

King Hussein

Hamas

Ayatollah Khomeini

Islamic fundamentalism

Taliban

Saddam Hussein

Persian Gulf War

Kurds

The Impact of Geography

The Middle East has been a crossroads for people of Africa, Asia, and Europe since ancient times. This fact has led to an enormous diversity of peoples, belief systems, and cultures. These differences have sometimes led to conflict.

The discovery of oil in the region brought power to some Middle Eastern nations. Oil is a vital part of the global economy. Oil resources, however, are not evenly distributed across the region. As a result, Middle Eastern countries have gone to war over control of oil-rich lands. Dependence on oil is one reason why countries around the world take an active interest in conflicts in the Middle East.

The
**Big
Idea**

In the Middle East, since 1945:

• the creation of Israel has led to conflicts between Jews and Arabs.

• the search for peace between Jews and Arabs has met with some success.

• a revolution in Iran has led to an Islamic republic.

• Iraq has been involved in several international conflicts.

• many Muslims have urged a return to Islamic government and law.

Key People and Terms

Place each of the key people and terms into these three categories: politics, conflict/cooperation, and belief system.

Preparing for the Regents

• What impact has geography had on the culture and history of the Middle East?

Forces Shaping the Middle East

Religious and Ethnic Differences	Natural Resources	Governments	Islamic Traditions
• Muslims, Christians, and Jews • Different sects within religions • More than 30 languages • Religious, racial, and cultural prejudices • Desire for a united Arab state	• Largest oil fields in the world • Oil-rich nations gain wealth and political and economic power • Limited water supply • Arguments over dams and water rights	• Democracy in Israel and Turkey • Rule by royal family in Jordan and Saudi Arabia • Single-party dictators in Iraq and Syria	• Laws of Islam influence government, society, and personal life • Antiwestern feelings • 1990s revival of Islamic traditions

A Jewish State Among Arab Nations

Large numbers of Jews had begun migrating to Palestine from Europe in the late 1800s as part of the Zionist movement. During World War I, the British made conflicting promises to the Jews and Palestinians about creating a Jewish homeland in the area. After World War II and the Holocaust, there was increased support for a Jewish state in Palestine. However, both Jews and Palestinian Arabs claimed a right to the land of Palestine. Jews claimed that they were entitled to return to a land they had once ruled 3,000 years ago. The Palestinian Arabs claimed they were entitled to the land they had been living in since Roman times. Many violent clashes between these two groups have occurred since 1947.

Creation of Israel

In 1947, the United Nations drew up a plan to divide Palestine, which was under British rule, into an Arab state and a Jewish state. Jews accepted the plan, but Arabs did not. In 1948, Great Britain withdrew, and Jews proclaimed the independent state of Israel, which was recognized by both the United States and the Soviet Union.

Israel developed rapidly. Between 1948 and the mid-1980s, nearly two million Jews migrated to Israel, some to escape persecution. The government built towns for settlers. A skilled workforce expanded the economy. American aid helped Israel as well.

Palestinians and Arab-Israeli Wars

When the state of Israel was created, Arab nations vowed to drive the Jews out and restore Palestine as an Arab nation. Since 1948, there have been four full-scale wars and several smaller conflicts between Israel and the Arab states.

War of Independence The first Arab-Israeli war occurred in 1948 when six Arab states—Egypt, Iraq, Jordan, Lebanon, Syria, and Saudi Arabia—invaded Israel. Israel defeated the invaders and gained control of land which doubled its size. Over 700,000 Arabs became refugees. Most were refused entry by neighboring Arab countries and were placed in temporary refugee camps, which became permanent over time. The poverty and discrimination experienced by these Palestinian Arabs fueled anger. Many dreamed of an Arab Palestinian state. Resistance to the state of Israel took many forms.

Palestine Liberation Organization (PLO) In 1964, the Palestine Liberation Organization (PLO) was formed to destroy Israel and win self-rule for the Palestinians. Led by Yasir Arafat, the PLO used terrorist tactics and fought a guerilla war against Israelis at home and abroad. Many Israeli civilians were killed by PLO terrorists.

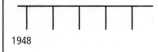

Further Wars Another war was fought over the Suez Canal in 1956. In 1967, during the Six-Day War, Israel overran the Sinai Peninsula, the Golan Heights on the Syrian border, and East Jerusalem. In 1973, Egypt and Syria launched a war against Israel on the Jewish high holy day of Yom Kippur. The Israelis won all of these wars.

Intifada In 1987, young Palestinians, who had grown up in the Israeli-occupied West Bank and Gaza, and who were frustrated with the lack of progress in gaining a Palestinian state, began widespread acts of civil disobedience called the intifada, or "uprising." Palestinians used boycotts, demonstrations, and attacks on Israeli soldiers by unarmed teenagers throwing rocks and bombs. The intifada continued into the 1990s. Crackdowns by the Israelis led to a wave of sympathy throughout the world for the Palestinians.

Israel's Changing Borders

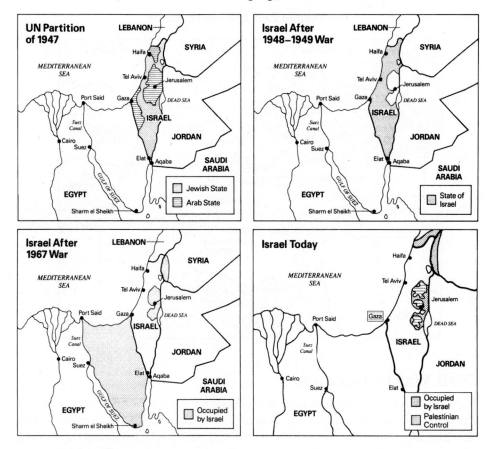

Israel's Changing Borders
Modern Israel was established in 1948. Israel and its Arab neighbors fought three wars—in 1956, 1967, and 1973. In these wars, Israel defeated Arab forces and gained more land.

Preparing for the Regents

• Practice your map skills by answering the following questions.

1. What countries border Israel?

2. What areas were gained by Israel after the 1967 war?

Attempts at Peace

Numerous attempts have been made to resolve the situation in Palestine. Limited progress has been made.

Camp David Accords In 1979, President Jimmy Carter invited President Anwar Sadat of Egypt and Prime Minister Menachem Begin of Israel to discuss terms of peace. The resulting treaty, the Camp David Accords, was based on the concept of "land for peace." Israel returned the Sinai Peninsula to Egypt in exchange for Egypt's recognition of Israel's right to exist. Sadat was later assassinated by a group of Muslim extremists angered by Egypt's peace with Israel.

Oslo Peace Accords In 1993, direct talks were held for the first time between Israel and the PLO. Arafat had renounced the use of terrorism, which opened the

Vocabulary Builder

renounce—(rih NOWNS) *v.* to reject; to publicly say or show that you no longer believe in something, or will no longer behave in a particular way

Preparing for the Regents

• Why does the Arab-Israeli conflict continue today?

door for Israeli Prime Minister **Yitzhak Rabin** to sign an agreement giving Palestinians in the Gaza Strip and West Bank limited self-rule. A year later, Jordan, led by **King Hussein,** also made a peace agreement with Israel. In 1995, Rabin was assassinated by right-wing Jewish extremists, opposed to making concessions to the Palestinians.

Israelis continues to build settlements in lands that Palestinians claim while Palestinian riots and suicide bombers began increasing. In 2002, Israeli military forces invaded Palestinian-ruled areas that were centers of terrorist activities. They arrested or assassinated PLO and other Palestinian leaders. Many Palestinian civilians also died. The United States, United Nations, European Union, and Russia outlined a roadmap of peace. This plan would establish a Palestinian state, but the PLO had to make democratic reforms and end the use of terrorism. Peace prospects improved when Palestinian leader Yasir Arafat died in 2004.

The Middle East and North Africa

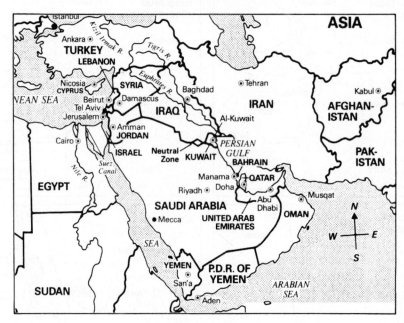

The Middle East and North Africa
The Middle East controls large oil resources and important waterways such as the Persian Gulf. Western nations have tried to prevent regional powers from interfering with the oil supply.

Preparing for the Regents

• Which nations border the Persian Gulf?

Key Themes and Concepts

Diversity
The diverse population of Lebanon, as well as outside political forces, led to civil war in Lebanon. Diversity has contributed to conflict throughout the Middle East.

Civil War in Lebanon

North of Israel, Lebanon had gained independence after World War II. It was a thriving commercial center with a diverse population. There, Christians and Muslims lived together peacefully. However, as Palestinian refugees entered Lebanon, especially after 1967, they created a Muslim majority. The PLO became powerful in Palestinian refugee camps.

A civil war between Christians and Muslims began in 1975. Israeli and Syrian forces participated in the conflict. By 1990, a degree of order had returned to Lebanon. In 2000, Israel withdrew its forces, and Syria followed reluctantly in 2005. In May 2005, Lebanon held its first legislative elections since the civil war. In 2006, Hezbollah, a radical Shi'a group, captured two Israeli soldiers, leading to a 34-day conflict with Israel.

Islamic Fundamentalism

Beginning in the 1970s, increasing numbers of Muslims opposed westernization. They wanted to apply Islamic principles to the problems in their nations. This movement for reform, called Islamic fundamentalism by many Westerners, has played a key role in the Middle East.

- **Libya** In 1969, Muammar al-Qaddafi established a government based on Islamic principles. He supported revolutionary organizations and activities in the Middle East and around the world. Qaddafi renounced terrorism in 1999.
- **Algeria** In 1992, the Algerian Islamic political party did well in elections. The ruling party feared that an Islamic revolution might occur. The military therefore seized power and took harsh measures against Islamic activists, resulting in the deaths of thousands of people. Since 2005, a newly elected government's offer of amnesty to terrorists who lay down their arms has not ended terrorist attacks by groups who want to return to strict Islamic rule.
- **Turkey** Throughout the 1900s, the government of Turkey based many of its policies on Western models. In the 1990s, however, Islamic political parties gained increasing support and influence. They hoped to restore traditional Islamic government to Turkey.
- **Afghanistan** From 1979 to 1989, Afghanistan fought a Soviet invasion whose goal was to strengthen the Afghan Communist government. Following the Soviet withdrawal, the country was torn by civil war. An Islamic group, the **Taliban**, seized power in 1996 and set up an Islamic government.

The Iranian Revolution

In 1953, Great Britain and the United States helped Muhammad Reza Pahlavi gain control of the Iranian government. He proclaimed himself the shah. He westernized and modernized the country; he also ruled as a dictator.

In the 1970s, opposition to the shah was led by the exiled **Ayatollah Khomeini.** *Ayatollah* is a title given to learned Shiite legal experts. With protests mounting, the shah fled Iran in 1979. Soon afterward, Khomeini returned, declaring Iran an Islamic republic based on Islamic fundamental beliefs. In 1989, Khomeini died, and more moderate leaders took control. Then, in 2005, elections put conservatives back in power. World concerns grew over Iran's nuclear program, which President Mahmoud Ahmadinejad refused to curb.

Impact of the Revolution

The Iranian revolution of 1979 had effects in Iran and beyond.

- The new Iranian government was extremely hostile to the West, especially to the United States. Western books, music, and movies were banned.
- The government required strict adherence to Islamic fundamental beliefs. There was no separation of religion and government.
- Many rights were taken away from women.
- Iranian militants seized the American embassy in Tehran and held a group of Americans hostage for more than a year.
- Iran encouraged Muslims in other countries to work to overthrow secular governments and establish Islamic republics.

Main Cause	Event Iranian Revolution	Effects

Saddam Hussein and Iraq

Under the leadership of dictator **Saddam Hussein,** Iraq was involved in several conflicts in the Middle East.

Iran-Iraq War

In 1980, Hussein's forces seized control of a disputed border area between Iraq and Iran. War broke out between the two nations. When both sides attacked oil tankers in the Persian Gulf, the United States Navy began to protect shipping lanes in the region. The war continued until 1988 and created extreme hardship in both nations.

Persian Gulf War

In 1990, Iraq invaded Kuwait and seized its oil fields. The United States saw the Iraqi action as a threat to Saudi Arabia and to the flow of oil from the Middle East. The first response of the United States was to organize a trade embargo of Iraq. Peacekeeping troops from many Western and Middle Eastern countries were sent to Saudi Arabia. When Iraq refused to withdraw from Kuwait, the 1991 **Persian Gulf War** began. The United States and its allies quickly won the war, and Kuwait was liberated. The United States continued to view Iraqi dictator Saddam Hussein as a very dangerous force. They hoped that the war would topple his dictatorship. He remained in power, however.

Over the next 12 years, Saddam Hussein's rhetoric, tight military control, and human rights abuses alienated many countries. His actions, including allegedly stockpiling weapons of mass destruction, created fear in his own people as well as in Western countries.

Summary

The Middle East is an area of great diversity and economic importance. It is also an area of great conflict. The creation of the state of Israel in 1948, and the refusal of neighboring Arab nations to accept Israel, set off years of conflict between Arabs and Jews. A revolution occurred in Iran that created an Islamic republic. A growing influence in the area is that of Islamic fundamentalism, a movement to return to traditional Islamic ways. The aggressive actions of Iraqi leader Saddam Hussein led to a war that involved many countries of the world.

Key Themes and Concepts

Interdependence
Because the world economy depends so strongly on oil, the Iraqi takeover of Kuwaiti oil fields in 1990 provoked a reaction throughout the world.

Preparing for the Regents

- What factors have contributed to conflict in the Middle East?

UNIT 3
Section 6
Collapse of Communism and the Soviet Union

Section Overview

Eastern Europe underwent great change in the 1980s and 1990s. The Soviet invasion of Afghanistan heightened Cold War tensions and added to Soviet economic problems. Mikhail Gorbachev came to power in the Soviet Union and took steps to reform the economy and allow more openness. His policies contributed to the collapse of communism in Eastern Europe and the breakup of the Soviet Union. By 1989, Germany was reunited. The former Soviet Union and its satellites experienced varying degrees of difficulty as they tried to establish new political and economic systems in their countries. New nations emerged in Eastern Europe, sometimes accompanied by violent ethnic conflict.

Key Themes and Concepts

As you review this section, take special note of the following key themes and concepts:

Change What were the causes and impacts of the collapse of the Soviet Union?

Diversity and Conflict How has ethnic diversity contributed to conflict in Eastern Europe?

Political and Economic Systems What kinds of problems did Eastern European countries face in the transition to democracy and a market economy?

Key People and Terms

As you review this section, be sure you understand the significance of these key people and terms:

détente	Vladimir Putin
Mikhail Gorbachev	Lech Walesa
perestroika	Solidarity
glasnost	

Easing of Cold War Tensions

By the 1970s, the Cold War had been going on for more than 25 years. Both the United States and the Soviet Union realized that the tension could end in mutual destruction. Large amounts of money were spent by both powers on weapons. Under their leaders, Richard Nixon and Leonid Brezhnev, the United States and the Soviet Union promoted a period of **détente,** or lessening of tension. Détente involved:

- arms control talks and treaties
- cultural exchanges
- trade agreements

The
Big
Idea

Between 1970 and 1990, the Soviet Union broke up, and communist control of Eastern Europe ended. During this period:

- the invasion of Afghanistan weakened the Soviet Union.

- Gorbachev's reforms led to the end of the Soviet Union.

- communist governments fell in Eastern Europe.

- ethnic divisions led to civil wars and the creation of new nations.

Key People and Terms

For each of the key people and terms, write a sentence explaining its significance.

Soviet Invasion of Afghanistan

Détente came to a sudden end with the Soviet invasion of Afghanistan in 1979. The Soviet Union had invaded Afghanistan in order to keep a procommunist government in power there. This move convinced many in the West that the Soviet Union was still an aggressive force.

Relations between the two superpowers worsened. The United States increased defense spending to match the buildup of Soviet arms that had continued during the period of détente. In the Soviet Union, however, the war in Afghanistan was very unpopular.

Gorbachev in the Soviet Union

In 1985, **Mikhail Gorbachev** came to power in the Soviet Union. Gorbachev wanted to end Cold War tensions. He pulled troops out of Afghanistan. He also reformed the Soviet government and economy.

Perestroika

Gorbachev restructured the failing state-run command economy in a process called **perestroika.** The goals were to stimulate economic growth and to make industry more efficient. Gorbachev also backed free market reforms. Perestroika had some negative effects, however. Inflation increased, and there were shortages of food and medicine.

Glasnost

Gorbachev also called for **glasnost,** or openness. This policy ended censorship and encouraged people to discuss openly the problems in the Soviet Union. Gorbachev hoped to win support for his policies both among ordinary citizens and among members of the Communist Party.

The Fall of the Soviet Union
The Cold War between the United States and the Soviet Union lasted almost 50 years. In the years around 1990, the struggle finally ended with the fall of the Soviet Union. After 69 years, the Soviet Union ceased to exist.

The Fall of the Soviet Union

CAUSES
• Leadership of Mikhail Gorbachev
• Openness to democratic ideas (glasnost)
• Reshaping of economy and government (perestroika)
• Economic problems
• Freedom movement in Eastern Europe

Fall of the Soviet Union

EFFECTS
• Formation of the Commonwealth of Independent States
• Loss of role as world superpower
• End of the Cold War
• Economic hardships
• Conflicts between procommunist and prodemocratic groups
• Minority revolts and civil conflicts

Breakup of the Soviet Union

As Gorbachev eased political restrictions, people began to voice their nationalist sentiments. As you have learned, the Soviet Union was a multinational state. People in the non-Russian republics opposed Russian domination. In 1991, the Baltic republics of Estonia, Latvia, and Lithuania regained their independence. Soon, all the Soviet republics declared their independence. The Soviet Union ceased to exist.

In mid-1991, communist hardliners tried to overthrow Gorbachev and restore the previous order. Their attempt failed, but Gorbachev soon resigned. However, Gorbachev's reforms had helped to end communism throughout Eastern Europe. His policies also contributed to the breakup of the Soviet Union.

Preparing for the Regents

- Explain the meaning of the political cartoon on this page.

Source: Reprinted By Permission of Bob Englehart, The Hartford Courant

Difficult Challenges for Russia

Boris Yeltsin became the Russian president. Yeltsin struggled to make the transition from communism to democracy. One of the most difficult challenges was converting the state-run command economy to a market economy. Industries and farms were privatized. Still, economic problems grew worse. Food shortages increased and unemployment rose.

Yeltsin retired in 1999. To succeed him, voters chose **Vladimir Putin** and, in 2008, his chosen successor, Dmitry Medvedev. For the first time in Russian history, power passed peacefully from one elected leader to another. Putin curbed the power of regional leaders and exerted control over the Duma, Russia's legislature, and continued to wield power as Medvedev's prime minister. Although Putin's policies have led to economic growth, there are growing concerns about his suppression of dissents and the future of democracy in Russia. In 2002, Russia and the United States signed a nuclear arms reduction agreement and a new START Treaty in 2010, but tensions between Russia, Europe and the United States increased over the Ukraine and Russia's support of the Syrian government.

Note Taking

Reading Skill:
Summarize
Make a table. Summarize each leader's time in power.

Soviet Union/Russian Leaders	
Gorbachev	
Yeltsin	
Putin	
Medvedev	

Preparing for the Regents

- Identify and explain three key events in the fall of communism in Eastern Europe.

Cause and Effects

List the effects of the Solidarity union in Poland.

Eastern Europe Transformed

Throughout Eastern Europe, Gorbachev's reforms had sparked demands for democracy and national independence. Poland, East Germany, Romania, Bulgaria, and other countries of Eastern Europe broke away from Soviet control. Through much of the region, there were attempts to enact democratic reforms and make the transition from a command economy to a market economy.

Lech Walesa and Solidarity in Poland

In the 1980s in Poland, economic hardships caused labor unrest. Led by **Lech Walesa,** workers organized **Solidarity,** an independent trade union. With millions of members, Solidarity called for political change.

At first, the Soviet Union pressured the Polish government to suppress Solidarity. The government outlawed the union and arrested Walesa and other leaders. However, communism's power was weakening. International pressure as well as internal pressure led to reform. In 1989, the first free elections in 50 years were held, and Solidarity candidates won. Lech Walesa became president. Poland joined NATO in 1999 and the European Union in 2004.

East and West Germany United

Since World War II, Germany had been divided into a democratic western state and a communist eastern state. The Berlin Wall had been built in 1961 to keep East Germans from fleeing to the West.

The Fall of the Berlin Wall East Germans wanted to share the prosperity and freedom enjoyed by West Germans. By 1989, East German leaders could no longer count on support from the Soviet Union. A rising wave of protests forced the communist government from power. In November 1989, the Berlin Wall was torn down by joyous Germans.

The Fall of Communism in Eastern Europe

Before 1990, the Soviet Union controlled Eastern Europe by force. As the Soviet Union weakened, Eastern Europeans demanded an end to Soviet domination.

The Fall of Communism in Eastern Europe

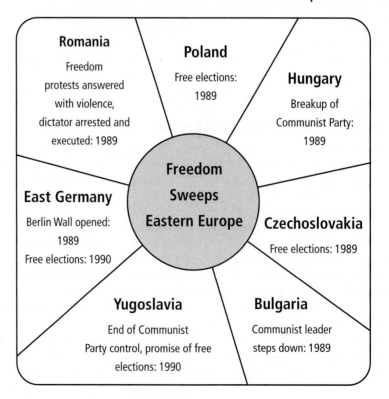

Impact of Reunification The people of Germany welcomed reunification of their country, but there were problems. West Germans had to pay higher taxes to finance the rebuilding of impoverished East Germany. Unemployment rose in East Germany during the transition to a market economy. Social unrest followed, with some right-wing extremists trying to revive Nazi ideology. Foreign workers, many of whom came from Turkey, were attacked. However, by the beginning of the twenty-first century, Germany had regained its position as the dominant economy in Europe. It was a major player on the formation of the European Union and continues to be a dominant presence in that organization.

Ethnic Tensions Surface

Under communism, ethnic tensions in multinational states had been suppressed. With the fall of the Soviet Union, they resurfaced. Czechoslovakia split peacefully into two separate countries, the Czech Republic and Slovakia. Elsewhere, however, ethnic divisions often resulted in open warfare. In the early 1990s, for example, Armenia and neighboring Azerbaijan fought over a small area in Azerbaijan where many Armenians lived. Armenia eventually gained control of the area. In the Balkan peninsula, ethnic conflict ripped apart the country of Yugoslavia. The Chechen people, whose Muslim culture is very different from that of the Russians, have fought for independence from Russia for over 150 years. In 1991, when the Soviet Union collapsed, Russia refused to recognize Chechnya as an independent nation. A bitter war began between the Russian army and Chechen separatists. Russian troops and air attacks destroyed sections of Chechnya, while Chechen terrorists conducted deadly attacks on civilians across Russia, including in Moscow theaters. Although Chechnya continues to declare its independence and carry out terrorist attacks, Moscow refuses to recognize the area as an independent nation.

Summary

Cold War tensions eased in the 1970s, though they flared with the Soviet invasion of Afghanistan. During the 1980s, worker unrest in Poland led to the toppling of the communist government. During the same period, the reforms brought by Mikhail Gorbachev helped bring about the end of the Soviet Union and the collapse of communism throughout Eastern Europe. Germany reunited, and new nations were born. Sometimes these changes led to continuing ethnic conflict. Russia also experienced difficulty in its transition from a command economy to a market economy.

Political and Economic Change in Latin America

Section Overview

Many of the nations of Latin America have experienced periods of unrest since 1945. In Argentina, a series of military regimes and repressive governments finally gave way to democracy in the last decades of the century. Guatemala endured a long civil war and has struggled to rebuild its society. Cuba underwent a revolution in 1959 that led to a communist dictatorship. In Nicaragua, years of strife between communists and counterrevolutionary groups gave way in the 1990s to a democratically elected government. Mexico has experienced more stability but has also had periods of revolt and unrest.

Key Themes and Concepts

As you review this section, take special note of the following key themes and concepts:

Conflict What factors led to continuing conflict in Latin America?

Change What types of political changes occurred in Latin American nations after 1945?

Political Systems What role does democracy play in Latin America today?

Key People and Terms

Key People and Terms

Place each of the key people and terms into these three categories: politics, economics, and cooperation.

As you review this section, be sure you understand the significance of these key people and terms:

Juan Perón

import substitution

dirty war

Mothers of the Plaza de Mayo

indigenous

Sandinistas

contras

Organization of American States

North American Free Trade Agreement

cartels

Sources of Unrest

Latin America is a diverse region with a great variety of peoples and cultures. Geographic barriers have discouraged unity, yet the nations of Latin America share similar problems. After World War II, political and social upheavals threatened stability in Latin America. Many Latin American nations looked to authoritarian leaders to provide solutions.

Argentina

By 1900, Argentina was the richest nation in Latin America. The Great Depression of the 1930s devastated the country, however. A military coup brought Juan Perón to power in 1946.

Juan Perón

Juan Perón was a former army colonel. He appealed to Argentine nationalism by limiting foreign-owned businesses and by promoting **import substitution,** in which local manufacturers produce goods at home to replace imported products.

Juan Perón

Perón gained popularity by boosting wages, strengthening labor unions, and beginning social welfare programs. Perón's government was repressive, however, and his economic policies led to huge debts. In 1955, he lost power in a military coup.

State Terrorism

Another military government took control in 1976. This government began a program of state terrorism against leftist guerrilla groups. In what came to be known as the **dirty war,** the military arrested, tortured, and killed thousands of people. As many as 20,000 people simply "disappeared."

Many of those who vanished were young people. Their mothers, organized as the **Mothers of the Plaza de Mayo,** marched silently every week in Buenos Aires for over thirty years, holding pictures of their missing children. Their protests demanding an accounting by the government of the whereabouts of their children won worldwide attention.

Democracy Restored

In 1983, Argentina held elections. Voters returned a democratic government to power. The new government worked to control the military and restore human rights. However, economic problems persisted. In 2001, an economic crisis rocked the nation. The hardships led to widespread protests and continued instability.

Guatemala

As you have learned, Cold War tensions caused the United States to view certain political movements in Latin America as threats. In Guatemala, the United States helped to overthrow Jacobo Arbenz in 1954, after his land reform program threatened United States business activities in Guatemala. Landowners and the military regained power.

A civil war soon began. The **indigenous** Indians, those who had lived there for thousands of years and who were in the majority, suffered. As many as 30,000 were killed in the fighting. Rebels finally laid down their arms in 1996, when a peace accord was reached. The accord brought hope for increased rights for all citizens of Guatemala, including its Indian population.

Nicaragua

From 1936 to 1979, the Somoza family had governed Nicaragua. The Somozas were repressive but had close ties to the United States because of their anti-communist stance. In 1979, the **Sandinistas,** a group that included both reform-minded nationalists and communists, overthrew the Somoza government.

Note Taking

Reading Skill:
Identify Main Ideas
Make a table. As you read, fill in the main ideas for each Latin American country in Section 7.

Change in Latin America		
Country	Political Change	Economic Change

Preparing for the Regents

• How did individual citizens make a difference in Argentina? What other examples of citizens making a difference can you think of in global history?

Key Themes and Concepts

Power
The United States has often intervened in the politics of Latin America. This intervention has caused resentment among many Latin Americans.

The Sandinistas in Power

The Sandinistas set up a government under the leadership of Daniel Ortega. Many in the government were Socialists or Communists. The new government introduced some reforms and socialized policies. At the same time, it grew closer to Cuba and other communist nations.

The Contras

Identify Central Issues

Why did the United States support the contras in Nicaragua in the 1980s?

In the 1980s, the Sandinistas faced armed opposition from the **contras,** a counterrevolutionary group. Fearing the spread of communism, the United States supported the contras in their fight against the Sandinistas. A civil war followed, leading to many deaths and weakening the Nicaraguan economy.

Other Central American countries helped reach a compromise. In 1990, the Sandinistas handed over power to a freely elected president, Violeta Chamorro. Nicaragua still had to struggle to rebuild its economy, however.

Mexico

Politics in Mexico

Preparing for the Regents

• Briefly explain causes of unrest in Latin America in each of the categories listed below.

Gap between rich and poor:

Social classes:

Population and poverty:

Urban growth:

After the Mexican Revolution, one party, the Institutional Revolutionary Party (PRI), dominated Mexican politics for 71 years. Between 1960 and 2000, there were periods of upheaval.

• In 1968, police and the military brutally suppressed the student protests.

• In 1994, armed Indian Zapatista rebels in the southern state of Chiapas demanded social and economic reforms, but the group's goals were not achieved.

• Many groups called for election reforms. In 2000, the PRI lost Mexico's presidential election to the National Action Party. Then, in 2012, the PRI retook power, but promised not to return to being an authoritarian party.

• In 2006, a nationwide military crackdown on Mexican drug cartels began. Drug lords struck back with daily killings that threaten the stability of Mexico. Drug-related violence continues to be a major issue for Mexico.

Causes of Unrest in Mexico

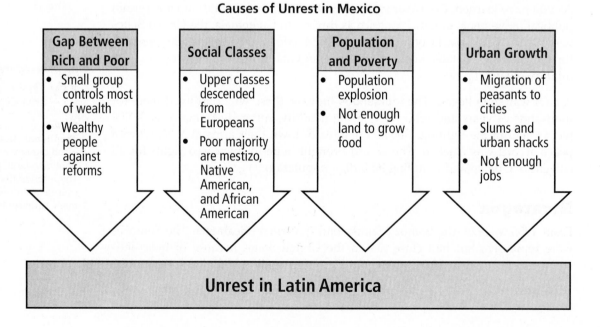

Gap Between Rich and Poor	Social Classes	Population and Poverty	Urban Growth
• Small group controls most of wealth • Wealthy people against reforms	• Upper classes descended from Europeans • Poor majority are mestizo, Native American, and African American	• Population explosion • Not enough land to grow food	• Migration of peasants to cities • Slums and urban shacks • Not enough jobs

Unrest in Latin America

Economic Links With the United States

In the 1950s, the **Organization of American States,** or the OAS, was formed to strengthen democracy, promote human rights, and confront shared problems such as poverty, terrorism, illegal drugs, and corruption. Thirty-five nations in the Western Hemisphere, including Canada and the United States, belong to the organization. The OAS expelled communist Cuba in 1962. Finally, in 2014, relations between Cuba and the United States began to move toward renewed economic and diplomatic relations.

In the 1990s, Mexico, the United States, and Canada signed the **North American Free Trade Agreement,** or NAFTA, a plan to allow free trade among the three nations. Many hoped that it would bring prosperity to Mexico by lowering trade barriers. Some business and investment did go to Mexico, but other manufacturers were hurt by competition from the United States.

Immigration provides another link between Mexico and the United States. Since the 1970s, millions of Mexicans have migrated to the United States, usually in search of better economic opportunities. The money they send back to Mexico is an important part of Mexico's economy.

Panama

In the late 1980s, United States officials suspected that the leader of Panama, Manuel Noriega, was helping criminal gangs called **cartels** smuggle drugs into the United States. United States troops invaded Panama in 1989 and arrested Noriega. Panama experienced greater stability in the 1990s.

The Panama Canal

The Panama Canal was constructed by the United States in the early 1900s. By connecting the Atlantic and Pacific oceans, the canal shortens voyages between the two oceans by thousands of miles. The United States had controlled the canal since it first opened in 1914. Then, in 1977, the United States and Panama signed a treaty designed to gradually turn over control of the canal to Panama. Panama assumed complete control of the Panama Canal on January 1, 2000.

The Role of Religion

The Catholic Church has played a major role in Latin American society since colonial times. Traditionally a conservative force, many church leaders became proponents of social reform during the late 1900s. Outspoken priests and nuns, for example, struggled against the oppressive military regimes that ruled many Latin American countries in the 1970s and 1980s. At the same time, evangelical Protestant groups have gained a growing following with the poor throughout Latin America.

Summary

Many of the nations of Latin America faced political unrest in the last decades of the twentieth century. Argentina suffered under military rule. Guatemala and Nicaragua experienced civil wars. Cuba was a Cold War battleground. Mexico also experienced unrest. Today, however, democracy is taking hold in the region. Still, some problems remain, including the presence and activity of international drug traffickers.

Draw Conclusions

- Why did the OAS expel Cuba in 1962?

Key Themes and Concepts

Political Systems
In Latin America and elsewhere around the world, drug trafficking causes political upheaval as well as social problems. Drug cartels put pressure on national governments and commit violent acts to gain their ends.

Vocabulary Builder

proponent—(pruh POH nunt) *n.* someone who supports something or persuades people to do something

Vocabulary Builder

evangelical—(ee van JEL ih kul) *adj.* evangelical Christians believe that they should persuade as many people as possible to become Christians

Multiple Choice

Directions: Review the Test-Taking Strategies section of this book. Then answer the following questions, drawn from actual Regents examinations. For each statement or question, choose the *number* of the word or expression that, of those given, best completes the statement or answers the question.

Base your answer to question 1 on the map below and on your knowledge of social studies.

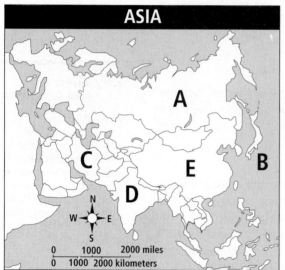

Source: *American History: Historical Outline Map Book With Lesson Ideas*, Prentice Hall, 1998 (adapted)

1   Which letter identifies the nation most closely associated with Mohandas Gandhi?

   (1) A

   (2) B

   (3) C

   (4) D

2   Border conflicts between India and Pakistan have most often occurred in

   (1) Kashmir

   (2) East Timor

   (3) Tibet

   (4) Afghanistan

3   The formation of the North Atlantic Treaty Organization (NATO), the division of Germany into East Germany and West Germany, and the Korean War were immediate reactions to

   (1) Japanese military aggression in the 1930s

   (2) the rise of German nationalism after World War I

   (3) ethnic conflict and civil war in Africa in the 1950s

   (4) communist expansion after World War II

4   Which headline concerning the Soviet Union refers to a Cold War event?

   (1) **"Yeltsin Assumes Power"**

   (2) **"Trotsky Forms Red Army"**

   (3) **"Germany Invades Soviet Union"**

   (4) **"Warsaw Pact Formed"**

5   "A group of planners makes all economic decisions. The group assigns natural, human, and capital resources to the production of those goods and services it wants. The group decides how to produce them and to whom to distribute them."

This description *best* applies to the

   (1) manorial economy of feudal Europe

   (2) mercantile economy of the 1700s in Europe

   (3) command economy of the Soviet Union

   (4) market economy of the United States

Source: Reprinted by permission of Bob Englehart,
The Hartford Courant

Base your answer to question 6 on the political cartoon above and on your knowledge of social studies.

6   What is the cartoonist saying about the impact of democracy on the Soviet Union?

(1) Democracy covered up hidden problems in the Soviet Union.

(2) Democracy led to the development of the Soviet Union.

 (3) Democracy had no impact on the Soviet Union.

(4) Democracy led to the breakup of the Soviet Union.

7   The main reason the Chinese Communists gained control of mainland China in 1949 was that

(1) they were supported by many warlords and upper-class Chinese

(2) the United States had supported the Chinese Communist party during World War II

(3) Mao was a dynamic leader who had the support of the peasant class

(4) they had the support of the Nationalists and of Japan

8   The Tiananmen Square massacre in China was a reaction to

(1) Deng Xiaoping's plan to revive the Cultural Revolution

(2) demands for greater individual rights and freedom of expression

(3) China's decision to seek Western investors

(4) Britain's decision to return Hong Kong to China

9   Which statement best explains why India was partitioned in 1947?

(1) The British feared a united India.

(2) One region wanted to remain under British control.

(3) Religious differences led to a political division.

(4) Communist supporters wanted a separate state.

10 From the perspective of the North Vietnamese, the war in Vietnam in the 1960s was a battle between

(1) fascism and liberalism

(2) nationalism and imperialism

(3) republicanism and totalitarianism

(4) theocracy and monarchy

11 One similarity shared by the Meiji emperors of Japan, Peter the Great of Russia, and Shah Reza Pahlavi of Iran was that they all supported policies that

(1) increased the power of the aristocracy

(2) introduced new religious beliefs

(3) kept their nations from industrial expansion

(4) westernized their nations

12 A nation governed by Islamic fundamentalists would be most likely to

(1) allow many different interpretations of the Quran

(2) adopt the values and culture of the West

(3) emphasize the traditional beliefs and values of the religion

(4) promote active participation of women in government

13 "Cuba today is a puppet still dancing after the puppet master's death."

In this 1993 newspaper quotation, which nation is referred to as the "puppet master"?

(1) Haiti

(2) Soviet Union

(3) Spain

(4) United States

14 One similarity between Lenin's New Economic Policy and Gorbachev's policy of perestroika is that both policies

(1) supported collectivization of farms in the Soviet Union

(2) allowed some aspects of capitalism in the Soviet economy

(3) increased citizen participation in the Soviet government

(4) strengthened governmental control over the Soviet republics

15 "Take sides. Neutrality helps the oppressor, never the victim. Silence encourages the tormentor, never the tormented."

—*Elie Wiesel, Holocaust survivor*

According to this quotation, which situation would have most concerned Elie Wiesel?

(1) formation of the United Nations

(2) the world's initial reaction to ethnic cleansing in Bosnia

(3) Arab reaction to the creation of Israel in 1948

(4) dismantling of the Berlin Wall

In developing your answer, be sure to keep these general definitions in mind:

   (a) <u>explain</u> means "to make plain or clear; render understandable or intelligible"
   (b) <u>describe</u> means "to illustrate something in words or tell about it"
   (c) <u>evaluate</u> means "to judge or determine the significance, worth, or quality of"

Directions: Write a well-organized essay that includes an introduction, several paragraphs addressing the task below, and a conclusion.

Theme: Interdependence

> Throughout global history, the world has been growing more and more interdependent. This process has accelerated in the twenty-first century.

Task:

> - Explain what is meant by *global interdependence*.
> - Describe two examples of interdependence.
> - Evaluate the positive and negative effects of the examples of interdependence you have chosen on individuals and nations.

  You may discuss any nations or regions and any example of interdependence from your study of global history and geography. Some suggestions you may wish to consider are economic interdependence, political interdependence, military interdependence, cultural interdependence, and technological interdependence.

You are not limited to these suggestions.
Do not use the United States in your answer.

Guidelines:

  In your essay, be sure to
  - Develop all aspects of the task
  - Support the theme with relevant facts, examples, and details
  - Use a logical and clear plan of organization, including an introduction and a conclusion that are beyond a simple restatement of the theme

Document-Based Question

This question is based on the accompanying documents. The question is designed to test your ability to work with historical documents. Some of the documents have been edited for the purposes of the question. As you analyze the documents, take into account the source of each document and any point of view that may be presented in the document.

Historical Context:

After World War II, the world became divided by the Cold War. The Cold War policies of both superpowers affected nations around the world.

Task: Using the information from the documents and your knowledge of global history, answer the questions that follow each document in Part A. Your answers to the questions will help you write the Part B essay in which you will be asked to

> • Describe and evaluate the ways in which the Cold War affected nations around the world

In developing your answers, be sure to keep this general definition in mind:

> <u>discuss</u> means "to make observations about something using facts, reasoning, and argument; to present in some detail.

Part A: Short Answer

Directions: Analyze the documents and answer the question or questions that follow each document, using the space provided.

Document #1

> *A shadow has fallen upon the scenes so lately lighted by the Allied victories. . . . From Stettin in the Baltic to Trieste in the Adriatic, an iron curtain has descended across the Continent. Warsaw, Berlin, Prague, Vienna, Budapest, Belgrade, Bucharest, and Sofia, all these famous cities and populations around them lie in what I must call the Soviet sphere and all are subject to a very high and, in many cases, increasing measure of control from Moscow.*
>
> **—Winston Churchill, from a speech given in Fulton, Missouri, 1946**

1. What image does Churchill use to talk about the division of Europe? Why is this image appropriate?

_____

_____

Document-Based Question

Document #2

Europe After World War II

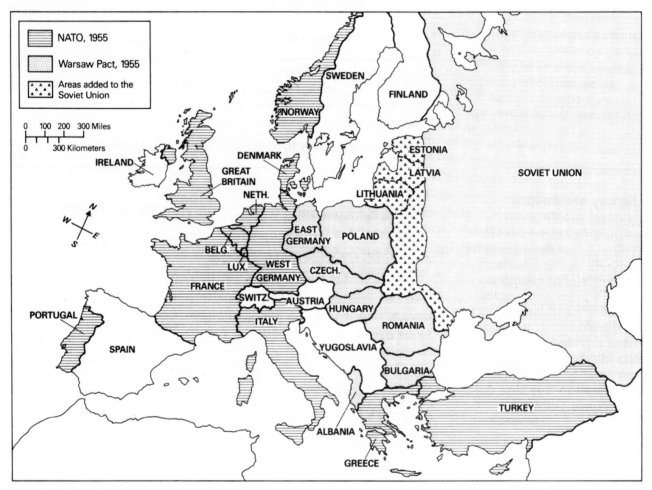

2. Name two European countries that were allies of the Soviet Union during the Cold War.

_____

_____

3. Name two European countries that were allies of the United States during the Cold War.

_____

_____

Document #3

The divisive force is international communism. . . . It strives to break the ties that unite the free. And it strives to capture—to exploit [use selfishly] for its own greater power—all forces of change in the world, especially the needs of the hungry and hopes of the oppressed. . . . To counter the threat of those who seek to rule by force, we must pay the costs of our own needed military strength, and help to build the security of others.

—Dwight D. Eisenhower, Second Inaugural Address, January 21, 1957

4. What did President Eisenhower promise to do in response to international communism? Why?

_____

_____

Document #4

United States Intervention in Latin America

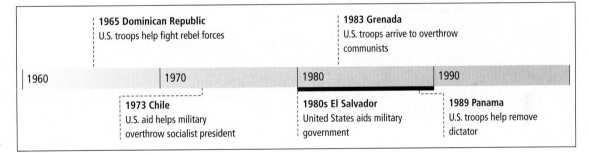

1965 Dominican Republic
U.S. troops help fight rebel forces

1983 Grenada
U.S. troops arrive to overthrow communists

1960   1970   1980   1990

1973 Chile
U.S. aid helps military overthrow socialist president

1980s El Salvador
United States aids military government

1989 Panama
U.S. troops help remove dictator

5. Explain how one event on this timeline was an effect of the Cold War.

_____

_____

Part B

Essay

Directions: Write a well-organized essay that includes an introduction, several paragraphs, and a conclusion. Use evidence from *at least **three*** documents in your essay. Support your response with relevant facts, examples, and details. Include additional outside information.

Historical Context:

After World War II, the world became divided by the Cold War. The Cold War policies of both superpowers affected nations around the world.

Task:

Using information from the documents and your knowledge of United States history, write an essay in which you:

> • Describe and evaluate several effects of Cold War policies on nations around the world

Guidelines:

In your essay, be sure to
- Develop all aspects of the task
- Incorporate information from *at least **three*** of the documents
- Incorporate relevant outside information
- Support the theme with relevant facts, examples, and details
- Use a logical and clear plan of organization, including an introduction and a conclusion that are beyond a restatement of the theme

The World Today:
Connections and Interactions
(1980–The Present)

Section 1: **Economic Trends**

Section 2: **Conflicts and Peace Efforts**

Section 3: **Social Patterns and Political Change**

Section 4: **Science and Technology**

Section 5: **The Environment**

Unit Overview

The years since 1980 have been a time of great change. Developing nations face challenges as they strive to progress economically despite rising populations and huge debt. There have been many regional conflicts, and international terrorism remains a great threat to world order. The United Nations addresses many of these issues.

As many nations look to the future, they struggle with the tension between modernization and traditional values. Changes come at a quick pace. Advances in computer technology, space exploration, and medicine have changed the way people live. Still, many problems remain, especially in the global environment. Whatever may be the long-term solutions to these problems, they depend on nations working together toward common goals.

Using Good Social Studies Practices

Context

Some of the many themes developed in Unit 4 are:

economic systems
interdependence
movement of people and goods
change

urbanization
science and technology
environment
power

Choose one of the themes listed above. As you review Unit 4, identify changes to the world that have occurred on the theme you have chosen. Focus on major developments and key turning points having to do with your theme. For each of those, identify the context in which it occurred.

UNIT 4
Section
1

Economic Trends

The Big Idea

In the final decades of the 1900s, global economic trends included the following:

- The world became divided economically between the relatively prosperous North and the developing South.

- Developing countries struggled to overcome problems such as poor geographical conditions, economic dependence, failed economic policies, and political unrest.

- Economic interdependence linked national economies around the world.

Key People and Terms

What do all of the key terms have in common? Explain.

Preparing for the Regents

- What are the differences between the prosperous countries of the global North and the developing countries of the global South?

Section Overview

There is an economic division between the more prosperous countries of the global North and the developing countries of the global South. Developing countries face many obstacles, such as rapid population growth, debt, and unrest. In today's world, however, the global North and South are interdependent. Cooperation among nations can lead to improvements for all. However, problems in one area of the world may have powerful effects on the global economy.

Key Themes and Concepts

As you review this section, take special note of the following key themes and concepts:

Places and Regions What global economic divisions exist today?

Economic Systems Why have some developing nations failed to achieve their goals?

Interdependence How has economic interdependence affected the world?

Key Terms

As you review this section, be sure you understand the significance of these key terms:

post-colonialism
emerging economies
trade deficit
refugees
globalization
World Trade Organization

International Monetary Fund
multinational corporations
Association of Southeast
  Asian Nations
North American Free Trade
  Association

North and South: Differences in Development

There is an economic division between the relatively rich nations of the global North and the relatively poor nations of the global South.

Wealthy Nations

The global North includes the nations of Western Europe and North America, along with Japan and Australia. These nations are highly industrialized and have high literacy rates and high standards of living.

Poor Nations

The global South includes developing economies in Asia, Africa, and Latin America. Many were once colonies and remain poor and industrially undeveloped, experiencing the problems of **post-colonialism.** Policies established during the age of imperialism continued after 1945. As a result, some nations have remained economically dependent on their former colonial rulers.

Nations with Emerging Economies

Countries with **emerging economies** are developing businesses and industries at a fast rate. Some were poor nations that are now richer, although they may have many poor and unemployed people.

Obstacles to Development

Geography

Several factors have hindered progress in developing countries. Uncertain rainfall, lack of fertile land, and geographic barriers are problems faced by many nations. Some countries are small and have few resources.

Natural disasters such as earthquakes and hurricanes can be devastating to struggling economies. For example, in September 1998, Hurricane Mitch struck Central America. Flooding and mudslides led to deaths and left many survivors homeless. It takes years to rebuild damaged economies.

Population Growth

High birthrates and better medical care in many nations of the global South have led to overpopulation. Also, specific religious and cultural beliefs, economic need, and a lack of reproductive information have led to increasing populations in certain countries. Overpopulation can cause a lack of food, as well as inadequate housing, jobs, and medical care. By 2012, the world's population reached the milestone of over 7 billion people. Many developing nations have tried to reduce population growth, but only China is willing to force people to limit family size. Even there, the policy is being challenged because of culture, an aging population, and a growing economy.

Key Themes and Concepts

Geography
Natural disasters, such as the 2015 earthquake in Tibet, have a profound impact on the economy of a country. Industrial growth, tourism, and infrastructure are impacted and these countries, especially those with limited economies, need foreign aid until they recover.

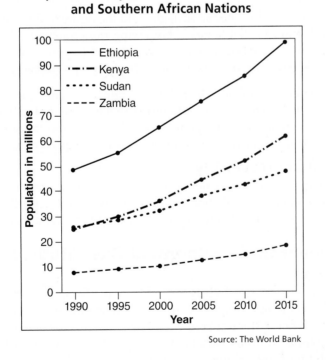

Population Projections for Selected Eastern and Southern African Nations

Population in millions (y-axis, 0–100); Year (x-axis, 1990–2015)

Legend: Ethiopia, Kenya, Sudan, Zambia

Source: The World Bank

Population Projections for Selected East and Southern African Nations
Because of population growth there may not be enough resources to meet people's basic needs. This can hurt efforts to improve living conditions.

Preparing for the Regents

• Practice your graph-reading skills by describing the general trend that this graph shows.

Past Economic Policies

After achieving independence, many new nations imposed socialist economic policies. Over time, socialism hindered economic growth. Beginning in the 1980s, some nations introduced market economies.

Economic Dependence, Trade Deficits, and Debt

For centuries, most people in Africa, Asia, and Latin America worked in agriculture. Today, much of the labor force in the global South is still engaged in agriculture and depends on developed nations for manufactured goods and technology while exporting cash crops or natural resources. These factors have led to trade deficits. A **trade deficit** is a situation in which a nation imports more than it exports.

Labor in Agriculture

	Agricultural workers	Nonagricultural workers	
Africa	65%	35%	Total labor force: 224,920,000
Asia*	62%	38%	Total labor force: 1,352,368,000
Latin America	28%	72%	Total labor force: 147,254,000
Australia and Oceania	18%	82%	Total labor force: 11,549,000
Europe†	12%	88%	Total labor force: 373,188,000
United States and Canada	3%	97%	Total labor force: 132,495,000

*Excluding Asian part of the former Soviet Union.
†Including Asian part of the former Soviet Union.

Source: FAO Production Yearbook, 1987, Food and Agricultural Organization of the United States. Figures are for 1987, prior to the breakup of the former Soviet Union.

Preparing for the Regents

• What evidence does this graph give of the economic division between the global North and the global South? How does having a large percentage of the population in agriculture affect a nation's economic progress?

Over the years, economic struggles and the desire to diversify their economies and develop quickly led to heavy borrowing from foreign banks. In the 1980s, interest rates rose, the global economy slowed, and resources were used to pay for high interest payments on these loans. This lowered productivity and increased debt.

Economic patterns are changing. Emerging economies, such as China, India, and Brazil, built factories and continue to develop advanced technology industries. They buy raw materials from poorer countries and build factories in some of the least developed countries. Poor countries no longer depend only on the richest countries.

Political Instability

In many developing nations, money is spent on warfare rather than on education or health care. People become **refugees** when they flee their homelands to seek safety elsewhere. This results in economic instability and a labor shortage.

Economic Development Case Studies

Congo

When, in 1960, Congo became independent from Belgium, it began years of civil war. People from some 200 different ethnic groups competed for power. In 1965, army general Mobutu Sese Seko seized control, renamed the country Zaire, and established a brutal dictatorship. Although it has vast natural resources, under Mobutu, Zaire's economy was ruined. Corrupt officials robbed the treasury. Roads were left to decay. Agriculture declined and mines closed. Finally in 1997, rebel forces removed Mobutu and the nation was renamed the Democratic Republic of Congo (DRC). Violence between rival groups continued and the DRC's government was tightly controlled. Millions have died because of violence between rebel groups, militias, ethnic groups, and the government. The International

Cycle of Poverty

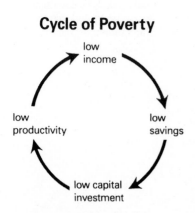

low income → low savings → low capital investment → low productivity → low income

Criminal Court convicted a powerful militia leader of using child soldiers. Today, DRC is among the poorest and hungriest countries in the world. Its violence and chaos has kept outside sources from investing in the country, and it is one of the least economically developed countries in the world.

China

In the past 30 years, political changes have allowed China to become a global economic superpower. It has the world's second-largest economy, but because it has so many poor people, its per capita income is not high. This economic inequality has caused unrest in both urban and rural regions. China's mixed economy focused on creating goods for export, and it is now the world's top exporter while the Chinese government is also encouraging the production and consumption of domestic goods, from steel to clothes. Multinational companies are successfully expanding into a growing Chinese market and Chinese companies are purchasing Western companies, partly because Chinese consumers trust Western products more than Chinese-made goods. Many Chinese consumers want Western products, like designer clothing and fast-food fried chicken. Internally, China has had problems with corruption, bribery, labor shortages, and labor strikes caused by poor working conditions. By 2015, China was experiencing a slowing of its economic growth. This was partly due to an industrial overcapacity of goods (such as ships and steel) and issues such as inefficiency and a heavy investment in manufacturing. Some Chinese companies have moved their operations to countries with lower wages, such as Cambodia. China is a major provider of aid to poor countries, especially in Southeast Asia and Africa.

Preparing for the Regents

Trace the political and economic changes in China that have led to the globalization of its economy.

Brazil

Military rulers controlled Brazil from the 1960s through the 1980s. Under their rule, Brazil experienced a boom due to foreign investment, exploitation of the Amazon rain forest, and reduction of oil imports (because they built hydroelectric plants). While the middle and upper classes of Brazil enjoyed prosperity, many workers remained in extreme poverty.

In the 1990s, democracy replaced military rule. Brazil faced serious economic troubles, but after 2000, its economy stabilized and it became an important emerging economic power. New reforms encouraged investment, economic growth, and judicial reform as well as reducing the deforestation of the Amazon. Brazil remains an economically divided society with high unemployment and a politically and economically unhappy middle class. After 2011, the worldwide recession began to affect Brazil's economy. This combined with low wages, concerns about public safety, and extensive government corruption has only intensified its economic problems. Increased problems flared as Brazil prepared for the 2014 World Cup and the 2016 Olympics. Protesters demonstrated against the eviction of people living in slums to make way for new sports venues and transportation systems. Continuing issues with unhealthy sanitation and unfinished projects continue to plague Brazil's cities and its political upheaval has limited the government's effectiveness in dealing with its problems.

Key Themes and Concepts

Environment and Society
Brazil is a good example of the relationship that can occur between economic development and environmental protection. Developing the Amazon region helps Brazil economically but it might have a negative global impact environmentally. Other countries want Brazil to balance economic and environmental concerns.

Economic Interdependence

Globalization

Although people and countries in different parts of the world have been linked by trade for centuries, a global economy, the integration of national economies into an international economy, began to develop in the late 1800s. Advances in science and technology in the late twentieth century accelerated the pace of this **globalization.** Today, raw materials flow from one country to factories in another,

Note Taking

Reading Skill:
Understand Effects
Make a table. As you read, list benefits and challenges of a global economy. Add boxes as needed.

A Global Economy	
Benefits	Challenges

Preparing for the Regents

Explain the global relationships depicted in the cartoon and the consequences of these events on the global market.

Key Themes and Concepts

Global Connections
Russia and the United States have become major exporters of oil. This has changed global economic and political dynamics and the power of OPEC, and affected oil prices.

while the finished products are sold in both emerging and rich nations. In the garment industry, this flow is often hidden, or indirect, so foreign companies and consumers have no idea of the conditions under which the product is made. Factories in Bangladesh have low wages, poor working conditions, as well as minimal and poorly enforced regulations. Its limited infrastructure, such as erratic electricity and transportation, has led to production delays and dangerous working conditions. These conditions allow lower cost, higher production, and better profit margins. Recent industrial accidents have caused some companies to rethink using the cheapest suppliers, many of which are based in countries such as Bangladesh. They are putting pressure on governments and factories to improve working conditions, especially worker safety.

Dependence on Oil Oil prices affect economies everywhere. When oil supplies are high, prices fall, and many economies benefit. However, when oil supplies are limited, prices rise, and many economies suffer. Inflation caused by high oil prices has contributed to debt crises in developing nations, while falling oil prices can damage economies that depend heavily on oil sales. Regional issues, such as civil unrest in Iraq, Libya, and Syria, have disrupted oil production. A European embargo on Iranian oil was imposed to limit its nuclear program, and influenced oil production. Regional crises such as these raise the worldwide price of oil. In recent years, China has become the world's biggest oil importer. It purchases 50 percent of Iran's oil, partly because it is less concerned with price than Western oil companies that are profit-driven. It is presently trying to invest in oil fields rather than just purchase oil. This will increase its role in globalization.

New methods of oil extraction, such as hydraulic fracturing, have affected the global oil market. In mid-2014, the price of oil dropped until by December it was half what it had been in June. The drop hurt the economies of countries, such as Russia and Saudi Arabia, that depend on oil sales. Oil importing countries benefited from the lower prices. Some governments, such as India's, responded with positive economic actions.

Global Banking and Financial Markets Finances can immediately flow across international boundaries via the Internet and whatever happens in one country has an effect on other places. Many Western banks make loans to developing nations to be used for modernization. As interest rates rose in the 1980s, the world economy slowed and poor nations struggled to repay their loans. The **International Monetary Fund** (IMF) and **World Bank** stepped in to work out agreements that included lower interest rates, new payment schedules, and a move to free market policies. Because financial markets are also linked, changes in stock prices in one part of the world can affect other markets. So when many Asian countries faced economic problems in the 1990s, stock markets all over the world were shaken. Microfinancing has made smaller loans available to clients who do not meet the qualifications for a loan from a larger institution. Low-income individuals without collateral are able to obtain small loans to improve or start their often home-based businesses.

Multinational Corporations Businesses that operate in many countries are called multinational corporations. Many of these companies are based in the global North or in countries with emerging economies. They make investments in the global South and bring new employment opportunities, infrastructure improvements, and technology. Sometimes they compete with and may ruin local industries. Because these corporations are foreign-owned, they respond to the economies in their home country while creating social and economic changes in the countries in which they are operating.

Regional and Global Cooperation
Nations have created regional trade agreements with each other, like the successful European Union. Each works on increasing economic cooperation and free trade to spur economic development and reduce poverty.

EU The European Union began in the early 1950s by integrating its six members' coal and steel industries. It has grown until it it now a political as well as economic organization with an elected parliament and 28 member states. it carries out economic policies, including trade regulations and has its own currency (the euro). It also conducts peacekeeping missions.

ASEAN The **Association of Southeast Asian Nations** (ASEAN), formed in 1967, is made up of ten Southeast Asian countries. It coordinates policies among members in trade and agriculture and focuses on peace and stability in the region.

NAFTA In 1994, the **North American Free Trade Agreement** (NAFTA) was set up to eliminate tariffs and trade restrictions among Canada, the United States, and Mexico.

World Trade Organization The World Trade Organization (WTO) was established in 1995 as a global organization to deal with the rules of trade between nations. It has 153 members and negotiates agreements, handles trade disputes, and provides assistance to developing countries. At many WTO meetings major protests are held by those who believe its policies favor rich nations and harm the environment.

G-20 The Group of 20 (G-20) are the finance ministers and central bank governors of 20 countries—both industrial countries, such as Germany and the United States, and countries with emerging economies, such as China, India, and Brazil. They first met in 1999 and focus on international economic development, including ways to avoid and/or control financial crises.

International Drug Trade
The United States declared a "war on drugs" in the 1980s and pressured many Latin American, African, and Asian countries to move against drug cartels. There has been some international cooperation to eliminate illegal drug trade. Sometimes the United States has linked this cooperation to trade or aid agreements.

Preparing for the Regents

- How has economic decision making become more global as national economies around the world become increasingly interdependent?

- How has that interdependence been tested by the global financial crisis?

Global Financial Crisis

In 2007, a financial crisis that began in the United States spread to many global financial institutions. Some were multinational companies, while others were affected because of investments or loans. In countries all over the world, unemployment rose as major financial institutions in the global North went out of business or had to seek governmental support. By 2008, trade had contracted because people in developed countries could afford fewer goods.

The G-20 and IMF worked with countries—developed, emerging, and poor—to create programs to limit the effects of the crisis. Although most countries were affected, by early 2010, emerging economies, such as China and India, were recovering. However, the decrease in demand for their goods and services in the United States and Europe meant a slow export market and long-term recovery.

In the more industrialized countries, like the United States and England, economic improvement moved much more slowly. Many developed countries cut government spending, as did private companies. Unemployment rose. The countries with the most critical financial problems, like Iceland and Greece, were not poor countries, but had large debts and deficits that grew worse during this crisis. The European Union helped its financially troubled members: Greece, Ireland, Portugal, Cyprus, and Spain. These countries made severe changes to their economies to get loans from the EU and international financial institutions. Ireland's economy is finally expanding, while others, like Greece and Cyprus, are recovering more slowly and continue to struggle with restrictions, taxes, high unemployment, and protests.

Preparing for the Regents

- Use this graph to identify which EU members are the slowest to recover from the recent global economic crisis.

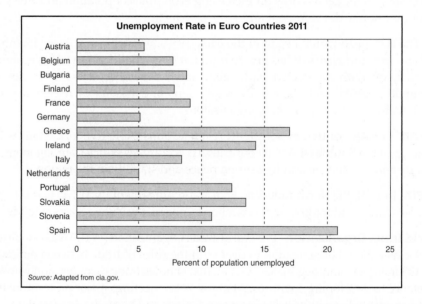

Source: Adapted from cia.gov.

Europe's slow recovery has had a global impact. Less developed countries, like those in Eastern Europe and the Caribbean, worry that European companies will pull out of their country or go bankrupt. This would harm their fragile economies.

Changing Globalization

Vocabulary Builder

austerity—(au STAIR it e) *n.* harsh or severe economy

In 2012, European governments that seemed to be recovering, like the Netherlands, elected new leaders because austerity budgets were very unpopular. This crisis has showed that the world economic picture is rebalancing. Trade between emerging economies and poor nations improved more quickly than trade with more developed countries. China overtook Germany as the biggest exporter in the world, although Chinese manufacturing has slowed. The countries that had been the biggest markets are not recovering quickly, so exporting countries have had to develop new markets. The continued fragile global economic recovery has been up-and-down for both high income and low income countries. Because of slow economic growth in most countries, including those that saw an initial spurt, multinational corporations are not making the profits they expected. The slow recovery, political issues, heavy fines, and taxes concern these corporations.

By 2016, many economists felt globalization was changing, but were cautious about predicting what future globalization would look like. They know there has been a steady drop in global trade and international investment. Some predictions include more trade barriers being enacted.

A recent and intense reaction to globalization came in 2016 when the British voted to leave the European Union ("Brexit"). This vote reflected a growing concern over the loss of nationalism and of increasing globalization and its effect on people in England. The Brexit vote was close, especially in England, but voters wanted more control over their borders and economy. When Britain leaves the EU, the way it deals with complex economic and immigration problems will change. It will eliminate the EU laws and trade agreements it now follows and create new ones of their own.

Not long after Brexit, the United States elected Donald Trump as its president. He also spoke about changing global trade agreements and emphasized nationalistic ideas like "America First." Since then, however, two EU countries have held elections. In both The Netherlands and France, candidates who supported the EU won over nationalists that wanted less globalization and to leave the EU.

At the same time increased "digital globalization" is occurring. More multinational companies manage themselves digitally rather than open offices in many different countries. Consumers shop online buying goods from all over the world. Finally, social media, such as Facebook, is creating a new international conversation.

Summary

There is a great economic gulf between the global North and the global South, but this has been changing in recent years. Developing countries struggle with obstacles that hinder their growth. Meanwhile, the global interdependence in banking and trade helped spread a global economic crisis. While globalization has resulted in benefits to almost all nations, there is considerable debate about whether developed nations have benefited at the expense of poorer countries. In recent years, emerging economics are playing a more important role in the global economy and in helping the developing economies of poor nations. The financial crisis forced many developed countries to reassess their economies, their debts, and their loans to other countries as they struggle to recover from deep debt and high unemployment.

Key Themes and Concepts

Movement of People and Goods
After Brexit is complete, it is likely people and goods will not move as freely between Britain and EU countries as they do now. This not only includes imports and exports, but also money, workers, tourists, and immigrants.

Preparing for the Regents

- Describe three policies that could help developing countries achieve greater economic prosperity.

Conflicts and Peace Efforts

As conflicts continue in various parts of the world, so do efforts to restore and maintain peace.

- Terrorism is a threat to global peace.

- Religious and ethnic conflicts continue to cause unrest.

- Conflicts have occurred in a number of post–Cold War hot spots.

- The United Nations attempts to maintain peace and promote social and economic well-being.

Section Overview

In the last several decades, some nations and organizations have continued to use violence and terrorism to achieve political goals. In its peacekeeping role, the United Nations (UN) has intervened in many conflicts, with varying degrees of success. The UN also promotes human rights and helps with disaster relief throughout the world. In many areas of the world, ethnic and religious differences have sparked conflict. Even with the end of the Cold War superpower struggles, various areas of the world have become hot spots.

Key Themes and Concepts

As you review this section, take special note of the following key themes and concepts:

Power For what purposes have various groups used terrorist tactics?

Belief Systems How have religious and ethnic differences contributed to instability and conflict?

Interdependence How does global interdependence cause local conflicts to have potentially global consequences?

Conflict How has the United Nations tried to promote world peace and security?

Key People and Terms

Place each of the key people and terms into one of these categories: belief system or conflict/cooperation.

Key People and Terms

As you review this section, be sure you understand the significance of these key people and terms:

terrorism	Saddam Hussein
al Qaeda	Kurds
Irish Republican Army	Darfur
ethnic cleansing	Universal Declaration of
Dalai Lama	Human Rights

Key Themes and Concepts

Interdependence
The United Nations is an international governing body. It is composed of more than 170 nations that cooperate to promote world peace and security.

The United Nations

Structure of the United Nations

The United Nations, or UN, was established in 1945. Its goals are to promote global peace and security as well as economic and social well-being. The UN has the power, through the votes of its more than 170 member nations, to take action against forces that threaten world peace.

The UN has five main bodies. The UN also has a number of specialized agencies. Some, such as the Food and Agriculture Organization (FAO) and the International Fund for Agricultural Development (IFAD), fight hunger through agricultural improvement. Others, such as the United Nations Children's Fund (UNICEF) and the World Health Organization (WHO), are concerned with health issues.

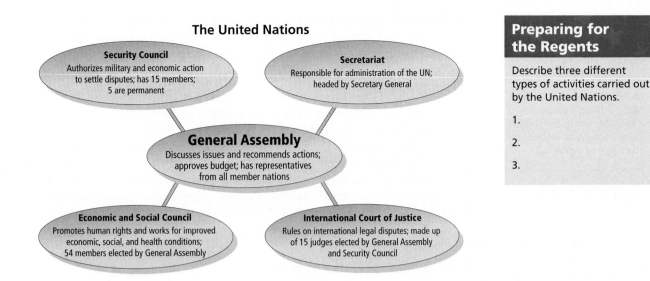

The United Nations

Security Council
Authorizes military and economic action to settle disputes; has 15 members; 5 are permanent

Secretariat
Responsible for administration of the UN; headed by Secretary General

General Assembly
Discusses issues and recommends actions; approves budget; has representatives from all member nations

Economic and Social Council
Promotes human rights and works for improved economic, social, and health conditions; 54 members elected by General Assembly

International Court of Justice
Rules on international legal disputes; made up of 15 judges elected by General Assembly and Security Council

Social and Economic Programs

The UN also promotes social and economic programs.

Human Rights In 1948, the United Nations adopted the **Universal Declaration of Human Rights.** This document states that human beings are born free and equal with dignity and rights. It goes on to list basic rights and freedoms that all people should have. Nevertheless, human rights are in peril in many parts of the world, including China and the Balkans.

Disaster Relief The United Nations has responded over the years to famine and other disasters.

- In the late 1960s, the UN helped save millions in Biafra from starvation during the Nigerian civil war.
- In the early 1990s, UN forces brought food to Somalians who were caught up in a civil war.
- The UN provides relief and recovery aid after natural disasters, such as the 2004 tsunami in Indonesia and Pakistan's 2005 earthquake and 2011 floods.
- In 2010, Haiti, already the poorest country in the Western Hemisphere, had a devastating earthquake. Millions in aid was provided by the UN and individual countries for relief, reforms, and rebuilding. In 2011, the UN observers monitored a presidential election in which Haiti's voters elected a singer, Michel Martelly, president, in the hopes that a political outsider would guide the country into recovery and a prosperous future. However, in 2012, over 600,000 still lived in displacement camps, agriculture had not recovered, and a cholera epidemic raged on.

Peacekeeping Operations

The United Nations has taken action to maintain peace or restore order in places all over the world. The UN has had mixed success in keeping the peace. Although no worldwide conflicts have occurred, the sovereignty of individual nations often makes it difficult for the UN to enforce its wishes. As part of its Department of Political Affairs, the UN also advises and monitors milestone elections, such as in the Democratic Republic of Congo and in Nepal.

Iraq In August 1990, Iraqi troops invaded oil-rich Kuwait. The United Nations voted to impose economic sanctions on Iraq to force the troops to withdraw. When Iraq did not withdraw, the Security Council sent a multinational force that drove Iraq out of Kuwait. More recently, it monitored Iraqi elections.

Haiti From 1957 through 1986, Haiti was ruled by brutal dictators. In 1990, Haiti held free elections. However, Jean-Bertrand Aristide, the victor, was later ousted by a military coup. Several years later, UN forces helped restore Aristide to power and build a functioning democracy in Haiti.

Sudan Sudan has been torn by civil war for most of its 52 years. Its cultural diversity has been a factor in these wars. In 2003, government-supported Arabic militias attacked black villagers and rebel groups in the **Darfur** region. In 2007, forces from the African Union joined UN peacekeepers to try to end the violence. In 2011, South Sudan split away from Sudan, and although tensions eased enough for the countries to resume trade and oil production, the violence in South Sudan's Darfur region has remained intense. Sudan's government refused to cooperate with the UN while the violence here hinders and threatens the UN peacekeepers and humanitarian workers who are working to help Darfur's displaced people.

The Threat of Terrorism

Nature of Terrorism

Terrorism is the deliberate use of unpredictable violence, especially against civilians, to gain revenge or to achieve political goals. Terrorism is often used by groups that do not have their own military power. Terrorists use tactics such as bombings, kidnappings, assassinations, and hijackings. In recent years, new fears about nuclear terrorism, chemical terrorism, and cyberterrorism have developed. Terrorism spreads fear throughout the world. Some terrorist groups raise money by ransoming the people they kidnap. Others raise it using secret donations or credit card fraud.

At first terrorism was local, such as disputes between nationalist groups that both claimed the same homeland (such as the Palestinians and the Israelis) or that claimed the same land (such as both India and Pakistan claiming Kashmir).

Then terrorism became more global with a developed central leadership. Al Qaeda trained terrorists, raised money, and supported conflicts between traditionalist groups and modern Western societies. It encouraged extremist attacks on Western societies.

A newer trend involves local terrorists who are not part of al Qaeda. These independent groups in Syria, Algeria, Kenya, and Nigeria often target civilians in their own countries by attacking hospitals, religious pilgrims, even shopping malls. Although many have religious affiliations, it is often the local issues—religious, political, or cultural—that motivate their actions. These independent groups are harder for the global community to battle than a central network. Some of the terrorist attacks have been in Western countries, such as France and England. Some terrorists are immigrants, but others were born and have lived their whole lives in Europe.

Ethnic and Religious Tensions

Religious beliefs and ethnic loyalties have united groups and sometimes led to the growth of nations. These forces have also divided peoples and led to persecution and violence. In every conflict, each group involved has its own point of view. In many instances, the violence is being renounced for more democratic, political methods of change.

Northern Ireland

Ireland won its independence from Britain in 1922. Britain, however, kept control of the six northern counties, which had a mostly Protestant population. The south was mostly Roman Catholic.

In Northern Ireland, violence increased in the 1970s because of extremists in both the Protestant and Roman Catholic communities. The **Irish Republican Army** (IRA) wanted Ireland to reunite and for British interference to end. They used violence to try and reach this goal. Protestant groups retaliated. Despite many attempts at peace, the violence and divisions continued until 2005, when the IRA ended its call for violence. In 2007, a new power-sharing government for Northern Ireland took control from the British government.

Spain and the Basques

A Basque separatist group had used violence, robbery, and terrorism since the 1950s to try to obtain a separate homeland for the Basques. In October, 2011, they ended their violent methods and vowed to work within Spain's democratic political system.

China and its Minorities

In 1951, the People's Republic of China invaded Tibet. The Chinese promised that Tibet would be an autonomous region of China. China's 1959 military crackdown on Tibetan rebels led to full-scale resistance. The **Dalai Lama,** the spiritual and political leader of Tibet, fled to India. China then began to impose Chinese culture on Tibet by creating land collectives and executing landlords. Protests against the Chinese flared again in 2008. The Chinese government reacted strongly, imposing curfews and strictly limiting access to Tibet. The Dalai Lama, in exile, accused the Chinese of cultural genocide and warned that Tibetan Buddhist culture was facing extinction. More recently, the Chinese government reacted to tensions with the Uyghur minority. These Muslims live in Western China but have conducted terrorist attacks across China. The government held huge show trials. In 2014, tens of thousands of pro-democracy demonstrators protested in Hong Kong. They wanted election reform and less control by the mainland communist government but police ended their protests.

South Asia and Southeast Asia

Ethnic and religious conflicts continue to produce violence on the Indian subcontinent.

- **Muslims, Hindus, and Sikhs** In India, both Muslims and Sikhs believe they are discriminated against by India's Hindu majority.
- **Indonesia** Indonesia's population is mostly Muslim, but in East Timor most people are Catholics. In 1999, East Timor demanded independence, and Indonesia's army responded with such force that less than a month later, international peacekeepers arrived. Despite free elections in 2007, newly independent Timor-Leste remains Asia's poorest country.
- **Sri Lanka** In 1976, the Tamil Tigers, a militant organization based in northern Sri Lanka, began a violent secessionist campaign to create an independent Tamil state. Approximately 80,000 people died by the time they were defeated in 2009.

Key Themes and Concepts

Belief Systems
Religious differences contributed to the political conflict in Northern Ireland. These religious and political conflicts have spilled into the rest of Ireland and into England.

Key Themes and Concepts

Human Rights
China's treatment of minorities and political protesters is not in line with the UN Universal Declaration of Human Rights. This sometimes causes diplomatic problems with other countries, such as the United States.

Ethnic Divisions in Yugoslavia Before 1990

Before 1990, Yugoslavia was made up of six republics, similar to states in the United States. Each republic had a dominant ethnic group, but they also had ethnic minorities. Most people spoke the same language, Serbo-Croatian, but had different religions. Others spoke minority languages.

Preparing for the Regents

• Practice your map skills by explaining how this map supports the idea that diversity led to conflict in the Balkans.

The Balkans

Yugoslavia was a multicultural state created after World War I. Orthodox Christian Serbs, Roman Catholic Croats, Muslim Albanians, and other ethnic groups lived there. Some areas were home to predominately one ethnic group, while several groups shared other regions.

By 1991, several of Yugoslavia's regions had declared independence. Some, like Slovenia, had only brief fighting. In more ethnically mixed areas, tensions flared. In Bosnia and Herzegovina, Serbs practiced **ethnic cleansing,** which is the act of removing or killing people of a certain ethnic group.

Ethnic Divisions in Yugoslavia Before 1990

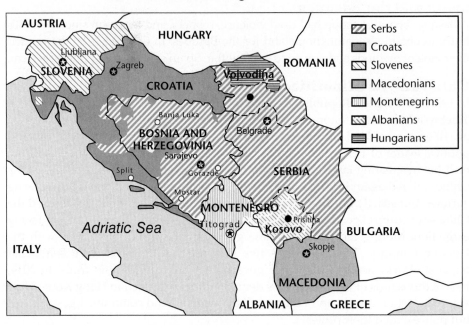

In 1992, **Slobodan Milosevic,** the Serbian leader of the Yugoslavian government, encouraged or ordered brutal campaigns of ethnic cleansing against non-Serbians, such as ethnic Albanians in Kosovo. In order to restore peace, NATO and the UN took military action.

In 2001, Milosevic was arrested and tried for war crimes and genocide by the UN's International Criminal Tribunal, but died before its verdict. After 2003, Yugoslavia changed its name to Serbia and Montenegro. By 2008, both Montenegro and Kosovo had gained their independence.

Copyright © 1994 by Jimmy Margulies, The Record, Hackensack, NJ

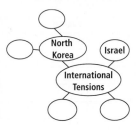
The Kurds

Most Kurds are Sunni Muslims but are not Arabs. Millions of Kurds live in Turkey, Iraq, Iran, Armenia, and Syria. Kurds have experienced harsh treatment and repression, especially in Turkey and Iraq. Since 1920 they have tried to create an independent Kurdish state, with land from all these countries. In 2005, the Kurds became participants in the new Iraqi government. In early 2008, Kurdish Iraq was invaded by the Turkish military in an attempt to stop Kurdish rebel attacks in Turkey. This is one conflict that continues to hinder Turkey's relationship with Iraq and the European Union. The Kurds' relationship with the United States is strong, as the Kurdish fighters are working with the United States military to fight ISIS in Syria and Iraq.

International Hot Spots

Throughout the world, continuing international tensions have the potential to cause local and global violence.

North Korea and South Korea

North Korea, is still ruled by a hard-line communist dictatorship that practices a foreign policy of brinksmanship, and it suffers from isolation and severe economic hardships including recurring famine. South Korea has a strong global economy but North Korea still hopes to unite the two Koreas under its rule and so still spends large sums of money on its military. It has one of the world's largest standing armies, although it is thought to be poorly trained and equipped. In 2006, North Korea became a nuclear power. Despite international warnings, sanctions, and unproductive disarmament talks, North Korea has conducted several more nuclear tests. Over the years, tensions have escalated between North and South Korea due to real or perceived hostile actions and verbal threats. When North Korea's longtime autocratic leader died, his son continued the militaristic government and policies of his father. He has made specific threats against South Korea and the United States, which has led to North Korea's continued political and economic isolation and the world's fear that it will take military, possibly

Note Taking

Reading Skill:
Summarize
Make a concept web. Summarize information about the international tensions described in this section. Add more circles if needed.

Preparing for the Regents

• Describe how isolation from the international economic community affects the people of North Korea.

nuclear, action. Since 2013, both military threats and new talks occurred between the two countries until North Korea once again violated UN agreements by test-firing medium-range missiles. Its actions sometimes affect the relationship between China and the United States. However, some analysts believe China is growing impatient with North Korea's erratic and embarrassing actions.

In 2017, the president of South Korea was impeached and her successor, Moon Jae-in, was elected. He will need to deal with strengthening the economy while making changes to laws affecting South Korea's huge family businesses. He will also have to address the continually fluctuating tensions with North Korea.

Israel and Its Neighbors

In 2005, when cease-fire talks began between Israel and the Palestinians, Israel began withdrawing settlers and soldiers from Gaza and parts of the West Bank. In a 2006 election, Palestinians elected **Hamas**, a party known for both its social services and its hard-line policies toward Israel. Hamas carried out its anti-Israeli policies using terrorists' methods, such as rockets and suicide bombings, to create chaos in Gaza before it assumed control.

To try to end Hamas's attacks, Israel and Egypt closed Gaza's borders. Economic sanctions destroyed the fragile Gaza economy, but a new economy developed using tunnels between Egypt and Gaza. In 2008, Israel launched a devastating attack on Hamas in Gaza. When it ended, much of Gaza was in ruins but Hamas remained in control. It reconciled with the less militant Fatah Party of the Palestinian Liberation Organization (PLO) to form a new joint Palestinian government for both Gaza and the West Bank. More recently individual young Palestinians with personal and financial problems have conducted uncoordinated attacks on Israeli citizens and security forces, especially in Jerusalem.

In 2011, the Palestinians asked the UN to give it full membership. Israel and its allies opposed this move, but in December 2012, the UN voted to give Palestine non-Member Observer State status. In 2015, Pope Francis recognized the Palestinian state.

Preparing for the Regents

Compare and contrast the factors affecting Israeli/Palestinian relations before 2005 with those affecting them more recently.

In recent years, Israel has lost support from its neighbors, such as Turkey. The downfall of President Mubarak of Egypt meant the loss of an ally. Because of the attacks on Gaza, which killed many women and children, Israel lost more international support. The war in Syria, one of Israel's most vocal enemies, leaves Israelis fearful of what will happen no matter who ends up in power. Israel fears a nuclear attack from Iran if its nuclear program is not stopped. Israel's isolation in the world has increased and peace talks have halted.

The Iraq War and its Aftermath

At the end of the Persian Gulf War, the United Nations required that Iraq destroy its nuclear, biological, and chemical weapons as well as its missiles. The UN sent inspection teams to ensure compliance until the late 1990s, when Iraq's leader, **Saddam Hussein,** refused to allow further inspections. In response, the United States and Britain staged air strikes against Iraq.

Saddam Hussein was a Sunni Muslim and his brutal dictatorship favored Sunnis while the majority of Iraqis are Shiite Muslims. These groups disagree on Iraq's culture, degree of westernization, and government.

In 2001, the United States accused Iraq of supporting terrorists, such as al Qaeda, and of hiding weapons of mass destruction. UN inspectors searched for these weapons, but found none. However, the grievances against Saddam Hussein included human rights abuses, such as the use of torture and poison gas against

Note Taking

Reading Skill:
Recognize Sequence
List the important events of the Iraq War. Record them in the order they occurred. Add boxes as needed.

Iraq War	
Date	Event

the Kurds. In March 2003, without UN support, the United States and its coalition forces invaded Iraq. Although the invasion led to a quick defeat of the Iraqi military, a violent insurgency developed against the coalition troops, the new Iraqi government, and workers repairing war damage. Saddam Hussein was captured in December 2003, convicted of crimes against humanity, and hanged.

In 2005, an Iraqi election took place amidst the violence. A new constitution was approved by voters and parliamentary elections were held. Sunnis, Shiites, and Kurds eventually agreed to a new government led by a compromise candidate, Nouri al-Maliki, as prime minister. In 2010, a second election with challenged results, more violence, and new alliances allowed Maliki to continue as prime minister. In 2011, the United States formally ended its military mission in Iraq. Subsequent elections did not bring factions together or provide the change necessary to make Iraq a safer place. Violence, including terrorism and battles sponsored by The Islamic State, combine with political divisions to leave this country torn by war and politics. Terrorist groups, such as those connected to Al Qaeda and the Islamic State, have a powerful presence in Iraq and deep ties to Syrian terrorists. Thousands of Iraqi civilians have died in car bombings and random killings in the unstable situation there.

Source: VIC HARVILLE/Stephens Media Group

Preparing for the Regents

• What political, religious, and social forces led the cartoonist to depict the Iraqi election in this way?

India and Pakistan

The long-standing hostility between India, with its Hindu majority, and Pakistan, with its Muslim majority, continued into the new century. Crises developed over control of Kashmir, a region divided between Pakistan and India; the 2001 Islamic terrorist attack on India's parliament; and the 2008 attacks on Mumbai by Pakistan-based terrorists. These crises raise fears of a nuclear conflict as both India and Pakistan have nuclear weapons. Relations between the two countries have improved and then disintegrated several times.

The Afghanistan War: Afghanistan and Pakistan

Soviet forces invaded Afghanistan in 1979 and supported a communist government there. More than three million Afghans fled, many to Pakistan. Afghan fighters resisted communist rule and finally forced the Soviets to withdraw. In the mid-1990s, the Taliban, a fundamentalist group, imposed an extreme form of Islam on Afghanistan. They also protected the terrorist group al Qaeda, which directed the 9/11 attacks on the United States in 2001.

Key Themes and Concepts

Belief systems
Some conflicts in Pakistan and Afghanistan are caused by differences in belief systems. Others are caused by a clash between modern and traditional values.

Key Themes
and Concepts

Geography
The landscape of the region
contributes to its cultural
diversity and the continuing
isolation of some cultural
groups as well as limited
communications and
suffering due to frequent
natural disasters.

In response to the 9/11 attacks, the United States launched an attack on Afghanistan that drove the Taliban from power. They sought al Qaeda's leaders, including Osama bin Laden. They were unsuccessful until 2011 when the Americans secretly located Osama bin Laden in Pakistan, and killed him. Because they did this without informing the Pakistani government, relations between the countries deteriorated.

In Afghanistan, the new remained weak and inconsistent, partly because of corruption, tribal loyalties, and the resentment of foreign intervention. Afghani's must also deal with a lack of modernization, land mines, thriving poppy fields that supply illegal opium, and a resurgence of the Taliban, al Qaeda and terrorists connected with the Islamic State.

Pakistan shares a mountainous border with Afghanistan. Violence, political problems, and tribal feuds are shared by both countries, and problems often spread back and forth between them. Neither country can control the border, and both countries resent United States' and NATOs military interference. The growing power and competition between terrorists in the region continues to create problems for both countries.

Since 2007, Pakistan's political stability has been shaky. Its former Prime Minister Benazir Bhutto returned from exile, only to be killed. It is suspected her death was planned by a Pakistani tribal leader with al Qaeda's help. The government failed to adequately respond to the devastating 2010 floods that displaced millions of Pakistanis. Aid from Islamic groups, such as the Taliban, and from the United States was necessary to rebuild the country's ruined infrastructure.

Terrorist bombings continue in both Pakistan and Afghanistan, but the goals of groups in these countries differ. In Afghanistan, the Taliban is trying to reassert its control over the government at the same time the Islamic State is terrorizing Afghani citizens in a Sunni against Shiite war. In Pakistan, terrorists focus on soft targets, such as hospitals and playgrounds. Many of these terrorists want to create a separate state in the northwest region of Pakistan. They are not after control of the whole country. Continuing attacks by the American military, especially by drones, on terrorist camps in Afghanistan and Pakistan along with the Pakistani government's reluctance to work against terrorists continues to weaken relations with the United States. Over the years, attacks by both terrorists and Americans have killed many Pakistani civilians, but many in the country depend on support and intervention by the United States.

President Obama changed the United States' military role in the region, several times. The use of unmanned drones has increased, as has the role of Afghani forces. Fewer countries provide military aid while the United States decided not to continue a full military withdrawal as it had planned. Peace talks between the Taliban and Afghan government have not yet lead to any positive outcomes.

Russia and Ukraine

Ukraine, located between Russia and Europe, has strong historic ties to Russia and was a republic in the Soviet Union. Many Ukrainian residents considered themselves more Russian than Ukrainian. Most of these people live in eastern Ukraine and the Crimea. Ukraine leased its Crimean ports to Russia for its Black Sea fleet and gas pipelines run between Russia and Europe across Ukraine.

Key Themes and Concepts

Interdependence
Ukraine's conflict with Russia is causing economic consequences in Europe.

In 2013, Russia objected to a trade agreement between Ukraine and the EU. The agreement was never signed, but protests led to a government crackdown on protestors.

The conflict became more intense, protests more violent, and protestors took over government buildings. When the corrupt, pro-Russian president disappeared, Parliament stripped him of his powers and planned a presidential election. Then, Russia took over Ukraine's Crimean ports. Crimea declared its independence and voted to merge with Russia. Russia, eager to have total control of Crimea, immediately put Russian laws into effect.

The crisis continued to grow and pro-Russian separatists in eastern Ukraine took control of entire towns. Russia moved troops to the Ukraine border and vowed to protect ethnic Russians inside Ukraine. They challenged the Ukrainian military, which was smaller, weaker, and operating with older equipment.

Preparing for the Regents

Analyze how the Ukrainian crisis contains many issues similar to those causing conflict in other parts of the world: control of a region for economic or military advantage; people protesting poor and corrupt governments; economic control by a very rich few; overreliance on major powers; and language and ethnic divisions.

Other countries placed economic and travel sanctions on Russian and Ukrainian officials although EU countries worried that Russia would cut off their supply of natural gas. Ukrainian refugees fled to EU countries, such as Poland. NATO ended cooperative activities with Russia. Ukraine experienced violent protests and military actions. Its government remained corrupt and unsettled. In 2014, a passenger plane carrying 298 people was shot down over eastern Ukraine. Russia and NATO disagree about who fired the missile. A ceasefire was finally agreed upon and has held for several months. Changes to Ukraine's government encouraged its Western supporters, but Russian troops patrol the border and continue to control Crimea.

Sub-Saharan African Terrorism

Many sub-Saharan countries became independent in the 1960s, but their governments have continued to be corrupt, repressive, and unstable. Some countries divided into several or have continual turmoil because of the cultural, economic, or religious differences of their people. Many men from these regions join terrorist organizations because they are unhappy with the political instability, corruption, extremely high unemployment, and increasing problems due to urbanization and climate change. These issues and their local implications are critical factors for many terrorist groups.

In Northern Nigeria, Boko Haram began by wanting to create a region that followed strict Islamic law. Today, it kidnaps children, such as the 276 girls it kidnapped from a school in 2014. Victims like these are forced to become wives, suicide bombers, or to raid villages and kill the inhabitants. Because farmers flee the violence little is growing in the region. Terrorists must kidnap animals and steal grain to eat.

Like in Afghanistan, African terrorist groups like Boko Haram are hard to stop because they are not under the control of one leader. Individuals and local groups have their own methods, goals, and what they will accept to establish peace. The future of this region is troubled and unpredictable.

Efforts to Stop Terrorism

The attacks on New York and Washington, D.C., on September 11, 2001, alarmed government leaders everywhere. The attacks showed how terrorism affects the security and stability of all nations. At the same time, leaders recognized that defeating terrorism will require a lengthy effort. Some nations not accustomed to cooperating are working together, while a few still harbor or support terrorists. After the 2014 to 2016 terrorist attacks in Europe, Western governments realized they had to do more sharing of information. At the same time demonstrators across Europe joined together to show they were against terrorism as well as the loss of personal rights in that battle.

Summary

In many areas of the world, local conflicts threaten to become global struggles. The United Nations has intervened in various conflicts around the world to try to bring peace. It has also worked to promote human rights and bring relief to victims of famine and disaster. Terrorists use various tactics, such as bombings and kidnappings, to achieve their political goals. Terrorist activity creates a climate of fear and can lead to further violence. Ethnic and religious differences have sparked conflict in areas such as Northern Ireland and the Middle East. Terrorist attacks in one part of the world have led to long wars in other parts of the world, affecting neighboring countries and changing governments and alliances.

Social Patterns and Political Change

Section Overview

Near the end of the twentieth century, modernization and industrialization created tensions. In some countries, these events have brought new opportunities to women; in others they have not. Excessive population growth is a problem facing many nations around the world today. Rapid urbanization is also a widespread change. Another trend is migration—people move to seek economic opportunity or political freedom.

Key Themes and Concepts

As you review this section, take special note of the following key themes and concepts:

Change What are the results of tension between tradition and modernization in societies today?

Culture What are the causes of overpopulation?

Urbanization What changes have resulted from the rapid urbanization that occurred in the late twentieth century?

Power How has modernization caused shifts in political power?

Movement of People and Goods How have changing patterns of migration created human rights issues?

Key Terms

As you review this section, be sure you understand the significance of these key terms:

westernization	urbanization	Arab Spring
overpopulation	shantytowns	human trafficking

Modernization and Tradition

In most societies, there is strain between the forces of modernization and those of tradition. This is especially true in non-Western societies. During the age of imperialism, modernization usually meant **westernization,** or the adoption of Western ways. Traditions were often weakened.

Many developing nations today work toward a balance between modernization and tradition. They want to embrace modern technology but preserve traditions and religious beliefs.

Japan

Japanese society has always been deeply traditional. The code of behavior that developed during feudal times gave each individual a very clear place in society. People had strictly defined duties toward each other. Families were patriarchal, or dominated by males. Individuals felt a strong sense of responsibility to their families or to a larger group. Personal desires mattered little. In modern Japan, many of these values survive, but create tensions with modern living.

The
Big Idea

In developing nations today, there are pressures for change.

- Strains between modernization and tradition have emerged.
- Overpopulation continues to be a difficult problem to solve.
- Urban areas have grown rapidly and produced social problems.
- People have migrated for better economic opportunities or more favorable political conditions.

Key People and Terms

For each of the key terms, write a sentence explaining its significance.

Key Themes and Concepts

Culture
Non-Western nations often want modern technology but do not want to lose completely their traditional culture and values.

Role of the Individual In the Japanese workplace, the sense of structure, duty, and individual sacrifice for the group remains strong. Japanese companies have always been based on teamwork. Although much was required of the worker, he or she had secure employment and was guaranteed advancement.

Recent economic difficulties, however, have weakened the Japanese economy and resulted in lost jobs. Devotion to the employer declined. At the same time, younger Japanese are less willing to sacrifice their personal lives for their jobs. Some Japanese are concerned about a weakening work ethic.

The Middle East

Muslim cultures of the Middle East are often traditional and place great importance on kinship ties and patriarchial families. Women are often subordinate to men and are expected to be modest and to remain secluded within their homes. In some conservative countries this includes the wearing of the **chador** in public, a kind of robe that completely covers the body and most of the face. Modernization and movement to cities have created tension regarding these traditions.

Great strains are clearly visible between the forces of westernization and tradition. Some Muslim countries, like Iran, have rejected Western values—though not Western technology. Some Muslims would like to abolish secular political systems and return to Islamic principles as a basis for government, including laws based on the Koran and Sharia.

Cultural strains in Saudi Arabia often stem from when many people moved to cities because of the oil industry. This weakened the traditional extended family structure. Some Saudi religious leaders worry about the influence of Western ideas, the place of women and their education in an Islamic society, and the effects of modern technology such as television and the Internet. Its conservative ruling family remains in control, but many Western ideas have taken hold in many areas. Because of global communications, Saudis are more aware of the freedoms available in other countries.

Urbanization

Urbanization, the movement of people to cities, is one of the most significant forces of social change, especially in the developing world.

Reasons for Urbanization

In developing countries, many people have moved to the cities to find jobs and escape the poverty of rural areas. Cities also offer other attractions, such as better health care, educational opportunities, stores, and modern conveniences.

Identify Effects

What are two effects of recent economic difficulties in Japan?

Vocabulary Builder

kinship—(KIN ship) *n.* a family relationship

Key Themes and Concepts

Change
Industrialization and urbanization are powerful agents of social change in developing nations. Traditional ways are often weakened in large industrial cities.

Percent of Population That Is Urban, 1950–2050

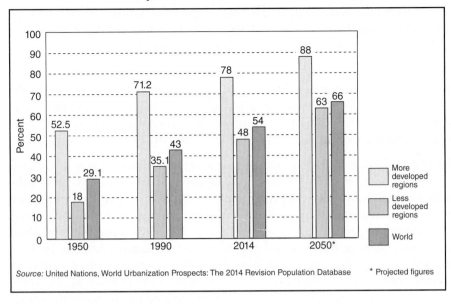

Source: United Nations, World Urbanization Prospects: The 2014 Revision Population Database   * Projected figures

Results of Urbanization

In the developing nations of Africa, South Asia, and Latin America, urbanization has had similar results.

Cultural Change In modern cities, people's traditional values and beliefs are often weakened. The caste system in India, for example, is not as strong in urban areas as in rural areas. Women have more opportunities in cities. Yet, some people feel cut off from their former communities and customs.

Poverty Those people who cannot afford to live in cities often settle nearby in **shantytowns,** areas of makeshift shacks that lack sewer systems, electricity, and other basic services. Their crowded conditions often lead to water pollution and other unhealthy effects. Lagos in Nigeria, Mumbai and Kolkata in India, and Mexico City in Mexico have been unable to cope with the waves of migration from rural areas.

Solving Urban Problems

Developing nations are trying to meet the needs that have resulted from urbanization. They sometimes rely on international relief organizations, such as the UN or the Roman Catholic Missionaries of Charity, founded by Mother Theresa in India. They must:

- Increase opportunities for education and better jobs
- Improve health care and working conditions
- Meet expanded demands on infrastructure: electricity, transportation, sewer and clean water

Human Rights

The global community has taken more notice of human rights abuses since World War II. The UN, various governments, and private nonprofit organizations work to ensure the rights of people all over the world. That hasn't stopped these abuses from happening.

Preparing for the Regents

Describe two problems that have resulted from urbanization in developing nations.

1.

2.

Key Themes and Concepts

Decision Making
Many social institutions, such as the family, religion, and education, change in developing nations in response to new urban problems.

Preparing for the Regents

- How do the background and political views of India's prime minister, Narendra Modi, reflect various urbanization and economic issues in India?

Status of Women		
Issue	What changed/ didn't change?	Where?

Vocabulary Builder

lucrative—(LOOK ruh tiv) *adj.* a job or activity that is lucrative lets you earn a lot of money

Status of Women

Women's status changed greatly in the 1900s in the West. Women gained the right to vote and entered the workforce in large numbers. Some developing countries have also expanded the role of women, while others have limited it.

In Japan, laws imposed after World War II ended some legal privileges given to Japanese males. Women gained many rights, including the right to vote. In the 1970s, they entered the workplace in great numbers. However, traditional views keep women in lower positions than men in the workplace. Few women have moved into higher-level jobs in business or government.

In the Middle East, the status of women varies greatly from country to country. Israel, for example, includes women in all facets of society, even as part of the military forces. Golda Meir was prime minister. The status of women in Muslim countries varies widely. In Turkey, Syria, and Egypt, many urban women gave up some traditional practices. In other countries, especially those with religious governments, such as Iran, women follow more traditional practices. In 2011, traditional Saudi Arabia granted women the right to vote and run for office in municipal elections but women are still unable to get a driver's license. However no matter what rights are granted to women, in some countries governments do not enforce them. The cultural attitudes toward women often remain traditional and sometimes repressive and abusive.

In most African and Southwest Asian nations, women won the right to vote when the countries gained independence, yet their social status often remains a subservient one. In rural areas, women traditionally work both at home and in the fields beside men. As men migrate to the cities to find work, women are left with more responsibilities. At the same time, women who go to the urban areas for jobs are both finding more freedom and are being attacked by men with traditional attitudes. In some societies, men who publicly gang rape, hang, or kidnap women are not seen as having committed a punishable crime. As these incidents become international news, international outrage grows and countries such as India and Pakistan are taking action.

Human Trafficking

One of the fastest-growing human rights issues in the world today is human trafficking. This is the recruiting and transporting of people for the purposes of slavery, forced labor, and servitude. Women are particularly at risk from sex trafficking. Criminals exploit the lack of opportunities these women have by promising them good jobs or opportunities to get an education. Then the victims are forced to become prostitutes. Thousands of children from Asia, Africa, and South America are sold into the global sex trade every year. Often they are kidnapped or orphaned, but sometimes they are actually sold by their own families to pay off debts or gain income. Other times they may be deceived about the prospects of training and a better life for their children. In West Africa, some trafficked children have lost one or both parents to the African AIDS crisis. Thousands of male (and sometimes female) children have been forced to be child soldiers. Trafficking is a fairly lucrative industry. In some areas, such as Russia, Eastern Europe, Hong Kong, Japan, and Colombia, trafficking is controlled by large criminal organizations.

Political Prisoners

Countries all over the world (developed, developing, and struggling) have been accused of human rights abuses in their treatment of political prisoners. Some prisoners were arrested for participating in protests. Others were accused of more serious crimes, like treason, even though they may only have joined an opposition party. In countries where the government tightly controls the media, such as in China and North Korea people do not have much freedom of speech. Once in prison, many of these people live in horrible conditions or solitary confinement, are used as forced labor, or undergo many hours of torturous questioning.

Arab Spring

Arab Spring is the period that began in Tunisia in December 2010, when a 26 year-old, college-educated street vendor set himself on fire to show his frustration with the government and police. This uprising's call for democratic changes spread across much of the Middle East via social media and the Internet.

- **Tunisia** This westernized North African country had a repressive government. Tunisian protests were photographed with cell phone cameras and sent around the world via the Internet. The protests spread quickly and the president fled the country. In October, 2011, Tunisia held its first free elections and elected a moderate Islamic party to run the country. Continuing tensions between ultraconservative Islamists and liberals have led to violent protests, a government crackdown on protestors, and a government promise for moderation. In 2014, after three years, the president lifted a "state of emergency" order.

- **Egypt** Social media played an important part in the revolution in Egypt, where more people use the Internet than in other Arab countries. Egyptians discussed their dissatisfaction with President Mubarak's government, and by 2011 videos and tweets calling for protest went viral. A Cairo protest was organized using Facebook®, Twitter®, and other social media, and spread quickly to other parts of the country. Within weeks, President Mubarak had resigned and the military had taken control of the government. This inspired people in other Middle Eastern countries to take action. In Egypt, demonstrations continued because many Egyptians feared the military would not relinquish power to elected officials. In 2012, Egyptians installed their first democratically elected parliament in 60 years, including many from the Muslim Brotherhood and ultraconservative Islamic parties. Mohamed Morsi of the Muslim Brotherhood was elected president. A year of popular protests centered on Egypt's poor economic conditions and political conflicts. These led to the Egyptian military forcing Morsi and the elected parliament out of office and making the Muslim Brotherhood illegal. The military arrested, tried, and convicted thousands of protesters, especially liberals and Islamists. A newly elected government is trying to control Egypt's economic and political instability.

- **Libya** Colonial Muammar Qaddafi led Libya for 40 years, the region's longest rule. Then, in February 2011, protestors held a "Day of Rage" against his brutal regime. Qaddafi's violent reaction against protestors included the use of artillery, helicopter gunships, and antiaircraft missile launchers. A civil war erupted with rebels setting up a transitional government that won the support of the UN and many Western countries. When Qaddafi ignored the UN's call for an end to the violence against civilians, the Western alliance began bombing. They continued until Qaddafi fled and the transitional government took control. A few months later, a cell phone video went viral showing a humbled Qaddafi in the streets just before his death. But in 2016, rival governments, Islamic State terrorists, and battles within the city continued to plague the country. A UN-backed unity government has attempted to take control of the chaotic situation.

- **Yemen** Yemen, the poorest country in the Arab world, still has a strong traditional tribal culture. It was unified in 1990 but a violent struggle to create a separate South Yemen has created unrest. In 2011, new clashes, inspired by the

Preparing for the Regents

Compare and contrast the causes and events of Arab Spring in three different countries.

Vocabulary Builder

to go <u>viral</u>—(VAHY ruhl) *adj.* to spread an image or video very rapidly on the Internet or by email

<u>secularist</u>—(SEK yoo lahr ist) *n.* someone who believes religion should not be part of government

Preparing for the Regents

- How do the events of Arab Spring show that modern technology is changing the culture in Middle Eastern countries?

Note Taking

Reading Skill:
Identify Supporting Details
List three ways social media helped create the events of Arab Spring.

events of Arab Spring, forced the resignation of the president of 33 years. Although deep divisions remain, many discussions are taking place between all sides. Since the 1990s, a branch of Al Qaeda in southern Yemen has been tied to terrorist attacks around the world. Yemen is working with the United States to combat the Al Qaeda threat and to train new government forces.

Country	Unique Elements to Arab Spring
Tunisia	• First uprising • Elected moderate Islamic government
Egypt	• Influential country, so uprising inspired others • Protests planned using Internet and social media • Competition for power between Islamists, secularists, and military
Libya	• Use of heavy military weapons against protestors led to bombing by Western countries • Leader Colonel Muammar Qaddafi killed by rebels
Syria	• Religious division between the majority of Syrians and those in power • Russia supports the government • Violence against demonstrators and towns where demonstrations were held • Refugees fleeing country and military shelling refugee camps in other countries • Becoming isolated from neighbors
Yemen	• Poorest Arab country • Division between north and south • South Yemen is home to a branch of Al Qaeda

Adapted from cia.gov

The events of Arab Spring touched other countries in the Middle East, as well. In some, divisions were exposed, refugees drained already shaky economies, or new political partnerships were formed. Some countries are becoming more isolated from their Arab neighbors and their traditional trade partners in the West. Arab Spring also revealed how much the world is changing due to modern communications technology.

Syria

Syria's civil war began as an incident during Arab Spring in March 2011. It quickly turned violent when the repressive government responded to demonstrations and rebels with tanks, massacres, and chemical weapons. Syria's religious divide adds a unique dimension. The government and well-armed military are controlled by Alawite Muslims, who comprise only about 12 percent of the country's population. The opposition is a fragmented group that includes various Islamic conservatives, mostly members of Syria's Sunni majority. Some countries have recognized the opposition, but it is so splintered, its members cannot agree on a course of action against the government and its forces. The government forces are being supported and supplied by Russia, Iran, and Hezbollah (a powerful Lebanese Shiite military and political party). The UN has not been able to initiate lasting ceasefires or peace talks but the Syrian government finally did agree to turn over its chemical weapons to the UN for destruction. At least most people thought so, until 2016 when the Syrian government used chemical weapons once again. Tensions between Syria and its neighbors, Israel and Turkey, are very high.

Key Themes and Concepts

Power
The Islamic State in Iraq and Syria (ISIS) is also called the Islamic State (IS) because its government is based only on Islamic law. It treats those who do not agree with them or who work against them with increasing violence and cruelty. Its power comes from the strength of its followers' beliefs and the fear it creates in anyone else.

Heavy bombing of the opposition forces by the Russians to support government troops and Russian insistence that the government remain in power has made the civil war an international issue.

Preparing for the Regents

Explain how the Syrian Civil War has changed since it began. Include how foreign support has affected the war.

The Islamic State and Terrorism

One opposition group in Syria, the Islamic State, has had many names including Islamic State in Iraq and Syria (ISIS). It broke away from al Qaeda because it was so violent and rigid. ISIS declared its own Islamic state incorporating parts of both Syria and Iraq but it has spread terrorism internationally. Its extreme tactics are often used against Westerners, Shiites, and those of religions other than Islam. But their suicide bombings often target places where people gather and so kill without discrimination. Because its members are Sunni, they have support from Sunnis in many countries. However, Shiite governments and their Western allies, are joining forces to stop ISIS. Religion, rigid and competing traditional attitudes, and westernization are mixing in new ways in response to these latest threats.

By 2017, both sides of the Syrian Civil War were taking back land controlled by the Islamic State. However, as they regained territory, thousands of civilians fled, were arrested, or died. Bombing by the Russians, Syrians, and the United States has destroyed cities and killed thousands. Civilians are caught between the three sides that are vying for control of each region.

The Islamic State has trained many terrorists who come to them from across the world. Their training camps in North Africa and Syria are targets for Western bombings. Terrorist acts in Africa, Libya, France, Belgium, and the United States have been caused by individuals or groups trained by the Islamic State, but not planned by a central organization. This makes them harder to investigate and prevent.

Patterns of Global Migration

Migration has grown due to economics, politics, and conflicts. There are always economic migrants, but a huge flood of migrants is arriving in Europe after fleeing war-torn and terrorized countries, like Mali, Afghanistan, Syria, and Iraq. Not since World War II has Europe had this many immigration and refugee issues.

Key Themes and Concepts

Movement of People
Ethnic tensions are often made worse by the migration of culturally different people into a region. This happens in the most developed countries and in places where diverse traditional cultures clash.

Preparing for the Regents

Identify the causes and effects of the changing migration patterns shown in this graph.

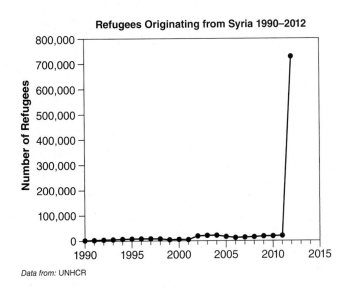

Refugees Originating from Syria 1990–2012

Data from: UNHCR

This huge wave of political and economic refugees and immigrants is surging toward Europe to escape the violence. They walk overland through the Balkans or pay human traffickers huge amounts to smuggle them across the Mediterranean into Greece or Italy. Thousands die when boats, loaded with many more people than they can safely hold, sink. Many end up in refugee camps, but most want to move on and resettle in Germany, France, or Sweden.

Europeans help the immigrants with food, housing, and jobs, but some resent them. Some countries, like Hungary, have closed their borders. Others put a limit on how many people they will accept for resettlement. Many Europeans fear that trained terrorists will arrive among the starving women and children. Others fear the social, cultural, and economic changes that occur with the immigrants. These migration and immigration issues and fears are influencing domestic politics in Europe and the United States. Similar tensions are occurring in Southeast Asia and North America.

Summary

As nations in the developing world have modernized, tensions between modern and traditional ways of living and thinking have emerged. Dissatisfaction with the ruling political system has created violence and change. Women have gained new rights and roles in some nations, but they have been kept in traditional roles in others. Throughout the developing world, there has been an increased use of technology including the media. This has spread political and economic ideas faster than repressive governments can control them. Although urbanization has created more opportunities for some individuals, cities find it difficult to provide basic services for a quickly increasing population. People migrate to seek better economic opportunities and to try to escape violence and political repression. These migrations produce their own tension and violence.

Preparing for the Regents

- To what extent are current migrations similar to earlier migrations? How are they different?

Science and Technology

Section Overview

In the last half of the twentieth century, science and technology have brought great changes. These changes are continuing today. The Green Revolution increased the food supply in developing countries. Computers and advances in telecommunications have brought an explosion of information and, with it, a greater need for education. Technology has allowed exploration of space. Medical breakthroughs have brought better health and longer life.

Key Themes and Concepts

As you review this section, take special note of the following key themes and concepts:

Science and Technology How did science and technology change life in the last half of the twentieth century?

Change What social and economic changes are being produced by the Computer Revolution?

Interdependence In what ways is the world more interdependent than ever before?

Key Terms

As you review this section, be sure you understand the significance of these key terms:

Green Revolution	Information	genetic engineering
Computer Revolution	Revolution	clone
Internet	literacy	AIDS

The Green Revolution

Increasing the Food Supply

Throughout the 1900s, scientists applied technology in a number of ways to increase food production.

- **Irrigation** Farmers installed pumps to bring water from far below the surface of the earth and used other irrigation systems to distribute water.
- **Machinery** Farmers used machines, especially those powered by gasoline and diesel fuel, to increase yields from their land.
- **Fertilizer and Pesticides** Farmers enriched their soil with fertilizers and eliminated insect pests with pesticides.
- **New Varieties of Grains and Livestock** Scientists developed new, hardier grains and bred livestock that produced more meat or milk.

In the 1960s, farmers in developing countries applied some of these methods to increase their production of wheat and rice. Their efforts were so successful that the result was called the Green Revolution. In some countries, such as India and Indonesia, the Green Revolution doubled food output.

The Big Idea

Science and technology have brought great change as:

- new agricultural methods increase the food supply.
- people are able to obtain, process, and transmit information more quickly than ever before.
- nations are exploring space.
- medical breakthroughs are improving the quality of life.

Key People and Terms

Place each of the key terms into one of these categories: technology or medicine.

Preparing for the Regents

- What were the benefits and limitations of the Green Revolution?

Key Themes and Concepts

Science and Technology
The benefits of technology are not enjoyed equally by the global North and the global South. Because technology is expensive, wealthier nations have an added advantage over poorer ones.

Note Taking

Reading Skill:
Categorize
Make a chart. List at least two advances in science and technology for each area.

Advances in Science and Technology	
Food Production	• •
Information Age	• •
Space Age	• •
Medicine	• •

Preparing for the Regents

- List three social, economic, or political changes to a traditional culture caused by modern technology.

Limits of the Green Revolution

The Green Revolution increased the food supply, but it did not solve the problems of world hunger and poverty. In some regions, population is still growing faster than food production. Also, technology has limitations. A region has to have enough water to start with to support new irrigation techniques. Also, irrigation systems, chemical fertilizers, and pesticides cost money that developing nations of the global South do not have. Poorer farmers usually cannot afford these innovations, and some have been forced off their land. Recently scientists have developed genetically modified food as another way to combat world hunger. Critics of this technology claim that malnutrition and hunger are often the result of politics that prevent food from reaching hungry people rather than lack of food. They say such foods are too expensive and that long-term effects of eating such foods are unknown.

The Information Age

The Computer Revolution

Probably the most revolutionary development since the mid-1900s is the computer. The first computers were enormous machines that filled a large room and worked slowly. After the invention of the silicon chip, computers were miniaturized. Computers have allowed people to obtain, process, and distribute information very quickly. Businesses today depend on computers for their accounting, word processing, ordering, and many other systems. This increase in the use of computers is often called the Computer Revolution. Today, access is more often on mobile devices, such as tablets and cell phones. New ways of providing access to the Internet for those who do not have it has become a priority.

The Information Revolution

The rapid spread of information, which began in the 1950s and increases with each passing year, is sometimes referred to as the **Information Revolution.** In the 1990s, the Internet began as a growing computer network that linked individuals, governments, and businesses all over the world. At first, people linked to the Internet through the telephone. Later, they connected by cable or with wireless devices, such as cell phones.

People use the Internet to communicate and do business more rapidly than ever before. The move to wireless and satellite technology has made the Internet available to people who previously were not able to be "connected."

At the same time access became easier, greater amounts of information became available. Facts, ideas, and opinions are openly discussed on websites, in emails, and on social media sites, such as Facebook®. Shopping, researching, gaming, and sharing are common activities. E-readers and tablets offer books that had been previously unavailable.

This access to information has had unexpected results. In 2010, many U.S. military and diplomatic files were published on the Internet by WikiLeaks. Disputes over the arrest or asylum of the WikiLeaks founder has created an international incident involving Great Britain, Ecuador, Sweden, and the United States. In 2009, many Iranians protested the results of their presidential election. Information and images from their protests and the government's violent response were sent all over the world via Internet-based sites such as Twitter® and YouTube®. Iranian authorities tried to limit Internet access, but the postings continued and soon contained ways to use social media to organize and take action. These events were duplicated during Arab Spring, as the protestors in one country learned about protests in other countries from the Internet and emails, and then organized their own demonstrations, often using Facebook and Twitter. Like Iran, most governments tried to control Internet access, but failed as protests continued and governments fell.

More recently, unforeseen consequences have developed in the globalization of the Internet. Hackers sent ransomware all over the world. They held computer files hostage until the owners paid a ransom. Also, hackers, probably from Russia, were accused of working to influence elections in the United States and several European countries.

Daily Life

New technology is affecting many parts of our daily life. Besides easy access to the Internet, wireless communications allow safer driving and even self-drive cars.

3D printing is developing quickly. It will allow goods to be made closer to the consumer, changing manufacturing. It will also allow for much more customization of goods. It may revolutionize manufacturing, the global economy, and even some aspects of health care.

Literacy and Education

The Information Revolution has had a great impact on both education and the job market in the global North. In these nations, there has been a gradual decline in the number of jobs in industry and agriculture. New jobs are often based on information and communications services. Such jobs require more education and new types of learning, especially about technology.

Gains continue to be made throughout the world in **literacy,** the ability to read and write. Developing countries have recognized that economic and social progress depends in part on having a literate population. For this reason, most nations of the world provide—and, in fact, require—education through at least age 14. Some emerging economies, such as China and India, have encouraged technology-based businesses. Factories in China build computers and cell phones. Businesses in India provide technological support to technology users in more developed countries.

Vocabulary Builder

ransomware—(RAN suhm) *n.* a computer program that is sent to other computers and then locks their files and holds them captive until money is paid

hacker—(HAK ur) *n.* a person who is able to break into others' computer systems without permission

Preparing for the Regents

• Why is education so important to progress in today's world?

Summarize

Write a summary statement about the benefits and limits of new technology.

New Technology: Benefits and Limits

Technology	Benefits (+)	Limits (−)
The Computer and Information Revolutions	• Creates new jobs • Links people, businesses, and nations • Makes more information available	• Threatens some jobs • Available only to those who can afford equipment • Widens gap between those with power and those without
Medical breakthroughs	• Prevents illnesses • Wipes out diseases • Increases life span	• Available only to nations and people who can afford them • Presents new problems of quality of life and care of the aged
Revolution in agriculture (The Green Revolution)	• Increases food production • Develops new food products	• May succeed only where rainfall is regular • Requires costly chemicals • High cost may force out small farmers

The Space Age

Space Exploration

The space age began in the late 1950s with a space race between the United States and the Soviet Union. In recent years the United States and Russia have cooperated on joint space ventures. At the permanent International Space Station scientific experiments are done by astronauts from many countries who stay in space longer and longer. Humans have walked on the moon; space probes have sent back huge amounts of information from Mars and other planets. The United States' space shuttle program ended in 2011, but private companies and countries (such as China, India, and Japan) have established successful space programs.

Satellites

A satellite is an object that is launched into orbit around the Earth, usually for observation or telecommunications purposes. Satellites can be used to:

- map and forecast weather
- navigate in ships and aircraft
- monitor changes in the natural environment
- aid in rapid worldwide communications

Satellites are used to transmit television and telephone signals globally. Signals are transmitted from one point on Earth to the satellite. The satellite transmits the signals to another point on Earth. This technology allows rapid reporting of events happening anywhere in the world.

Medical Technology

Since 1945, medical science has achieved amazing successes. Throughout the world, people are living longer, infant mortality rates are lower, and people can enjoy a better quality of life.

Important Advances

- **Antibiotics** Scientists have developed antibiotics to treat diseases.
- **Vaccines** Vaccines have wiped out diseases such as smallpox and prevented the spread of many other diseases. New vaccines are being researched and used.
- **Transplants** Surgeons developed and gradually improved procedures for the transplanting of organs to save lives.
- **Laser Surgery** Lasers, devices that make use of concentrated beams of light, have made surgery safer.
- **New Treatments** New ways to treat deadly problems, such as strokes, are being taught to doctors and hospitals. Sometimes these involve new machines or new medicines. Other times they involve new diagnostic procedures to correctly treat a patient.
- **New Medications** New medicines are being used to cure or slow the spread of many diseases and incurable ailments. Computers often help to design them.
- **New Diagnostic Procedures** New ways have been invented to identify what is wrong with someone use genes, blood, and other bodily samples.
- **New Medical Devices** New technological devices are being designed for people who have lost limbs or need help with some bodily function.

Difficult Challenges

- **Genetic Engineering** The process of genetic engineering, which involves changing the chemical codes carried by living things, holds promise for creating new drugs and curing disease. In 1997, the first **clone,** or exact genetic replica of an organism, was announced. Genetic engineering is controversial, however, because it has raised questions about how far science should go to change or create life.

- **New Epidemics** Challenges to medicine have arisen in recent decades. After the 1980s, the disease called **AIDS** (acquired immunodeficiency syndrome) resulted in millions of deaths. Scientists continue to search for a cure for it. Other epidemics include the pneumonic and bubonic plagues in southern India in 1994. Avian influenza (bird flu) spread from birds to humans across the world. Since the virus mutates easily, new outbreaks occur, as in China in 2013. In 2009, a flu virus created a pandemic by spreading throughout the world. Procedures to deal with a pandemic were tested. By mid-2010, over 18,000 people were known to have died from this flu. This pandemic revealed problems: rich countries with a surplus of vaccine, and poor countries were without the necessary vaccine. A cholera epidemic in Haiti was the largest outbreak in the world, with hundreds of thousands sick and over 7,000 dead from the disease. A vaccine exists, but did not reach the people who needed it. The 2014 Ebola epidemic affected several countries in West Africa. The interconnectedness of modern life was highlighted when people outside these countries were also diagnosed with Ebola. They had been in the African countries or were healthcare workers and carried the disease with them to other countries. New methods for identifying and fighting an epidemic were in place, but these did not stop the disease before it caused many deaths and affected both international travel and health care in distant countries such as the United States.

- **Drug-Resistant Microbes** The widespread use of antibiotics has allowed some types of microbes to become resistant to drugs. Certain diseases that the medical community thought were under control, such as tuberculosis, are becoming a threat again.

- **Destruction of Tropical Rain Forests** The world's tropical rain forests are the source of many medicinal plants. As these forests are being destroyed, scientists worry that valuable drugs in use today, as well as new ones that might have been discovered later, will be lost.

Summary

Better food production, an explosion in information and communication, the exploration of space, and medical breakthroughs have changed the world. In many ways, science and technology have benefited people's lives. Many problems, however, remain to be solved.

Note Taking

Reading Skill:
Summarize
Make a concept web. Complete it with information about the challenges of medical technology. Add more circles if needed.

Challenges of Medical Technology

The Environment

The
Big
Idea

Today, the world faces many important environmental issues and concerns. These include:

- pollution.
- deforestation.
- endangered species.
- desertification.
- nuclear safety.

Key People and Terms

What do four of the key terms have in common? Explain.

Preparing for the Regents

Describe the possible causes and impacts of the following environmental problems.

Acid rain:

Depletion of the ozone layer:

Global warming:

Section Overview

Many global environmental issues arose in the twentieth century. Pollution of water, land, and air threatens the health of all living things. Forests are being destroyed, species are disappearing, and deserts are growing. The safety of nuclear power plants and of nuclear waste disposal methods are additional environmental concerns.

Key Themes and Concepts

As you review this section, take special note of the following key themes and concepts:

Environment and Society What environmental problems exist today?

Interdependence How do these issues affect people globally?

Decision Making How are nations working together to make decisions that will solve environmental problems?

Key Terms

As you review this section, be sure you understand the significance of these key terms:

pollution	ozone layer	deforestation
acid rain	greenhouse effect	desertification
fossil fuels		

Pollution and Climate Change

Pollution is the contamination of the environment, including air, water, and soil. Pollution is harmful to humans as well as to plants and other animal life. It takes many forms. Factories and automobiles release gases and soot into the air. These substances can cause respiratory disease. They can even block sunlight, causing plants to grow more slowly. Water can become polluted by human wastes, fertilizers, pesticides, and toxic chemicals. These substances may lead to the development of cancers or even cause death. For this reason, many nations have set standards for both air and water quality.

In many developing countries, such as China and India, the rush to create a strong economy overrides pollution concerns. The impact of rapid industrialization and the accompanying urban growth often create a pollution crisis. Beijing and other cities in China are experiencing air pollution that is a thick, fog-like pollution. Thousands are dying from related respiratory diseases, plants are stunted, and tourism is suffering. The winds are blowing the pollution across the Pacific Ocean and it is affecting the western United States.

Air Pollution and Acid Rain

Acid rain occurs when rain falls through air that is polluted by the burning of fossil fuels. **Fossil fuels** include coal, oil, and natural gas. Factories, automobiles, and other sources release these chemicals. Acid rain damages forests, lakes, and farmland. Because of winds, air pollution in one part of the world can cause acid rain in another. International agreements have been signed to reduce emissions of the substances that cause acid rain.

Depletion of the Ozone Layer

Some scientists are concerned about depletion of the ozone layer, a layer of gases high in the atmosphere that protects the Earth from the dangerous ultraviolet rays of the sun. This layer is becoming thinner, perhaps because of the use of chlorofluorocarbons (CFCs) and other chemical pollutants. Depletion of the ozone layer could expose people to more solar radiation and result in increased skin cancer and eye disease. Ultraviolet rays might also damage crops and marine life. Many developed countries have agreed to eliminate production and use of CFCs and other harmful substances. In 2002, a scientific organization found that these limitations were helping reduce harmful pollutants.

Climate Change and Global Warming

Scientists are also concerned about a gradual rise in global temperatures. Since 1998, the world has experienced many of the warmest years on record. Many places around the world had their hottest temperatures ever measured. Abnormal cold was found in other places, such as Europe. Many scientists believe that this phenomenon is caused by the **greenhouse effect,** in which warm air becomes trapped in the lower atmosphere by CO_2, or carbon dioxide. The percentage of CO_2 in the air has been rapidly rising. Possible causes are the use of CFCs, the burning of fossil fuels, and the destruction of forests. This overall warming and related extreme weather events affect agriculture and cause coastal flooding as polar icecaps melt. In 2010, the arctic sea-ice was at the lowest level on record.

Climate change seems to be causing extreme events that affect people: destructive floods in Pakistan, Thailand, and Australia; droughts in the Amazon and Africa; and heat waves and record cold and snowfalls in Europe and Russia. Not only do these events kill people, but they destroy their ability to supply their basic needs. Rebuilding is often slow, especially in poor nations or those at war.

Since 1997, at UN meetings on global warming, attendees agreed to set limits on emissions that are thought to contribute to climate change. Those that emit the most, the United States and China, have not kept to limits. At the 2015 Climate Change Conference, almost 200 countries agreed to cooperate to limit climate change, preserve forests, and work to hold down unnecessary temperature increases.

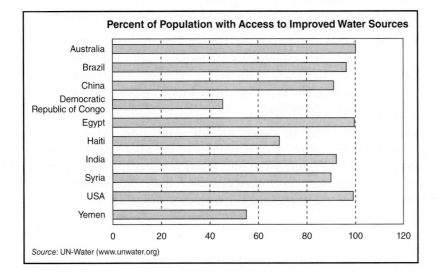

Percent of Population with Access to Improved Water Sources

Source: UN-Water (www.unwater.org)

Scarcity of Clean Water

Approximately one billion people worldwide lack access to clean water, many because of population growth, pollution, and climate change. In developing countries, the lack of clean water is linked to diseases such as malaria. Where nations share lakes and rivers, such as in Israel and Jordan, disputes over pollution or water supplies could lead to war. The deadly cholera epidemic in Haiti that began in 2010 was traced directly to a river polluted with raw sewage. Private industry and organizations such as the United Nations are developing clean water technologies, improving water quality, and ensuring people's access to clean water.

ⓒ

**Vocabulary
Builder**

erosion—(ee ROH zhun)
n. the process by which
something is gradually
reduced or destroyed

Deforestation

Deforestation is the destruction of forests, especially tropical rain forests. Deforestation is usually caused by development as nations harvest lumber or clear land to raise crops, graze cattle, or build homes. Some estimate that the world is losing more than 50 million acres of tropical forest each year. Brazil, India, and Indonesia are the nations where forests are disappearing at the highest rate.

Effects of Deforestation

The effects of deforestation include changes in local weather patterns, a buildup of carbon dioxide in the atmosphere (which may lead to the greenhouse effect), soil erosion, and extinction of certain plants and animals.

Global Solutions

Many of the world's great forests are in developing nations. These nations need the income that would come from using deforested land for agriculture. Those who want to save the forests say that the economic needs of developing nations must be balanced against needs of the global population. Many nations debated these and other environmental problems at the 1992 UN-sponsored Earth Summit in Rio de Janeiro, Brazil. In 2008, the Brazilian government announced a new policy to reduce the rate of the deforestation of its rainforest.

**Key Themes
and Concepts**

Needs and Wants
The economic progress
of some developing
countries conflicts with
protecting the environment.
Sometimes international
pressure and economic
support are used to help a
developing country protect
its environment and still
continue to develop a
strong economy.

Desertification
Causes and Effects

Desertification is the changeover from arable land (land that can be farmed) into desert. Desertification is caused mostly by human activity, especially the following:

- **Overgrazing** by livestock, such as sheep and cattle, eliminates the grasses that hold the soil together to prevent erosion.
- **Cutting down forests** robs the land of another barrier to soil erosion.

As grass and trees are eliminated, the soil loses its nutrients. Without plant roots to hold the soil, wind erosion removes the fertile topsoil. The land is then unable to sustain plant life. The Sahara in Africa, for example, is expanding at the rate of about 50 miles per year. The expansion of deserts is one cause of famine.

Controlling Desertification

Methods to control desertification include restricting livestock (to prevent overgrazing) and the planting of new trees to act as a barrier against erosion. These solutions are difficult to put into practice in developing countries, where farmers try to work as much land as possible. However, new farming methods, including improved irrigation, may help solve the problem.

**Preparing for
the Regents**

- Why are cooperative
solutions needed for
international problems
such as drug trafficking,
deforestation, and
the preservation of
endangered species?

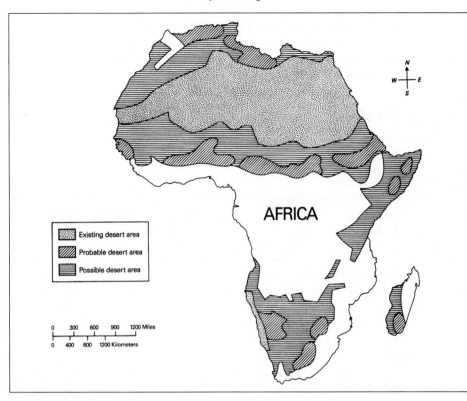

AFRICA

Existing desert area

Probable desert area

Possible desert area

0   300   600   900   1200 Miles

0   400   800   1200 Kilometers

The Spreading Desert
Desertification is a major problem in Africa, especially in the Sahel region just south of the Sahara Desert. Here, there has been a large loss of farmland and pastures.

Preparing for the Regents

Practice your map skills by answering these questions.

1. Where in Africa is the largest area of existing desert?

2. If desertification continues, what social conditions might result?

Endangered Species

Problems and Effects

A problem related to deforestation is the endangerment of various species of plants and animals. Various by-products of development—the clearing of land, the damming of waterways, and many types of pollution—all threaten to wipe out species of plants and animals.

If species are lost, the balance of the ecosystem of the world could be damaged severely. In addition, resources that people use for food and medicines may disappear.

Global Solutions

Several international agreements have attempted to address the topic of endangered species. Some agreements, for example, have banned the shipment and sale of endangered animals. Some people have suggested that these species can best be protected through preserving their habitats. The 1992 Earth Summit addressed this issue. Other agreements have been made about specific animals, such as whales and tuna, which have been endangered by commercial fishing and other economic practices.

Natural Disasters

Just as climate disasters affect people, so do natural disasters, such as volcanic activity. In 2010, a volcano in Iceland erupted and sent clouds of ash over Europe, stopping air traffic for weeks.

Earthquakes can cause untold disaster, no matter how prepared a country might be. Unprepared Haiti lost much of its capital city and much of the country's infrastructure in a 2010 earthquake. After several years, Haiti is still rebuilding,

Preparing for the Regents

• How do natural disasters affect governments, economies, and social structures?

hundreds of thousands still live in temporary camps, agriculture has not recovered, and a cholera epidemic has killed thousands. The much more prepared Japan had many earthquake-resistance standards in place, but was hit by one of the largest earthquakes ever recorded. The quake and resulting tidal wave swept away thousands of people, buildings, and farmland and caused one of the world's worst nuclear disasters.

Nuclear Proliferation

The use of nuclear energy and the proliferation, or spread, of nuclear weapons pose serious potential threats to the global environment.

Nuclear Accidents

In 1986, an accident at the Chernobyl nuclear power plant in the Soviet Union exposed people and crops to deadly radiation. Radiation was also blown across countries in Europe. This accident led to heightened concern about safe use of nuclear energy, but in spite of more regulations, another nuclear disaster happened.

Before 2011, one-third of Japan's electricity came from nuclear power plants. Then, a powerful earthquake sent a huge tsunami across part of Japan, including the Fukushima Daiichi Nuclear Power Station. Due to the water damage, the nuclear power plant experienced explosions, radiation leaks, contaminated water leaks, and partial meltdowns. Eventually, after a huge evacuation, most people were allowed to return home, if their home still remained standing. The reactor is so badly damaged and unstable that it will take many years before it can be completely sealed. Surprisingly, there was little immediate effect on people's health, but it did take a toll on the mental state of many. During the following year, Japan took almost all its nuclear reactors offline. By mid-2013, only two had been restarted.

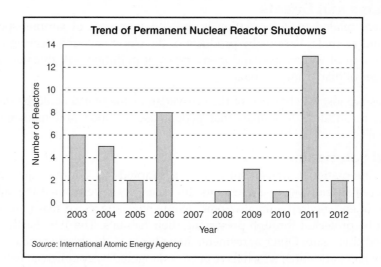

Note Taking

Reading Skill:
Identify Supporting Details
Make a word web. List the dangers of nuclear energy. Add boxes as you need them.

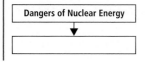

Key Themes and Ideas

Decision Making
Economics often play a role in a developing country's decision to build and maintain nuclear energy plants and nuclear weapons, and how they dispose of nuclear waste.

Nuclear Waste Disposal

Dangers are also posed by nuclear waste that is created by nuclear weapons production facilities. Nuclear waste is radioactive and remains that way for many years. Exposure to high levels of radioactivity is very harmful to humans. Earlier methods of disposing of nuclear waste included dumping it at sea or burying it in deep wells. Both of these methods have been banned by the international community. Within nations and across the globe, solutions are being sought for the safe disposal of nuclear waste. Effective cleanup of nuclear waste is expensive, however. This expense makes other solutions more attractive for many nations.

Nuclear Weapons

As the 1900s ended, the United States and Russia controlled over 90 percent of the world's nuclear weapons. China, Britain, France, India, and Pakistan were also publicly declared nuclear powers. It was widely accepted that Israel had a small, undeclared nuclear arsenal.

Several nations gave up their nuclear weapons in the 1990s. South Africa dismantled its nuclear weapons. The nuclear missiles stationed in the former Soviet republics of Belarus, Kazakhstan, and Ukraine were returned to Russia.

While tensions between the major nuclear powers have eased since the end of the Cold War, a continuing concern is that regional conflicts, such as the dispute between India and Pakistan, could escalate into a nuclear exchange. North Korea continues to test nuclear bombs although it offers to restart talks under certain conditions at the same time it threatens to launch rockets at South Korea and the United States. It continues to be an unstable nuclear threat and to shroud its nuclear activities in secrecy.

Iran also had a nuclear program which it claims is for developing nuclear material to use to generate electricity and for medical uses. However, the Middle East is an unpredictable region and Iran has threatened countries like Israel and the United States. In 2012, the UN, the United States, and the EU placed sanctions on Iran for its continued nuclear activity. Iran, in turn, threatened to close the Strait of Hormuz, a critical shipping lane for oil exports. Israel threatened to bomb the Iranian nuclear facilities, as they see Iran's program as a major threat to its security. Then, in 2013, a new, more moderate Iranian government agreed to temporarily halt its nuclear program. In 2015, Iran signed an agreement to limit its nuclear research, rid itself of some uranium, and submit to inspections. In exchange, the severe economic sanctions will be lifted.

This brought an end to some nuclear tensions, but another dangerous possibility looms over the world. That threat is that a terrorist group could obtain nuclear weapons.

Summary

Nations are working together to resolve the environmental issues that face the global community. These issues include air and water pollution, global warming, deforestation, desertification, and nuclear safety. Weather, climate disasters, and natural disasters often affect human activity, and the world continually reacts to them. Sometimes making decisions involves balancing the protection of the environment with the needs of individual nations. Only with global cooperation, however, will these problems be solved.

Make Inferences

Why might the United States and Russia not want to give up their nuclear weapons? Why might less developed countries, like North Korea, want them?

Preparing for the Regents

Analyze the economic, military, and political factors that led to the nuclear treaty with Iran. Determine how a successful implementation would affect these factors. What do countries that did not sign the treaty think of it?

Preparing for the Regents

How do environmental issues—both problems and solutions—demonstrate the interdependence of the modern world?

Questions for Regents Practice

Multiple Choice

Directions: Review the Test-Taking Strategies section of this book. Then answer the following questions, drawn from actual Regents examinations. For each statement or question, choose the *number* of the word or expression that, of those given, best completes the statement or answers the question.

Base your answer to question 1 on the graph below and on your knowledge of social studies.

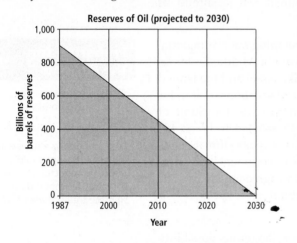

Reserves of Oil (projected to 2030)

1 Which action will help slow the trend indicated by the graph?
  (1) expanding Green Revolution technology
  (2) increasing industrialization in developing countries
  (3) using alternative energy sources
  (4) lowering worldwide oil prices

2 Bombings, kidnappings, and hijackings are tactics most often used by
  (1) imperialists
  (2) terrorists
  (3) nationalists
  (4) absolutists

3 Economic development in Latin American nations has been hindered most by
  (1) a scarcity of goods produced for trade and a lack of natural resources
  (2) governments that are primarily concerned with preserving the environment
  (3) problems of overpopulation, patterns of land distribution, and a lack of investment capital
  (4) corporations that are not interested in the use of modern technology

4 Which is the major reason that the United Nations has often been unsuccessful in solving international disputes?
  (1) The United Nations does not have sufficient funds to act.
  (2) The disputing nations are usually not members of the United Nations.
  (3) National sovereignty stands in the way of international cooperation.
  (4) The United Nations charter does not provide a means to settle disputes.

5 Since 1990, people in Timor, Kosovo, and Kurdish Iraq have all protested their lack of
  (1) membership in the European Union
  (2) economic stability
  (3) independent homelands
  (4) representation in the Arab League

6 In many developing nations, rising levels of pollution and continued housing shortages are a direct result of
  (1) increased urbanization
  (2) a reliance on single-crop economies
  (3) changing climatic conditions
  (4) increasing nationalism

7 In Middle Eastern societies, women have increasingly been at the center of a conflict between the forces of modernization and the

(1) values of traditional Islamic culture

(2) pressure for a Palestinian homeland

(3) shortage of capital for industrial development

(4) need to reduce the birthrate

8 The major goal of the Green Revolution has been to

(1) decrease the use of modern farm machinery

(2) decrease population growth

(3) increase agricultural output

(4) increase the number of traditional farms

9 A valid statement about the technology in the 1900s is that technology has

(1) eliminated famine and disease throughout the world

(2) delayed economic progress in developing countries

(3) led to the adoption of free trade policies

(4) accelerated the pace of cultural diffusion

10 A study of the accident at the Chernobyl nuclear power plant in the Soviet Union and of the severe air pollution in Mexico City would lead to the conclusion that

(1) technology can cause problems throughout the world

(2) international trade is more profitable than domestic commerce

(3) modern science cannot solve most political problems

(4) agricultural nations have caused major world environmental problems

11 A major environmental problem affecting Latin America, sub-Saharan Africa, and Southeast Asia has been

(1) air pollution

(2) deforestation

(3) disposal of nuclear waste

(4) acid rain

Thematic Essay Question

In developing your answer, be sure to keep these general definitions in mind:

      (a) <u>describe</u> means "to illustrate something in words or tell about it"
      (b) <u>evaluate</u> means "to judge or determine the significance, worth, or quality of"

Directions: Write a well-organized essay that includes an introduction, several paragraphs addressing the task below, and a conclusion.

Theme: **Science and Technology**

> Since 1945, technology has transformed human life. Advances have occurred in many different areas. These changes have had both positive and negative effects on human life.

Task:

- Describe one scientific or technological advance made since 1945 that has had a significant impact on global history.
- Give two examples of ways in which this advance has affected you or will have an effect on you in the future.
- Evaluate the positive and negative effects of that scientific or technological advance on the lives of human beings.

You may discuss any scientific or technological advance that has come about since 1945. Some types of advances that you may wish to consider are discovery of nuclear power, the widespread use of the computer or of Internet technology, and medical advances.

You are not limited to these suggestions.

Guidelines:

In your essay, be sure to
- Develop all aspects of the task
- Support the theme with relevant facts, examples, and details
- Use a logical and clear plan of organization, including an introduction and a conclusion that are beyond a simple restatement of the theme

This question is based on the accompanying documents. The question is designed to test your ability to work with historical documents. Some of the documents have been edited for the purposes of this question. As you analyze the documents, take into account the source of each document and any point of view that may be presented in the document.

Historical Context:

People have held differing views about human rights throughout history and in different cultures. In the 1900s, however, there have been movements all over the world to ensure basic human rights for all people.

Task: Using the information from the documents and your knowledge of global history, answer the questions that follow each document in Part A. Your answers to the questions will help you write the Part B essay in which you will be asked to

> • Describe and evaluate the progress of justice and human rights in the 1900s

In developing your answers, be sure to keep these general definitions in mind:

(a) <u>describe</u> means "to tell or depict in written or spoken words; give an account of"
(b) <u>evaluate</u> means "to examine and judge the significance, worth, or condition of; to determine the value of"

Document-Based Question

Part A: Short Answer

Directions: Analyze the documents and answer the question or questions that follow each document, using the space provided.

Document #1

Article 1 All human beings are born free and equal in dignity and rights. . . .
Article 2 Everyone is entitled to all the rights and freedoms . . . without distinction of any kind. . . .
Article 18 Everyone has the right to freedom of thought, conscience and religion. . . .
Article 19 Everyone has the right to freedom of opinion and expression. . . .
Article 25 Everyone has the right to a standard of living adequate for the health and well-being of himself and of his family, including food, clothing, housing and medical care. . . .
    —General Assembly of the United Nations, *The Universal Declaration of Human Rights,*
    adopted December 10, 1948

1. Describe one economic right to which Document 1 says all people are entitled.

_____

_____

2. Which article or articles in Document 1 most closely support freedom of speech? Explain the reason for your choice.

_____

_____

Document #2

In many parts of the world the people are searching for a solution which would link the two basic values: peace and justice. The two are like bread and salt for mankind. Every nation and every community have the inalienable right to these values. No conflicts can be resolved without doing everything possible to follow that road...
    —Lech Walesa, Nobel Peace Prize Lecture, 1983

3. What point was Walesa trying to make by comparing peace and justice to bread and salt?

_____

_____

Document #3

4. Explain why some people in this cartoon have been waiting for hours, while others have been waiting for years.

_____

_____

_____

_____

_____

Document-Based Question

Part B

Essay

Directions: Write a well-organized essay that includes an introduction, several paragraphs, and a conclusion. Use evidence from *at least **two*** documents in your essay. Support your response with relevant facts, examples, and details. Include additional outside information.

Historical Context:

People have held differing views about human rights throughout history and in different cultures. In the 1900s, however, there have been movements all over the world to ensure basic human rights for all.

Task:

Using information from the documents and your knowledge of global history and geography, write an essay in which you:

- Evaluate justice and human rights in the 1900s
- Describe advances in human rights as well as human rights violations
- Explain whether you think that the trend is toward greater human rights for all

Guidelines:

In your essay, be sure to
- Develop all aspects of the task
- Incorporate information from *at least **two*** documents
- Incorporate relevant outside information
- Support the theme with relevant facts, examples, and details
- Use a logical and clear plan of organization, including an introduction and a conclusion that are beyond a restatement of the theme

Thematic Review

The Regents Examination takes a thematic approach to history. This section of the book will help you to review the themes that are mostly likely to be tested on the thematic essay and document-based parts of the exam. It is important to remember that the themes used in this course span the entire two-year course. The events you choose to write about in the thematic essay may be taken from either ninth or tenth grade or both.

Change

Change means basic alterations in things, events, and ideas. Throughout global history, major changes have had significant and lasting impacts on human development.

- **Neolithic Revolution** Some 11,000 years ago, people first developed farming methods and lived in permanent settlements. As a result, the first civilizations emerged.
- **Industrial Revolution** This change began in Europe in the 1700s and gradually spread throughout the world. Power-driven machinery in factories became the dominant means of production. The results of this change have included urbanization, a higher standard of living, and pollution of the environment.
- **Chinese Communist Revolution** In 1948, Mao Zedong established a Chinese Communist state. Since then, China has become a world economic power. Today, it works to control its growing population, as well as to adapt communism to modern needs.

Other examples of change are the Crusades, the spread of bubonic plague, the Renaissance, the Scientific Revolution, the Enlightenment, the Agrarian Revolution, the Reformation, African independence movements, and the emergence of Pacific Rim nations.

Turning Points

Turning points are times when decisive changes occur. Turning points often have political, social, and cultural impacts.

- **Fall of Constantinople** This event, which occurred in 1453, marked the end of the Christian Byzantine empire and the emergence of the powerful Ottoman empire, a Muslim power that dominated the region for centuries.
- **Voyages of Columbus** The voyages of Columbus began the European race to colonize the Americas. A far-reaching exchange of people, plants, animals, and ideas occurred between Europe, the Americas, and Africa.
- **French Revolution** The French Revolution of 1789 had a powerful influence well beyond France, spreading democratic ideals and a spirit of nationalism throughout Europe and around the globe.
- **Collapse of Communism in the Soviet Union** The collapse of communism in the Soviet Union initiated years of change in Eastern Europe and brought an end to the Cold War.

Other examples of turning points include the signing of the Magna Carta, the American Revolution, independence movements in Latin America, and the Russian Revolution.

Thematic Review

Belief Systems

Belief systems are the established, orderly ways in which groups or individuals look at religious faith or philosophical tenets.

- **Hinduism** A religion more than 3,000 years old, Hinduism has had an enormous effect on India, Southeast Asia, and the rest of the world.
- **Buddhism** A religion founded in the 500s B.C. in India, Buddhism spread throughout Asia.
- **Judaism** The first great monotheistic religion, Judaism has had an important effect on several other world religions.
- **Christianity** Greatly influenced by Judaism, Christianity is a monotheistic religion centered on the teachings of Jesus Christ.
- **Islam** Also greatly influenced by Judaism, Islam is a monotheistic religion and has followers all over the world, especially in the Middle East, Africa, and Asia.

Other examples of belief systems are animism, Confucianism, Taoism, Shintoism, and Sikhism.

Geography and the Environment

This theme has to do with relationships among people, places, and environments. Environment means the surroundings, including natural elements and elements created by humans.

- **Early River Civilizations** Early civilizations grew up around rivers. Rivers provided water for crops and for drinking, as well as a means of transportation.
- **Chinese Influence on Japan** Through the bridge of Korea, China had a strong influence on the culture of Japan.
- **Industrialization in Great Britain** Great Britain's natural resources, together with such geographical factors as rivers and natural harbors, allowed the Industrial Revolution to begin there.
- **Industrial Revolution: Impact on Environment** The Industrial Revolution had a lasting impact on the natural environment. For example, new sources of energy often created new types of pollution. Urbanization changed the landscape as cities and their suburbs grew.

Other examples of the impact of geography and the environment are the development of city-states in ancient Greece, the importance of the Middle East as a crossroads between three continents, and environmental problems such as desertification and the destruction of tropical forests.

Economic Systems

Economic systems include traditional, command, market, and mixed systems. Each must answer the three basic economic questions: What goods and services are to be produced and in what quantities? How shall these goods and services be produced? For whom shall these goods and services be produced?

- **Traditional Economy** An economic system based on farming, often subsistence farming, is a traditional economy.

- **Manorialism** The economic system of Western Europe in medieval times was called manorialism. It was based on the manor, an estate that often included one or more villages and the surrounding lands.
- **Mercantilism** The economic policy in which nations sought to export more than they imported is known as mercantilism. Overseas empires were central to mercantilism, which led to imperialism.
- **Capitalism (Market Economy)** Capitalism is an economic system in which the means of production are privately owned and operated for profit. It developed as an economic system in the 1500s.
- **Marxist Socialism (Command Economy)** Marxist socialism is the economic system found in communist states such as the former Soviet Union and its satellites. It is characterized by ownership of property and operation of businesses by the state rather than by private individuals.

Other examples of topics connected with economic systems are laissez-faire economics, the commercial revolution, cash crop economies, and imperialism.

Political Systems

Political systems, such as monarchies, dictatorships, and democracies, address certain basic questions of government such as: What should a government have the power to do? What should a government not have the power to do?

- **Monarchy** In monarchies, a king or queen exercises central power. Monarchies have been common since ancient times, and a few are still in existence today.
- **Feudalism** Feudalism was most prominent in medieval Europe and in Japan from about 1600 to the mid-1800s. It is a decentralized political system. In Europe, it declined with the growth of nation-states.
- **Democracy** Democracy, a system in which the people hold the ruling power— either directly or through elected representatives—had its roots in ancient Greece. It is a primary political system in the countries of the West today.
- **Totalitarianism** In a totalitarian system, a one-party dictatorship regulates every aspect of its citizens' lives. The Soviet Union under Stalin was a totalitarian state.

Other examples of political systems are the limited democracy of Athens, the militarism of Sparta and of Japan, absolutism, theocracy, communism, fascism, and apartheid.

Culture and Intellectual Life

Culture includes the patterns of human behavior (encompassing ideas, beliefs, values, artifacts, and ways of making a living) that a society transmits to succeeding generations to meet its fundamental needs. Intellectual life involves ways of thinking, studying, and reflecting on aspects of life.

- **Roman Civilization** Rome left a great cultural and intellectual legacy to the Western world, including a commitment to law and justice, the Latin language, and a body of great literature.
- **Gupta Golden Age** In India, from A.D. 320 through 550, lasting achievements in mathematics, medicine, arts, and architecture occurred, supported by the stable reign of the Gupta dynasty.

- **Islamic Golden Age** Between A.D. 750 and 1350, Islamic empires experienced a golden age. The roots of modern mathematics and science can be traced to this period.
- **African Civilizations** From the mid-1200s through the mid-1500s, Africa was the site of great activity in scholarship and art.
- **Renaissance Europe** The Renaissance in Europe, which began in the mid-1300s, was a time of great cultural and intellectual activity. Humanism—which recognized the importance of individual worth in a secular society—guided the Renaissance.

Other important eras of cultural and intellectual activity included early river civilizations, classical Chinese civilization, Mesoamerican civilizations, and the Enlightenment in Europe.

Nationalism

Nationalism is a feeling of pride in and devotion to one's country or the desire of a people to control their own government. It is sometimes a divisive force and sometimes a force that unifies. In many cases, it is a source of conflict.

- **German and Italian Unification** In the mid-1800s, both Germany and Italy experienced unification. In each case, many small states joined into one nation.
- **India** Ideals of Western democracy, as well as devotion to traditional Hindu and Muslim culture, sustained Indian nationalism through the first half of the 1900s, leading to independence in 1948.
- **Zionism** Since Roman times, Jews had dreamed of returning to Palestine. This dream grew into an international movement in the 1900s. By 1948, the nation of Israel had been created.
- **African Independence Movements** In 1945, just four European powers controlled nearly all of Africa. Less than 25 years later, a tide of nationalism had liberated many African peoples and set them on the road to self-determination.

Other historical situations in which nationalism had an impact are the development of the nation of Turkey, conflicts in the Balkans, the breakup of the Ottoman empire, Latin America in the 1800s and 1900s, Pan-Africanism, and Pan-Arabism.

Imperialism

Imperialism is the domination by one country of the political and economic life of another country or region. Imperialism has had both positive and negative effects on colonies.

- **British in India** The British controlled India by the late 1700s. Although railroads and the British educational system benefited some Indians, local industries and Indian culture suffered, and Indians were treated as inferiors. India gained its independence in 1948.
- **European Powers in Africa** European nations carved up the continent of Africa in the late 1880s. Africa was a continent made up mainly of colonies until after 1945, when African peoples began to demand independence. The legacy of imperialism still affects Africa today.

- **Japan** An imperialist power from the Meiji period, Japan ruled Korea from 1910 to the end of World War II. It also controlled areas in China and Southeast Asia. Japanese imperialism was a cause of World War II.
- **Imperial Rivalry** Competition between imperial powers was one of the causes of World War I. Germany and France, especially, clashed over territory in Africa. Imperial rivalry was also a cause of many smaller wars.

Other civilizations that practiced imperialism include the Chinese Han dynasty, the Romans, the Byzantines, and the Mongols. The collapse of European imperialism still affects many regions of the world today.

Diversity and Interdependence

Diversity involves understanding and respecting oneself and others, including differences in language, gender, socioeconomic class, religion, and other human characteristics and traits. It is closely related to interdependence, the reliance upon others in mutually beneficial interactions and exchanges. Sometimes the refusal to accept diversity leads to conflict.

- **Byzantine Empire** The Byzantine empire blended many diverse cultures. This diversity allowed it to preserve many differing traditions.
- **Balkans** This region of Eastern Europe has always been an area of great religious and ethnic diversity. Often this diversity has led to conflict.
- **Global Economy** In the 1900s, the world economy became more interdependent, a process that started during the age of imperialism. Today, the world's economy is truly global.
- **Environmental Issues** The global population shares the Earth, and what occurs in one part of the world often has an impact on many other areas. Increasingly, environmental decisions are reached by many nations working together for mutual benefit.

Other examples of diversity and interdependence include the links between the East and the West during the time of the Mongol empire, tensions that have arisen as a result of Islamic fundamentalism, and interactions among Muslims, Hindus, and Sikhs in India.

Justice and Human Rights

Justice is fair, equal, proportional, or appropriate treatment given to individuals in interpersonal, societal, or government interactions. Human rights are those basic political, economic, and social rights to which all human beings are entitled. At times throughout history, justice and human rights have been violated.

- **Code of Hammurabi** Because the Code of Hammurabi was carved on a pillar in Babylon (around 1800 B.C.), all people could see what the laws were. This was the first major collection of laws in history.
- **English Bill of Rights** The English Bill of Rights was an important document because it limited the power of the monarchy and returned traditional rights to English citizens.
- **Irish Potato Famine** A blight that affected the main food crop for the Irish people in the mid-1800s created widespread famine when the British, who ruled

the island, continued to export crops that could have fed the Irish. At least a million Irish people died during the famine, also called the Great Hunger.

- **Tiananmen Square** When students in China demanded greater political freedom in the late 1980s, Chinese Communist authorities cracked down, wounding and killing many demonstrators.

Other examples of important developments in justice and human rights include the Laws of the Twelve Tables, Justinian's Code, the Sharia, and the Magna Carta. Violations of human rights include the Armenian massacres, the Holocaust, apartheid, the Khmer Rouge in Cambodia, and international terrorism.

Movement of People and Goods

Cultural diffusion is the constant exchange of people, ideas, products, technology, and institutions from one region or civilization to another. Cultural diffusion has occurred throughout history.

- **Muslim Influence on Africa** Muslim traders spread Islam across Africa. Their contacts with diverse cultures allowed them to spread a great number of other ideas and technologies along with the religion of Islam.
- **Silk Road** This 4,000-mile trade route stretched from western China to the Mediterranean. For centuries, from the A.D. 100s onward, goods, ideas, and technology flowed along this route from East to West and back again.
- **Crusades** From the late 1000s through the late 1200s, Christian and Muslim armies battled for control of Palestine. A great deal of cultural diffusion occurred during and after the Crusades, as Europe increased its interest in goods and ideas from the Middle East.
- **Modern Communication** In today's world, computers, the Internet, and satellite communications allow ideas to be passed in moments over great distances.

Other examples of movement of peoples, goods, and ideas include the spread of belief systems (such as Buddhism and Confucianism to Japan), the Muslim influence on Europe, and patterns of global migration.

Science and Technology

Science and technology means the tools and methods used by people to get what they need and want.

- **Neolithic Revolution** When people developed the knowledge and technology for farming and domesticating animals, permanent settlements grew.
- **Invention of the Printing Press** The printing press was a crucial breakthrough in technology, allowing ideas to spread.
- **Computer Revolution** Since the 1950s, our society has become increasingly dependent on computers and on digitized information.
- **Space Explorations** Humans have populated Earth and moved into the solar system. In recent years, space exploration has been a shared venture among major world powers.

Other examples of breakthroughs in science and technology are the improved standard of living that occurred in the 1800s, the Green Revolution, and advances in genetics.

Conflict

Conflict has occurred throughout history, and its costs have sometimes been very high. The causes of conflict may be political, social, or economic.

- **Religious Conflicts** Conflicts between peoples of differing belief systems began in ancient times and still exist today in places as widespread as Northern Ireland, India, and the Middle East.
- **Political Revolutions** Violent revolutions occurred within nations from the late 1700s through the 1800s as groups sought democratic reform, national independence, or both.
- **World War I** Sparked by several complex causes, World War I was the first modern, fully industrialized war and the first truly global conflict.
- **The Cold War** After 1945, the United States and its allies were engaged in a global competition with the Soviet Union and its allies. Surrogate conflicts occurred as the two superpowers—the United States and the Soviet Union—exerted their influence throughout the world.

Other examples of conflict include the Crusades, World War II, the Russian Revolution, ethnic disputes in the Balkans and Africa, and Arab-Israeli conflict in the Middle East.

Modern Global Connections and Interactions

Today's world is a web of connections and interactions. On every level, the people of the world meet, connect, interact, and sometimes collide. These interactions involve politics, economics, culture, or the environment.

- **Global Environmental Cooperation** Nations are becoming increasingly interdependent in their decisions about environmental issues, acknowledging that various peoples share one world.
- **Global Migrations** The last half of the 1900s was a time of great migration, especially from Africa, Asia, and Latin America to Europe and North America. Many people migrated to improve their economic conditions.
- **International Terrorism** Modern technology and transportation systems have allowed violent groups to express their frustration and anger globally through random acts of violence.
- **The United Nations** Created after World War II, the United Nations remains an organization through which nations can come together to seek peaceful solutions to global problems and conflicts.

Other examples of modern global connections and interactions include economic interdependence, nuclear proliferation, and the sharing of technology and ideas through the Internet.

Glossary

A

absolutism: political system in which autocratic rulers have complete authority over the government and the lives of people in their nations

acid rain: toxic mixture that is produced when rain falls through polluted air

African National Congress: group formed by opponents to apartheid in South Africa that encouraged political activism by blacks

Agrarian Revolution: change in farming methods in the 1600s that improved the quality and quantity of farm products

agribusiness: large commercial farm owned by multinational corporation

AIDS: acquired immunodeficiency syndrome

Allied Powers: World War I alliance of Great Britain, France, and Russia, later joined by Italy, the United States, and others

animism: the belief that every living and nonliving thing in nature has a spirit

antibiotic: drug that attacks or weakens the bacteria that cause many diseases

anti-Semitism: prejudice against Jews

apartheid: South African government policy calling for separation of the races

appeasement: policy of giving in to an aggressor's demands in order to keep the peace

apprentice: young person who is learning a trade from a master

aqueduct: bridgelike stone structure that brings water from hills to cities, first used by ancient Romans

Arabic numeral: type of numeral first developed in India and used by many Western countries today (1, 2, 3, etc.)

aristocracy: a government ruled by an upper class

armistice: agreement to end fighting

Association of Southeast Asian Nations: formed in 1967, group of nine Southeast Asian countries that coordinate policies among members in areas such as trade and agriculture

astrolabe: instrument used to determine latitude by measuring the position of the stars

asylum: protection from arrest or from being returned to a dangerous place from which one fled

artifact: an item made by humans that is used by archeologists to learn about past cultures

autocrat: a single ruler with complete authority

B

balance of power: distribution of political and economic power that prevents any one nation from becoming too strong

balance of trade: difference between how much a country imports and how much it exports

Bataan Death March: forced march of Allied prisoners by the Japanese during World War II

Bible: the sacred scriptures of Christianity

blitz: massive bombing

Boer War: war occurring from 1899 to 1902 between the British and the Boers, Dutch farmers; it began after the British tried to annex the Boer republics

Bolshevik: member of 1917 Russian revolutionary group

bourgeoisie: middle class in Marxism; it refers to capitalists

Boxer Rebellion: event in 1900 in which a group known as Boxers assaulted foreign communities across China

brahman: single unifying spirit of Hindu belief

bubonic plague: a contagious disease that devastated the world in the 1300s

bureaucracy: system of managing government through departments run by appointed officials

bushido: code of conduct for samurai during feudal period in Japan

C

caliph: successor to Muhammad as political and religious leader of the Muslims

calligraphy: fine handwriting

capitalism: economic system in which the means of production are privately owned and operated for profit

cartel: an association of businesspeople; used to refer to the criminal gangs that produce and smuggle drugs internationally

cartographer: mapmaker

cash crop economy: economy based on the raising and selling of one crop or a small number of crops

caudillo: military dictator in Latin America

Central Powers: World War I alliance of Germany, Austria-Hungary, and the Ottoman empire (later joined by Bulgaria)

chador: cloak worn by some Muslim women

chivalry: the code of conduct followed by knights during the Middle Ages

civil disobedience: the refusal to obey unjust laws

civilization: community characterized by elements such as a system of writing, development of social classes, and cities

clone: exact genetic replica

Cold War: continuing state of tension and hostility between the United States and the Soviet Union after 1945 because of differences in political and economic philosophies

collective: large farm owned and operated by workers as a group

Columbian exchange: global exchange of people, plants, animals, ideas, and technology that began in the late 1400s

command economy: economy in which government officials make all basic economic decisions

commercial revolution: the business revolution that occurred in Europe after the Middle Ages

common law: uniform system of justice, developed in England, based on court decisions that became accepted legal principles

Common Market: See *European Community*

commune: community of people who live and work together and hold property in common

Computer Revolution: great increase in the use of computers

concentration camp: detention centers instituted by Adolf Hitler where Jews and others were starved, shot, or gassed to death

Congress of Vienna: conference held in 1815 among European diplomats that had the purpose of restoring order and stability to Europe

conquistador: name, meaning "conqueror," for certain explorers of the 1500s and 1600s

conservatism: set of beliefs held by those who want to preserve traditional ways

Constitutional monarchy: a government in which the power of the king is limited by law

containment: Cold War policy that involved limiting communism to areas already under Soviet control

contras: counterrevolutionary group in Nicaragua that opposed the Sandinistas

Counter-Reformation: actions taken by the Catholic Church in the 1600s to oppose Protestantism

coup d'état: a revolt by a small group intended to overthrow a government

Crusades: series of religious wars fought between Christians and Muslims from the late 1000s to the mid-1200s

cultural diffusion: the exchange of ideas, customs, goods, and technologies among cultures

Cultural Revolution: program launched in 1966 by Mao Zedong to renew loyalty to communism and purge China of nonrevolutionary tendencies

cuneiform: wedge-shaped writing formed by pressing a penlike instrument into clay

czar: term for autocratic ruler of Russia; Russian word for *Caesar*

D

daimyo: in feudal Japan, warrior lords who held a place below the shogun

decimal system: number system based on 10

Declaration of Independence: document drafted by Thomas Jefferson that declared American independence from Great Britain

decolonization: the process by which European colonies in Africa and Asia became independent states

deforestation: destruction of forests, especially tropical rain forests

desaparecidos: word meaning "the disappeared ones," used to describe the thousands of people in Argentina who disappeared during the dirty war

desert: dry, barren land

desertification: the changeover of arable land into desert

despot: absolute ruler

détente: period in the 1970s during which there was an easing of tensions between the United States and the Soviet Union

developed nation: nation with established agriculture and industry, advanced technology, and a strong educational system

developing nation: nation with limited resources that faces obstacles in achieving modern industrial economies

dharma: in Hinduism, the moral and religious duties that are expected of an individual

diaspora: a scattering of people, as when the Jewish people were forced to leave their homeland in Palestine

direct democracy: system of government in which citizens participate directly rather than through elected representatives

Dirty War: period beginning in the late 1970s in Argentina during which the military arrested, tortured, and killed thousands of people

divine right: belief that a ruler's authority comes directly from God

Domino Theory: the belief that if one nation in Southeast Asia fell to Communism, the rest would soon follow

dynasty: ruling family

E

empire: group of states or territories governed by one ruler

enclosure: process of taking over and fencing off land once shared by peasant farmers

encomienda: system created by Spanish government in the Americas allowing colonists to demand labor or tribute from Native Americans

English Bill of Rights: a set of acts passed by Parliament to ensure its superiority over the monarchy and guarantee certain rights to citizens

enlightened despot: absolute ruler who used royal power to reform society

Enlightenment: the period in the 1700s in which people rejected traditional ideas and supported a belief in human reason

epidemic: an outbreak of disease that spreads quickly and affects a large number of people

Estates General: a French legislative body made up of clergy, nobles, and common people, such as businesspeople and peasants

ethnic cleansing: policy of forcibly removing or killing people of a certain ethnic group

ethnocentrism: the belief in the superiority of one's own race, culture, or nation

euro: European currency introduced in 1999

European Community: group of nations established in 1957 to expand free trade in Europe; also called *Common Market*

European Union: expansion of the European Community in the 1980s and 1990s; sometimes abbreviated EU

excommunicate: to exclude from the Roman Catholic Church as a penalty for refusing to obey Church laws

F

factory: place in which workers and machines are brought together to produce large quantities of goods

fascism: the rule of a people by a dictatorial government that is nationalistic and imperialistic

feudalism: system of government in which local lords control their own lands but owe military service and other support to a greater lord

five-year plan: one of a series of plans instituted by Joseph Stalin to build industry and increase farm output in the Soviet Union

fossil fuels: fuels such as coal, oil, and natural gas

G

genetic engineering: process of changing the chemical codes carried by living things to produce cures for disease, better drugs, and so on

genocide: attempt to destroy an entire ethnic or religious group

gentry: wealthy landowning class

germ theory: medical theory stating that many diseases are caused by microorganisms

glasnost: period of openness called for in the mid-1980s by Mikhail Gorbachev in the Soviet Union

globalization: the growing integration of economies and societies around the world

Glorious Revolution: in Great Britain, nonviolent overthrow of the government of James II that resulted in the reign of William and Mary

Gothic: style of European church architecture characterized by pointed arches and flying buttresses

Great Depression: global economic downturn that began in 1929

Great Leap Forward: program begun by Mao Zedong in China in 1958 to increase agricultural and industrial output

Green Revolution: development of new varieties of plants and improved agricultural techniques that resulted in greatly increased crop yields

greenhouse effect: process in which excess carbon dioxide in the atmosphere traps heat and causes rising global temperatures

guild: a type of trade association of merchants or artisans that was active in the Middle Ages

Guomindang: Chinese nationalist party formed by Sun Yixian

H

haiku: form of Japanese poetry that expresses a feeling, thought, or idea in three lines

Hanseatic League: trade association of northern German towns in the mid-1300s

heliocentric: sun-centered

Hellenistic: type of culture, resulting from Alexander the Great's conquests, that blended Eastern and Western influences

hijra: Muhammad's flight from Mecca to Medina in 622; also spelled *hegira*

heresy: a religious belief that is opposed to the official teachings of a church

Holocaust: act of genocide by the Nazis during World War II in which more than six million Jews died

Holy Land: Palestine, a land holy to Jews, Christians, and Muslims

humanism: intellectual movement at the heart of the Renaissance that focused on worldly subjects rather than religious ones

I

icon: holy image of Jesus, the Virgin Mary, or a saint of the Orthodox Christian Church

imperialism: domination by one country of the political, economic, or cultural life of another country or region

Indian National Congress: group formed by Hindu nationalist leaders in India in the late 1800s to gain greater democracy and eventual self-rule

indigenous: native to a country or region

indulgence: a pardon (forgiveness) for sins that was sold by the Catholic Church

Industrial Revolution: period in which production of goods shifted from using hand tools to using power-driven machines and from human and animal power to steam power

Information Revolution: the rapid spread of information that began in the 1950s and increases with each passing year

International Monetary Fund: in the 1980s, group that stepped in to work out agreements to help debtor nations repay their loans

Internet: vast computer network that ties together millions of computers

Interpol: the International Criminal Police Network

intifada: uprising mounted in 1987 by Palestinians in territory held by Israel

iron curtain: the imaginary line through Europe that divided the democracies of the West from the communist countries of the East

Islamic fundamentalism: movement by Muslim reformers who oppose westernization and want to apply Islamic principles to problems in their nations

J

janissaries: members of an elite force in the army of the Ottoman empire

Justinian's Code: code of laws organized by the Byzantine emperor Justinian in the 500s

K

kabuki: form of Japanese drama developed in the 1600s

kaiser: German word meaning "emperor," used for German kings of the late 1800s and early 1900s

kami: according to Japanese tradition, the spirits in all living and nonliving things

karma: in Hinduism, all the deeds of a person's life that affect existence in the next life

Koran: holy book of Islam

L

laissez faire: policy allowing business to operate with little or no government interference

Laws of the Twelve Tables: laws of ancient Rome written on twelve tablets and displayed in the marketplace

League of Nations: group of more than 40 countries formed after World War I with the goal of settling problems through negotiation, not war

liberalism: way of thinking that supports personal freedom, democracy, and reform

limited monarchy: government in which a legislative body limits the monarch's powers

literacy: the ability to read and write

Long March: 1934 retreat by Mao Zedong and his followers from the Guomindang

M

Magna Carta: a charter signed by the English king John in 1215 that placed limits on the king's power

mandate: after World War I, a territory that was administered by a foreign power

Mandate of Heaven: according to Chinese tradition, the divine right to rule

manorialism: an economic system structured around a lord's manor, or estate

Marshall Plan: American aid package for Europe proposed in 1947 to strengthen democratic governments and lessen the appeal of communism

medieval: the name for the period of the Middle Ages, from about 500 to the middle of the 1400s

Meiji Restoration: period from 1868 to 1912 in Japan in which Japan industrialized and modernized

mercantilism: economic policy by which a nation sought to export more than it imported in order to build its national wealth

Messiah: Jewish word for a savior sent by God

mestizo: a person of mixed parentage in Latin America

Middle Kingdom: traditional name for Chinese civilization, so-called because the Chinese believed China was the center of the Earth

Middle Passage: the voyage from Africa to the Americas on slave ships

militarism: the glorification of military power

millet: within the Ottoman empire, a religious community of non-Muslims

missionary: person dedicated to spreading a religion

mixed economy: economic system with both private and state-run enterprises

monastery: community where men or women focus on spiritual goals

monopoly: complete control of a product or business by one person or group

monotheistic: believing in one god

mosaic: picture or design formed by inlaid pieces of stone or other materials

mosque: Muslim house of worship

multinational corporation: a business that operates in many countries

Munich Pact: 1938 agreement between Great Britain, France, Italy, and Germany that allowed Hitler to seize the Sudentenland

Muslim League: group formed by Muslims in India in the early 1900s to protect Muslim interests

N

Napoleonic Code: legal code of Napoleon that included many Enlightenment ideas

National Assembly: group formed mostly by the third estate in France in 1789 with the intention of writing a new constitution

nationalism: a feeling of pride in and devotion to one's country

NATO: acronym for the North Atlantic Treaty Organization, a pact between Western nations who pledged to support each other if any member nation was attacked

natural laws: according to some philosophers, rules that govern human nature

Neolithic: the period of human culture characterized by the development of a system of settled agriculture; also called the New Stone Age

neutral: not supporting either side in a conflict

New Economic Policy: plan instituted by Lenin in 1921 that privatized some industries

95 Theses: list of 95 arguments against indulgences, posted by Martin Luther on the door of a church in Wittenberg, Germany, in 1517

nirvana: in Buddhism, union with the universe and release from the cycle of death and rebirth

nomad: person who moves from place to place in search of food

nonalignment: policy of not supporting either side in a conflict, such as the Cold War

O

oligarchy: government in which ruling power belongs to a few people

OPEC: acronym for the Organization of Petroleum Exporting Countries, a trade group that attempts to set world oil prices by controlling oil production

Opium War: conflict between Great Britain and China in 1839 over the opium trade

Organization of African Unity (OAU): group founded in 1963 by Kwame Nkrumah to promote Pan-Africanism and the end of colonialism in Africa

overpopulation: overabundance of people in a region or country that lacks sufficient resources to adequately provide for them

ozone layer: layer of gases high in the atmosphere that protects the Earth from the dangerous ultraviolet rays of the sun

P

Pacific Rim: group of nations in Asia and the Americas that border the Pacific Ocean

pagoda: Buddhist temple with many levels and a roof that curves up at the corners

Palestine Liberation Organization (PLO): group formed in 1964 that represents many Palestinian nationalist groups

Pan-Africanism: movement emphasizing the unity of Africans and people of African descent all over the world

Pan-Arabism: movement emphasizing the unity of all peoples sharing a common Arab cultural heritage

Pan-Slavism: nationalistic movement that sought to unite Slavic peoples

Parliament: representative assembly of England

patriarch: the highest church official in the Orthodox Christian Church

patriarchal: family order in which the father or oldest male heads the household

patrician: member of the landholding upper class in ancient Rome

Pax Mongolia: period of stability through much of Asia created by Mongol rule from the late 1200s through the mid-1300s

Pax Romana: term meaning "Roman Peace" for a period covering about 200 years beginning with the reign of Augustus

peninsulares: European-born elite in Latin America

perestroika: restructuring of the government and the economy in the Soviet Union under Mikhail Gorbachev in the mid-1980s

Persian Gulf War: war in 1991 prompted by the Iraqi invasion of Kuwait in which a coalition of European and Arab powers drove Iraq out of Kuwait

pharaoh: ruler of ancient Egypt

philosophe: thinkers of the Enlightenment

plantation: large estate run by an owner or overseer

plebeian: member of the lower class in ancient Rome, which included farmers, merchants, artisans, and traders

PLO: (Palestine Liberation Organization) originally a terrorist group dedicated to the destruction of Israel;

later became an official organization representing Palestinians in negotiations with Israel

pogrom: violent attack on a Jewish community

polis: city-state in ancient Greece

pollution: contamination of the environment, including air, water, and soil

polytheistic: believing in many gods

porcelain: hard, shiny pottery

post-colonialism: term used to describe conditions shared by nations that were once colonies

propaganda: the spreading of ideas to promote a certain cause or to damage an opposing cause

Protestant Reformation: period when Europeans broke away from the Roman Catholic Church and formed new Christian churches

purge: the process of eliminating a nation of undesirable people

Puritans: group in England in the 1600s who sought to purify the church of England by eliminating Catholic practices

Q

quipus: knotted strings used by Incan officials for keeping records

Quran: the sacred scriptures of Islam

R

radioactivity: powerful form of energy released by certain substances

Reconquista: a campaign begun by Christians in the 700s to recapture Spain from the Muslims

Red Guards: groups of radical students formed in China during the Cultural Revolution

refugee: person who flees his or her homeland to seek safety elsewhere

reincarnation: in Hinduism, the rebirth of the soul in a new body

Renaissance: period of great creativity and change in Europe from the 1300s through the 1600s; the word means "rebirth"

reparations: payment for war damages

republic: system of government in which officials are chosen by the people

Russification: attempt by Russian rulers to make all groups under Russian rule think, act, and believe as Russians

Russo-Japanese War: war occurring from 1904 to 1905 between Japan and Russia; won by Japan

S

samurai: member of the warrior class in Japanese feudal society

Sandinistas: group of revolutionaries that overthrew the Nicaraguan government in 1979

satellite: a smaller country that is economically or politically dependent on a more powerful country

savanna: grassy plain

schism: permanent split

scientific method: a method of discovering truth based on experimentation and observation rather than on past authorities

Scientific Revolution: period in the 1500s and 1600s in which scientific thinkers challenged traditional ideas and relied on observation and experimentation

secondary source: written information that is based on original or primary sources

secular: having to do with worldly rather than religious matters

Senate: the most powerful governing body of ancient Rome

sepoy: Indian soldier serving in the army set up by the British or French East India Companies

Sepoy Mutiny: rebellion fought by Hindu and Muslim sepoys against British rule in India in the mid-1800s

serf: in medieval Europe, peasant bound to the lord's land

shantytown: area of shacks that grows up around a city that is experiencing rapid growth

Sharia: the system of Islamic law

Shiite: one of the two main divisions of Islam

Shinto: traditional Japanese religion

shogun: in Japanese feudal society, top military commander

Silk Road: ancient trade route that linked China with lands to the west

Sino-Japanese War: war that lasted from 1894 to 1895 between Japan and China

socialism: system in which the people as a whole rather than private individuals own all property and operate all businesses

Solidarity: independent trade union formed in Poland in 1980

soviet: council of workers and soldiers set up by Russian revolutionaries in 1917

sphere of influence: area in which an outside power claims exclusive trade privileges

stupa: large dome-shaped Buddhist shrine

suffrage: the right to vote

sultan: Muslim ruler

Sunni: one of the two main divisions of Islam

superpower: name after 1945 for both the United States and the Soviet Union, the two nations that dominated global politics for more than four decades

surrogate: word for a representative state; used to describe smaller countries whose actions represented the interests of either the United States or the Soviet Union during the Cold War

Swahili: language that mixed Arabic words with Bantu, an African language

T

Taiping Rebellion: peasant rebellion in China occurring between 1850 and 1864

tariff: a tax on imports

technology: tools and skills people use to meet their basic needs

terrace: a flat area of land on a steep hillside

terrorism: deliberate use of unpredictable violence, especially against civilians, to gain revenge or achieve political goals

Torah: the most sacred scriptures of Judaism

totalitarian state: form of government in which a one-party dictatorship attempts to regulate every aspect of the lives of citizens

total war: the channeling of all of a nation's resources into a war effort

trade deficit: a situation in which a nation imports more than it exports

trade fair: site of regular trading activity in medieval Europe

trench warfare: type of warfare in which troops dig trenches and fight from them

tributary state: independent state that must acknowledge the supremacy of another state and pay tribute to its ruler

Truman Doctrine: an economic and military program of the United States designed in 1947 to help other countries resist Soviet aggression

U

United Nations: international group formed in 1945 to provide a place to discuss world problems and develop solutions

Universal Declaration of Human Rights: document adopted in 1948 by the United Nations that sets out the basic human rights of all individuals

Untouchables: within the ancient Indian caste system, outcasts who lived harsh lives

urbanization: movement of people to cities

utopian: a plan for creating a perfect social order

W

Warsaw Pact: defensive alliance among the Soviet Union and its satellites promising mutual military cooperation

westernization: process of adopting Western ways

Y

Young Turks: movement established by Turks in the late 1800s to reform the Ottoman Empire

Z

zaibatsu: Japanese families that became powerful in banking and industry

Zen Buddhism: sect of Buddhism that spread throughout Japan

Zionism: movement dedicated to building a Jewish state in Palestine

Index

A

absolutism, 8, 14–16
acid rain, 168–169
Afghanistan, 115, 117–118, 121, 151–153
Africa, 1, 12, 18, 35–38, 40, 53, 55, 66, 73, 92–95, 104, 107–111, 114, 136, 140, 154, 158
African Union, 108, 146
Agrarian Revolution, 25–26, 31
al Qaeda, 146, 150–151
Algeria, 115
American Revolution, 6–7
Americas, the, 6, 31, 35
Angola, 93
apartheid, 108–110
appeasement, 73
Arab Spring, 159–160
Arafat, Yasir, 112, 114
Argentina, 13, 122–123, 125
Armenia, 23, 53, 121, 149
arms race, 92
arts, 30–31, 62, 68
Asia, 17
Austria, 5, 9–11, 14–16, 21–22, 51, 54, 66, 73
Austria-Hungary, 24, 53–55, 66
Azerbaijan, 121

B

Balkans, 148
Bangladesh, 105
Basques, 147
Belgium, 15, 26, 37, 54–55, 74
belief systems, 111, 147
Biafra, 108, 145
Boko Haram, 154
Bolivia, 13
Bosnia, 54, 142
Bosnia-Herzegovina, 121
Brazil, 139, 170
Brexit, 143
Buddhism/Buddhists, 143
Bulgaria, 24, 55, 120
Burma, 110

C

Cambodia, 110
Canada, 31, 68, 76, 125, 138, 140
capitalism, 27–29, 69, 95
cash crop economies, 18, 107
caste system, 68, 105–106, 157
Castro, Fidel, 93–94
Central America, 124, 137

Chechnya, 121
China, 38–40, 66, 68, 73, 147, 173
China (People's Republic), 74, 100–103, 137, 143. see also Taiwan (Republic of China)
Christianity/Christians, 23, 53, 67, 108, 114, 142
Churchill, Winston, 74–75
cities/urbanization, 26–27, 59, 124, 156–157
climate change, 168–170
Cold War, 90–94, 105
collectivization, 63
Colombia, 13
command economies, 62–63, 95–96
Common Market, 98
Commonwealth of Independent States, 118
Communism, 60–63, 68, 77, 89–93, 101–103, 118, 120
Computer Revolution, 164
Congo, Democratic Republic of the, 138
Congo, the, 93, 145
conservatism, 15
Croatia, 143
Cuba, 93–94
cultural nationalism, 19
Cultural Revolution, 102
Curie, Marie, 51
Czech Republic, 121
Czechoslovakia, 66, 73, 90–92, 121

D

Daimyo, 33
Dalai Lama, 147
Darfur, 108, 146
de Klerk, F. W., 109
Declaration of Independence, 7, 9, 12
deforestation, 139, 170
democracy/democracies, 2, 5, 12, 16–17, 22–23, 68–69, 71, 73, 77, 88–89, 98, 105, 117, 119–120, 122–123, 125, 139, 145–146
Deng Xiaoping, 100, 102–103
Denmark, 22, 38, 74, 98
depression, worldwide, 64, 69–70
desertification, 108, 170–171
developing countries, 136–137, 139–140, 156–157
digital globalization, 143
disaster relief, 145
drug trafficking, 125
dynasty/dynasties, 38–39, 67

E

East Germany, 77, 91, 120
economic imperialism, 18
economic interdependence, 99, 139–140
economic issues, 95–99
economic nationalism, 19
economic unification, 97–98
economy, global, 31, 143
Ecuador, 13
Edison, Thomas, 50
education, 30–31, 156–157, 165
Egypt, 93, 96–97, 99, 150, 158, 159
Einstein, Albert, 51
emerging nations, 138
empires, 11, 66
enclosure, 26
endangered species, 171
energy, 26, 51, 99, 139
England (Great Britain), 9, 11, 26, 29–30, 36, 53, 67–68, 74, 76, 77, 88–89, 103–104, 112, 143, 146, 147, 173
enlightenment, 4–7
enslaved people/Africans, 12
environmental concerns, 168–173
Estonia, 61, 66, 119
Ethiopia, 37, 73, 137
ethnic cleansing, 148
ethnic conflicts, 142–145, 146, 148
Europe, 14–16, 21–24, 68, 77, 88, 90–91, 96–98, 106, 142–143
European Community (EC), 98
European Union (EU), 98

F

Facebook, 143
fascism, 69, 71
Ferdinand, Archduke Francis, 54
feudalism, 16–17
Finland, 68
food supply, 163–164
fossil fuels, 168–169
France, 8–12, 15, 20, 30, 53, 67, 68, 74–75, 89, 143, 146, 173
French Revolution, 8–12, 13, 14–16, 19
Freud, Sigmund, 51

G

Galilei, Galileo, 3
Gandhi, Indira, 105–106
Gandhi, Mohandas, 67–68, 104
genetic engineering, 167
Germany, 16, 21–22, 30, 53, 56, 61, 65–66, 68, 70–71, 73–77, 89, 91, 97, 120–121

Ghana, 106
glasnost, 118
Global North, 136, 140
global North, 143
Global South, 136–137, 140
global South, 143
global warming, 169
Glorious Revolution, 9
Gold Coast, 106
Gorbachev, Mikhail, 118
Great Britain. *see* England (Great Britain)
Great Depression, 69
Great Leap Forward, 101–102
Greece, 90
Green Revolution, 163–164
Guatemala, 123

H

Haiti, 12, 146
Hamas, 150
Herzegovina, 54, 142
Hinduism/Hindus, 105, 143, 151
Hiroshima, 75
Hitler, Adolf, 70–71, 74–76
Ho Chi Minh, 110
Holocaust, 76–77, 89
Hong Kong, 99, 103
human rights, 76, 103, 145, 147, 157–161
human trafficking, 158
Hungary, 66, 91
Hussein, Saddam, 116, 150–151

I

imperialism, 17, 35–40, 53, 104
independence movements, Latin
 American, 12–13
India, 22–23, 67–68, 94, 96, 104–106, 143,
 151, 157, 158, 170, 173
Indian National Congress, 22–23
Indonesia, 143, 147, 170
Industrial Revolution, 26–28
Information Age, 164–165
Information Revolution, 164–165
Internet, 164
intifada, 113
Iran, 67, 93, 99, 115, 116, 149
Iraq, 67, 93, 99, 116, 145, 149
Iraq War, 116, 150–151
Ireland, 31, 142, 147
Irish Republican Army (IRA), 147
Islamic State, 161
Islam/Muslims, 23, 105, 114, 143, 147, 151
Israel, 89, 93, 99, 112–114, 150, 173
Italy, 15–16, 21, 55, 66, 70, 73–75

J

Japan, 66, 71, 73–75, 77, 89, 96, 98,
 155–156

Jefferson, Thomas, 7
Judaism/Jews, 17, 22, 67, 76, 112

K

Kenya, 106, 137
Kenyatta, Jomo, 106
Korea. *see* North Korea; South Korea
Korean War, 92
Kosovo, 142, 148
Kurds, 149, 151
Kuwait, 99, 116, 145

L

labor unions, 29–30, 49
Latin America, 12–13, 17–18, 93, 97,
 122–125
Latvia, 61, 66, 119
League of Nations, 65, 71, 72
Lebanon, 67, 114
Lenin, Vladimir, 60–61, 63
liberalism, 15
Libya, 115, 159
literacy, 165
Lithuania, 61, 66, 119
Long March, 101

M

Macedonia, 143
Mandela, Nelson, 108–109
Mao Zedong, 101
market economies, 95–96
Marshall Plan, 91
Marxist socialism, 29
medical technology, 166–167
medicine, 48–49
Meiji Restoration, 33–34
Mexican Revolution, 18–19
Mexico, 18–19, 124–125
Middle East, 112–116, 143, 156
migration, 31, 105, 124, 161–162
militarism, 53, 71, 73
Milosevic, Slobodan, 142, 148
money, 97
Montenegro, 148
multinational corporations, 139–140
Muslim League, 23
Muslims. *see* Islam/Muslims
Mussolini, Benito, 70
Myanmar, 110

N

Nagasaki, 75
Napoleon Bonaparte, 10–12
nationalism, 5, 12, 15, 19–24, 35–36, 53,
 59, 61, 67–68, 96, 106–109, 119, 148
natural disasters, 171–172
Nehru, Jawaharlal, 104
Netherlands, the, 74, 143

Newton, Isaac, 3
Ngo Dinh Diem, 110
Nicaragua, 123–124
Nigeria, 108, 154
Nkrumah, Kwame, 106
North American Free Trade Agreement
 (NAFTA), 140
North Atlantic Treaty Organization
 (NATO), 91, 121, 142
North Korea, 92, 149–150, 173
North Vietnam, 110
Northern Ireland, 142, 147
Norway, 74
nuclear accidents, 172
nuclear proliferation, 172–173
nuclear waste, 172
nuclear weapons, 173

O

oil, 111, 139
Organization of African Unity (OAU), 106
Organization of Petroleum Exporting
 Countries (OPEC), 99
Ottoman empire, 23, 53–54, 66

P

Pacific Rim, 98–99
Pakistan, 105, 151–153, 158, 173
Palestine, 22, 67, 112–114
Palestinian Arabs, 112–114, 144, 150
Palestinian Liberation Organization
 (PLO), 150
Pan-Africanism, 106
Panama, 125
Pan-Arabism, 67
Pan-Slavism, 24, 53
peacekeeping, 145
Perestroika, 118
Perón, Juan, 123
Peru, 13
Philippines, the, 77
Poland, 15, 61, 65, 74, 77, 90–91, 120
political prisoners, 158–159
political revolutions, 6–13, 15–16, 18–20
pollution, 168–170
population growth, 26, 50–51, 97,
 124, 137
poverty, 157
prisoners, 158–159

R

Rabin, Yitzhak, 113–114
red guards, 102
religious conflicts, 104–105, 142–145, 146
Renaissance, 2
revolutions, 1–5, 6–13, 14–19, 20, 22, 24,
 25–31, 35, 39, 47, 49, 57–60, 63, 91,
 93–94, 100, 102, 115–116, 122, 124,
 163–164

Roman Catholic Church, 4, 18, 21, 125
Romania, 66, 120
Roosevelt, Franklin Delano, 74–75, 106
Russia, 5, 11, 14, 16–17, 19, 22–24, 33–34,
   47, 52–57, 58–63, 66–67, 75, 77, 114,
   119, 153–154, 173. *see also* Soviet
   Union
Russification, 17, 59, 62
Russo-Japanese War, 34, 59
Rwanda, 108

S

samurai, 33
satellites, 165–166
Saudi Arabia, 99, 112, 116
Scientific Revolution, 2–5
scientific theories, 51
Sepoy Mutiny, 36
Serbia, 24, 53–54, 142, 148
Sikhism/Sikhs, 106, 143, 147
Singapore, 99
Sino-Japanese War, 34
slave trade, 35, 37–38
slaves/slavery, 12, 76, 158
Slovakia, 121
Slovenia, 142
Smith, Adam, 27–28
social classes, 8, 27–28, 59, 124
social Darwinism, 28–29, 36
social media, 143
socialism, 29, 137
solidarity, 120
South Africa, 93, 104, 108–110, 173
South America, 12–13, 17, 158
South Korea, 92, 99, 149–150, 173
South Vietnam, 110
Southeast Asia, 35, 98, 104, 109–110,
   140, 143
Soviet Union, 29, 61–63, 72–75, 77,
   87–94, 95–97, 112, 117–121

Space Age, 165–166
space exploration, 165–166
Spain, 12–13, 18, 93, 147
Sri Lanka, 147
Stalin, Joseph, 58, 61–63, 73, 75,
   88, 90–91
sub-Saharan Africa, 154
Sudan, 108, 137, 146
Suu Kyi, Aung San, 110
Sweden, 68
Syria, 67, 93, 112, 114, 149, 158, 160–161

T

Taiwan (Republic of China), 34, 99–101
technology, 26–27, 33–34, 47–48, 50–51,
   52, 55–57, 72, 75, 92, 135, 137,
   139–140, 163–167
terrorism, 113–115, 123, 125, 135,
   141–142, 146, 150–151, 154, 161
Tibet, 143, 147
total war, 56, 76
trade, European, 21
trade, global, 18, 31, 32, 34, 38–39,
   69, 96, 98–99, 102–103, 107, 125,
   139–140, 158
trade restrictions, 27, 93–94, 109, 116
tribalism, 108
Triple Alliance, 53
Triple Entente, 53
Trump, Donald, 143
Tunisia, 159
Turkey, 20, 23, 53, 66–67, 90, 115, 149, 158
Tutu, Desmond, 109

U

Ukraine, 142–143, 153–154
United Kingdom. *see* England
   (Great Britain)
United Nations (UN), 72, 77, 88, 92, 94,
   102, 112, 135, 141, 144–147, 169

United States, 6–7, 18, 26, 31, 32–33, 35,
   50, 52, 55–56, 61, 64–65, 68–69, 72,
   74–77, 87–94, 95–99, 102–103, 110,
   112, 114–116, 117–119, 123–125, 140,
   150–151, 173
Universal Declaration of Human
   Rights, 145
urbanization. *see* cities/urbanization

V

Venezuela, 13, 99
Vietnam, 92–93, 109–110

W

Walesa, Lech, 120
War Crime Trials, 77
Warsaw Pact, 91
water, 170
West Germany, 77, 88–89, 91, 94, 95,
   97, 120–121
Westernization, 115, 155
women, 5, 19, 28, 34, 56, 64, 67–68, 76,
   89, 101, 106, 115, 158
women's suffrage movement, 64, 68
World War I, 23–24, 47, 52–57, 58–60,
   63–71, 112, 120, 122
World War II, 72–77, 88–92, 95–99, 101,
   104, 106, 109–110, 112

Y

Yeltsin, Boris, 119
Yemen, 159–160
Yugoslavia, 66, 94, 121, 142, 148

Z

Zaibatsu, 33
Zaire, 93, 138
Zambia, 137
Zionism, 22, 67

Acknowledgments

Photographs

Every effort has been made to secure permission and provide appropriate credit for photographic material. The publisher deeply regrets any omission and pledges to correct errors called to its attention in subsequent editions.

Unless otherwise acknowledged, all photographs are the property of Pearson Education, Inc.

Photo locators denoted as follows: Top (T), Center (C), Bottom (B), Left (L), Right (R), Background (Bkgd)

Cover ©JustASC/Shutterstock; **i** (C) ©JustASC/Shutterstock; **xxii** Rex Babin; **xxiii** Universal Press Syndicate; **1** (R) Gretchen Medeiros; **16** (C) ©emei/Shutterstock; **35** (R) Gretchen Medeiros; **46** (TL) ©Sufi/Shutterstock; **47** Leslie Deeb; **51** Eugene Gordan; **71** Library of Congress; **87** Art Resource, NY; **108** Library of Congress; **128** (L) Demetrio Carrasco/©DK Images; **139** Currier and Ives/Library of Congress; **149** Library of Congress; **183** ©The Granger Collection, NY; **185** Library of Congress; **199** Comrade Lenin Cleans the World of Filth (1920), lithograph. Viktor Nikolayevich Deni/©The Granger Collection, NY; **225** U. S. Air Force Photo; **241** United Media; **257** Bob Englehart/Hartford Courant; **261** Library of Congress; **265** Bob Englehart/Hartford Courant; **287** Stephens Media; **285** North Jersey Media; **288** zorani/Getty Images; **311** John Trever.

Regents Exams: January 2017 3 Camel, approx. 690–750. China; Shaanxi province or Henan province, Tang dynasty (618–906). Glazed low-fired ceramic. Asian Art Museum of San Francisco, The Avery Brundage Collection, B60S95. Photograph © Asian Art Museum of San Francisco; **6** Greene in the New York Evening Telegram, Literary Digest, August 30, 1919 (adapted); **August 2017 5** Source: Joseph C. Miller, *Way of Death: Merchant Capitalism and the Angolan Slave Trade 1730–1830,* The University of Wisconsin Press (adapted); **8** Source: Henry Bateman, Victoria and Albert Museum 1939–1945 (adapted); **9** Source: Edmund S. Valtman, The Hartford Times, August 31, 1961 (adapted); **10** Rob Rogers, Used with permission from Andrews McMeel Syndication; **10** Nick Anderson Editorial Cartoon used with the permission of Nick Anderson, the Washington Post Writers Group and the Cartoonist Group. All rights reserved.; **18** Punch, Volume 17, 1849 (adapted); **June 2016 4** Getty Images; **6** Punch, September 25, 1852 (adapted); **12** Source: Leonard Raven-Hill, Punch (adapted); **Draft Prototypes for Global History and Geography II, Draft April 2016 4** *The Little Journal,* published in France, January 16, 1898 (Biblioteque Nationale de France); **6** Reprinted with permission from Compton's by Britannica, © 2010 by Encyclopedia Britannica, Inc.; **24** The University of the State of New York Regents used under CC-BY-SA license https://en.wikipedia.org/wiki/File:Partition_of_India-en.svg; **January 2016 04** © Paula J. Becker, **11** General Photographic Agency/Getty Images, **18** AP Photo/File; **August 2015 04** Peter N. Stearns et al., World Civilizations: The Global Experience, Pearson Longman (adapted), **08** The University of Iowa, Special Collections and University Archives, **09** "Another type of fossil fuel." (May 7, 2008) by Glenn McCoy, Universal UClick, **18** Pig Iron and Cattle in the Soviet Union, 1920–1940 from A History of the Modern World by Palmer and Colton. Copyright (c) Alfred A Knopf, an imprint of Random House., **22** Source: Ben Kiernan, The Pol Pot Regime, Yale University Press, 1996 (adapted); **June 2015 05** The Granger Collection, New York, **17** Reprinted with permission from Compton's by Britannica, © 2010 by Encyclopædia Britannica, Inc.

Text

Grateful acknowledgment is made to the following for copyrighted material:

Regents Exams: January 2017 4 Michael W. Dols, Viator: *Mediaeval and Renaissance Studies, Volume 5*; **6 Friedrich Engels; 9** CIA World Factbook; **11** The Young Turks, A. Sarrou, trans., Paris, 1912; **14** Charles Messenger, *British Army,* Bramley Books, 1997; **15** Lawrence James, *Raj: The Making and Unmaking of British India,* St. Martin's Griffin, 1997 (adapted); **16** Milton Jay Belasco, *India-Pakistan: History, Culture, People,* Cambridge Book Company, 1968; **19** Letter from M. K. Gandhi, Esq. to the Viceroy, Lord Irwin, March 2, 1930; **20** Warshaw and Bromwell with A. J. Tudisco, *India Emerges: A Concise History of India from Its Origin to the Present,* Benziger, 1975; **21** Jawaharlal Nehru, The Discovery of India, The John Day Company, 1946; **22** William Goodwin, India, Lucent Books; **August 2016 2** Tarini J. Carr, *"The Harappan Civilization"* (adapted); **4** The Edict of 1635 Addressed to the Joint Bugyo– of Nagasaki; **6** Karl Marx and Friedrich Engels, *The Communist Manifesto*; **7** Arthur G. Empey, "Over The Top," G. P. Putnam's Sons; **15** Rathje and Murphy, *Rubbish! The Archaeology of Garbage,* Harper Collins Publishers, 1992; **16** William Stearns Davis, *A Day in Old Athens,* Allyn and Bacon (adapted); **17** *What Life Was Like in the Age of Chivalry: Medieval Europe AD 800-1500,* Time-Life Books (adapted); **22** Source: *Geography Theme Activities, Global Insights: People and Cultures,* Glencoe/McGraw-Hill; **June 2016 3** Erik Christian Haugaard, *The Samurai's Tale,* Houghton Mifflin; **5** French National Assembly, 1789; **5** Olympe de Gouges, 1791; **7** *Japan: A Country Study,* Library of Congress; **8** Bishop Desmond Tutu, *The Rainbow People of God: The Making of a Peaceful Revolution*; **19** Balfour Declaration, 1917; **21** Source: Based on The Avalon Project at Yale Law and The Jewish Virtual Library; **Draft Prototypes for Global History and Geography II, Draft April 2016 2** Montesquieu, The Spirit of the Laws; **8** Winston Churchill, *"The Sinews of Peace,"* March 5, 1946, The Churchill Centre; **12** The Versailles Treaty June 28, 1919; **15** Dr. Tatsuichiro Akizuki, Nagasaki 1945. Quartet Books Ltd. **16** Macgregor Laird and R. A. K. Oldfield, Narrative of an Expedition into the Interior of Africa by the River Niger in the Steam-Vessels Quorra and Alburkah in 1832, 1833, 1834, Volume II, London, Richard Bentley, 1837;

Acknowledgements

17 Nnamdi Azikiwe speech, Cambridge University Press-US-Journals **20** Julius Streicher, member of the Nazi Party, March 31, 1933. Routledge Publishing, Inc. **24** United Nations General Assembly, December 9, 1948, Resolution 260 (III) A.; **January 2016 06** The Physical and Moral Condition of the Children and Young Persons employed in Mines and Manufactures, 1843/British Library, **07** The Communist Manifesto/Karl Mark & Friedrich Engels, **07** New York Times, **09** Lyrics from "East is Red," **14** From "Sources of the Japanese Tradition", © Columbia University Press. All Rights Reserved., **15** "Sankin Kotai and the Hostage System," from Nakasendo Way © Walk Japan, **16** A People's History of the World/©Verso Books, **17** From J. Noakes and G. Pridham, eds., Documents on Nazism, 1919–1945, The Viking Press, **17** From J. Noakes and G. Pridham, eds., Documents on Nazism, 1919–1945, The Viking Press, **18** The Jewish Victims of the Holocaust, © Enslow Publishers, **19** The Holocaust Chronicle, Publications International, © 2000, **20** Native Laws Amendment Act, Act No. 54 of 1952, Digital Innovation South Africa online, **20** "This is Apartheid", © Christian Action, London, **21** "Tell Freedom: Memories of Africa", © Alfred A. Knopf, **22** "South Africa", Children's Press, a division of Scholastic, Inc.; **August 2015 07** "A History of the World in 6 Glasses," Copyright © Walker Publishing Company, **09** From Iran Awakening: One Woman's Journey to Reclaim Her Life and Country, Copyright © Random House., **13** From "Modern History; the Rise of a Democratic, Scientific, and Industrial Civilization" by Carl L. Becker. Copyright © Pearson Education., **16** From "Eyewitness: Russia," published by Dorling Kindersley, **17** Stalin: Russia's Man of Steel, © Puffin Books, a division of Penguin Random House, **18** From A History of the Modern World, Copyright © Alfred A. Knopf, **20** To Destroy You Is No Loss: The Odyssey of a Cambodian Family, Anchor Books, 1989, **20** "Memoir of a Child's Nightmare," Children of Cambodia's Killing Fields, Yale University Press, 1997, **22** The Pol Pot Regime, Yale University Press, 1996; **June 2015 02** Library of Congress, **02** National Geographic Traveler: India, 2007, **07** New York Times Company, **07** Worldpress.org, a division of All Media, Inc., **13** West, Louis C. "The Economic Collapse of the Roman Empire." The Classical Journal 28.2 (1932): 96-106. Web., **14** Steven Kreis, The History Guide: Lectures on Ancient and Medieval European History, Lecture 17, History Guide online, **15** "Ottoman Empire (1301–1922)," BBC online, 2009, **16** "European Imperialism and the Balkan Crisis," The Ottomans, World Cultures, **16** A History of the Middle East, Viking, **18** Indian Independence and the Question of Pakistan, Choices Program, Watson Institute for International Studies, Brown University, **19** Scholastic World Cultures: Western Europe, Scholastic, 1988

Note: Every effort has been made to locate the copyright owner of material reproduced on this component. Omissions brought to our attention will be corrected in subsequent editions.

This section contains an actual Regents Examination in Global History and Geography that was given in New York State in January 2017.

Circle your answers to Part 1. Write your responses to the short-answer questions in the spaces provided. Write your thematic essay and document-based essay on separate sheets of paper. Be sure to refer to the test-taking strategies in the front of this book as you prepare to answer the test questions.

Part I

Answer all questions in this part.

Directions (1–50): For each statement or question, record on your separate answer sheet the *number* of the word or expression that, of those given, best completes the statement or answers the question.

Base your answer to question 1 on the map below and on your knowledge of social studies.

Inner Asia's Major Ecological Zones

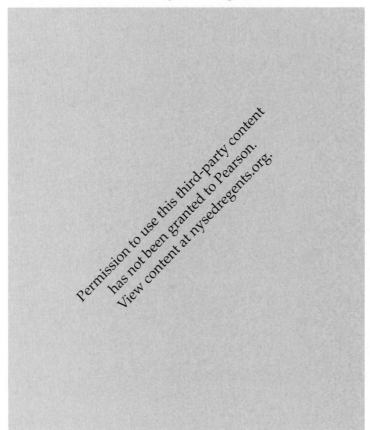

1 Which modification to the environment would most likely need to be made to grow cotton in the region directly south of the Aral Sea?

(1) Terraces would need to be constructed.
(2) Irrigation systems would need to be established.
(3) Desalination plants would need to be built.
(4) Floating gardens would need to be developed.

2 Historians need to determine the authenticity of a source in order to

(1) establish its usefulness
(2) reinforce popular opinion
(3) demonstrate the significance of religious beliefs
(4) determine the characteristics of propaganda

3 In a traditional economy, habits, customs, and rituals function as

(1) territorial boundaries
(2) incentives to change
(3) independent theories
(4) primary considerations in decision making

4 Which title best completes the partial outline below?

> I. _____
>   A. City-states depended on goods exchanged directly with Mediterranean peoples
>   B. Political loyalty centered on the city-state
>   C. A common enemy, Persia, threatened city-states' autonomy

(1) Features of Gupta Empire
(2) Attributes of Indus Valley Civilizations
(3) Characteristics of Ancient Greece
(4) Traits of Ancient China

5 The Hellenistic culture, associated with the rule of Alexander the Great, developed as a result of

(1) ethnocentrism   (3) direct democracy
(2) cultural diffusion   (4) embargoes

6 The pyramids of ancient Mesoamerica and the aqueducts of ancient Rome demonstrate that these early civilizations

(1) used large wooden structures for protection
(2) practiced religious toleration
(3) were able to prevent flooding
(4) had advanced technology

7 One similarity between Confucianism and Christianity is that both belief systems emphasize

(1) respecting others
(2) praying five times a day
(3) converting others to their teachings
(4) making pilgrimages to holy shrines

8 Interactions between the Byzantine Empire and Kievan Russia influenced the Russians to

(1) recognize the absolute political authority of the Pope
(2) adopt Orthodox Christianity
(3) call for an alliance with the Muslims
(4) terrorize Charlemagne's empire

Base your answer to question 9 on the artifact below and on your knowledge of social studies.

Artifact from the Tang Dynasty

Source: The Avery Brundage Collection, Asian Art Museum online

9 In what way does this artifact represent the culture of the Tang dynasty?

(1) Camels were used by traders along the Silk Roads.
(2) Decorative ceramics were primarily imported from Japan.
(3) Farmers used camels to plow fields in the Gobi Desert region.
(4) Iron stirrups were developed and traded with the Mongols.

10 Throughout Japan's early history, a major factor contributing to its ability to resist invasion was its

(1) island location
(2) superior military technology
(3) alliances with neighbors on the continent
(4) decentralized government structures

Base your answer to question 11 on the passage below and on your knowledge of social studies.

. . .The impact of the pandemic on Christian Europe is fairly well known since the Black Death has been the subject of considerable scholarly attention. This interest has led to a misconception of the Black Death as primarily a European phenomenon. Regrettably, the Black Death in the Orient has not attracted a comparable interest, but this neglect should not be interpreted as an indication of its lack of historical significance. The famous fourteenth-century Muslim historian, Ibn Khaldūn, who lost his parents and a number of his teachers during the Black Death in Tunis, recognized the import of the pandemic for Islamic civilization: . . .

— Michael W. Dols, *Viator* (adapted)

11 Which statement expresses the author's argument regarding misconceptions related to the Black Death?

(1) Primary sources have been difficult to find.
(2) Testimonies about the Black Death are unreliable.
(3) The causes of the Black Death are not understood by historians.
(4) Historical study has focused more on one region rather than on others.

12 The influence of Greek and Roman culture on some Renaissance art is reflected in

(1) a realistic portrayal of the human body
(2) challenges made to ancient religious ideals
(3) the impact of William Shakespeare's writing in southern Europe
(4) competition promoted between northern and southern European artists

13 Which situation was a direct result of the Protestant Reformation in western Europe?

(1) The Pope was removed as leader of the Catholic Church.
(2) The religions of the people of Europe became more diverse.
(3) Women assumed leadership in most Christian denominations.
(4) European rulers established religious freedom for their subjects.

14 Knowledge about trade wind patterns and the ability of sailors to utilize them on the Indian and Atlantic Oceans demonstrate that

(1) government monopolies affect trade
(2) geography and technology influence economic activity
(3) economic concepts dominate the study of transportation
(4) laws and customs regulate exchanges across international waters

15 The Spanish encomienda system established in the Spanish colonies of Latin America was most similar to European

(1) guild systems
(2) joint stock companies
(3) subsistence agriculture
(4) feudal land grants

16 Which statement about Louis XIV is an opinion rather than a fact?

(1) He insisted that Huguenots convert to Catholicism.
(2) He strengthened the monarchy by centralizing the government.
(3) The wars he engaged in were the least successful in the history of France.
(4) The palace he built at Versailles was part of his plan for controlling the nobles.

17 The idea that all people are born with the natural rights of life, liberty, and property is most directly associated with the writings of

(1) Baron de Montesquieu
(2) Thomas Hobbes
(3) Jacques-Bénigne Bossuet
(4) John Locke

18 What influence did the Scientific Revolution have on the Enlightenment in Europe?

(1) Natural laws were used to explain human affairs.
(2) Economic growth was slowed by the lack of useable technology.
(3) Scientific truths were used to justify absolute monarchies.
(4) The emphasis on religious doctrine led to the rejection of scientific ideas.

Base your answer to question 19 on the map below and on your knowledge of social studies.

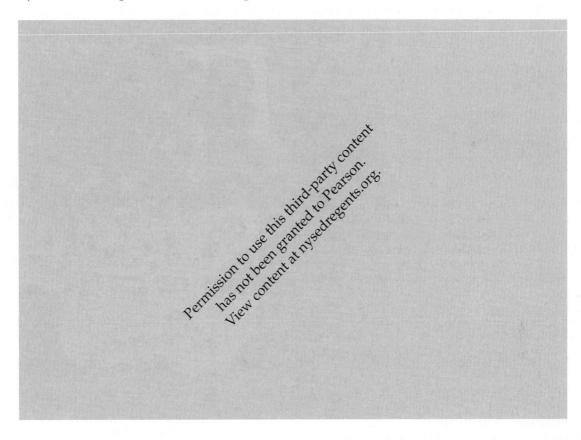

Permission to use this third-party content has not been granted to Pearson. View content at nysedregents.org.

19 This map shows that at the height of the Ottoman Empire, the empire

 (1) controlled the port cities of Barcelona and Marseille
 (2) governed the Persian Empire
 (3) included territory in Europe, Africa, and Asia
 (4) completely surrounded the Red Sea

20 Which geographic feature aided industrialization in Great Britain?

 (1) good harbors   (3) highland climate
 (2) large forests   (4) monsoon winds

21 Capitalism is to private ownership as communism is to

 (1) supply and demand   (3) state control
 (2) laissez-faire   (4) self-determination

22 The terms of the Treaty of Nanjing and of the Treaty of Kanagawa demonstrate the

 (1) unequal relationships that characterized imperialism
 (2) humanitarian ideals that accompanied missionary activity
 (3) importance of technology in developing economies
 (4) changing roles of men and women associated with modernization

Base your answers to questions 23 and 24 on the excerpts below and on your knowledge of social studies.

. . . The following serious accidents (minor injuries are not reported) were recorded in the *Manchester Guardian* between June 12th and August 3rd, 1844:

. . .15th June, 1844: A youth from Saddleworth died of dreadful injuries after being caught in a machine.

29th June, 1844: A young man of Greenacres Moor, near Manchester, working in a machine shop, had two ribs broken and suffered from many cuts as a result of falling under a grindstone. . . .

3rd August, 1844: A Dukinfield bobbin turner was caught in a belt and had all his ribs broken. . . .

— Friedrich Engels

23 Friedrich Engels is using these examples to draw attention to the

(1) efficiency of the factory system
(2) working conditions in factories
(3) living conditions in cities
(4) quality of care in urban hospitals

24 The Parliamentary response to circumstances like these was to

(1) ship most manufacturing overseas
(2) take over poorly run businesses
(3) offer support to striking workers
(4) adopt safety reforms

25 • Japan fights China. (1894)
• Japan defeats Russia. (1905)
• Japan annexes Korea. (1910)

These events reflect the growing power of Japan and its desire to

(1) spread Shinto
(2) acquire warm-water ports
(3) obtain natural resources
(4) suppress the Boxer Rebellion

Base your answer to question 26 on the cartoon below and on your knowledge of social studies.

TURN ON THE HOSE

Source: Greene in the *New York Evening Telegram, Literary Digest,* August 30, 1919 (adapted)

26 The situation shown in this 1919 cartoon is most directly associated with

(1) efforts to stabilize the global economy
(2) the removal of Lenin from power
(3) widespread German victories
(4) the aftermath of war

27 • Development of secret alliances
• Assassination of Archduke Franz Ferdinand
• Stalemate along the trenches

Which conflict is directly associated with these events?

(1) Austro-Prussian War   (3) World War I
(2) Boer War   (4) World War II

28 The term *Zionism* can be defined as a form of
  (1) nonalignment   (3) nationalism
  (2) collective security   (4) pacifism

29
  • Bitterness over the Treaty of Versailles
  • Loss of the Ruhr and overseas colonies
  • Rising inflation and unemployment

These factors are most closely associated with
  (1) the rise of fascism in Germany
  (2) the Russian Revolution of 1917
  (3) French imperialism in Africa
  (4) the communist revolution in China

30 Which geographic factor most directly contributed to the early success of the Nazi blitzkrieg during World War II?
  (1) Alps Mountain Range
  (2) English Channel
  (3) Thames River
  (4) Northern European Plain

31 Use of the term *Iron Curtain* is meant to symbolize and highlight differences in
  (1) religious philosophy
  (2) political ideology
  (3) art and architecture
  (4) resources and climate

32 One reason Mao Zedong, Ho Chi Minh, and Fidel Castro rose to power was that these leaders
  (1) promoted capitalism and democracy
  (2) gained the support of the peasants
  (3) represented the interests of rich landowners
  (4) wanted their countries to stress religious values

33 The organization of campaigns in South Africa against the policy of racial separation and segregation are most closely associated with
  (1) Jomo Kenyatta   (3) Nelson Mandela
  (2) Cecil Rhodes   (4) Kwame Nkrumah

34 Beginning in the late 1970s, one of Deng Xiaoping's major goals for the People's Republic of China was to
  (1) encourage economic growth through modernization
  (2) support the practice of traditional religions
  (3) lessen control over the bureaucracy
  (4) protect the purity of revolutionary doctrine

35
  • Sale of nuclear materials on the black market
  • Reassertion of cultural identities in Ukraine and Moldova
  • Application for membership in the European Union by the Czech Republic

Which event most directly influenced these conditions?
  (1) collapse of the Soviet Union
  (2) failure of the Berlin blockade
  (3) revolution in Iran
  (4) pro-democracy protests in Tiananmen Square

36 A major goal of both the World Bank and the International Monetary Fund (IMF) has been to
  (1) control oil prices
  (2) promote the development of rain forests
  (3) expand governmental control of industry
  (4) encourage economic development

Base your answer to question 37 on the cartoon below and on your knowledge of social studies.

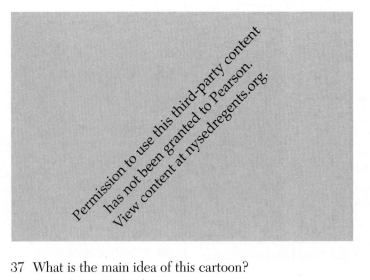

Permission to use this third-party content has not been granted to Pearson. View content at nysedregents.org.

37 What is the main idea of this cartoon?

(1) Peace talks have led to a cease-fire.
(2) The conflict is near an end.
(3) Negotiations have failed.
(4) Key groups have been brought to the peace table.

38 One way in which Hiroshima and Chernobyl are similar is that people in both places were

(1) displaced by earthquakes
(2) harmed by nuclear radiation
(3) affected by massive oil spills
(4) devastated by biological warfare

39 One way in which the motives for the Arab Spring and for the French Revolution are similar is that people wanted to

(1) rid society of secular beliefs
(2) alter the government to bring about reform
(3) create change through nonviolent means
(4) end economic inequalities using social media

40 One way in which the conversion of the Hagia Sophia into an Islamic mosque and the tearing down of the Berlin Wall are similar is that both occurred due to

(1) shifts in political power
(2) forced migrations of religious groups
(3) adoption of steel technology
(4) the restoration of international trade

Base your answers to questions 41 and 42 on the chart below and on your knowledge of social studies.

Selected Countries of the World

Country	Population in Millions	Area in Thousands of Sq. Kilometers	People Per Sq. Kilometer	% Urban	% Arable	Literacy Rate Male/Female		Life Expectancy in Years Male/Female	
France	66.0	643.8	102.5	85.0	33.5	99.0	99.0	78.5	84.8
Japan	127.3	377.9	336.1	91.3	11.3	99.0	99.0	80.9	87.7
Nigeria	174.5	923.8	188.9	49.6	39.0	72.1	50.4	49.4	55.8
Pakistan	193.2	796.1	242.7	36.2	26.0	69.5	45.8	64.8	68.7
Poland	38.4	312.7	122.8	60.9	35.5	99.9	99.6	72.5	80.6
Venezuela	28.5	912.0	31.3	93.0	2.9	95.7	95.4	71.1	77.5

— CIA World Factbook

41 Based on this chart, which statement about these countries is most accurate?

(1) Nigeria has the lowest literacy rate for men and women.
(2) Japan is the most densely populated country.
(3) Venezuela has the lowest percentage of urbanization.
(4) France has the largest population.

42 Which generalization can best be supported using the data in this chart?

(1) The higher the population of a country is, the larger the area will be.
(2) The less arable land a country has, the lower the literacy rate will be.
(3) Longer life expectancies tend to correlate with higher literacy rates for men and women.
(4) The more people per square kilometer a country has, the more likely it is to have a higher percentage of urban population.

---

43 Which development occurred during the Neolithic Revolution?

(1) Food was grown on haciendas.
(2) Stone tools were used for the first time.
(3) The factory system replaced the domestic system.
(4) Permanent settlements were established in river valleys.

44 Expansion of the Hanseatic League, prosperity of Italian city-states, and growth of trade fairs all influenced the

(1) spread of Islamic beliefs
(2) development of Pax Romana
(3) growth of commercial activity in Europe
(4) maintenance of military outposts in West Africa

Base your answers to questions 45 and 46 on the image below and on your knowledge of social studies.

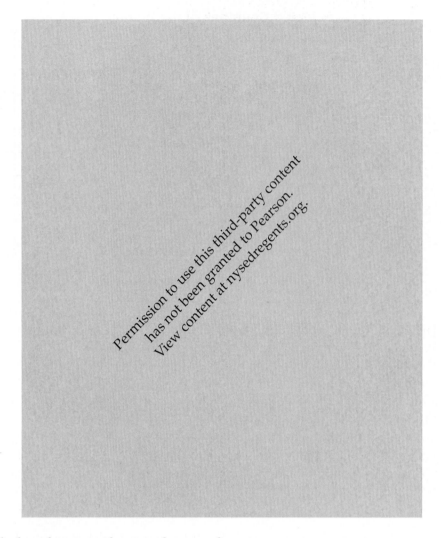

Permission to use this third-party content has not been granted to Pearson. View content at nysedregents.org.

45 Which civilization is shown in this image?

    (1) Maurya   (3) Islamic

    (2) Maya   (4) Cambodian

46 Some of the items shown in this image directly contributed to the

    (1) age of European exploration   (3) fall of the Zulu

    (2) invasions by the Central Asians   (4) formation of the Justinian Code

47 The voyages of Zheng He, development of blue and white porcelain, and the establishment of the Forbidden City are all associated with the

(1) Tokugawa shogunate (3) Axum Kingdom
(2) Ming dynasty   (4) Umayyad dynasty

48 • Emperor Montezuma falls from power.
   • Large numbers of Native Americans died from smallpox and other diseases.

These events occurred as a result of the

(1) Encounter
(2) Latin American independence movements
(3) Mexican Revolution
(4) Cuban Revolution

49 One similarity between the rule of Peter the Great and the rule of Emperor Meiji is that their governments

(1) encouraged the people to convert to Christianity
(2) supported isolationist policies
(3) implemented democratic elections for legislative bodies
(4) began to modernize by adopting Western technology

Base your answer to question 50 on the excerpt below and on your knowledge of social studies.

The Young Turks: Proclamation for the Ottoman Empire, 1908

. . . 7. The Turkish tongue will remain the official state language. Official correspondence and discussion will take place in Turk. . . .

9. Every citizen will enjoy complete liberty and equality, regardless of nationality or religion, and be submitted to the same obligations. All Ottomans, being equal before the law as regards rights and duties relative to the State, are eligible for government posts, according to their individual capacity and their education. Non-Muslims will be equally liable to the military law. . . .

—"The Young Turks," A. Sarrou, trans., Paris, 1912

50 This proclamation incorporates the principle of

(1) national identity   (3) Social Darwinism
(2) divine right   (4) Marxism

Answers to the essay questions are to be written in the separate essay booklet.

In developing your answer to Part II, be sure to keep these general definitions in mind:

(a) <u>explain</u> means "to make plain or understandable; to give reasons for or causes of; to show the logical development or relationships of"

(b) <u>discuss</u> means "to make observations about something using facts, reasoning, and argument; to present in some detail"

Part II

THEMATIC ESSAY QUESTION

Directions: Write a well-organized essay that includes an introduction, several paragraphs addressing the task below, and a conclusion.

Theme: Needs and Wants

> Throughout history, the need and desire for certain natural resources and products have significantly influenced the development of civilizations, empires, and regions. Availability and access to these natural resources and products have helped and hindered their development.

Task:

> Select *two* different natural resources and/or products and for *each*
> - Explain why people needed or desired this natural resource and/or product
> - Discuss how this natural resource and/or product has significantly influenced the development of a civilization, an empire, *and/or* a region

You may use any natural resource or product from your study of global history and geography. Some suggestions you might wish to consider include coal, oil, diamonds, water, salt, wood, rubber, tea, cotton, spices, and sugar.

You are *not* limited to these suggestions.

Do *not* write about the United States and its resources.

Guidelines:

In your essay, be sure to
- Develop all aspects of the task
- Support the theme with relevant facts, examples, and details
- Use a logical and clear plan of organization, including an introduction and a conclusion that are beyond a restatement of the theme

NAME _____   SCHOOL _____

Part III

DOCUMENT-BASED QUESTION

This question is based on the accompanying documents. The question is designed to test your ability to work with historical documents. Some of these documents have been edited for the purposes of this question. As you analyze the documents, take into account the source of each document and any point of view that may be presented in the document. Keep in mind that the language used in a document may reflect the historical context of the time in which it was written.

Historical Context:

> During the rule of the British Crown known as the Raj (1857–1947), the British took many actions to strengthen and maintain their rule over the Indian subcontinent. The impact of British rule on the people and the region can be viewed from a variety of perspectives.

Task: Using the information from the documents and your knowledge of global history and geography, answer the questions that follow each document in Part A. Your answers to the questions will help you write the Part B essay in which you will be asked to

---

- Discuss how actions taken by the British strengthened and/or maintained their rule over the Indian subcontinent between 1857 and 1947
- Discuss, from different perspectives, the impact of British rule on the people *and/or* the region

---

In developing your answers to Part III, be sure to keep this general definition in mind:

> **discuss** means "to make observations about something using facts, reasoning, and argument; to present in some detail"

Part A
Short-Answer Questions

Directions: Analyze the documents and answer the short-answer questions that follow each document in the space provided.

Document 1

> . . .The Indian Mutiny [1857] had come as a nasty shock, especially since British rule in India had appeared so secure. In order to prevent such an outbreak again, the authority for governing British India was removed from John Company [the British East India Company] and placed in the hands of the Crown. Queen Victoria became Empress of India, and her personal representative in the country was to be the Viceroy, who replaced the Governor-General, the administration of India being controlled by the India Office in London. The British Army presence in the country, as opposed to what was now called the Indian Army, was increased to 65,000 men, and as a general principle every garrison was now to contain at least one British regiment. . . .

Source: Charles Messenger, *British Army*, Bramley Books, 1997

1 According to Charles Messenger, what is **one** way the British attempted to strengthen their control over the Indian subcontinent after the Indian Mutiny? [1]

_____

_____

Score ☐

Document 2

. . .How the Raj treated the famines of the 1870s and 1890s says much about its character. Original prognoses [predictions] about railway and canal expansion were probably correct, although there is no exact method of calculating precisely the numbers saved by food distributed by rail. Many more would have died if there had been no extension of the rail network; of this we can be certain. Likewise, as [British Viceroy] Curzon appreciated in 1903 when he initiated a new, ambitious policy of digging more canals, artificial irrigation saved lives. But humanitarianism was always balanced by pragmatism [practicality] and the Raj never lost sight of the need to pay its way. Technical improvements which made Indians less vulnerable to the wayward forces of nature were also contrived [planned] to enrich them [Indians] and, through taxation, the government. The waterways which rendered hitherto arid regions of the Sind and the Punjab fruitful added to the government's revenue. A Punjabi district which had been assessed at £15,000 annually before irrigation was rated at £24,000 afterwards. . . .

Source: Lawrence James, *Raj: The Making and Unmaking of British India*, St. Martin's Griffin, 1997 (adapted)

2 According to Lawrence James, what is **one** action taken by the Raj that aided the Indian people and strengthened British rule? [1]

_____

_____

Score [ ]

Document 3

. . .New schools were started by the British, by princely governments, by missionaries, and by private enterprise. These schools were at all levels, including universities. The English language was used in all schools of higher education. Though only a tiny minority of Indians attended these schools, those who did received a fine English education (facility [fluency] in English became the badge of an educated man). They studied English ideas about democracy and nationalism, and became the eventual leaders of the movement for Indian independence. . . .

Source: Milton Jay Belasco, *India-Pakistan: History, Culture, People,* Cambridge Book Company, 1968

3 According to Milton Jay Belasco, what is *one* way the British and others influenced Indian culture? [1]

_____

_____

Score ☐

Document 4

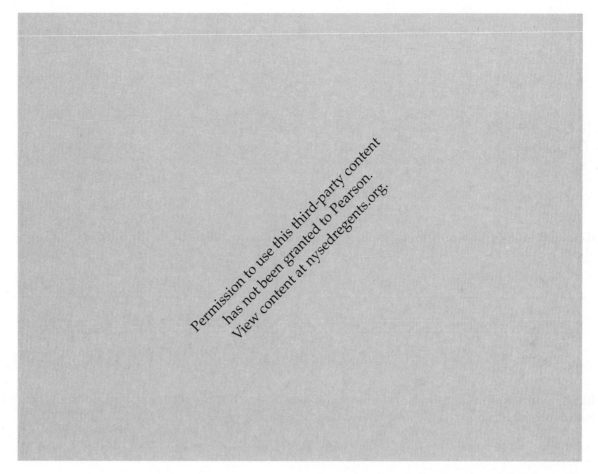

4a What is **one** way Sir Reginald Coupland believes the British Raj improved life for the Indians? [1]

_____

_____

Score ☐

b Based on this excerpt, what is Sir Reginald Coupland's view of Indian people? [1]

_____

_____

Score ☐

Document 5

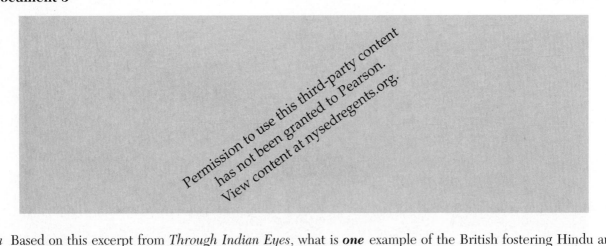

5a Based on this excerpt from *Through Indian Eyes*, what is **one** example of the British fostering Hindu and Muslim animosities? [1]

_____

_____

Score ☐

b Based on this excerpt from *Through Indian Eyes*, what is an action taken by the Muslim League because it feared a Hindu majority? [1]

_____

_____

Score ☐

Document 6

> . . .And why do I regard the British rule as a curse?
>
> It has impoverished the dumb millions by a system of progressive exploitation and by a ruinously expensive military and civil administration which the country can never afford.
>
> It has reduced us politically to serfdom. It has sapped the foundations of our culture. And, by the policy of disarmament, it has degraded us spiritually. Lacking the inward strength, we have been reduced, by all but universal disarmament, to a State bordering on cowardly helplessness. . . .

Source: Letter from M.K. Gandhi, Esq. to the Viceroy, Lord Irwin, March 2, 1930

6 According to Gandhi, what is **one** problem created by British rule? [1]

_____

_____

Score ▢

Document 7

> ...The India Act of 1935 had two parts, each of which became amendments to the Constitution. The first part, put into effect in 1937, gave the provincial assemblies and administrations full autonomy in government. The Viceroy retained the right to overrule them, however. The Act's second part attempted to establish a federal union combining the British-held territories with the more than 560 Princely States. The British-held territories by this time included Bengal, Assam, Punjab, Sind, Bihar, Orissa, Madras, North-West Frontier Provinces, Central Provinces, United Provinces, and Bombay....

Source: Warshaw and Bromwell with A.J. Tudisco,
India Emerges: A Concise History of India from Its Origin to the Present, Benziger, 1975

7 Based on this excerpt from *India Emerges*, what is **one** way the British government maintained control in India under the India Act of 1935? [1]

Score ☐

Document 8

British Rule in India (1946)

...Thus India had to bear [support] the cost of her own conquest, and then of her transfer (or sale) from the East India Company to the British crown, and for the extension of the British empire to Burma and elsewhere, and expeditions to Africa, Persia, etc., and for her defense against Indians themselves. She was not only used as a base for imperial purposes, without any reimbursement for this, but she had further to pay for the training of part of the British Army in England—"capitation" charges these were called. Indeed India was charged for all manner of other expenses incurred [contracted] by Britain, such as the maintenance of British diplomatic and consular establishments in China and Persia, the entire cost of the telegraph line from England to India, part of the expenses of the British Mediterranean fleet, and even the receptions given to the sultan of Turkey in London. . . .

Source: Jawaharlal Nehru, *The Discovery of India*, The John Day Company, 1946

8 According to Nehru, what is **one** way India had to support the costs of the British Empire?   [1]

_____

_____

Score ☐

Document 9

> ...During World War II, Britain made its last demands on India as its colony. It took stringent [harsh] police measures to preserve the Raj against increasing Indian nationalism while England used India as both a supply and operations base. Many Indians served in the British military forces, and Indian industry was expanded to supply the war effort. While some parts of India benefited from the increased industrial production, war-related factors combined with lack of rain led to food shortages that resulted in 2 million deaths by starvation in Bengal between 1942 and 1944. ...

Source: William Goodwin, *India*, Lucent Books

9 According to William Goodwin, what are *two* ways India was asked to support Great Britain in the 1940s? [2]

(1) _____

_____

Score ☐

(2) _____

_____

Score ☐

Part B
Essay

Directions: Write a well-organized essay that includes an introduction, several paragraphs, and a conclusion. Use evidence from at *least five* documents in your essay. Support your response with relevant facts, examples, and details. Include additional outside information.

Historical Context:

During the rule of the British Crown known as the Raj (1857–1947), the British took many actions to strengthen and maintain their rule over the Indian subcontinent. The impact of British rule on the people and the region can be viewed from a variety of perspectives.

Task: Using the information from the documents and your knowledge of global history and geography, write an essay in which you

- Discuss how actions taken by the British strengthened and/or maintained their rule over the Indian subcontinent between 1857 and 1947
- Discuss, from different perspectives, the impact of British rule on the people *and/or* the region

Guidelines:

In your essay, be sure to
- Develop all aspects of the task
- Incorporate information from *at least five* documents
- Incorporate relevant outside information
- Support the theme with relevant facts, examples, and details
- Use a logical and clear plan of organization, including an introduction and a conclusion that are beyond a restatement of the theme

This section contains an actual Regents Examination in Global History and Geography that was given in New York State in August 2016.

Circle your answers to Part 1. Write your responses to the short-answer questions in the spaces provided. Write your thematic essay and document-based essay on separate sheets of paper. Be sure to refer to the test-taking strategies in the front of this book as you prepare to answer the test questions.

Part I

Answer all questions in this part.

Directions (1–50): For each statement or question, record on your separate answer sheet the *number* of the word or expression that, of those given, best completes the statement or answers the question.

Base your answers to questions 1 and 2 on the model below and on your knowledge of social studies.

Egyptian Model

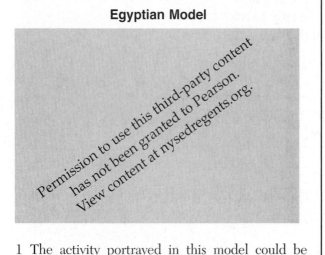

1 The activity portrayed in this model could be used as evidence to argue that Egyptians

(1) lived in settled communities
(2) relied on slash-and-burn technology
(3) practiced hunting
(4) engaged in foraging

2 An examination of this model would suggest that

(1) peasants are excluded from political activity
(2) this society lacks a social class system
(3) art can provide an understanding of history
(4) everyday life is based on religious beliefs

3 Which field of study primarily focuses on governmental powers and the rights of citizens?

(1) economics   (3) archaeology
(2) geography   (4) political science

4 One explanation for the fall of the Roman Empire and of the Han dynasty is that they both

(1) refused the aid of foreign mercenaries
(2) grew too large to govern their territories effectively
(3) banned long-distance trade causing economic strain
(4) required devotion to a single religion

Base your answer to question 5 on the passage below and on your knowledge of social studies.

Some several thousand years ago there once thrived a civilization in the Indus Valley. Located in what's now Pakistan and western India, it was the earliest known urban culture of the Indian subcontinent. The Indus Valley Civilization, as it is called, covered an area the size of western Europe. It was the largest of the four ancient civilizations of Egypt, Mesopotamia, India and China. However, of all these civilizations the least is known about the Indus Valley people. This is because the Indus script has not yet been deciphered. There are many remnants of the script on pottery vessels, seals, and amulets, but without a "Rosetta Stone" linguists and archaeologists have been unable to decipher it. . . .

— Tarini J. Carr, "The Harappan Civilization" (adapted)

5 Based on this passage, what is a valid conclusion about civilization in the Indus Valley?

(1) Lack of a Rosetta stone has hindered linguists from deciphering Indus Valley script.
(2) The absence of pottery vessels and seals from the Indus Valley indicates limited urban development.
(3) The Indus Valley civilization controlled a territory that extended from western Europe to China.
(4) Artifacts suggest the Indus Valley civilization is older than the civilizations in Egypt and Mesopotamia.

6 The Bantu migration is most closely associated with the spread of

(1) bureaucratic governments
(2) agricultural skills
(3) the diamond trade
(4) the principles of Sharia

Base your answers to questions 7 and 8 on the map below and on your knowledge of social studies.

Established Trade Routes, ca. A.D. 600

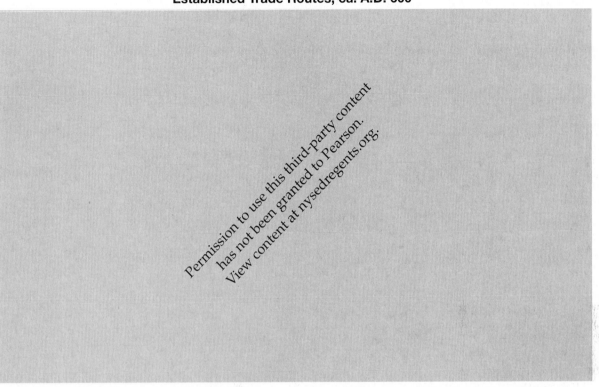

Permission to use this third-party content has not been granted to Pearson. View content at nysedregents.org.

7 Which aspect of geography is the primary focus of this map?

  (1) latitude and longitude
  (2) climate and culture
  (3) humans interacting on Earth
  (4) humans adapting their environment

8 Based on this map, which statement is true of trade routes around A.D. 600?

  (1) Most trade was occurring across the Pacific Ocean.
  (2) Trade began in Ghana and spread down the Niger River.
  (3) Northern Africa was isolated from trade with Asia.
  (4) Trade took place over a network of land and sea routes.

9 Which statement about the Gupta Empire is a fact rather than an opinion?

  (1) India's strongest leaders came from the Gupta Empire.
  (2) The Gupta Empire developed advancements in the areas of mathematics and science.
  (3) The achievements of the Gupta Empire surpassed those of the Tang dynasty in China.
  (4) Gupta paintings found on the walls of the Ajanta caves were superior to the art produced during the Mauryan Empire.

10 What was a major contribution of the Byzantine Empire?

  (1) adoption of democratic ideas from Russia
  (2) spread of humanism and secularism across Europe
  (3) reunification of eastern and western Christendom
  (4) preservation of Greek and Roman culture

11 Which technological innovation was essential to stimulate the expansion of the gold-salt trade in West Africa?

(1) lateen sail   (3) camel caravans
(2) iron cannons   (4) moveable type

12 Which geographic factor of Korea most directly influenced the spread of Chinese culture to Japan?

(1) rivers   (3) climate
(2) mountains   (4) location

Base your answer to question 13 on the excerpt below and on your knowledge of social studies.

---

1. Japanese ships are strictly forbidden to leave for foreign countries.
2. No Japanese is permitted to go abroad. If there is anyone who attempts to do so secretly, he must be executed. The ship so involved must be impounded and its owner arrested, and the matter must be reported to the higher authority.
3. If any Japanese returns from overseas after residing there, he must be put to death. . . .

— The Edict of 1635 Addressed to the Joint Bugyō of Nagasaki

---

13 These rules were made by the Japanese in an attempt to

(1) further cultural diffusion and strengthen interdependence
(2) limit the influence of foreigners in their country
(3) regulate prisoner exchanges with overseas neighbors
(4) reduce the power of the shogun and the emperor

14 A major reason the Renaissance began in the Italian city-states was their

(1) military success against the Seljuk Turks
(2) access to goods from the Americas
(3) location on the Mediterranean Sea
(4) dependence on the teachings of the Catholic Church

15 What was a consequence of the Protestant Reformation?

(1) Secular rulers became more powerful.
(2) Judaism dominated southern Europe.
(3) The Holy Roman Empire became a republic.
(4) Religious differences were peacefully settled.

16 What was one reason China ended overseas exploration after the death of Zheng He in 1433?

(1) China's fleet of ships was destroyed by European navies.
(2) Tribute payments to the Japanese shogunate drained the Ming treasury.
(3) The Ming dynasty ended the authority of Confucian scholars.
(4) The Chinese government decided to focus its efforts on internal affairs.

17 • Use of cannons, foot soldiers, and muskets
• Capture of Constantinople in 1453
• Formation of the janissaries as an effective fighting force

Which empire is associated with these characteristics?

(1) Austro-Hungarian   (3) Spanish
(2) Ottoman   (4) Mughal

18 Inca farmers adapted their environment by growing food in

(1) flooded rice paddies
(2) terraced fields
(3) clear-cut rain forests
(4) expansive plantations

19 The policy of mercantilism was intended to

(1) enrich European governments
(2) end slavery in the Americas
(3) promote the isolation of Asia
(4) establish religious freedom in New Spain

Base your answer to question 20 on the map below and on your knowledge of social studies.

Southern Atlantic Sailing Routes

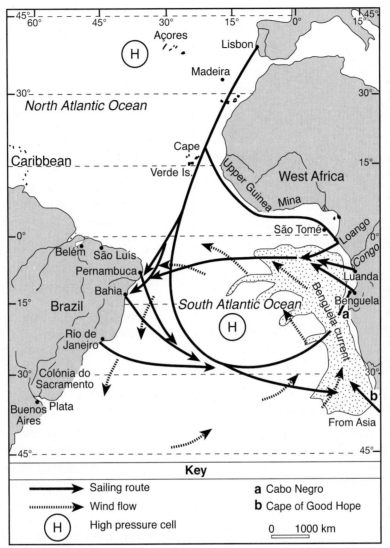

Source: Joseph C. Miller, *Way of Death: Merchant Capitalism and the Angolan Slave Trade 1730–1830,* The University of Wisconsin Press (adapted)

20 This map would be most useful in the study of the

(1) spread of Islam

(2) pilgrimage of Mansa Musa

(3) routes of the Middle Passage

(4) commercial connections in East Africa

21 Which statement would Louis XIV, Philip II, and Peter the Great most likely support?

(1) "The king is entitled to unquestioning obedience."
(2) "Parliament should represent the best interests of the people."
(3) "People have the right to revolt against an unjust government."
(4) "Government should be administered by people of all beliefs."

22 The heliocentric model of the universe developed by Copernicus and Galileo was considered heresy during their lives because it

(1) linked astronomy to the teachings of Muhammad
(2) supported the world view of the ancient Greeks
(3) challenged the secular power of absolute monarchs
(4) conflicted with the official doctrine of the Roman Catholic Church

23 Which statement about the French and Latin American revolutions is accurate?

(1) People in both regions were fighting for freedom from England.
(2) Strong French monarchs led revolutions in Latin America.
(3) Revolutions in both regions were based on the idea of natural rights.
(4) The French Revolution was modeled after revolutions in Latin America.

24 • Bismarck uses "blood and iron" to unify Germany (1864–1870).
   • Theodor Herzl organizes Zionist efforts (1897).

Which concept is most closely associated with these movements?

(1) assimilation   (3) conservatism
(2) modernization   (4) nationalism

25 During the Industrial Revolution, locating factories near concentrations of natural resources and transportation routes most directly promoted

(1) annexations and unequal treaties
(2) migration and urbanization
(3) legislative reforms and formation of unions
(4) communal fields and the domestic system

Base your answer to question 26 on the passage below and on your knowledge of social studies.

...The bourgeoisie, during its rule of scarcely one hundred years, has created more massive and more colossal productive forces than have all preceding generations together. Subjection [control] of Nature's forces to man, machinery, application of chemistry to industry and agriculture, steam-navigation, railways, electric telegraphs, clearing of whole continents for cultivation, canalization [channeling] of rivers, whole populations conjured [brought up] out of the ground—what earlier century had even a presentiment [previous notion] that such productive forces slumbered in the lap of social labor? ...

— Karl Marx and Friedrich Engels, *The Communist Manifesto*

26 In this passage, Marx and Engels state that the bourgeoisie

(1) implemented policies of ethnocentrism
(2) expanded the manufacturing capacity
(3) was controlled by natural forces
(4) replaced railways with canals

27 During the 19th century, the economies in most Latin American countries relied primarily on the export of

(1) cash crops
(2) service jobs
(3) hydroelectric power
(4) factory-made goods

28 The poem "White Man's Burden" is most directly associated with the concept of

(1) neutrality   (3) reparations
(2) appeasement   (4) imperialism

29 Why was the outcome of the Russo-Japanese War a concern for European governments?

(1) Japan was able to defeat a western power.
(2) Russia had surrendered without a fight.
(3) Japan had developed a superior air force.
(4) The Russian monarch had been assassinated.

Base your answer to question 30 on the passage below and on your knowledge of social studies.

Permission to use this third-party content has not been granted to Pearson. View content at nysedregents.org.

30 This *BBC News* article suggests that scholars often have

(1) differing historical perspectives of the same events
(2) difficulty knowing the order in which events have occurred
(3) serious obstacles in bringing those responsible for atrocities to trial
(4) trouble determining the role religion plays in events

31 In the 1930s and 1940s, Japan expanded its empire to include parts of

(1) eastern Europe and southwest Asia
(2) China and southeast Asia
(3) Turkey and the Soviet Union
(4) Australia and Latin America

Base your answers to questions 32 and 33 on the passage below and on your knowledge of social studies.

. . .Gas travels quickly, so you must not lose any time; you generally have about eighteen or twenty seconds in which to adjust your gas helmet. . . .

For a minute, pandemonium [chaos] reigned in our trench,—Tommies adjusting their helmets, bombers running here and there, and men turning out of the dugouts with fixed bayonets, to man the fire step. . . .

Our gun's crew were busy mounting the machine gun on the parapet and bringing up extra ammunition from the dugout. . . .

— Arthur G. Empey, *"Over The Top,"*
G. P. Putnam's Sons

32 Which aspect of warfare is emphasized in this passage about World War I?

(1) importance of civilian support
(2) impact of government propaganda
(3) shortage of manpower on the battlefield
(4) role of military technology

33 Which type of source does this passage best represent?

(1) census study
(2) government decree
(3) first person account
(4) encyclopedia article

34 Which description best fits the Salt March conducted by Mohandas Gandhi?

(1) an act of civil disobedience against the British
(2) a statement of support for dividing India
(3) a protest against the Sepoy Mutiny
(4) a rally for the British during World War II

35 During its climb to power in the 1930s and 1940s, the Chinese Communist Party under Mao Zedong developed a strategy that focused on

(1) taking over cities
(2) building peasant support
(3) sponsoring nonviolent protests
(4) strengthening traditional Confucian values

Base your answer to question 36 on the posters below and on your knowledge of social studies.

Strive on to Victory!
Save electricity, save light bulbs.

Source: Henry Bateman, *Victoria and Albert Museum*,
1939–1945 (adapted)

36 Which aspects of World War II home-front culture do these 1940s posters reflect?

(1) national pride and employment opportunities
(2) mobilization and draft
(3) military expenditures and regulations
(4) conserving resources and sacrificing

37 After World War II, a key reason the Soviet Union established satellite nations in Eastern Europe was to

(1) ease tensions with the Chinese government
(2) expand trade opportunities with Western Europe
(3) protect its western border from attack
(4) maintain freedom of the seas

38 Which factor was a major consideration at the time India was being partitioned?

(1) creation of uniform land areas
(2) equal distribution of natural resources
(3) tensions between Hindus and Muslims
(4) territorial disputes between Britain and France

Base your answer to question 39 on the cartoon below and on your knowledge of social studies.

'WHAT YOU NEED, MAN, IS A REVOLUTION LIKE MINE'

Source: Edmund S. Valtman, *The Hartford Times*, August 31, 1961 (adapted)

39 The artist uses this cartoon as a way to express

(1) skepticism about the success of Castro's revolution
(2) support for a revolution in Brazil
(3) admiration for Castro's bold plan
(4) confusion about Brazil's economic needs

40 One way in which Soviet leader Mikhail Gorbachev and Chinese leader Deng Xiaoping are similar is that both

(1) granted autonomy to satellite countries
(2) promoted a multiparty political system
(3) encouraged religious dissenters to seek freedom
(4) incorporated capitalist ideas into communist societies

Base your answer to question 41 on the picture below and on your knowledge of social studies.

Keeping a Country Afloat

Permission to use this third-party content has not been granted to Pearson. View content at nysedregents.org.

41 The primary purpose of these floating gardens is to

(1) increase regional food supplies
(2) provide more goods for export
(3) serve as an island bridge to the mainland
(4) expand recreational areas for children

42 Nelson Mandela and Aung San Suu Kyi are closely associated with movements to

(1) establish theocratic rule
(2) guarantee rights and liberties
(3) introduce socialistic economic principles
(4) support military juntas

Base your answer to question 43 on the cartoons below and on your knowledge of social studies.

Source: Rob Rogers, *Pittsburgh Post-Gazette*, 2012   Source: Nick Anderson, *Houston Chronicle*, 8-16-13

43 These cartoons suggest that the government of Egypt reacted to the situation by
  (1) discouraging technological advances
  (2) suppressing dissenting points of view
  (3) eliminating most acts of terrorism
  (4) rejecting the use of foreign military aid

44 One way in which the withdrawal of Belgian control in Rwanda and the fall of communism in Yugoslavia are similar is that they both led directly to
  (1) ethnic conflict
  (2) open multiparty elections
  (3) membership in the EU (European Union)
  (4) intervention by NATO (North Atlantic Treaty Organization)

45 "OPEC Meets To Discuss Production Restrictions"
  "European Union Threatens Sanctions Against Nonmembers"
  "China Granted Most Favored Nation Status by United States"

  These headlines illustrate the economic concept of
  (1) interdependence   (3) communism
  (2) imperialism   (4) self-sufficiency

46 Pax Romana, the Golden Age of Islam, and the Renaissance were all periods of
  (1) cultural isolationism
  (2) censorship and regulation
  (3) advancements in arts and in knowledge
  (4) decreasing influence of religion on cultural practices

47 Portugal's attempt to participate directly in the global spice trade was a factor leading to the
  (1) Age of Exploration
  (2) formation of the Hanseatic League
  (3) Berlin Conference
  (4) creation of the Council of Trent

Base your answer to question 48 on the cartoon below and on your knowledge of social studies.

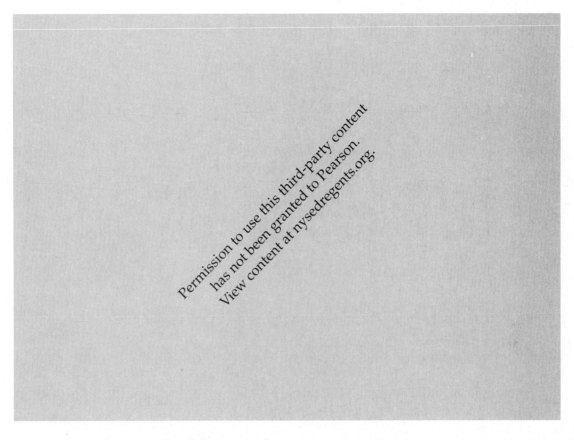

Permission to use this third-party content has not been granted to Pearson. View content at nysedregents.org.

48 What is the main idea of this cartoon?

   (1) Fences were built to prevent the spread of illness and suffering.
   (2) The world continues to ignore human rights violations.
   (3) The people of Darfur are reaching out to those suffering in Europe.
   (4) Poverty affects both the people of Darfur and of Europe.

49 The fall of the Aztec Empire, the encomienda system, and the missionary work of the Roman Catholic Church are all associated with

   (1) ethnic tensions in the Balkans
   (2) oil politics in the Middle East
   (3) colonialism in Latin America
   (4) migration in sub-Saharan Africa

50 Which event in the history of Russia and the Soviet Union occurred *first*?

   (1) establishment of Joseph Stalin as dictator
   (2) end of the Cold War
   (3) introduction of Lenin's New Economic Policy
   (4) crowning of Czar Nicholas II

This page left blank intentionally.

Answers to the essay questions are to be written in the separate essay booklet.

In developing your answer to Part II, be sure to keep these general definitions in mind:

(a) <u>describe</u> means "to illustrate something in words or tell about it"

(b) <u>discuss</u> means "to make observations about something using facts, reasoning, and argument; to present in some detail"

Part II

THEMATIC ESSAY QUESTION

Directions: Write a well-organized essay that includes an introduction, several paragraphs addressing the task below, and a conclusion.

Theme: Belief Systems

> Throughout history, belief systems and their practices have influenced societies and regions.

Task:

> Select *two* belief systems and for *each*
> - Describe the beliefs *and/or* practices of this belief system
> - Discuss how this belief system influenced a society or region in which it was practiced

You may use any belief system from your study of global history and geography. Some suggestions you might wish to consider include Buddhism, Christianity, communism, Confucianism, humanism, Islam, Judaism, legalism, and Shinto.

You are *not* limited to these suggestions.

Do *not* use the United States as the society or region influenced in your answer.

Guidelines:

In your essay, be sure to
- Develop all aspects of the task
- Support the theme with relevant facts, examples, and details
- Use a logical and clear plan of organization, including an introduction and a conclusion that are beyond a restatement of the theme

NAME _____ SCHOOL _____

Part III

DOCUMENT-BASED QUESTION

This question is based on the accompanying documents. The question is designed to test your ability to work with historical documents. Some of these documents have been edited for the purposes of this question. As you analyze the documents, take into account the source of each document and any point of view that may be presented in the document. Keep in mind that the language used in a document may reflect the historical context of the time in which it was written.

Historical Context:

> Throughout history, humans have created waste and pollution. Urbanization and industrialization have contributed to the pollution of the land, water, and air. As urbanization and industrialization have increased, humans have attempted to address the problems of waste and pollution through different means with varying degrees of success.

Task: Using the information from the documents and your knowledge of global history and geography, answer the questions that follow each document in Part A. Your answers to the questions will help you write the Part B essay in which you will be asked to

> - Describe problems that humans face because of pollution caused by urbanization and industrialization
> - Discuss attempts to address problems related to pollution **and** whether or not these attempts have been successful

In developing your answers to Part III, be sure to keep these general definitions in mind:

(a) <u>describe</u> means "to illustrate something in words or tell about it"

(b) <u>discuss</u> means "to make observations about something using facts, reasoning, and argument; to present in some detail"

Part A
Short-Answer Questions

Directions: Analyze the documents and answer the short-answer questions that follow each document in the space provided.

Document 1

> . . .It was the threat of disease, finally, that made garbage removal at least partially a public responsibility in Europe and the United States. One obstacle these days to a calm and measured approach to garbage problems is a collective memory restricted to the human lifespan of about seventy-five years. It is difficult for anyone alive now to appreciate how appalling, as recently as a century ago, were the conditions of daily life in all of the cities of the Western world, even in the wealthier parts of town. "For thousands of years," Lewis Mumford wrote in *The City in History*, "city dwellers put up with defective, often quite vile, sanitary arrangements, wallowing in rubbish and filth they certainly had the power to remove." The stupefying level of wrack [rubbish] and rejectamenta [refuse] in one's immediate vicinity that was accepted as normal from prehistory through the Enlightenment was raised horribly by the Industrial Revolution, which drew millions of people into already congested cities and at the same time increased the volume of consumer goods—future throwaways—by many orders of magnitude. . . .

Source: Rathje and Murphy, *Rubbish! The Archaeology of Garbage,* HarperCollins Publishers, 1992

1a According to Rathje and Murphy, which problem influenced cities to take responsibility for waste removal? [1]

_____

_____

Score ☐

b According to Rathje and Murphy, what is **one** factor that has accelerated the production of garbage in cities? [1]

_____

_____

Score ☐

Document 2

Description of Ancient Athens

...**The Streets and House Fronts of Athens.** — Progress is slower near the Market Place because of the extreme narrowness of the streets. They are only fifteen feet wide or even less, — intolerable alleys a later age would call them, — and dirty to boot. Sometimes they are muddy, more often extremely dusty. Worse still, they are contaminated by great accumulations of filth; for the city is without an efficient sewer system or regular scavengers. Even as the crowd elbows along, a house door will frequently open, an ill-favored slave boy show his head, and with the yell, "Out of the way!" slap a bucket of dirty water into the street. There are many things to offend the nose as well as the eyes of men of a later race. It is fortunate indeed that the Athenians are otherwise a healthy folk, or they would seem liable to perpetual pestilence [disease]; even so, great plagues have in past years harried [attacked] the city. . . .

Source: William Stearns Davis, *A Day in Old Athens,* Allyn and Bacon (adapted)

2 As a result of poor sanitation, what was *one* problem faced by the city of ancient Athens according to William Stearns Davis? [1]

_____

_____

Score [ ]

Document 3

As more and more people left the countryside and moved into towns and cities, waste disposal and public hygiene in the increasingly congested areas became major concerns. Sewage and animal cadavers were thrown into the rivers; butchers let the blood of slaughtered animals flow into the gutters, as did dyers the contaminated water from their vats. From fishmongers' shops. . . , unsold fish were tossed into the street at the end of the day.

For the most part municipal hygiene laws did little to prevent these practices, and those citizens who, like the man [shown] wearing clogs to stay above the muck, tried to sweep up the accumulated refuse often had to compete with the free-roaming pigs that rooted in the garbage. Some towns tried to restrict the activities of porcine [pig] scavengers, imposing a fine on owners who let their pigs run free on a Sunday—and an even higher fine if the offending animal was a sow [female pig].

Source: *What Life Was Like in the Age of Chivalry: Medieval Europe AD 800–1500,* Time-Life Books (adapted)

3a According to this excerpt from *What Life Was Like in the Age of Chivalry,* what was **one** cause of unsanitary conditions in European medieval cities? [1]

_____

_____

Score ☐

b According to this excerpt from *What Life Was Like in the Age of Chivalry,* what was **one** attempt made to address the issue of municipal waste? [1]

_____

_____

Score ☐

Document 4a

Poem About the Thames River in London

THE WATER THAT JOHN DRINKS.

THIS is the water that JOHN drinks.

This is the Thames with its cento* of stink,
That supplies the water that JOHN drinks.

These are the fish that float in the ink-
-y stream of the Thames with its cento of stink,
That supplies the water that JOHN drinks.

This is the sewer, from cesspool and sink,
That feeds the fish that float in the ink-
-y stream of the Thames with its cento of stink,
That supplies the water that JOHN drinks.

These are vested int'rests,** that fill to the brink,
The network of sewers from cesspool and sink,
That feed the fish that float in the ink-
-y stream of the Thames, with its cento of stink,
That supplies the water that JOHN drinks.

This is the price that we pay to wink
At the vested int'rests that fill to the brink,
The network of sewers from cesspool and sink,
That feed the fish that float in the ink-
-y stream of the Thames with its cento of stink,
That supplies the water that JOHN drinks.

Source: *Punch,* Volume 17, 1849 (adapted)

*cento: a mixture

**vested int'rests: a person or group having a personal stake or financial involvement

4a According to this 1849 illustrated poem, what was *one* reason London's drinking water was polluted? [1]

_____

_____

Score

Document 4b

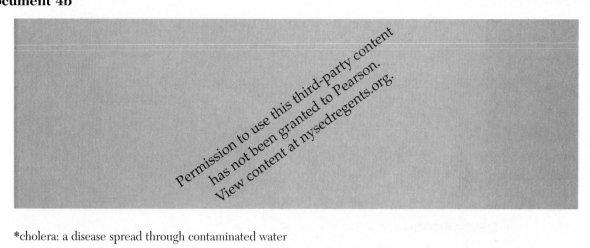

*cholera: a disease spread through contaminated water

4b According to Stephanie True Peters, what was **one** action taken in London to reduce the number of people being affected by cholera? [1]

_____

_____

Score [ ]

Document 5

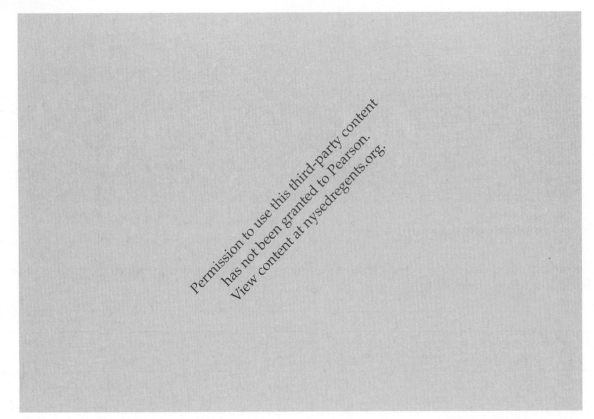

Permission to use this third-party content has not been granted to Pearson. View content at nysedregents.org.

5a According to Amberly Polidor, what is *one* problem pollution has created in the Ganges River region? [1]

_____

_____

Score ☐

b According to Amberly Polidor, what is *one* reason attempts made by the government of India to address the problems of pollution in the Ganges River region have been unsuccessful? [1]

_____

_____

Score ☐

Document 6

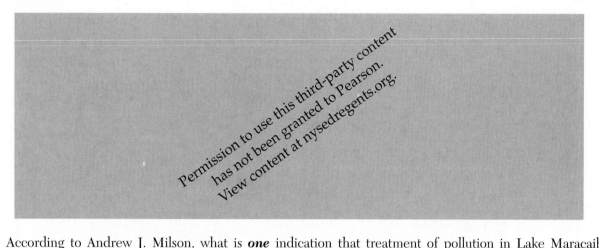

Permission to use this third-party content has not been granted to Pearson. View content at nysedregents.org.

6 According to Andrew J. Milson, what is **one** indication that treatment of pollution in Lake Maracaibo, Venezuela is lacking or is not effective? [1]

_____

_____

Score ☐

Document 7

. . . Mexico City residents once viewed the forest of smokestacks and their congested highways with pride. They saw these developments as symbols of modernization and proof of a growing economy. In recent years, however, air pollution has begun to have a serious impact on their lives. Several times during 1992, for instance, Mexico City's ozone level climbed well over the "very dangerous" point on the official index and remained there for days. Each time the government declared an emergency. Car use was restricted, and industries were required to cut back operations. One result of such events is that more and more people are beginning to equate the city's factories and cars with environmental destruction. . . .

Source: Geography Theme Activities, *Global Insights: People and Cultures,* Glencoe/McGraw-Hill

7a Based on this document, what is a major cause of pollution in Mexico City? [1]

_____

_____

Score ☐

b Based on this document, what is **one** action taken by the government in an attempt to address the issue of pollution in Mexico City? [1]

_____

_____

Score ☐

Document 8

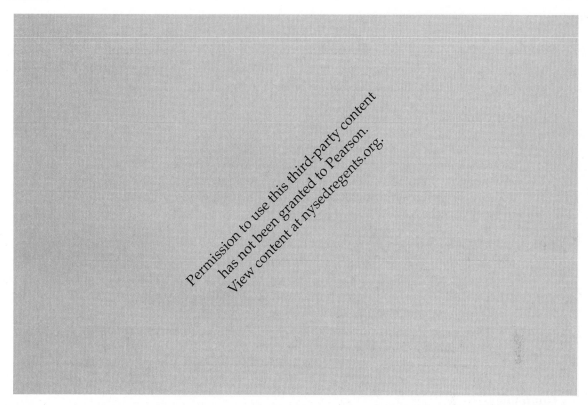

8*a* According to Rylan Sekiguchi, what is **one** environmental problem China faces as a result of burning coal? [1]

_____

_____

Score ☐

b According to Rylan Sekiguchi, what is **one** challenge China faces as it attempts to shift to renewable sources of energy? [1]

_____

_____

Score ☐

Part B
Essay

Directions: Write a well-organized essay that includes an introduction, several paragraphs, and a conclusion. Use evidence from *at least five* documents in your essay. Support your response with relevant facts, examples, and details. Include additional outside information.

Historical Context:

Throughout history, humans have created waste and pollution. Urbanization and industrialization have contributed to the pollution of the land, water, and air. As urbanization and industrialization have increased, humans have attempted to address the problems of waste and pollution through different means with varying degrees of success.

Task: Using the information from the documents and your knowledge of global history and geography, write an essay in which you

- Describe problems that humans face because of pollution caused by urbanization and industrialization
- Discuss attempts to address problems related to pollution *and* whether or not these attempts have been successful

Guidelines:

In your essay, be sure to

- Develop all aspects of the task
- Incorporate information from *at least five* documents
- Incorporate relevant outside information
- Support the theme with relevant facts, examples, and details
- Use a logical and clear plan of organization, including an introduction and a conclusion that are beyond a restatement of the theme

This section contains an actual Regents Examination in Global History and Geography that was given in New York State in June 2016.

Circle your answers to Part 1. Write your responses to the short-answer questions in the spaces provided. Write your thematic essay and document-based essay on separate sheets of paper. Be sure to refer to the test-taking strategies in the front of this book as you prepare to answer the test questions.

Part I

Answer all questions in this part.

Directions (1–50): For each statement or question, record on your separate answer sheet the *number* of the word or expression that, of those given, best completes the statement or answers the question.

1 Historians rely on primary sources because these sources

   (1) are more detailed than secondary sources
   (2) provide eyewitness accounts of events
   (3) have the approval of religious authorities
   (4) establish rules for writing history

2 • Studies systems of government
   • Formulates public policy proposals
   • Analyzes election polls and results

   A person who specializes in these activities is called

   (1) an economist   (3) a sociologist
   (2) a political scientist (4) an anthropologist

3 Which pair of countries is most affected by monsoons?

   (1) Ghana and Argentina
   (2) Algeria and Turkey
   (3) India and China
   (4) Cuba and Afghanistan

4 The Neolithic Revolution is seen as a turning point in human history mainly because

   (1) farming led to settled communities
   (2) people started using animal skins for clothing
   (3) copper was first used to improve stone tools
   (4) cave paintings recorded the activities of nomadic groups

5 Which action is most closely associated with the early Mesopotamian civilizations?

   (1) building floating gardens to grow corn
   (2) establishing representative democracies
   (3) developing a writing system using cuneiform
   (4) constructing Hindu temples

6 Which two major regions were directly connected by the Silk Road?

   (1) Europe and South America
   (2) Central America and Africa
   (3) Asia and Africa
   (4) Asia and Europe

7 The belief systems of Daoism, Shinto, and animism stress

   (1) harmony with nature to live in peace
   (2) acceptance of monotheism to achieve salvation
   (3) proper behavior to maintain social order
   (4) obedience to caste rules to achieve moksha

8 • Justinian imposes new code of law.
   • Completion of Hagia Sophia adds beauty to Constantinople.
   • Greco-Roman tradition preserved.

   Which empire is described in these statements?

   (1) Byzantine   (3) Mauryan
   (2) Persian   (4) Ottoman

9 What was one effect of the expansion of Islam between 632 and 750?

   (1) Armed conquest was forbidden by the caliphs.
   (2) Cultural and commercial connections were established over a sizable region.
   (3) A majority of the western European population converted.
   (4) A single centralized authority governed an area from the Mediterranean Sea to the Indus River.

10 What was a final outcome of the Crusades?

   (1) The Seljuk Turks conquered Spain.
   (2) Jerusalem remained under the control of Muslims.
   (3) Charlemagne established the Frankish Empire.
   (4) The pope became the leader of the Eastern Orthodox Church.

Base your answer to question 11 on the chart below and on your knowledge of social studies.

Mongol Rule in Russia, Persia, and China

Russia
• Mongols allowed Russian princes to rule and required them to pay tribute.
• Mongols tolerated local religious practices.

Persia
• Mongols used Persians to serve as lower government officials, governors, and state officials.
• Most Mongols in Persia converted to Islam.

China
• Mongols brought in foreign administrators to run the government.
• Mongols ended the privileges of Confucian scholars and destroyed the Confucian examination system.

11 Based on the information in this chart, which statement best summarizes the influence of Mongol rule in Russia, Persia, and China?

(1) Local officials were allowed to rule throughout the Mongol Empire.

(2) The Mongols demanded that those who were conquered convert to Islam.

(3) The Mongols used various methods to rule the different people they conquered.

(4) Civil service examinations were used to select government officials in all conquered areas.

12 Which statement about the bubonic plague in the 14th century is most accurate?

(1) Improved sanitation systems eliminated the threat of the plague.

(2) Advances in medicine halted the spread of the plague.

(3) Trade between Europe and Asia stopped just before the plague began.

(4) The death toll from the plague led to labor shortages.

13 What is a major reason the Renaissance began in the Italian city-states?

(1) The Rhine River provided power to Italian industries.

(2) The Alps isolated these city-states from the rest of Europe.

(3) The Mediterranean location of these city-states encouraged trade.

(4) The favorable climate of Italy led to a reliance on agricultural products.

Base your answer to question 14 on the dialogue below and on your knowledge of social studies.

…"Then I must remain loyal to Lord Akiyama, regardless of what he does — even if he is disloyal to Lord Takeda?" I asked.

"Certainly!" There was no shade of doubt in Kansuke's reply. "Your lord is like your father, you must follow him wherever he leads, even into death, to the road to the west."…

— Erik Christian Haugaard, *The Samurai's Tale*,
Houghton Mifflin

14 Which traditional belief is being expressed in this excerpt from *The Samurai's Tale*?

(1) reincarnation   (3) hajj

(2) bushido   (4) nirvana

Base your answer to question 15 on the illustration below and on your knowledge of social studies.

Source: *Ancient Middle America*, University of Minnesota at Duluth

15 To achieve the degree of development shown, the Aztecs first had to

(1) invent wheeled vehicles to move construction materials
(2) use domesticated animals to assist in agriculture
(3) establish an organized government and a specialized work force
(4) adopt advanced engineering techniques diffused from European cultures

16 The kingdoms of Ghana, Mali, and Songhai were all able to achieve golden ages in part because of their

(1) reliance on sugar plantations in the Niger delta
(2) control of trans-Saharan trade routes
(3) discovery of oil reserves in the Gulf of Guinea
(4) ability to use the natural harbors on the Atlantic Ocean coast

17 By the late 1500s, the Ottoman Empire governed an area that extended from

(1) southwestern Asia to eastern Europe and into northern Africa
(2) the Arabian Peninsula across northern Africa and into southern Spain
(3) Mongolia across the central Asian kingdoms
(4) the Indian subcontinent to the Straits of Malacca

Base your answer to question 18 on the document excerpts below and on your knowledge of social studies.

Declaration of the Rights of Man and of the Citizen

1. Men are born and remain free and equal in rights. Social distinctions may be founded only upon the general good.

2. The aim of all political association is the preservation of the natural and imprescriptible [inalienable] rights of man. These rights are liberty, property, security, and resistance to oppression....

— French National Assembly, 1789

Declaration of the Rights of Woman and Female Citizen

1. Woman is born free and remains equal to man in rights. Social distinctions can only be founded on common service.

2. The aim of all political associations is to preserve the natural and inalienable rights of Woman and Man: these are the rights to liberty, ownership, safety and, above all, resistance to oppression....

— Olympe de Gouges, 1791

18 Based on these excerpts, which action would most likely be supported by Olympe de Gouges?

(1) executing the king
(2) restricting access to education
(3) creating more radical military strategies
(4) expanding the definition of equality

19 Which change is most closely associated with Peter the Great of Russia?

(1) establishment of Moscow as the capital city
(2) extension of Russia's borders to the Northern Caucuses and Ukraine
(3) westernization and modernization of the country
(4) emancipation of the serfs on private estates

20 What was an economic result of the Columbian exchange?

(1) establishment of a feudal land system in Europe
(2) development of a European-dominated global trade network
(3) introduction of slash-and-burn farming techniques in the Americas
(4) creation of the Hanseatic League

21 Which term is defined as land grants and taxation policies used in colonial Latin America by the Spanish to provide labor in the fields?

(1) encomienda system   (3) Middle Passage
(2) mercantilism   (4) capitalism

22 Which heading best completes the partial outline below?

I. _____
   A. "Blood and Iron"
   B. Austro-Prussian War
   C. Franco-Prussian War
   D. Kaiser Wilhelm I

(1) Congress of Vienna
(2) Scramble for Africa
(3) Age of Absolutism
(4) Unification of Germany

23 The primary purpose of both the Suez and the Panama canals was to

(1) control immigration to the colonies
(2) limit the slave trade
(3) expand irrigation systems
(4) decrease the distance of trade routes

Base your answer to question 24 on the drawing below and on your knowledge of social studies.

A COURT FOR KING CHOLERA.

Source: *Punch*, September 25, 1852 (adapted)

24 This 1852 drawing most likely would have been used to argue for improvements in

    (1) workhouse rules   (3) factory conditions

    (2) sanitation regulations   (4) suffrage laws

Base your answers to questions 25 and 26 on the passage below and on your knowledge of social studies.

…Economic reforms included a unified modern currency based on the yen, banking, commercial and tax laws, stock exchanges, and a communications network. Establishment of a modern institutional framework conducive to an advanced capitalist economy took time but was completed by the 1890s. By this time, the government had largely relinquished direct control of the modernization process, primarily for budgetary reasons. Many of the former *daimyo*, whose pensions had been paid in a lump sum, benefited greatly through investments they made in emerging industries. Those who had been informally involved in foreign trade before the Meiji Restoration also flourished. Old *bakufu*-serving firms that clung to their traditional ways failed in the new business environment.…

— *Japan: A Country Study*, Library of Congress

25 According to this passage, what was this country trying to do?

(1) provide benefits to the daimyo
(2) develop a safety net for traditional businesses
(3) become an industrialized nation-state
(4) relinquish control over foreign trade

26 Which set of factors directly advanced the modernization process described in this passage?

(1) isolationist policies, taxation policies, lump sum payments
(2) capital investments, government influences, economic reforms
(3) foreign trade, direct governmental control, old bakufu-serving firms
(4) communication networks, customary practices, revoking pensions

27 The Armenian massacre (1910s) and the forced famine in Ukraine (1930s) are examples of

(1) international terrorism
(2) religious conflicts
(3) guerrilla warfare
(4) human rights violations

28 Censorship, a one-party dictatorship, and the replacement of religious ideals with those of the state are all characteristics of a

(1) democratic government
(2) limited monarchy
(3) totalitarian government
(4) parliamentary system

29 The primary purpose of Joseph Stalin's five-year plans was to

(1) increase agricultural and industrial output
(2) limit the wealth of the upper class
(3) increase the production of consumer goods
(4) limit immigration of ethnic minorities

30 During the 1930s, Japan's policy of imperialism was primarily driven by

(1) revenge for the bombing of its cities
(2) the need for natural resources
(3) a desire to retain its traditional values
(4) a determination to spread Zen Buddhism

31 • Great Leap Forward
• Cultural Revolution
• Four Modernizations

All of these policies are associated with

(1) India   (3) Chile
(2) Italy   (4) China

32 In which region are most member-nations of the Organization of Petroleum Exporting Countries (OPEC) located?

(1) Latin America   (3) Middle East
(2) Europe   (4) East Asia

Base your answer to question 33 on the cartoon below and on your knowledge of social studies.

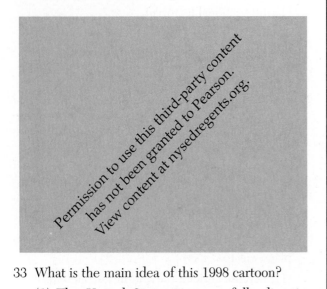

Permission to use this third-party content has not been granted to Pearson. View content at nysedregents.org.

33 What is the main idea of this 1998 cartoon?

(1) The United States is successfully directing Russia's economic changes.
(2) Russia is having difficulty changing from communism to capitalism.
(3) Most Russians support a return to communism.
(4) The Russian government has failed to maintain order.

34 The Universal Declaration of Human Rights was written in response to

(1) atrocities committed during World War II
(2) the burning of Hutu homes in Rwanda
(3) demands for better treatment of Latin American peasants in Guatemala
(4) the forced migrations of city people under the rule of the Khmer Rouge

35 The 20th-century term *Green Revolution* refers to significant advancements made in the field of

(1) electronic communication
(2) food production
(3) zero population growth
(4) biological warfare

Base your answer to question 36 on the passage below and on your knowledge of social studies.

…They stood in the voting queues [lines] together—white, black, Colored, Indian—and they discovered that they were compatriots [countrymen]. White South Africans found that a heavy weight of guilt had been lifted from their shoulders. They are discovering what we used to tell them—that freedom is indivisible, that black liberation inexorably [inevitably] meant white liberation. We have seen a miracle unfolding before our very eyes—it is a dream coming true. It is a victory for all South Africans. It is a victory for democracy and freedom.…

— Bishop Desmond Tutu, *The Rainbow People of God:
The Making of a Peaceful Revolution*

36 The event described in this passage signifies the end of which policy?

(1) apartheid   (3) colonialism
(2) détente   (4) appeasement

Base your answer to question 37 on the passage below and on your knowledge of social studies.

JOHANNESBURG—Africa is often depicted as a place of war, disease and poverty, with a begging bowl extended to the world. But a new report paints a much more optimistic portrait of a continent with growing national economies and an expanding consumer class that offers foreign investors the highest rates of return in the developing world.…

— "Report Offers Optimistic View of Africa's Economies,"
New York Times, June 24, 2010

37 What additional evidence would best support the argument in this passage?

(1) a rise in poverty rates for most African countries
(2) increases in the mortality rate of African children
(3) growth in the gross domestic product for some African countries
(4) continuously high inflation rates throughout Africa

Base your answer to question 38 on the map and graph below and on your knowledge of social studies.

Permission to use this third-party content has not been granted to Pearson. View content at nysedregents.org.

38 Based on the information provided by this map and graph, which statement is accurate?

(1) Women have gained national leadership positions only in Western democracies.
(2) The political power of women has declined steadily since the 1960s.
(3) Women national leaders have been dominant in African governments.
(4) Women have been national leaders in nearly every world region.

Base your answer to question 39 on the cartoon below and on your knowledge of social studies.

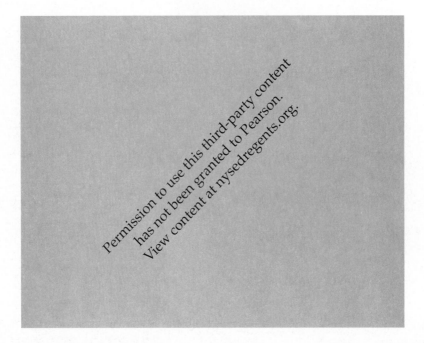

39 What is the main idea of this cartoon?

(1) After the earthquake, the government of Haiti responded quickly to the needs of the people.

(2) The people of Haiti had been facing serious economic problems before the 2010 earthquake.

(3) The earthquake of 2010 brought financial relief to the people of Haiti.

(4) Although the earthquake resulted in massive property damage, few Haitians were injured or lost their lives.

40 "Cambodia's Highest Court Begins Review of Election Complaints"

"Incumbent Declared Winner in Kenya's Disputed Election"

"Robert Mugabe Vote-Rigging Allegations Mar Zimbabwe Elections"

These headlines illustrate that in some countries there is an ongoing struggle to

(1) create fair democratic processes
(2) protect freedom of the press
(3) establish courts that are unbiased
(4) guarantee freedom of assembly

41 The title of the article "Can Minority Languages be Saved?" in *The Futurist* magazine best suggests the conflict of

(1) productivity vs. income
(2) liberty vs. dictatorship
(3) religion vs. secularism
(4) globalization vs. diversity

42 What was a major reason the cities of Babylon, Harappa, and Kiev became important centers of civilization?

(1) River valley trade made them key economic areas.

(2) Their control of nearby straits made them powerful.

(3) Direct access to the ocean made them pilgrimage sites.

(4) Their locations near mountain passes made them gateways to other regions.

43 • Galileo used the telescope and challenged the teachings of the day.
• Sir Isaac Newton discovered the laws of gravity.
• Copernicus determined that the Sun is the center of the universe.

Which period is most directly associated with these events?

(1) Early Middle Ages
(2) Scientific Revolution
(3) Protestant Reformation
(4) Industrial Revolution

44 Which of these technological innovations was developed *first*?

(1) steam engine   (3) wooden plow
(2) gunpowder   (4) caravel

45 • King James II of England flees to France.
• William and Mary ascend the English throne.
• English Bill of Rights established.

Which event in English history is most directly associated with these actions?

(1) founding of the Anglican Church
(2) defeat of the Spanish Armada
(3) Glorious Revolution
(4) Puritan Revolution

Base your answer to question 46 on the speakers' statements below and on your knowledge of social studies.

Speaker A: Trade fairs and guilds emerged during my lifetime. I traveled from town to town to trade with artisans and to find new products imported from the east along established trade routes.

Speaker B: National boundaries and loyalties became less important during my lifetime. Many countries eliminated tariffs and a new international trading organization was created.

Speaker C: Our family worked independently on our own land. We grew enough food to feed ourselves and met nearly all of our needs through our own labor.

46 Which topic is the main focus of these speakers' statements?

(1) citizenship   (3) human rights
(2) urbanization   (4) economics

47 A comparison of the French Revolution (1789) and the Russian Revolution (1917) illustrates that

(1) political and economic inequalities often lead to demands for change
(2) democratic governments generally result from revolutions
(3) revolutions are based on a single grievance
(4) privatization eventually leads to class struggle

48 A goal of the Sepoy Rebellion in India and of the Zulu Resistance in South Africa was to

(1) divide their country
(2) establish theocratic governments
(3) oppose nationalist movements
(4) end foreign control

Base your answers to questions 49 and 50 on the cartoon below and on your knowledge of social studies.

The Gap in the Bridge

Source: Leonard Raven-Hill, *Punch* (adapted)

49 This cartoonist is commenting on international politics immediately after which conflict?

(1) the Napoleonic Wars   (3) World War II
(2) World War I   (4) the Cold War

50 This cartoonist is suggesting the League of Nations will fail because

(1) France and England control the keystone
(2) the United States is relying too much on England and Italy for support
(3) the United States has not become a member
(4) England and Italy do not want help from Belgium and France

Answers to the essay questions are to be written in the separate essay booklet.

In developing your answer to Part II, be sure to keep these general definitions in mind:

(a) <u>explain</u> means "to make plain or understandable; to give reasons for or causes of; to show the logical development or relationships of"

(b) <u>discuss</u> means "to make observations about something using facts, reasoning, and argument; to present in some detail"

Part II

THEMATIC ESSAY QUESTION

Directions: Write a well-organized essay that includes an introduction, several paragraphs addressing the task below, and a conclusion.

Theme: Human and Physical Geography

> Natural geographic features sometimes present challenges for societies. Societies have used various technological innovations to overcome these challenges resulting in change.

Task:

> Select *two* natural geographic features that presented challenges to a society and for *each*
>
> • Explain why this natural geographic feature presented a challenge for a society
> • Discuss changes brought about by the use of technological innovations to overcome the challenge presented by this geographic feature

You may use any natural geographic feature from your study of global history and geography. Some natural geographic features you might wish to consider include the Atlantic Ocean (caravel), Andes Mountains (roads), Sahara Desert (camel caravans), Amazon rain forest (fire/cutting equipment), Russia's tundra (specialized drilling equipment), Indian Ocean monsoons (lateen sail), China's eastern flowing rivers (Grand Canal), and Nile River flooding (dams).

You are *not* limited to these suggestions.

Do *not* use natural geographic features that presented challenges for the United States in your answer.

Guidelines:

In your essay, be sure to

• Develop all aspects of the task
• Support the theme with relevant facts, examples, and details
• Use a logical and clear plan of organization, including an introduction and a conclusion that are beyond a restatement of the theme

This page left blank intentionally.

GO ON TO THE NEXT PAGE ⇨

NAME _____ SCHOOL _____

Part III

DOCUMENT-BASED QUESTION

This question is based on the accompanying documents. The question is designed to test your ability to work with historical documents. Some of these documents have been edited for the purposes of this question. As you analyze the documents, take into account the source of each document and any point of view that may be presented in the document. Keep in mind that the language used in a document may reflect the historical context of the time in which it was written.

Historical Context:

> After World War II, ***Germany***, ***Palestine***, and ***British India*** were divided for various reasons. Each division has affected the people of this region, the region, and other countries.

Task: Using the information from the documents and your knowledge of global history, answer the questions that follow each document in Part A. Your answers to the questions will help you write the Part B essay in which you will be asked to

> Choose ***two*** regions mentioned in the historical context and for ***each***
> - Describe the historical circumstances that led to the division
> - Discuss how the division of this region has affected people of this region, the region, and/or other countries

In developing your answers to Part III, be sure to keep these general definitions in mind:

(a) <u>describe</u> means "to illustrate something in words or tell about it"

(b) <u>discuss</u> means "to make observations about something using facts, reasoning, and argument; to present in some detail"

Part A
Short-Answer Questions

Directions: Analyze the documents and answer the short-answer questions that follow each document in the space provided.

Document 1

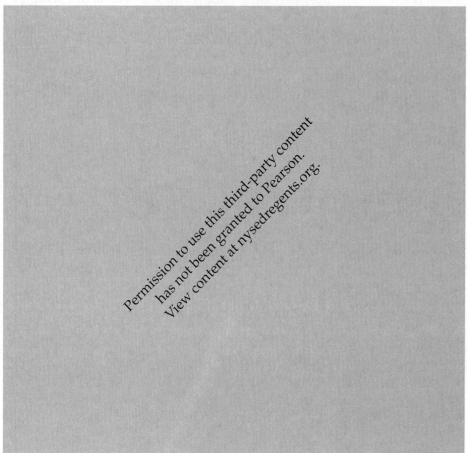

* The Protectorate of Slovakia remained independent although it was aligned with Germany.

1 Based on this map, identify *one* territory annexed by Germany between 1938 and 1939. [1]

_____

_____

Score ☐

Document 2

Post–World War II Germany

Berlin, 1948–1989

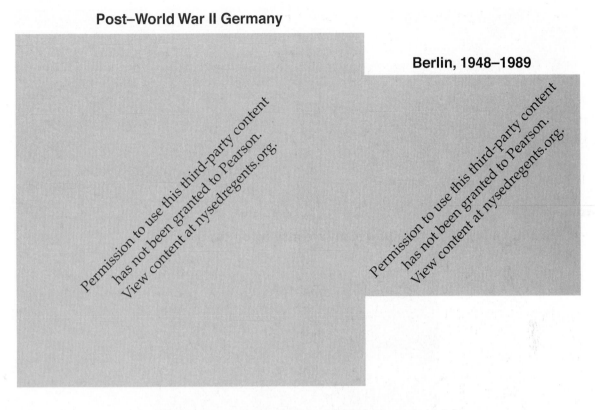

2 Based on these maps, identify *two* impacts World War II had on Germany.   [2]

(1)_____

_____   Score ☐

(2)_____

_____   Score ☐

Document 3a

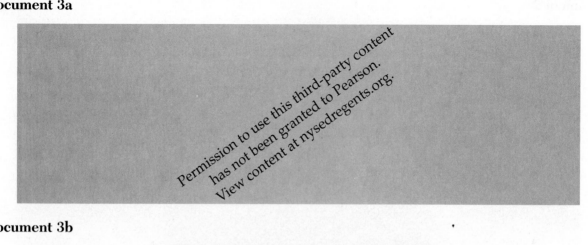

Document 3b

"See how many are staying on our side."

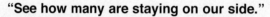
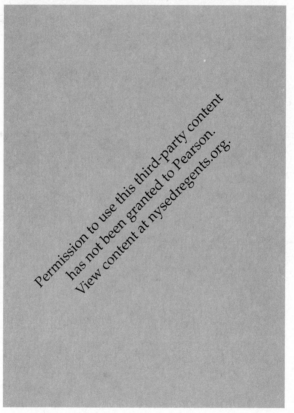

3 Based on these documents, state *one* result the construction of the Berlin Wall had on the people of Berlin. [1]

_____

_____

Score

Document 4

> November 2nd, 1917
>
> Dear Lord Rothschild,
>
> I have much pleasure in conveying to you, on behalf of His Majesty's Government [British], the following declaration of sympathy with Jewish Zionist aspirations which has been submitted to, and approved by, the Cabinet.
>
> "His Majesty's Government view with favour the establishment in Palestine of a national home for the Jewish people, and will use their best endeavours to facilitate the achievement of this object, it being clearly understood that nothing shall be done which may prejudice [harm] the civil and religious rights of existing non-Jewish communities in Palestine, or the rights and political status enjoyed by Jews in any other country."
>
> I should be grateful if you would bring this declaration to the knowledge of the Zionist Federation.
>
> Yours sincerely,
>
> Arthur James Balfour

Source: Balfour Declaration, 1917

4a According to the Balfour Declaration, what support does the British government offer to the Jewish people in 1917? [1]

_____

_____

Score ☐

b According to the Balfour Declaration, what assurance does the British government make to the non-Jewish communities in Palestine? [1]

_____

_____

Score ☐

Document 5a   **Document 5b**

                                        United Nations' Partition Plan, 1947

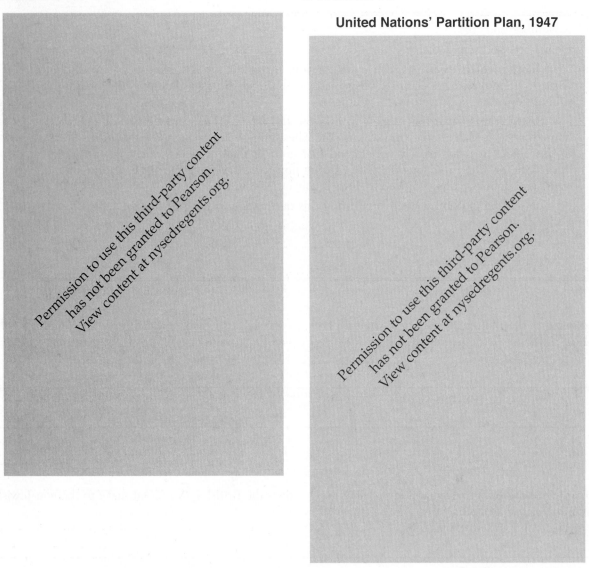

5a According to the BBC News, what is **one** reason for the recommended division of Palestine? [1]

_____

_____

                                                              Score ☐

b Based on the borders shown on this map, what is **one** problem that could result from the United Nations plan for partition? [1]

_____

_____

                                                              Score ☐

Document 6

Events in the Israeli-Palestinian Region
1948–1950

1948	• Israel declares itself an independent country. • War breaks out. • United Nations efforts to bring about peace fail. • United Nations Resolution 194 includes a provision that would allow refugees wishing to return to their homes and live in peace be allowed to do so at the earliest practical date and compensation should be paid for the property of those choosing not to return. [Although the resolution has been voted on numerous times, it has never been implemented.]
1949	• Armistice agreements signed between Israel and Egypt, Lebanon, Jordan, and Syria. • West Bank is under Jordanian rule. • Gaza Strip is under Egyptian occupation.
1950	• West Bank including East Jerusalem is annexed by the Kingdom of Jordan.

Source: Based on The Avalon Project at Yale Law and The Jewish Virtual Library

6 Based on this chart, state *one* result of the failure of the 1947 United Nations plan for partition in the Israeli-Palestinian region. [1]

_____

_____

Score ☐

Document 7

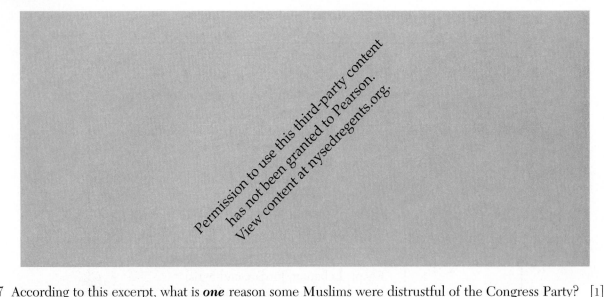

Permission to use this third-party content has not been granted to Pearson. View content at nysedregents.org.

7 According to this excerpt, what is **one** reason some Muslims were distrustful of the Congress Party? [1]

_____

_____

Score ☐

Document 8

Partition of India

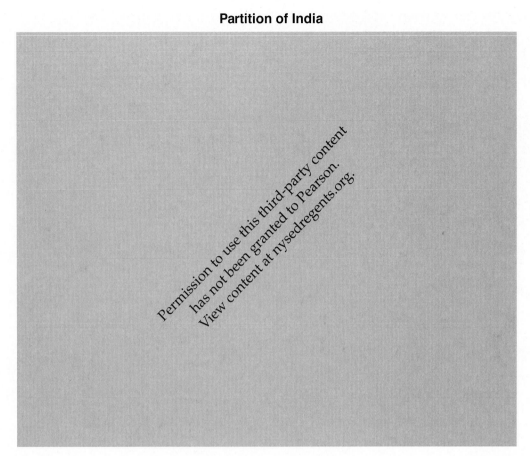

8 Based on this map, state **one** impact of the partition of India. [1]

_____

_____

Score ☐

Document 9a

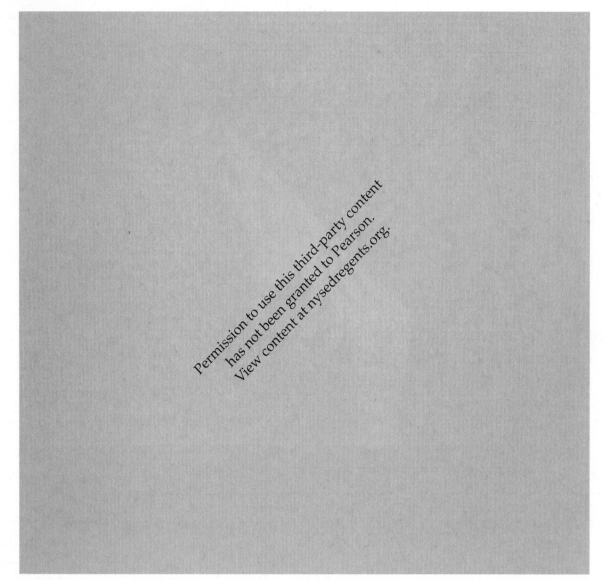

Document 9b

This is an excerpt from an interview with Mohammad Sadiq, a Kashmiri hotel manager. The hotel is located in Kargil in the Indian-administered area of Kashmir.

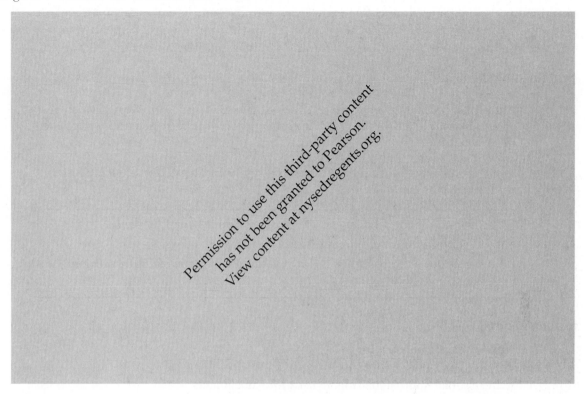

Permission to use this third-party content has not been granted to Pearson. View content at nysedregents.org.

9 Based on these documents, what are **two** results of the border tensions between India and Pakistan? [2]

(1)_____

_____

Score ☐

(2)_____

_____

Score ☐

Part B
Essay

Directions: Write a well-organized essay that includes an introduction, several paragraphs, and a conclusion. Use evidence from *at least* **four** documents to support your response. Support your response with relevant facts, examples, and details. Include additional outside information.

Historical Context:

After World War II, **Germany**, **Palestine**, and **British India** were divided for various reasons. Each division has affected the people of this region, the region, and other countries.

Task: Using the information from the documents and your knowledge of global history, write an essay in which you

> Choose **two** regions mentioned in the historical context and for **each**
> - Describe the historical circumstances that led to the division
> - Discuss how the division of this region has affected people of this region, the region, and/or other countries

Guidelines:

In your essay, be sure to:
- Develop all aspects of the task
- Incorporate information from *at least* **four** documents
- Incorporate relevant outside information
- Support the theme with relevant facts, examples, and details
- Use a logical and clear plan of organization, including an introduction and a conclusion that are beyond a restatement of the theme

This section contains an actual Regents Examination in Global History and Geography that was given in New York State in January 2016.

Circle your answers to Part 1. Write your responses to the short-answer questions in the spaces provided. Write your thematic essay and document-based essay on separate sheets of paper. Be sure to refer to the test-taking strategies in the front of this book as you prepare to answer the test questions.

1ˢᵗ June, 2018
Friday

Part I

Answer all questions in this part.

Directions (1–50): For each statement or question, record on your separate answer sheet the *number* of the word or expression that, of those given, best completes the statement or answers the question.

1 Which social scientists focus their studies on scarcity, resources, and profit motives?
   (1) archaeologists   (3) economists
   (2) historians   (4) sociologists

2 A geographer attempts to understand and interpret patterns and processes primarily by
   (1) examining political theories
   (2) authenticating oral histories
   (3) studying supply and demand models
   (4) analyzing spatial data at different scales

3 In a parliamentary system with multiple political parties in which no single party gains a majority, elections usually result in
   (1) command economies
   (2) religious conflict
   (3) coalition governments
   (4) secessionist movements

4 Which factor most influenced the construction of semipermanent settlements during the Neolithic period?
   (1) production of surplus food
   (2) drawings on cave walls
   (3) ability to harness fire
   (4) introduction of fishing nets

5 Which geographic feature was central in helping the Romans unify their empire?
   (1) Alps   (3) Mediterranean Sea
   (2) Tiber River   (4) Great Rift Valley

6 Which region was the birthplace of Confucianism, Buddhism, and Hinduism?
   (1) Africa   (3) Europe
   (2) Asia   (4) South America

7 Which area served as a cultural bridge between early China and Japan?
   (1) Persia   (3) India
   (2) Russia   (4) Korea

8 The role of Muslim religious leaders in Africa was to
   (1) spread the Four Noble Truths
   (2) emphasize the importance of ancestor worship
   (3) promote the caste system
   (4) introduce the teachings of the Qur'an (Koran)

9 The Abbasid and Ummayad empires are most closely associated with
   (1) causing the fall of the western Roman Empire
   (2) creating an Islamic Golden Age
   (3) controlling trade in the Strait of Malacca
   (4) inventing the compass and gunpowder

10 The European system of manorialism is most closely associated with
   (1) promoting social mobility
   (2) reviving and preserving learning
   (3) serving the spiritual needs of society
   (4) maintaining economic self-sufficiency

Base your answers to questions 11 and 12 on the map below and on your knowledge of social studies.

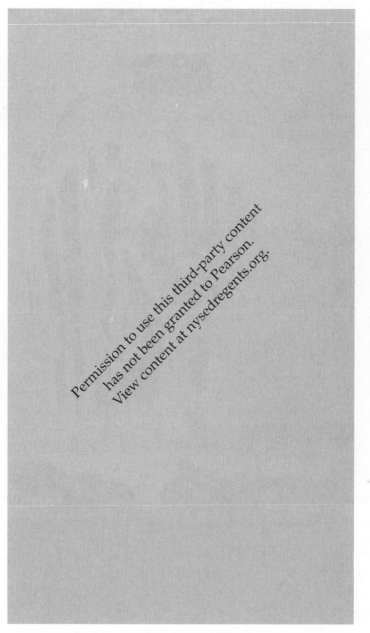

Permission to use this third-party content has not been granted to Pearson. View content at nysedregents.org.

11 Based on this map, in which area did Europeans locate most of their trading bases?

   (1) banks of the Ganges River   (3) coast of the Arabian Sea

   (2) banks of the Indus River   (4) Bay of Bengal region

12 Which conclusion about the Indian economy during the Mughal period can best be supported using the information shown on this map?

   (1) Cinnamon and pepper were the major products of Kashmir.

   (2) Most textile-related goods were produced north of the Deccan Sultanate.

   (3) Diamonds and gold were mined in the Bengal region.

   (4) Many tropical products were raised near Delhi.

Base your answer to question 13 on the cartoon below and on your knowledge of social studies.

The Wittenberg Church

Source: Paula J. Becker (adapted)

13 Which period began as a result of the actions shown in this cartoon?

   (1) Italian Renaissance   (3) Scientific Revolution

   (2) Protestant Reformation   (4) Glorious Revolution

14 The kingdoms of Ghana and Mali became prosperous and powerful because of

   (1) their participation in the gold and salt trade

   (2) the military protection provided to them by the Egyptians

   (3) their dependence on legalism to enforce social control

   (4) the tax revenue they collected from Christian missionaries

15 The Chinese belief that China was the Middle Kingdom is an example of

   (1) extraterritoriality

   (2) ethnocentrism

   (3) filial piety

   (4) the Mandate of Heaven

Base your answer to question 16 on the graphic organizer below and on your knowledge of social studies.

Inca Civilization

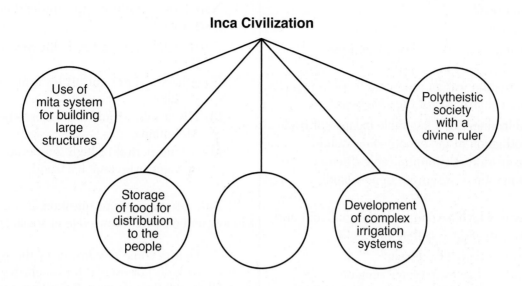

16 Which phrase best completes this graphic organizer?

(1) Building thousands of miles of roads
(2) Maintenance of a large naval fleet
(3) Establishment of a national library filled with hundreds of books
(4) Reliance on camel caravans

17 • Some Central Asian nomads made their living by fostering commerce along the Silk Road.
• Central Asian nomads invaded villages and cities when climate changes affected their food supply.
• Some Central Asian nomads adopted Islam and some embraced Islamic cultures.

Based on these statements, which generalization about Central Asian nomads can best be supported?

(1) They posed few challenges to settled societies.
(2) They allied with settled neighbors to repel common enemies.
(3) They interacted with settled societies.
(4) They contributed little to the culture of their settled neighbors.

18 The Ottoman Turks viewed Constantinople as being strategically important because it

(1) was the birthplace of the Prophet Muhammad
(2) would allow them to control the Vatican
(3) was a crossroads between Europe and Asia
(4) would provide them with access to the Persian Gulf

19 One way in which the voyages of Zheng He authorized by Emperor Yongle of China and the explorations funded by King Ferdinand and Queen Isabella of Spain are similar is that these voyages and explorations resulted in

(1) an increasing effort to preserve the status quo
(2) trade and cultural diffusion
(3) the creation of colonial empires
(4) naval wars between rival powers

20 Which country is located in the region known as Latin America?

(1) Portugal   (3) Vietnam
(2) Somalia   (4) Argentina

21 Which situation was an unintended consequence of Spain's colonization of the Americas?

(1) establishment of a favorable balance of trade
(2) introduction of the encomienda system
(3) transmission of communicable diseases
(4) exploitation of resources in new lands

22 One way in which Suleiman the Magnificent and Louis XIV are similar is that they both

(1) centralized political power
(2) introduced a new national religion
(3) strengthened the authority of the nobility
(4) freed peasants from feudal obligations

23 In the 16th and 17th centuries, the heliocentric theory became the centerpiece for debate between

(1) capitalism and communism
(2) science and religion
(3) colonialism and nationalism
(4) isolationism and globalism

24 In which way did the ideas of the Enlightenment influence the French Revolution?

(1) Superstition and ignorance were promoted.
(2) The principles of mercantilism were glorified.
(3) The divine right theory of kings was challenged.
(4) Punishments for criminal acts were rooted in vengeance.

25 In which way did the geographic diversity of Latin America affect newly independent countries?

(1) limiting the military power of Creoles
(2) forcing the Church to guarantee land reform
(3) making political unity difficult
(4) necessitating a reliance on Spain

26 Which statement best describes a consequence of Napoleon's failure to understand Russian geography?

(1) Rough waters in the Baltic Sea destroyed his fleet.
(2) A harsh winter cut off his army from needed supplies.
(3) His armies could not cross the high Ural Mountains.
(4) A long period of high temperatures and lack of water overcame his troops.

Base your answer to question 27 on the excerpt below and on your knowledge of social studies.

. . .That in some few instances the regular hours of work do not exceed ten, exclusive of the time allowed for meals; sometimes they are eleven, but more commonly twelve; and in great numbers of instances the employment is continued for fifteen, sixteen, and even eighteen hours consecutively.

That in almost every instance the Children work as long as the adults; being sometimes kept at work sixteen, and even eighteen hours, without any intermission. . . .

— *The Physical and Moral Condition of the Children and Young Persons Employed in Mines and Manufactures*, 1843

27 This type of evidence was used in the argument for

(1) modifying laissez-faire practices
(2) opposing the spread of communism
(3) restricting voting rights
(4) reforming the landholding system

Base your answer to question 28 on the passage below and on your knowledge of social studies.

. . .The bourgeoisie, by the rapid improvement of all instruments of production, by the immensely facilitated means of communication, draws all nations, even the most barbarian, into civilisation. The cheap prices of its commodities are the heavy artillery with which it batters down all Chinese walls, with which it forces the barbarians' intensely obstinate [persistent] hatred of foreigners to capitulate [give in]. It compels all nations, on pain of extinction, to adopt the bourgeois mode of production; it compels them to introduce what it calls civilisation into their midst, *i.e.*, to become bourgeois themselves. In a word, it creates a world after its own image. . . .

— Karl Marx and Friedrich Engels

28 Which statement supports the point of view expressed in this passage?

(1) The bourgeoisie needs to use military force to open markets.

(2) The bourgeoisie are backward compared to the barbarians.

(3) Foreigners and the bourgeoisie must work together to end the extinction of cultures.

(4) Cheap prices and industrial improvements are tools used by the bourgeoisie to impose its values.

29 • 1791—Declaration of the Rights of Women and the Female Citizen (France)

• 1829—Prohibition of sati (India)

• 1857, 1882—Married Women's Property Acts (Great Britain)

Which change in perception is suggested by these international developments regarding women?

(1) a decrease in political power for women

(2) a decline in the economic status of women

(3) a growing concern for the treatment of women

(4) an increase in the global exploitation of women

30 The Haitian Revolution and the Sepoy Rebellion happened in response to

(1) European colonial policies

(2) indigenous ethnic rivalries

(3) urban development

(4) religious divisions

Base your answer to question 31 on the notice below and on your knowledge of social studies.

NOTICE!
Travelers intending to embark on the Atlantic voyage are reminded that a state of war exists between Germany and her allies and Great Britain and her allies; that the zone of war includes the waters adjacent to the British Isles: that, in accordance with formal notice given by the Imperial German Government, vessels flying the flag of Great Britain, or any of her allies, are liable to destruction in those waters and that travelers sailing in the war zone on ships of Great Britain or her allies do so at their own risk.
IMPERIAL GERMAN EMBASSY,
Washington, D. C., April 22, 1915.

Source: *New York Times*, May 1, 1915 (adapted)

31 Which technological innovation of World War I is most closely associated with this German notice?

(1) tanks   (3) submarines

(2) airplanes   (4) machine guns

32 What was the main goal of Zionism?

(1) forming a representative government in China

(2) establishing a Jewish homeland in the region of Palestine

(3) improving the standard of living in developing countries

(4) creating an international peacekeeping organization to solve global conflicts

33 Which of these events that occurred in the Soviet Union was a direct cause of the other three?

(1) famine in Ukraine

(2) implementation of five-year plans

(3) establishment of collective farms

(4) development of heavy industry

Base your answer to question 34 on the map below and on your knowledge of social studies.

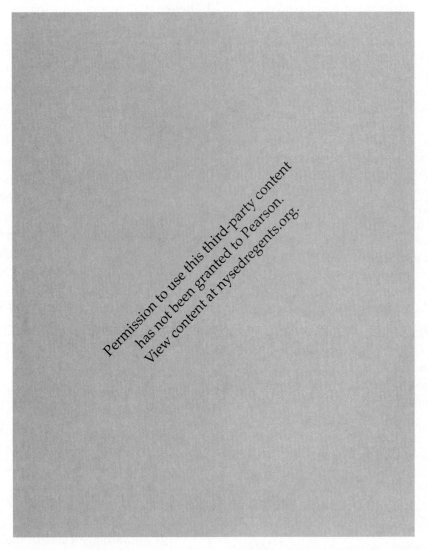

34 Based on this map, which region experienced the most severe drop in industrial production between 1929 and 1932?

    (1) western Europe   (3) central Europe

    (2) northern Europe   (4) southeastern Europe

35 Extreme nationalism, individuals existing for the good of the state, and unquestioning loyalty to the leader are the defining characteristics of

    (1) fascism   (3) democracy

    (2) liberalism   (4) theocracy

36 The Soviet Union's response to the formation of the North Atlantic Treaty Organization (NATO) was to create the

    (1) Marshall Plan   (3) Truman Doctrine

    (2) Warsaw Pact   (4) European Union

Base your answer to question 37 on the cartoon below and on your knowledge of social studies.

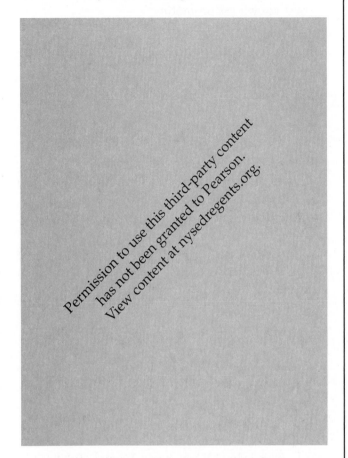

Permission to use this third-party content has not been granted to Pearson. View content at nysedregents.org.

37 Hitler's actions as expressed by this cartoon led Stalin to

(1) adopt a policy of appeasement
(2) take over Germany's industry
(3) join the Allies in the fight against Germany
(4) reduce the size of the Soviet army

38 Which statement about the impact of geography on the culture and history of the Middle East region in the 20th century is most accurate?

(1) Deserts have prevented military invasions.
(2) The uneven distribution of resources has led to conflict.
(3) The abundance of water has contributed to agricultural self-sufficiency.
(4) Mountains have halted cultural diffusion.

Base your answers to questions 39 and 40 on the song lyrics below and on your knowledge of social studies.

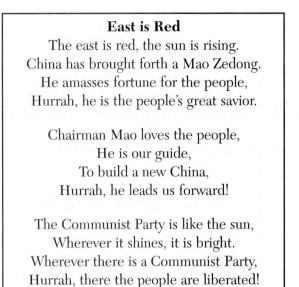

East is Red
The east is red, the sun is rising.
China has brought forth a Mao Zedong.
He amasses fortune for the people,
Hurrah, he is the people's great savior.

Chairman Mao loves the people,
He is our guide,
To build a new China,
Hurrah, he leads us forward!

The Communist Party is like the sun,
Wherever it shines, it is bright.
Wherever there is a Communist Party,
Hurrah, there the people are liberated!

39 What is the main idea of this 1960s Chinese song?

(1) The Sun will never set on Chinese communism.
(2) Communist policies will liberate Mao Zedong.
(3) The Chinese people will become wealthy under communism.
(4) Mao Zedong will lead the Communist Party in building a new China.

40 This 1960s Chinese song would most likely have been sung during the

(1) return of Hong Kong
(2) Cultural Revolution
(3) Boxer Rebellion
(4) Tiananmen Square incident

41 During the Cold War, India's decision to support neither the United States nor the Soviet Union was based on its policy of

(1) nonalignment   (3) containment
(2) isolationism   (4) separatism

42 • Vietcong disappeared into jungle cover.
 • Sandstorms halted helicopter flights in Iraq.
 • Afghan mountain caves sheltered Osama bin Laden.

Which generalization can best be applied to these situations?

(1) Advanced technology ensures victory.
(2) Religious tensions often promote disagreements.
(3) Most military confrontations involve biological weapons.
(4) Geography often has an influence on the course of a conflict.

43 A major obstacle to creating policies that address the issue of global warming is the conflict between

(1) migrant labor and native workers
(2) socialist governments and democratic governments
(3) nations possessing nuclear weapons and those without
(4) economic development and environmental protection

44 The practices of allowing animals to overgraze grasses and shrubs and of clearing trees to use for fuel have caused

(1) coastal pollution   (3) acid rain
(2) desertification   (4) desalination

45 In the late 1970s, the Chinese government created the one-child policy because its leaders realized that there is a direct relationship between population growth and

(1) military strength
(2) economic development
(3) social mobility
(4) political toleration

46 One way in which the Indian leaders Asoka and Akbar the Great are similar is that they are both best known for promoting

(1) religious toleration
(2) enslavement of prisoners
(3) special taxes for Hindus
(4) the spread of Buddhism

47 The Russian adoption of Orthodox Christianity and of the Cyrillic alphabet demonstrates the

(1) impact of Ibn Battuta's travels
(2) role of the printing press during the Reformation
(3) leadership of Peter the Great
(4) influence of the Byzantine Empire

48 Austria-Hungary's ultimatum to Serbia in 1914 and the United States military actions in Afghanistan beginning in 2001 are both reactions to acts of

(1) imperialism   (3) communism
(2) isolationism   (4) terrorism

49 Which leaders are most directly associated with the Cuban Revolution of 1959?

(1) Emiliano Zapata and Francisco Villa
(2) Juan Perón and Hugo Chávez
(3) Fidel Castro and Che Guevara
(4) Bernardo O'Higgins and Miguel Hidalgo

Base your answer to question 50 on the photographs below and on your knowledge of social studies.

Kemal Atatürk

Source: İlhan Akşit, Compiler,
Mustafa Kemal Atatürk, Akşit

Reza Pahlavi

Source: Iran Politics Club online,
Mohamad Reza Shah Pahlavi Photo Album

50 The style of clothing worn by Kemal Atatürk of Turkey and Reza Pahlavi of Iran in these photographs indicates these leaders' desire to

(1) westernize their nation

(2) support nationalist movements

(3) enforce fundamental Islamic principles

(4) adapt to the physical climate of their country

Answers to the essay questions are to be written in the separate essay booklet.

In developing your answer to Part II, be sure to keep this general definition in mind:

<u>discuss</u> means "to make observations about something using facts, reasoning, and argument; to present in some detail"

Part II

THEMATIC ESSAY QUESTION

Directions: Write a well-organized essay that includes an introduction, several paragraphs addressing the task below, and a conclusion.

Theme: Imperialism

Since 1500, countries have pursued a policy of expansion known as imperialism for a variety of reasons. The effects of this policy can be viewed from different perspectives.

Task:

Select *one* country that engaged in imperialism since 1500 and

- Discuss the reasons this country engaged in imperialism
- Discuss the effects of imperialism from the perspective of the people or society taken over *and/or* from the perspective of the conqueror

You may use any country that engaged in imperialism since 1500 from your study of global history and geography. Some suggestions you might wish to consider include Portugal, Spain, Great Britain, France, Italy, Belgium, and Japan.

You are *not* limited to these suggestions.

Do *not* use the United States as the focus of your response.

Guidelines:

In your essay, be sure to

- Develop all aspects of the task
- Support the theme with relevant facts, examples, and details
- Use a logical and clear plan of organization, including an introduction and a conclusion that are beyond a restatement of the theme

NAME _____ SCHOOL _____

Part III

DOCUMENT-BASED QUESTION

   This question is based on the accompanying documents. The question is designed to test your ability to work with historical documents. Some of these documents have been edited for the purposes of this question. As you analyze the documents, take into account the source of each document and any point of view that may be presented in the document. Keep in mind that the language used in a document may reflect the historical context of the time in which it was written.

Historical Context:

> Throughout history, governments have developed and established laws and orders for a variety of reasons. The ***laws for the warriors under the Tokugawa Shogunate, the Nazi orders and laws of the Third Reich***, and ***the pass laws of the Republic of South Africa*** had many impacts on societies, regions, and groups of people.

Task: Using the information from the documents and your knowledge of global history, answer the questions that follow each document in Part A. Your answers to the questions will help you write the Part B essay in which you will be asked to

> Select ***two*** sets of laws and/or orders mentioned in the historical context and for ***each***
>
> • Explain what the government hoped to achieve by establishing these laws and/or orders
> • Discuss the impacts of these laws and/or orders on a specific society, region, or group of people

In developing your answers to Part III, be sure to keep these general definitions in mind:

(a) <u>explain</u> means "to make plain or understandable; to give reasons for or causes of; to show the logical development or relationships of"

(b) <u>discuss</u> means "to make observations about something using facts, reasoning, and argument; to present in some detail"

Part A
Short-Answer Questions

Directions: Analyze the documents and answer the short-answer questions that follow each document in the space provided.

Document 1

By 1603, Tokugawa Ieyasu had won the civil war and had become the supreme ruler of Japan, the Shogun. His successor, Shogun Hidetada, put forth laws for military households. These households included members of the warrior class: the daimyo, the greater samurai, and the lesser samurai.

Laws Governing Military Households (1615), Excerpts

. . . [4] Great lords (daimyō), the lesser lords, and officials should immediately expel from their domains any among their retainers [vassals] or henchmen who have been charged with treason or murder. . . .

[6] Whenever it is intended to make repairs on a castle of one of the feudal domains, the [shogunate] authorities should be notified. The construction of any new castles is to be halted and stringently [strictly] prohibited.

"Big castles are a danger to the state." Walls and moats are the cause of great disorders.

[7] Immediate report should be made of innovations which are being planned or of factional conspiracies [schemes by dissenting groups] being formed in neighboring domains. . . .

Source: Compiled by Ryusaku Tsunoda, et al., *Sources of the Japanese Tradition*, Columbia University Press (adapted)

1 Based on this document, what is *one* way these laws limited the actions of the warrior class? [1]

_____

_____

Score [ ]

Document 2

The sankin kotai or hostage system was included as part of the warrior class laws.

> Alternate residence duty, or sankin kotai, was a system developed in the Warring States period and perfected by the Tokugawa shogunate. In essence, the system demanded simply that daimyo reside in the Tokugawa castle at Edo for periods of time, alternating with residence at the daimyo's own castle. When a daimyo was not residing in the Tokugawa castle, he was required to leave his family at his overlord's [shogun's] castle town. It was, at its simplest, a hostage system which required that either the daimyo or his family (including the very important heir) always be physically subject to the whim of the overlord. . . .

Source: "Sankin Kotai and the Hostage System," *Nakasendo Way*, Walk Japan

2 Based on this document, what is **one** way the daimyo were affected by the Tokugawa hostage system (alternate residence duty)? [1]

_____

_____

Score ☐

Document 3

. . . These measures [the hostage system, the isolation policy, and the banning of guns] succeeded in bringing the bloody wars of the previous period to an end. But the Shoguns could not stop the society beneath them continuing to change. The concentration of the lords and their families in Edo led to a growing trade in rice to feed them and their retainers, and to a proliferation [increase] of urban craftspeople and traders catering to their needs. Japan's cities grew to be some of the biggest in the world. The merchant class, although supposedly of very low standing, became increasingly important, and a new urban culture of popular poetry, plays and novels developed, different in many ways from the official culture of the state. A relaxation of the ban on western books after 1720 led to some intellectuals showing an interest in western ideas, and a 'School of Dutch learning' began to undertake studies in science, agronomy [agriculture] and Copernican astronomy. As money became increasingly important, many of the *samurai* became poor, forced to sell their weapons and to take up agriculture or crafts in order to pay their debts. Meanwhile repeated famines hit the peasantry—almost a million died in 1732 (out of a population of 26 million), 200,000 in 1775, and several hundred thousands in the 1780s—and there were a succession of local peasant uprisings. The Tokugawa political superstructure remained completely intact. But beneath it social forces were developing with some similarities to those in western Europe during the Renaissance period. . . .

Source: Chris Harman, *A People's History of the World*, Verso (adapted)

3 According to Chris Harman, what is **one** change that occurred in Japan as a consequence of the hostage system and isolationist policy? [1]

_____

_____

Score ☐

Document 4a

Excerpts of the [Nazi] Party Boycott Order, 28 March 1933

> . . . 3. The action committees must at once popularize the boycott by means of propaganda and enlightenment. The principle is: No German must any longer buy from a Jew or let him and his backers promote their goods. The boycott must be general. It must be supported by the whole German people and must hit Jewry in its most sensitive place. . . .
>
> 8. The boycott must be coordinated and set in motion everywhere at the same time, so that all preparations must be carried out immediately. Orders are being sent to the SA and SS so that from the moment of the boycott the population will be warned by guards not to enter Jewish shops. The start of the boycott is to be announced by posters, through the press and leaflets, etc. The boycott will commence on Saturday, 1 April on the stroke of 10 o'clock. It will be continued until an order comes from the Party leadership for it to stop. . . .

Source: J. Noakes and G. Pridham, eds., *Documents on Nazism, 1919–1945*, The Viking Press

4a In 1933, what is **one** action the Nazi Party wanted the German people to take against the Jews based on this excerpt? [1]

_____

_____

Score ☐

Document 4b

Decree Eliminating Jews from German Economic Life, 12 November 1938

> . . . *Article 1*
> 1. From 1 January 1939 the running of retail shops, mail order houses and the practice of independent trades are forbidden to Jews. . . .

Source: J. Noakes and G. Pridham, eds., *Documents on Nazism, 1919–1945*, The Viking Press

4b As a result of this Nazi decree, what is **one** specific economic situation faced by the Jewish people? [1]

_____

_____

Score ☐

Document 5a

"The Night of Broken Glass"

Source: Anne Frank Guide online

Document 5b

. . . The Nazis claimed that Kristallnacht was an uprising by ordinary Germans. Actually, it was carefully planned. The government ordered squads of Brownshirts into the streets. Their job was to destroy and terrorize. The Gestapo, or secret police, received orders not to stop the violence. Instead, they were to sweep through the burning neighborhoods, arresting Jews.

Kristallnacht was a turning point. The Nazis stepped up their efforts to "Aryanize" the German economy. Jews had been losing their property since Hitler came to power. Now, taking it from them became an official policy.

On November 12, the government levied a fine of one billion *reichmarks* on the German Jewish community. This was punishment for the act of one troubled teenager.* In addition to this, Jewish victims of Kristallnacht had to pay for the damage out of their own pockets. They could not collect insurance to cover their losses. . . .

Source: Linda J. Altman, *The Jewish Victims of the Holocaust*, Enslow Publishers (adapted)

*Herschel Grynszpan had killed a German at the German embassy in Paris out of anger over his parents' deportation. This act was used by the government to justify its actions on Kristallnacht.

5 Based on this photograph and passage, what are *two* impacts of the policy of Kristallnacht on the Jewish population in Germany? [2]

(1)_____

_____

Score ☐

(2)_____

_____

Score ☐

Document 6

- September 1996: A report by London's *Jewish Chronicle* claims that $4 billion ($65 billion in 1996 dollars*) looted by the Nazis from Jews and others during World War II was diverted to Swiss banks. The sum is about 20 times the amount previously acknowledged by the Swiss; . . .

- October 29, 1996: . . .Art, coins, and other items looted by Nazis from the homes of Austrian Jews are sold at a benefit auction in Vienna. It is the intent of the auction organizers to keep the items in the Jewish community. By day's end, the auction grosses $13.2 million, with proceeds going to aid Holocaust survivors and their heirs. . . .

- February 12, 1997: Switzerland, stung by allegations that the wartime government accepted and laundered [concealed the source of] funds from Nazi Germany that had been looted from Jews, agrees to create a $71 million fund for Holocaust survivors and their heirs.

Source: *The Holocaust Chronicle*, Publications International, 2000

*Four billion dollars during World War II had the approximate value of $65 billion in 1996.

6 Based on this information from the *The Holocaust Chronicle*, state **one** action taken in an attempt to compensate Holocaust survivors and their heirs many years after World War II ended.   [1]

_____

_____

Score ☐

Document 7a

Native Laws Amendment Act, Act No. 54 of 1952, Union of South Africa

. . . 29 (1) Whenever any authorized officer has reason to believe that any native [black South African] within an urban area or an area proclaimed in terms of section *twenty-three*—

(a) is an idle person in that—

(i) he is habitually unemployed and has no sufficient honest means of livelihood. . .

he [authorized officer] may, without warrant arrest that native or cause him to be arrested and any European police officer or officer appointed under sub-section (1) of section *twenty-two* may thereupon bring such a native before a native commissioner or magistrate who shall require the native to give a good and satisfactory account of himself. . . .

Source: Native Laws Amendment Act, Act No. 54 of 1952, Digital Innovation South Africa online (adapted)

7a Under the Union of South Africa Act No. 54 of 1952, what could happen to a native person who was habitually unemployed? [1]

_____

_____

Score ☐

Document 7b

Natives (Abolition of Passes and Coordination of Documents) Act, Act No. 67 of 1952, Union of South Africa

. . . Any policeman may at any time call upon an African [black] who has attained the age of sixteen years to produce his reference [pass] book. If a reference book has been issued to him but he fails to produce it because it is not in his possession at the time, he commits a criminal offence and is liable to a fine not exceeding ten pounds or imprisonment for a period not exceeding one month. . . .

Source: Leslie Rubin and Neville Rubin, *This is Apartheid*, Christian Action, London (adapted)

7b Under the Union of South Africa Act No. 67 of 1952, what penalty could be given to a sixteen-year-old or older African black if he failed to produce his reference book? [1]

_____

_____

Score ☐

Document 8

This excerpt is based on Peter Abrahams's memories and his conversation with his black South African boss, Jim.

> . . . When Jim left his Pedi village in the northern Transvaal he had to go to the nearest police station or Native Affairs Department. There he got a Trek Pass. This permitted him to make the journey to Johannesburg. On reaching the city he got an Identification Pass and a Six-Day Special Pass. He paid two shillings each month for the Identification Pass. The Six-Day Special was his protection while he looked for work. He did not find work during his first six days in the city. He did not go to the pass office to renew his Six-Day Special. He was picked up on the eighth day and spent two weeks in jail as a vagrant [person without residence or work]. That taught him to go to the pass office regularly. . . .

Source: Peter Abrahams, *Tell Freedom: Memories of Africa*, Alfred A. Knopf

8 According to Peter Abrahams, what was **one** way the pass laws affected his boss, Jim? [1]

_____

_____

Score [ ]

Document 9

Resistance to white domination was continuous but unsuccessful. The South African police and the army were called out every time blacks rose up against the apartheid laws that made their lives so miserable. On March 21, 1960, a group of unarmed blacks made their way to the police station in Sharpeville (a black township) to hold a peaceful protest against the passbook laws. No black in South Africa could travel, live, or work without a passbook. This hated document was the record of a person's life as defined by the white government. Thousands of demonstrators left their passbooks at home, expecting to be arrested. They thought this would show the government's policy could not continue if it had to arrest thousands. But the peaceful demonstration was met with gunfire. When it was over, sixty-nine blacks were dead, shot in the back by the police as they tried to flee when the shooting began. Their deaths sparked a nationwide protest.

Source: Blauer and Lauré, *South Africa*, Children's Press

9a Based on this document, what action did black South Africans take to oppose the pass laws? [1]

_____

_____

Score ☐

b Based on this document, what was the South African government's response to the situation in Sharpeville on March 21, 1960? [1]

_____

_____

Score ☐

Part B
Essay

Directions: Write a well-organized essay that includes an introduction, several paragraphs, and a conclusion. Use evidence from *at least four* documents in your essay. Support your response with relevant facts, examples, and details. Include additional outside information.

Historical Context:

Throughout history, governments have developed and established laws and orders for a variety of reasons. The ***laws for the warriors under the Tokugawa Shogunate, the Nazi orders and laws of the Third Reich,*** and ***the pass laws of the Republic of South Africa*** had many impacts on societies, regions, and groups of people.

Task: Using the information from the documents and your knowledge of global history, write an essay in which you

> Select *two* sets of laws and/or orders mentioned in the historical context and for *each*
>
> - Explain what the government hoped to achieve by establishing these laws and/or orders
> - Discuss the impacts of these laws and/or orders on a specific society, region, or group of people

Guidelines:

In your essay, be sure to

- Develop all aspects of the task
- Incorporate information from *at least four* documents
- Incorporate relevant outside information
- Support the theme with relevant facts, examples, and details
- Use a logical and clear plan of organization, including an introduction and a conclusion that are beyond a restatement of the theme

This section contains an actual Regents Examination in Global History and Geography that was given in New York State in August 2015.

Circle your answers to Part 1. Write your responses to the short-answer questions in the spaces provided. Write your thematic essay and document-based essay on separate sheets of paper. Be sure to refer to the test-taking strategies in the front of this book as you prepare to answer the test questions.

Part I

Answer all questions in this part.

Directions (1–50): For each statement or question, record on your separate answer sheet the *number* of the word or expression that, of those given, best completes the statement or answers the question.

1 The Europeans referred to China as the *Far East*. The Chinese referred to China as the *Middle Kingdom*. What do these terms illustrate?

(1) The names of places refer to significant physical features.

(2) Most people do not understand geography.

(3) The point of view of people influences geographic labels.

(4) Place names sometimes commemorate important events.

2 In which economic system does the government make most major decisions about what to produce, how much to produce, and for whom the goods and services will be produced?

(1) traditional   (3) command

(2) mixed   (4) market

3 Throughout history, a basic purpose of government has been to provide

(1) equal rights for all people

(2) laws to maintain order

(3) representation for all social classes

(4) separate political and religious systems

4 The Neolithic Revolution is considered a turning point in global history because it led to

(1) increasing migrations of people in search of food

(2) increasing use of animal skins for clothing

(3) a belief in a spiritual world

(4) the development of civilization

5 The primary reason ancient peoples of the Nile River valley built levees, dikes, and reservoirs was to

(1) purify sacred waters

(2) create a shorter route to distant cities

(3) defend against invaders

(4) increase agricultural production

6 In the practice of religion, the Ten Commandments are to Christianity as the Eightfold Path is to

(1) Buddhism   (3) Islam

(2) Daoism   (4) Shinto

7 Mandate of Heaven, production of silk, and reverence for ancestors are all characteristics associated with civilizations in

(1) India   (3) Greece

(2) China   (4) West Africa

8 • Made advances in mathematics, science, and medicine

• Preserved Greek and Roman learning

• Influenced Spanish architecture and literature

These achievements are most closely associated with the

(1) Golden Age of Islam

(2) Maya Empire

(3) Gupta Empire

(4) Tang dynasty

9 Which country has acted as a cultural bridge between China and Japan?

(1) Philippines   (3) Korea

(2) Vietnam   (4) Bangladesh

10 After the fall of the Mongol Empire, which city emerged as the new political and cultural center of Russia?

(1) Moscow   (3) Novgorod

(2) Warsaw   (4) Kiev

Base your answer to question 11 on the chart below and on your knowledge of social studies.

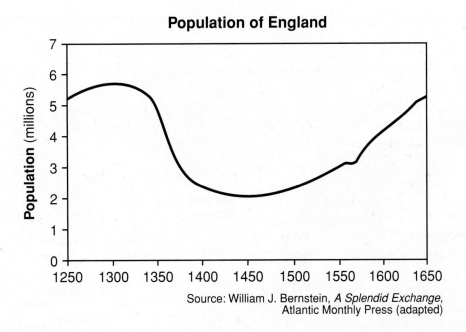

Population of England

Source: William J. Bernstein, *A Splendid Exchange*,
Atlantic Monthly Press (adapted)

11 The population trend from 1350 to 1450 is most likely the result of the
    (1) development of trade with the Americas
    (2) raids by Vikings on coastal cities
    (3) defeat of the Spanish Armada by England
    (4) spread of the bubonic plague in England

12 Which characteristic was common to the cities of the Hanseatic League in Europe and the cities of the African kingdom of Ghana?

    (1) location on key trade routes
    (2) indirect control by the papacy
    (3) management of local gold mines
    (4) development as centers of woolen industry

13 Which leader started the Protestant Reformation by speaking out against papal abuses and the sale of indulgences in the Ninety-five Theses?
    (1) John Calvin   (3) John Wycliffe
    (2) Henry VIII   (4) Martin Luther

14 What was one important result of Mansa Musa's pilgrimage to Mecca?
    (1) creation of a large navy
    (2) translation of the Qur'an from Arabic to Swahili
    (3) establishment of diplomatic ties with other Muslim states
    (4) preservation of animistic traditions in the Arabian Peninsula

Base your answer to question 15 on the map below and on your knowledge of social studies.

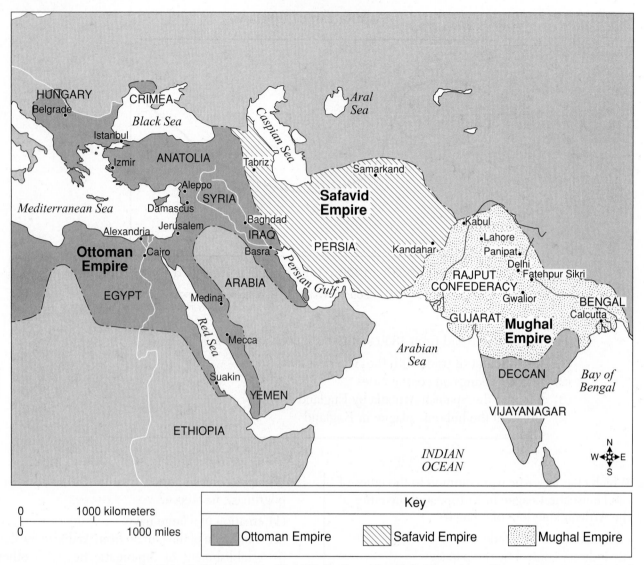

Source: Peter N. Stearns et al., *World Civilizations: The Global Experience*, Pearson Longman (adapted)

15 Which statement can best be supported by the information shown on this map?

(1) The Ottoman Empire included parts of northern Africa.

(2) The Safavid Empire controlled the entire Indian subcontinent.

(3) The Mughal Empire occupied territory adjacent to the Mediterranean Sea.

(4) The Ottoman Empire conquered less territory than either the Safavid or the Mughal Empire.

Base your answers to questions 16 and 17 on the speakers' statements below and on your knowledge of social studies.

Speaker A: It was a combination of the Protestant wind and the island nature of our nation that protected us. Surely, Philip must be upset at his defeat.

Speaker B: Our archipelago and divine winds have protected us once again. The Mongols may have taken China, but they cannot conquer us.

Speaker C: To support our growing population, we must find a suitable way to farm. With floating gardens on our lake, we should be able to grow enough to meet our demand.

Speaker D: We have connected highland and lowland areas by building networks of roads and bridges. We have also built terraces into our mountainsides to grow crops.

16 Which two speakers discuss how their society modified their environment?

(1) *A* and *B*   (3) *C* and *D*
(2) *B* and *C*   (4) *D* and *A*

17 Which speaker is most likely from 16th-century England?

(1) *A*   (3) *C*
(2) *B*   (4) *D*

18 Which statement best describes a key aspect of mercantilism?

(1) removing tariffs to increase free trade between empires
(2) acquiring colonies to provide a favorable balance of trade
(3) eliminating private ownership of the means of production
(4) encouraging subsistence agriculture

19 One way in which Suleiman the Magnificent and Peter the Great are similar is that they both

(1) modernized their military
(2) promoted free speech
(3) isolated their people from outside influences
(4) reduced taxes levied on their people

20 The Magna Carta and the English Bill of Rights both served to

(1) extend the voting privileges of commoners
(2) abolish the government's role in levying taxes
(3) limit the power of the monarchy
(4) support the theory of the divine right of kings

21 Which individual suggested the idea that if a government fails to protect its people's natural rights of life, liberty, and property, the people have the right to overthrow it?

(1) Karl Marx
(2) John Locke
(3) Thomas Hobbes
(4) Niccolò Machiavelli

22 One scientific belief held by both René Descartes and Isaac Newton is that

(1) reasoned thought is the way to discover truth
(2) new theories should be made to fit existing traditional ideas
(3) the method by which discoveries are made is unimportant
(4) difficult problems should be solved by reading religious texts

23 Simón Bolívar, Toussaint L'Ouverture, and José de San Martín are all associated with revolutions in

(1) Africa   (3) South Asia
(2) Europe   (4) Latin America

Base your answers to questions 24 and 25 on the maps below and on your knowledge of social studies.

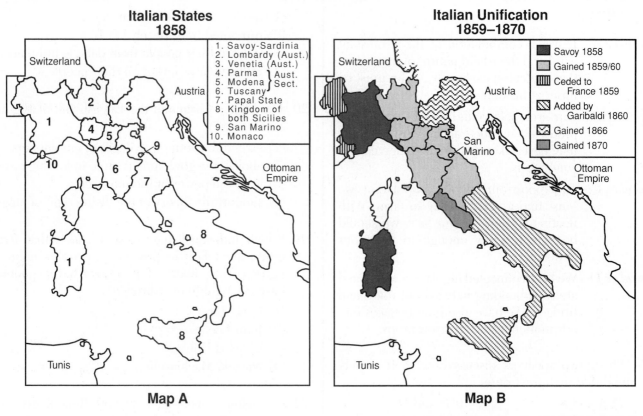

**Italian States
1858**

Switzerland

Austria

1. Savoy-Sardinia
2. Lombardy (Aust.)
3. Venetia (Aust.)
4. Parma ⎱ Aust.
5. Modena ⎰ Sect.
6. Tuscany
7. Papal State
8. Kingdom of
   both Sicilies
9. San Marino
10. Monaco

Ottoman
Empire

Tunis

Map A

**Italian Unification
1859–1870**

Switzerland

Austria

San
Marino

■ Savoy 1858
▨ Gained 1859/60
▥ Ceded to
   France 1859
▨ Added by
   Garibaldi 1860
▨ Gained 1866
▨ Gained 1870

Ottoman
Empire

Tunis

Map B

Source: Alexander Ganse, 2000 (adapted)

24 Which factor provided the motivation for the changes that took place between 1858 and 1870 as indicated on these maps?

(1) exploration (3) religion
(2) appeasement (4) nationalism

25 Which pair of individuals played a direct role in the changes that took place between Map A and Map B?

(1) Otto Von Bismarck and Wilhelm II
(2) Klemens von Metternich and Victor Emmanuel III
(3) Camillo di Cavour and Guiseppe Mazzini
(4) Alexander II and Frederick the Great

26 In the late 1700s, the Industrial Revolution developed in Britain because Britain

(1) possessed key factors of production
(2) excluded foreign investors
(3) suppressed the enclosure movement
(4) required a minimum wage be paid to workers

Base your answers to questions 27 and 28 on the passage below and on your knowledge of social studies.

… The Opium War of 1839–42 was short and one-sided, due to the superiority of European weapons, which came as a complete surprise to the Chinese. In the first skirmish alone, in July 1839, two British warships defeated twenty-nine Chinese ships. On land, the Chinese and their medieval weapons were no match for British troops armed with state-of-the-art muskets. By the middle of 1842 British troops had seized Hong Kong, taken control of the key river deltas, and occupied Shanghai and several other cities. The Chinese were forced to sign a peace treaty that granted Hong Kong to the British, opened five ports for the free trade of all goods, and required the payment of reparations to the British in silver, including compensation for the opium that had been destroyed by Commissioner Lin….

— Tom Standage

27 Which term best characterizes the events described in this passage?

(1) industrialization   (3) containment
(2) imperialism   (4) cultural diffusion

28 What was an immediate result of the Opium War described in this passage?

(1) signing the Treaty of Nanking
(2) forming the Guomindang
(3) beginning the Boxer Rebellion
(4) organizing the Taiping Rebellion

29 Which event sparked the outbreak of World War I?

(1) attack on Pearl Harbor by Japan
(2) Germany's invasion of Poland
(3) Bolshevik coup d'état in Russia
(4) assassination of the Austrian Archduke

30 Which agreement was labeled by the Nazis as unfair to Germany?

(1) Treaty of Versailles
(2) Soviet Nonaggression Pact
(3) Munich Pact
(4) Treaty of Brest-Litovsk

31 Japan expanded her empire in the 1930s and 1940s to include parts of

(1) eastern Europe and the Middle East
(2) China and Southeast Asia
(3) Turkey and the Soviet Union
(4) Australia and India

32 Which geographic factor enabled the German blitzkrieg to succeed?

(1) swift running rivers
(2) mountain ranges
(3) relatively flat terrain
(4) tropical climate

33 Which action is most closely associated with totalitarian governments?

(1) allowing public discussion of issues and building consensus
(2) accepting criticism and permitting dissent
(3) engaging in censorship and propaganda campaigns
(4) having open and transparent elections with multiple political parties

34 The purpose of Mohandas Gandhi's actions such as the Salt March and the textile boycott was to

(1) begin a cycle of armed revolution
(2) draw attention to critical issues
(3) increase the strength of the military
(4) resist the power of religious leaders

Base your answer to question 35 on the cartoon below and on your knowledge of social studies.

We Tried Everything but Dynamite

Source: J. N. "Ding" Darling, *Des Moines Register*, October 4, 1948 (adapted)

35 What is the main idea of this cartoon?

   (1) The United Nations is usually successful in freeing nations from communist control.

   (2) Western nations are frustrated by the strength of communist control in Eastern Europe.

   (3) Nations of the West are willing to negotiate with the Soviet Union.

   (4) The Soviet Union will usually cooperate with the United Nations.

36 The 38th parallel in Korea and the 17th parallel in Vietnam were used to mark

   (1) boundaries created by mountain ranges

   (2) demarcation lines instituted by papal authority

   (3) territorial claims disputed between ethnic minorities

   (4) political divisions established between communist and noncommunist territories

37 Prior to 1947, the Indian National Congress and the Muslim League worked together seeking to end

   (1) nonviolence   (3) foreign rule

   (2) religious diversity   (4) nonalignment

38 What was an immediate result of the Great Leap Forward (1958)?

(1) independence of Kenya from Great Britain
(2) the breakup of the Soviet Union
(3) the relocation of Bosnian refugees
(4) increased famine in China

Base your answer to question 39 on the passage below and on your knowledge of social studies.

… The grim statutes [laws] that I would spend the rest of my life fighting stared back at me from the page: the value of a woman's life was half that of a man (for instance, if a car hit both on the street, the cash compensation due to the woman's family was half that due the man's); a woman's testimony in court as a witness to a crime counted only half as much as a man's; a woman had to ask her husband's permission for divorce. The drafters of the penal code had apparently consulted the seventh century for legal advice. The laws, in short, turned the clock back fourteen hundred years, to the early days of Islam's spread, the days when stoning women for adultery and chopping off the hands of thieves were considered appropriate sentences.…

— Shirin Ebadi, *Iran Awakening*

39 Based on this passage, which statement is a valid conclusion about Iran following the revolution in 1979?

(1) Men were often penalized for their treatment of women.
(2) Laws were changed to reflect Western legal principles.
(3) The legal system discriminated against women.
(4) Legal decisions were based on economic values.

40 Which sequence of 20th-century Cold War events is in the correct chronological order?

(1) fall of the Berlin Wall → Cuban missile crisis → adoption of the Marshall Plan
(2) Cuban missile crisis → fall of the Berlin Wall → adoption of the Marshall Plan
(3) fall of the Berlin Wall → adoption of the Marshall Plan → Cuban missile crisis
(4) adoption of the Marshall Plan → Cuban missile crisis → fall of the Berlin Wall

Base your answer to question 41 on the cartoon below and on your knowledge of social studies.

Source: Glenn McCoy, Universal Press Syndicate, May, 2008 (adapted)

41 What is the main idea of this cartoon?

(1) Many people have died as a result of consuming ethanol.
(2) Ethanol is produced from fossils and plants.
(3) Biofuel production is contributing to the world hunger problem.
(4) Biofuel production is the source of deadly greenhouse gases.

42 **"Dalit [Untouchable] Families Forbidden to Use Public Water-Tap"**
"Nepal Bans Bias Against Untouchables in Move to End Hindu Caste System"

These headlines reflect a conflict between

(1) traditional customs and modern law
(2) child labor and industrialization
(3) national self-determination and ethnic diversity
(4) access to resources and forced migration

43 Which region is most closely associated with the expansion of the Sahel and overgrazing in the savanna regions?

(1) South America   (3) Africa
(2) China   (4) Southeast Asia

44 Feudalism and manorialism played an important role in western European society during the

(1) medieval period
(2) Pax Romana
(3) Enlightenment
(4) Age of Exploration

45 Pope Urban II, Saladin, and King Richard the Lion-Hearted are leaders associated with the

(1) Age of Charlemagne
(2) Crusades
(3) Glorious Revolution
(4) Counter Reformation

46 One way in which the travels of Marco Polo and the voyages of Zheng He are similar is that both

(1) established colonial territories
(2) stimulated trade
(3) encouraged mass migrations
(4) led to discoveries in Africa

47 Which civilization is credited with recording data with quipu, developing an elaborate road system, and constructing Machu Picchu?

(1) Roman
(2) Egyptian
(3) Mesopotamian
(4) Inca

Base your answer to question 48 on the outline below and on your knowledge of social studies.

I. _____
   A. Rule of Porfirio Diaz
   B. Peasant support for Francisco Pancho Villa
   C. Constitution of 1917
   D. Land reform

48 Which revolution best completes this partial outline?

(1) Mexican
(2) Chinese
(3) Cuban
(4) Iranian

49 Some of the ethnic strife in Africa today can be traced back to the European division of Africa resulting from the

(1) Treaty of Tordesillas
(2) Congress of Vienna
(3) Berlin Conference
(4) Yalta Conference

50 One way in which the Armenians in the Ottoman Empire (1915) and the Tutsis in Rwanda (1994) are similar is that both groups

(1) sought safe haven in the Soviet Union
(2) suffered human rights violations
(3) seceded to create an independent state
(4) fled to escape a severe flood

Answers to the essay questions are to be written in the separate essay booklet.

In developing your answer to Part II, be sure to keep these general definitions in mind:

   (a) <u>explain</u> means "to make plain or understandable; to give reasons for or causes of; to show the logical development or relationships of"

   (b) <u>discuss</u> means "to make observations about something using facts, reasoning, and argument; to present in some detail"

Part II

THEMATIC ESSAY QUESTION

Directions: Write a well-organized essay that includes an introduction, several paragraphs addressing the task below, and a conclusion.

Theme: Movement of People and Goods

> Goods and ideas have moved from one place to another for a variety of reasons. The changes that resulted from the movement of these goods and ideas to new places significantly influenced groups of people, societies, and regions.

Task:

> Select *two* goods and/or ideas that moved from one place to another and for *each*
> - Explain how this good or idea moved from one place to another
> - Discuss how the movement of this good or idea significantly influenced a group of people, a society, *and/or* a region

You may use any goods or ideas from your study of global history and geography. Some suggestions you might wish to consider include the *goods* silk, salt, sugar, gold, wheat, oil, horses, and gunpowder, and the *ideas* of Buddhism, Christianity, Islam, and the authority of government comes from the people.

You are *not* limited to these suggestions.

Do *not* make the United States the focus of your answer.

Guidelines:

   In your essay, be sure to
   - Develop all aspects of the task
   - Support the theme with relevant facts, examples, and details
   - Use a logical and clear plan of organization, including an introduction and a conclusion that are beyond a restatement of the theme

NAME _____   SCHOOL _____

Part III

DOCUMENT-BASED QUESTION

    This question is based on the accompanying documents. The question is designed to test your ability to work with historical documents. Some of these documents have been edited for the purposes of this question. As you analyze the documents, take into account the source of each document and any point of view that may be presented in the document. Keep in mind that the language used in a document may reflect the historical context of the time in which it was written.

    Historical Context:

> Throughout history, leaders and governments have taken actions to increase power and to control their people. Three such leaders include ***Louis XIV of France, Joseph Stalin of the Soviet Union,*** and ***Pol Pot of Cambodia.*** The actions taken by these leaders and governments had a significant impact on their people and their society.

Task: Using the information from the documents and your knowledge of global history, answer the questions that follow each document in Part A. Your answers to the questions will help you write the Part B essay in which you will be asked to

---

Choose ***two*** leaders mentioned in the historical context and for ***each***

- Describe actions taken by the leader and his government to increase his power ***and/or*** to control his people
- Discuss an impact the actions had on his people *or* society

---

In developing your answers to Part III, be sure to keep these general definitions in mind:

    (a) <u>describe</u> means "to illustrate something in words or tell about it"

    (b) <u>discuss</u> means "to make observations about something using facts, reasoning, and argument; to present in some detail"

Part A
Short-Answer Questions

Directions: Analyze the documents and answer the short-answer questions that follow each document in the space provided.

Document 1

...How Louis obtained money enough to govern as he pleased.

The first need of a king who wished to rule as he pleased was money. Louis had little trouble in raising money, for the reason that he did not need to ask for it, as the English kings did. The institution in France which resembled the English Parliament was the Estates General. But this body had never met frequently, and it could scarcely be said to exist any more, since it had not been assembled for nearly fifty years. Louis was therefore free to collect taxes and use the money as he saw fit....

Source: Carl L. Becker, *Modern History*, Silver, Burdett and Company

1 According to Carl L. Becker, what was **one** way Louis XIV exercised power over the finances of France? [1]

_____

_____

Score ☐

Document 2

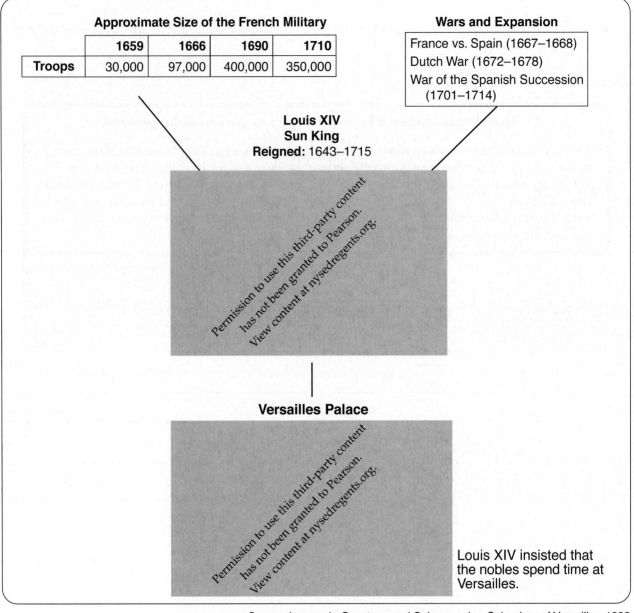

Approximate Size of the French Military

	1659	1666	1690	1710
Troops	30,000	97,000	400,000	350,000

Wars and Expansion

France vs. Spain (1667–1668)
Dutch War (1672–1678)
War of the Spanish Succession
(1701–1714)

**Louis XIV
Sun King
Reigned:** 1643–1715

Permission to use this third-party content has not been granted to Pearson. View content at nysedregents.org.

Versailles Palace

Permission to use this third-party content has not been granted to Pearson. View content at nysedregents.org.

Louis XIV insisted that the nobles spend time at Versailles.

Source: Images in Constans and Salmon, eds., *Splendors of Versailles*, 1998

2 Based on the information in this graphic organizer, identify **one** way the rule of Louis XIV had an impact on France. [1]

_____

_____

Score

Document 3

Revocation [removal] of the Edict of Nantes

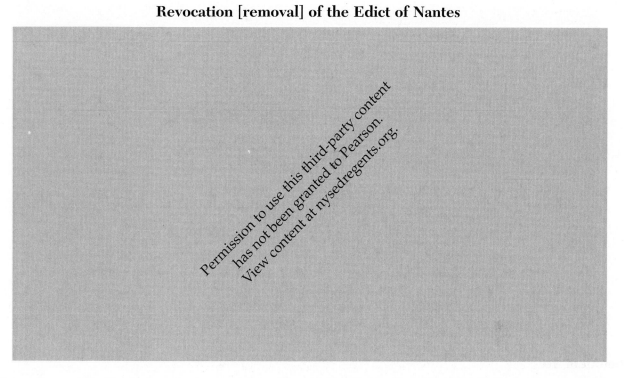

3 According to Martha Glaser, what is **one** impact the removal of the Edict of Nantes had on French society? [1]

_____

_____

Score ⬜

Document 4a

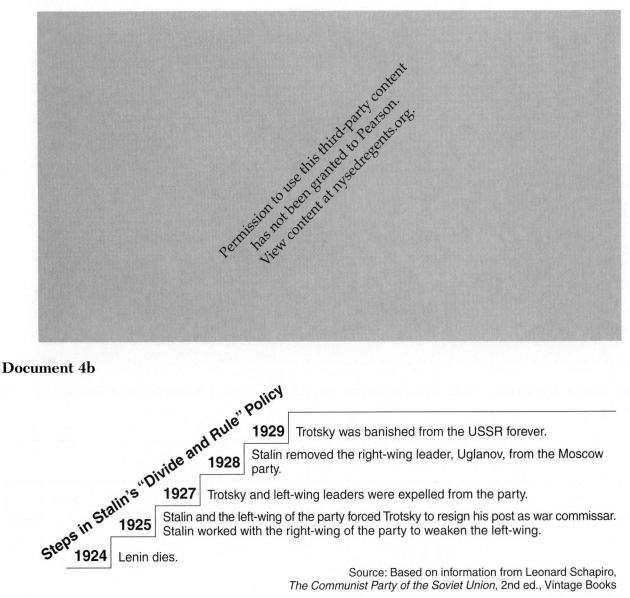

Permission to use this third-party content has not been granted to Pearson. View content at nysedregents.org.

Document 4b

Steps in Stalin's "Divide and Rule" Policy

1929	Trotsky was banished from the USSR forever.
1928	Stalin removed the right-wing leader, Uglanov, from the Moscow party.
1927	Trotsky and left-wing leaders were expelled from the party.
1925	Stalin and the left-wing of the party forced Trotsky to resign his post as war commissar. Stalin worked with the right-wing of the party to weaken the left-wing.
1924	Lenin dies.

Source: Based on information from Leonard Schapiro, *The Communist Party of the Soviet Union*, 2nd ed., Vintage Books

4 Based on these documents, identify *two* actions Stalin took to increase his power in the Soviet Union. [2]

(1) _____

_____

Score ☐

(2) _____

_____

Score ☐

Document 5

… The purge began its last, and deadliest, phase in the spring of 1937. Until then it had claimed thousands of victims from among the ruling classes. Now it began to claim millions of ordinary citizens who had nothing to do with politics.

Stalin knew that these people, let alone their families, hadn't committed treason and probably never would. He also knew the Russian proverb: "Fear has big eyes." He believed that arresting suspects for real crimes wasn't as useful as arresting the innocent. Arresting someone for a crime that could be proven would allow everyone else to feel safe. And safety bred confidence, and confidence drew people together. Fear, however, sowed suspicion. It built walls between people, preventing them from uniting against his tyranny. And the best way to create fear was to strike the innocent. Millions of innocent lives were, to Stalin, a small price to pay for safeguarding his power.

Creating fear was easy. The NKVD [Soviet secret police] had blanketed the country with informers. Like the secret police itself, informers were everywhere. An informer was stationed in every apartment house in every street in every Soviet town. Every office, shop, factory, and army barracks had its informers. He or she could be anyone: the janitor, the bank teller, the nice lady across the hall—or your best friend. Informers sat in the theaters, rode the trains, and strolled in the parks, eavesdropping on conversations. Although there is no way of checking, it was said that one person in five was a stool pigeon [informer]….

Source: Albert Marrin, *Stalin*, Puffin Books, 1988

5 According to Albert Marrin, what is **one** impact Stalin's policy had on the Soviet Union? [1]

_____

_____

Score ☐

Document 6a

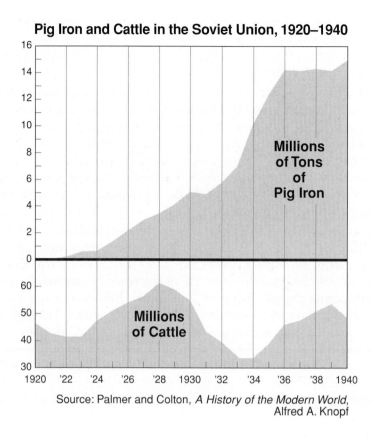

Pig Iron and Cattle in the Soviet Union, 1920–1940

Source: Palmer and Colton, *A History of the Modern World*,
Alfred A. Knopf

Document 6b

PIG IRON AND CATTLE IN THE SOVIET UNION, 1920–1940

… If pig iron [cast iron] is taken as a measure of industrial activity and number of cattle as a similar indication for agriculture, the chart reveals clearly what happened in the twenty years after the Revolution—an enormous build-up of heavy industry at the expense of food supplies. Iron mines and forges, in the disorganization of the Revolution and civil war, were producing almost nothing in 1920. By the late 1920s, output of pig iron regained the pre-Revolutionary level, but the great upsurge came with the Second Five-Year Plan. By 1940 Russia produced more pig iron than Germany, and far more than Britain or France. Numbers of cattle grew in the 1920s, but fell catastrophically during the collectivization of agriculture after 1929, and by 1940 hardly exceeded the figure for 1920. Since 1940 the industrial development of the Soviet Union has been impressive, but agricultural production has continued to be a problem.…

Source: Palmer and Colton, *A History of the Modern World*, Alfred A. Knopf

6 According to Palmer and Colton, what was *one* impact of Stalin's control of the Soviet economy? [1]

_____

_____

Score ☐

Document 7

This passage recounts Teeda Butt Mam's experience in April, 1975 when Pol Pot and the Khmer Rouge took over Phnom Penh, the capital city of Cambodia.

> Khmer Rouge soldiers were on the streets when I awakened before dawn. Four- to six-man patrols moved through the avenues and alleys of Phnom Penh evicting everyone from homes, shops, and shelters. No delays were permitted. No requests allowed. Troublemakers were killed on the spot. Often, animals were slaughtered to intimidate owners.
>
> Already, on this second day of evacuation, orphanages and monasteries, hotels and hospitals, stood empty. Within hours of the takeover, people staying in these places had been driven from the city at gunpoint. Doctors and staff were killed if they resisted expulsion. Hospital patients too weak to walk were shot in their beds. Others, carrying still-attached plasma bottles, hobbled from the wards. Hospital beds, filled with the sick and dying, were pushed through the streets by relatives and friends....

Source: Criddle and Mam, *To Destroy You Is No Loss: The Odyssey of a Cambodian Family,* Anchor Books, 1989

7 According to Teeda Butt Mam, what was **one** action the Khmer Rouge took to control the people of Phnom Penh? [1]

_____

_____

Score ☐

Document 8a

Pol Pot's Khmer Rouge government, referred to as Angka, attempted to create an agrarian society. It established collective farms throughout Cambodia. This passage reflects the experiences of Sopheap K. Hang during this time period.

> … When the registration of the remaining people was over, a leader of Angka [Khmer Rouge] showed up. He stood before the people holding a microphone in one hand. He gathered the new people [primarily city people] to listen to his speech. "I am the new leader of Cambodia. From now on you have to address the new government as Angka. There are no homes for you to return to. You have to work as a group from now on. No one can own property. Everything you own belongs to Angka [the government]. No more city lifestyle. Everyone has to dress in black uniforms." My mother looked at my father with concern. "No one can question Angka," he said. "If you have courage to question Angka, you will be taken to the reeducation learning institution." That meant we would be executed. Everyone, including my parents, was numb. We could not think. Our bodies were shaking and our minds were paralyzed by the imposing speech of Angka.…

Source: Sopheap K. Hang, "Memoir of a Child's Nightmare," *Children of Cambodia's Killing Fields,*
Yale University Press, 1997

8a According to Sopheap K. Hang, what was **one** action taken by Angka, Pol Pot's government, to control the Cambodian people? [1]

_____

_____

Score ☐

Document 8b

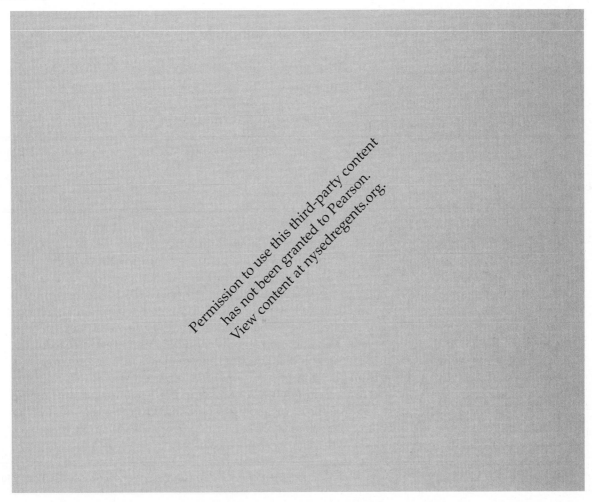

8b Based on this illustration by Sitha Sao, state **one** way the actions of Pol Pot's government affected the people. [1]

_____

_____

Score ☐

Document 9a

Approximate Death Tolls in Democratic Kampuchea [Cambodia], 1975–1979			
	1975 Population	Number who perished	Percent who perished
Total Cambodia	7,890,000	1,671,000	21

Source: Ben Kiernan, *The Pol Pot Regime,* Yale University Press, 1996 (adapted)

Document 9b

… I initially estimated the DK [Democratic Kampuchea] death toll at around 1.5 million people. This estimate was based on my own detailed interviews with 500 Cambodian survivors, including 100 refugees in France in 1979 and nearly 400 inside Cambodia in 1980. It was also supported by a survey carried out among a different sample, the refugees on the Thai-Cambodian border. In early 1980, Milton Osborne interviewed 100 Khmer refugees in eight different camps. This group included 59 refugees of non-elite background: 42 former farmers and fishermen and 17 former low-level urban workers. Twenty-seven of these people, and 13 of the other 41 interviewees, had had close family members executed in the Pol Pot period. The 100 refugees reported a total of 88 killings of their nuclear family members. 20 of the interviewees (14 of them from the non-elite group) also reported losing forty nuclear family members to starvation and disease during the Pol Pot period. This sample of 100 families (around 500 people) thus lost 128 members, or about 25 percent. Projected nationally, this points to a toll of around 1.5 million. The 39 farmers had lost 25 (of, say, 195) family members, suggesting a toll of 13 percent among the Cambodian peasantry.…

Source: Ben Kiernan, *The Pol Pot Regime,* Yale University Press, 1996 (adapted)

9 According to Ben Kiernan, what was **one** way the actions of Pol Pot's government affected the people of Cambodia? [1]

_____

_____

Score ☐

Part B
Essay

Directions: Write a well-organized essay that includes an introduction, several paragraphs, and a conclusion. Use evidence from *at least four* documents in your essay. Support your response with relevant facts, examples, and details. Include additional outside information.

Historical Context:

Throughout history, leaders and governments have taken actions to increase power and to control their people. Three such leaders include **Louis XIV of France, Joseph Stalin of the Soviet Union,** and **Pol Pot of Cambodia.** The actions taken by these leaders and governments had a significant impact on their people and their society.

Task: Using the information from the documents and your knowledge of global history, write an essay in which you

> Choose **two** leaders mentioned in the historical context and for **each**
> - Describe actions taken by the leader and his government to increase his power **and/or** to control his people
> - Discuss an impact the actions had on his people *or* society

Guidelines:

In your essay, be sure to

- Develop all aspects of the task
- Incorporate information from *at least four* documents
- Incorporate relevant outside information
- Support the theme with relevant facts, examples, and details
- Use a logical and clear plan of organization, including an introduction and a conclusion that are beyond a restatement of the theme

This section contains an actual Regents Examination in Global History and Geography that was given in New York State in June 2015.

Circle your answers to Part 1. Write your responses to the short-answer questions in the spaces provided. Write your thematic essay and document-based essay on separate sheets of paper. Be sure to refer to the test-taking strategies in the front of this book as you prepare to answer the test questions.

Part I

Answer all questions in this part.

Directions (1–50): For each statement or question, record on your separate answer sheet the *number* of the word or expression that, of those given, best completes the statement or answers the question.

Base your answer to question 1 on the passage below and on your knowledge of social studies.

… Oral histories are as old as human beings. Before the invention of writing, information passed from generation to generation through the spoken word. Many people around the world continue to use oral traditions to pass along knowledge and wisdom. Interviews and recordings of community elders and witnesses to historical events provide exciting stories, anecdotes, and other information about the past….

—Library of Congress

1 Based on this passage, historians should treat oral histories and oral traditions as

(1) persuasive arguments
(2) statistical data
(3) unbiased sources
(4) cultural evidence

2 Which academic discipline focuses study on the roles and functions of government?

(1) political science   (3) geography
(2) anthropology   (4) economics

3 During the Neolithic Revolution, production of a food surplus led directly to

(1) a nomadic lifestyle
(2) a reliance on stone weaponry
(3) an increase in population
(4) a dependence on hunting and gathering

4 Discovery of streets arranged in a grid-like pattern and a system of pipes for moving water in Harappa and Mohenjo-Daro suggest that these ancient river valley cities in South Asia had

(1) organized governments
(2) subsistence-based economies
(3) polytheistic beliefs
(4) rigid social classes

Base your answer to question 5 on the passage below and on your knowledge of social studies.

… Monsoons are relied upon throughout the country to provide water for growing crops. Heavy monsoons, however, can bring floods that often have a high death toll. These floods have been exacerbated [made worse] by deforestation of the hills for industrial and agricultural purposes. It is a fine balance between having plenty of water to flood the rice fields and having too much so that crops, homes, and even lives are lost. The alternative to the floods may be famines. However, India's infrastructure can now deal successfully with these: When the monsoon fails in one area, the army is able to move supplies to the drought-stricken area. As a result of this organization, few lives were lost in the Maharashtra famines of 1965–66 and 1974–75, while more than two million people died in the Bengal famine of 1943.

—Louise Nicholson, *National Geographic Traveler: India*, 2007

5 Based on this passage, how have the negative effects of the monsoons been reduced in recent years?

(1) The army is building dams to hold back the floods.
(2) Farmers have begun to grow crops that require less water.
(3) Home construction in flood areas has been controlled by government regulations.
(4) An improved infrastructure makes it possible to bring supplies to areas in need of help.

6 The Egyptians used hieroglyphics in the same way as the Sumerians used

(1) ideographs   (3) cuneiform
(2) calligraphy   (4) letters

7 Which geographic feature served as a barrier to political unity and encouraged the rise of independent city-states in ancient Greece?

(1) broad plains   (3) navigable rivers
(2) mountain ranges   (4) numerous ports

8 The Tang dynasty contributed to the development of Chinese culture by

(1) creating a shogunate
(2) producing porcelain and block printing
(3) introducing Hinduism as a major philosophy
(4) devising a set of laws and carving them on rocks and pillars

9 A primary goal of European Crusaders fighting in the Middle East was to

(1) establish markets for Italian merchants
(2) rescue Pope Urban II from the Byzantines
(3) halt the advance of Mongol armies in the Asian steppes
(4) secure access to Christian holy sites in Jerusalem

10 Increases in trade and commerce that occurred during the late Middle Ages in Europe resulted in

(1) lower living standards for guild members
(2) the development of more towns and cities
(3) a decline in rivalries between kings
(4) an increase in the number of self-sufficient manors

11 The writings of both Marco Polo and Ibn Battuta inspired

(1) exploration and trade
(2) important military expeditions
(3) movements for political freedom
(4) the spread of Islam to Southeast Asia

12 Nanjing, Venice, and Mogadishu were powerful and influential cities in the 13th century because they all

(1) developed agrarian-based economies
(2) served as religious pilgrimage sites
(3) established democratic governments
(4) took advantage of the factors of location

13 The West African empires of Ghana, Mali, and Songhai were able to thrive because

(1) they controlled the gold-salt trade
(2) their herds of cattle were in demand
(3) their armies took control of much of Africa
(4) they adopted Christianity as their primary religion

14 What was an immediate result of the Black Death?

(1) labor shortages
(2) overseas exploration
(3) decrease in anti-Semitism
(4) improvements in medical science

15 Which statement best expresses the philosophy of humanism?

(1) God selects those to be saved.
(2) The pope expresses the ultimate word of God.
(3) People have potential and can improve themselves by learning.
(4) A person's life on Earth is merely preparation for the afterlife.

16 Which development is most closely associated with early Inca achievements?

(1) inventing the wheel as a transportation device
(2) improving iron weapons
(3) expanding global trade
(4) adapting a mountainous environment

17 What was a major effect of the Columbian exchange?

(1) economic collapse in Europe
(2) introduction of new food crops to Europe
(3) decrease in European population
(4) expansion of democratic rights throughout Europe

18 Which policy is a country using when it regulates its colonies' imports and exports to produce a favorable balance of trade?

(1) embargo   (3) mercantilism
(2) outsourcing   (4) transmigration

Base your answer to question 19 on the diagram below and on your knowledge of social studies.

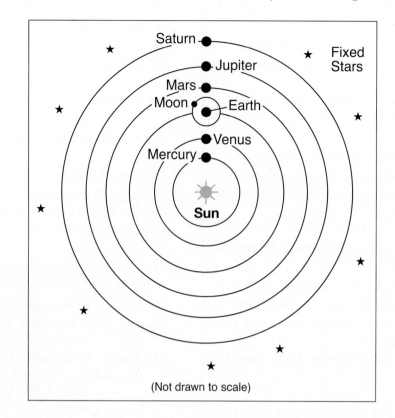

(Not drawn to scale)

19 Which scientist is most directly associated with formulating this view of the solar system?

(1) Ptolemy
(2) Descartes
(3) Copernicus
(4) Newton

20 Akbar the Great tried to unify the Mughal Empire and create peace between the different people of India by

(1) promoting a policy of religious toleration
(2) forcing all people to adopt modern dress
(3) building the Taj Mahal to inspire healing
(4) establishing Buddhism as the state religion

21 • Signing of the Magna Carta
• Signing of the Petition of Right
• Passage of the English Bill of Rights

In England, these events were instrumental in

(1) supporting a disarmament policy
(2) promoting government control of the economy
(3) justifying the acquisition of territory in foreign lands
(4) developing parliamentary democracy

22 Between 1500 and 1750, which commercial products were produced on Latin American plantations using enslaved laborers?

(1) corn and squash
(2) bananas and tea
(3) sugar and tobacco
(4) potatoes and wool

23 The ideas of Enlightenment philosophers were based on

(1) efforts to achieve salvation
(2) faith in human reason
(3) traditional practices
(4) the inevitability of poverty

24 Toussaint L'Ouverture and José de San Martín are leaders best known for

(1) leading independence movements
(2) supporting religious reforms
(3) promoting civil disobedience
(4) opposing democracy

Base your answer to question 25 on the poster below and on your knowledge of social studies.

**The Tsar, the Priest and the Rich Man
on the Shoulders of the Labouring People**

ЦАРЬ, ПОП И БОГАЧ

НА ПЛЕЧАХ У ТРУДОВОГО НАРОДА.

Source: A. Apsit, Coloured Lithograph, 1918 (adapted)

25 In early 20th-century Russia, which group may have gained support by circulating this poster?

(1) aristocracy   (3) monarchists
(2) Bolsheviks   (4) Orthodox clergy

26 Which course of action does the theory of laissez-faire suggest a government should follow?

   (1) providing help for people in need

   (2) establishing businesses to create jobs

   (3) letting natural laws regulate the economy

   (4) controlling the mineral resources of a country

27 One effect of the British landlord system in Ireland in the mid-1800s and in India in the early 1900s was that these landlord systems

   (1) contributed to famine and suffering

   (2) allowed local economies to prosper

   (3) emphasized food crops over mining

   (4) led to an agrarian revolution

28 Commodore Matthew Perry is best known for taking which action?

   (1) leading the British East India Company

   (2) rescuing Europeans during the Boxer Rebellion

   (3) justifying European spheres of influence in China

   (4) opening Japan to American and European influences

29 During World War I, developments in military technology led to

   (1) an early victory by the Allied powers

   (2) the establishment of industrial capitalism

   (3) the use of poisonous gas and submarine attacks

   (4) an increase in ethnic tension in western Europe

30 One major reason the League of Nations failed was that it

   (1) was not included in the Versailles Treaty

   (2) was controlled by communist Russia

   (3) frightened many nations with its large military force

   (4) lacked the support of many of the major world powers during crises

31 Which geographic characteristic of Japan most influenced its decision to engage in imperialism in the early to mid-20th century?

   (1) mountainous terrain

   (2) lack of natural resources

   (3) abundance of rivers

   (4) island location

32 Which condition was a result of Joseph Stalin's command economy?

   (1) Peasants were encouraged to sell surplus grain for personal profit.

   (2) The production of consumer goods increased.

   (3) National revenue increased allowing for greater individual spending.

   (4) The government controlled agriculture through collective farms.

33 After World War I, the rise of Benito Mussolini in Italy and the rise of Adolf Hitler in Germany are most closely associated with

   (1) the development of fascism

   (2) the desire for containment

   (3) an emphasis on democratic traditions

   (4) a return to conservative religious practices

34 What was a major reason the Soviet Union established satellite states in Eastern Europe after World War II?

   (1) developing better trade relations with the West

   (2) creating a buffer zone against future invasions

   (3) participating in United Nations peacekeeping missions

   (4) controlling the Organization of Petroleum Exporting Countries (OPEC)

Base your answer to question 35 on the excerpt below and on your knowledge of social studies.

... The achievement gap between black and white students in South Africa is enormous. In the province of Western Cape, only 2 out of 1,000 sixth-graders in predominantly black schools performed at grade level on a math test in 2005, compared with 2 out of 3 children in schools once reserved for whites that are now integrated, but generally in more affluent [wealthier] neighborhoods....

— Celia W. Dugger

35 Which underlying historical factor most significantly contributed to this achievement gap?

(1) inequalities existing between the races under apartheid
(2) economic sanctions placed on school communities
(3) lack of governmental support for white educational programs
(4) a period of political assassinations and civil war

36 "India Partitioned at Independence"
"Serbs Fuel Conflict in Kosovo"
"Grievances Divide Hutu and Tutsi"

Which conclusion do these headlines support?

(1) Cultural diversity leads to stable societies.
(2) Ethnic and religious differences have been sources of tension.
(3) Economic cooperation can overcome political issues.
(4) Gender differences are more powerful than differences in social status.

37 Many conflicts in the Middle East during the post–World War II period have directly resulted from

(1) the dissolution of the Arab League
(2) border clashes between Iran and China
(3) disputes related to Palestine
(4) the partition of Egypt

Base your answer to question 38 on the passage below and on your knowledge of social studies.

... More than 30 years after "Year Zero" and more than a decade after the "return to democracy," Cambodia remains in a league of its own — miserable, corrupt and compassionless. Only the toughest and the most unscrupulous can "make it" and get ahead. There is hardly any social net to speak of; the savage insanity of the Khmer Rouge has been replaced with savage capitalism, but often with the same people in charge....

— Andre Vitchek,
"A Tortured History and Unanswered Questions"

38 What does the author of this 2006 passage conclude?

(1) As democracy develops, circumstances will improve.
(2) Though governments change, circumstances often remain the same.
(3) New leadership is determined to replace the Khmer Rouge.
(4) Harsh living conditions have caused people to rely extensively on a social net.

39 Which action was taken by Deng Xiaoping to improve the economy of China?

(1) discouraging foreign investment
(2) encouraging some capitalist practices
(3) organizing the Red Guard
(4) practicing glasnost

40 Which revolution led to increases in global food production as a result of using genetically altered seeds and large amounts of chemical fertilizers and pesticides?

(1) Cultural   (3) Scientific
(2) Glorious   (4) Green

Base your answer to question 41 on the cartoon below and on your knowledge of social studies.

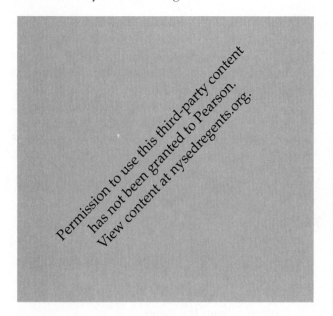

Permission to use this third-party content has not been granted to Pearson. View content at nysedregents.org.

41 What is the main idea of this 2010 cartoon?

(1) Pakistan plays a minor role in the affairs of Afghanistan.

(2) The United States and Pakistan will join forces to remove the Taliban.

(3) Disputes over water rights between Pakistan and Afghanistan continue to create challenges.

(4) The Taliban will pose a threat to Afghanistan when the United States leaves.

42 The World Trade Organization (WTO), North American Free Trade Agreement (NAFTA), and European Union (EU) all share the primary goal of

(1) promoting space exploration and maintaining satellites

(2) increasing economic aid to developing nations

(3) encouraging trade between countries and lowering trade barriers

(4) developing regulations to preserve the environment

43 The use of the decimal system, advancements in medicine, and construction of Hindu temples are most closely associated with the golden age of the

(1) Abbassid dynasty   (3) Gupta Empire

(2) Han dynasty   (4) Roman Empire

44 One reason the Justinian Code was significant was that it

(1) became the foundation of the modern legal systems of many Western countries

(2) established the basis for the development of the Code of Hammurabi

(3) incorporated laws from all over Asia and Europe

(4) led to the protection of inalienable rights in Roman territories

45 Which technological development contributed most directly to the success of the Protestant Reformation?

(1) astrolabe   (3) wheel

(2) compass   (4) printing press

46 "Liberty, Equality, Fraternity" and "Peace, Land, and Bread" are slogans used by revolutionaries to represent

(1) frameworks for economic stability

(2) political and economic ideals

(3) plans for maintaining the social hierarchy

(4) methods of political reform

47 One way in which Otto von Bismarck and Camillo Cavour are similar is that both leaders

(1) followed a policy of isolationism

(2) adopted papal policies

(3) led an African independence movement

(4) promoted unification to form a new nation-state

48 Which title best completes the partial outline below?

> I._____
>
>   A. During the early 1800s, Napoleon Bonaparte's grand army sweeps across eastern Europe.
>
>   B. During World War I, Germany invades France through Belgium.
>
>   C. During World War II, Germans blitzkrieg western Europe.

(1) Importance of Rivers as Invasion Routes
(2) Stalemate of Trench Warfare
(3) Use of the Northern Plain for Conquest
(4) Role of Naval Blockades in Wars

49 One way in which the rule of Peter the Great in Russia and the rule of Emperor Meiji in Japan are similar is that both leaders

(1) emancipated serfs
(2) granted equality to women
(3) encouraged modernization
(4) ruled according to a constitution

50 One purpose of the Nuremberg Trials and of the Truth and Reconciliation Commission in South Africa was to

(1) address human rights abuses
(2) support the establishment of democratic governments
(3) establish free trade zones throughout the world
(4) provide encouragement to people behind the Iron Curtain

Answers to the essay questions are to be written in the separate essay booklet.

In developing your answer to Part II, be sure to keep this general definition in mind:

discuss means "to make observations about something using facts, reasoning, and argument; to present in some detail"

Part II

THEMATIC ESSAY QUESTION

Directions: Write a well-organized essay that includes an introduction, several paragraphs addressing the task below, and a conclusion.

Theme: Belief Systems—Movements

Belief systems are an established, orderly way that groups or individuals look at religious faith or philosophical principles. Some belief systems have spread outside their places of origin. The diffusion of these belief systems has affected other societies and regions in various ways.

Task:

Select *two* belief systems that have spread outside their place of origin and for *each*

- Discuss a central principle of this belief system
- Discuss how this belief system spread to another region
- Discuss an effect of the spread of this belief system on a society or region

You may use any belief system from your study of global history and geography. Some suggestions you might wish to consider include Buddhism, Confucianism, Judaism, Christianity, Islam, and communism.

You are *not* limited to these suggestions.

Do *not* use the United States as a region to which a belief system has spread.

Guidelines:

In your essay, be sure to

- Develop all aspects of the task
- Support the theme with relevant facts, examples, and details
- Use a logical and clear plan of organization, including an introduction and a conclusion that are beyond a restatement of the theme

NAME _____   SCHOOL _____

Part III

DOCUMENT-BASED QUESTION

This question is based on the accompanying documents. The question is designed to test your ability to work with historical documents. Some of these documents have been edited for the purposes of this question. As you analyze the documents, take into account the source of each document and any point of view that may be presented in the document. Keep in mind that the language used in a document may reflect the historical context of the time in which it was written.

Historical Context:

>   Throughout history, empires such as the ***Roman***, the ***Ottoman***, and the ***British*** have faced various problems that led to their decline. The decline of these empires has influenced changes in societies and regions.

Task: Using the information from the documents and your knowledge of global history, answer the questions that follow each document in Part A. Your answers to the questions will help you write the Part B essay in which you will be asked to

> Select ***two*** empires mentioned in the historical context and for ***each***
> * Describe problems that led to this empire's decline
> * Discuss how this empire's decline influenced change in a society and/or a region

In developing your answers to Part III, be sure to keep these general definitions in mind:

(a) <u>describe</u> means "to illustrate something in words or tell about it"

(b) <u>discuss</u> means "to make observations about something using facts, reasoning, and argument; to present in some detail"

Part A
Short-Answer Questions

Directions: Analyze the documents and answer the short-answer questions that follow each document in the space provided.

Document 1

Roman Empire A.D. 350–476

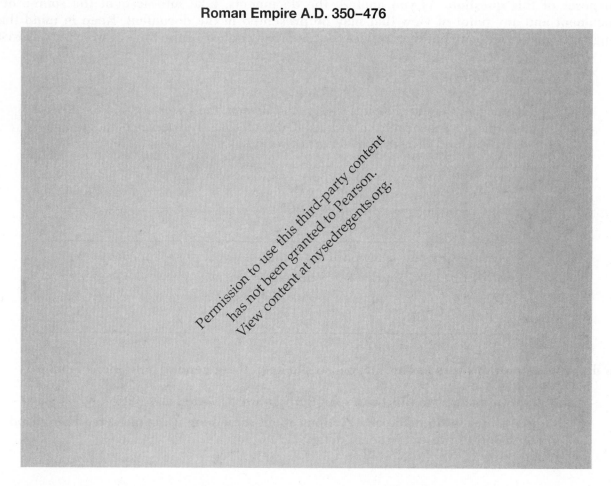

1 Based on the information shown on this map, state *one* problem that helped bring about the decline of the Roman Empire. [1]

_____

_____

Score ☐

Document 2

> … By the middle of the second century Italy [within the Roman Empire] was in a state of decline. By the time of Diocletian, at the opening of the fourth century, decay was apparent throughout the empire. Commerce had largely disappeared owing to the lack of customers, to piracy on the seas, and to insecurity of the roads on land. Generally speaking, purchasing power at that time was confined to the public officials, to the army officers, and to the great landowners. Trade in the everyday objects of daily use had all but disappeared, but trade in luxuries prospered. The cities in the west, omitting the places where government centered, were usually in decline; their commercial and industrial classes had disappeared, the old traders having been replaced by the traveling eastern merchant, of whom the Syrian was the most notorious. Foreign trade was sharply curtailed. At various times the government attempted to prohibit the export of various commodities, among them wine, oil, grain, salt, arms, iron, and gold. With this curbing of exports there was also an effort made to control certain imports such as is evidenced by the state monopoly in silk. These two movements hampered commercial contracts outside the empire and all but killed what was left of foreign trade.…

Source: Louis C. West, "The Economic Collapse of the Roman Empire," *The Classical Journal*, November 1932

2 According to Louis C. West, what were *two* economic problems the Roman Empire faced during its period of decline? [2]

(1) _____

_____

Score ☐

(2) _____

_____

Score ☐

Document 3

> ... As western Europe fell to the Germanic invasions, imperial power shifted to the Byzantine Empire, that is, the eastern part of the Roman Empire, with its capital at Constantinople. The eastern provinces of the former Roman Empire had always outnumbered those in the west. Its civilization was far older and it had larger cities, which were also more numerous than in the west....

Source: Steven Kreis, *The History Guide: Lectures on Ancient and Medieval European History*, Lecture 17, History Guide online

3 According to Steven Kreis, what was **one** change that resulted from the fall of the western half of the Roman Empire? [1]

_____

_____

Score ▢

Document 4

> The power of the [Ottoman] Empire was waning [fading] by 1683 when the second and last attempt was made to conquer Vienna. It failed. Without the conquest of Europe and the acquisition of significant new wealth, the Empire lost momentum and went into a slow decline.
>
> Several other factors contributed to the [Ottoman] Empire's decline:
> - Competition from trade from the Americas
> - Competition from cheap products from India and the Far East
> - Development of other trade routes
> - Rising unemployment within the Empire
> - Ottoman Empire became less centralised, and central control weakened
> - Sultans being less severe in maintaining rigorous standards of integrity in the administration of the Empire
> - Sultans becoming less sensitive to public opinion

Source: "Ottoman Empire (1301–1922)," BBC online, 2009 (adapted)

4a According to the BBC, what was *one economic* problem that contributed to the decline of the Ottoman Empire? [1]

_____

_____

Score ☐

b According to the BBC, what was *one political* problem that contributed to the decline of the Ottoman Empire? [1]

_____

_____

Score ☐

Document 5

> ... In 1875, the Slavic peoples living in the Ottoman provinces of Bosnia and Herzegovina (currently the state of Bosnia-Herzegovina), led an uprising against the Ottomans in order to gain their freedom. The general weakness of the Ottomans led two independent, neighbor Slavic states, Montenegro and Serbia, to aid the rebellion. Within a year, the rebellion spread to the Ottoman province of Bulgaria. The rebellion was part of a larger political movement called the Pan-Slavic movement, which had as its goal the unification of all Slavic peoples— most of whom were under the control of Austria, Germany, and the Ottoman Empire—into a single political unity under the protection of Russia. Anxious also to conquer the Ottomans themselves and seize Istanbul, the Russians allied with the rebels, Serbia, and Montenegro and declared war against the Ottomans....

Source: Richard Hooker, "European Imperialism and the Balkan Crisis," *The Ottomans*, World Cultures

5 According to Richard Hooker, what was **one** problem faced by the Ottomans during the decline of their Empire? [1]

_____

_____

Score ☐

Document 6

> ... Mustafa Kemal [Atatürk] was a secular nationalist who believed that all the inheritance of the Ottoman Empire should be abandoned and Turkey should be transformed into a modern European state. This involved less of a sudden break with the past than might appear. The *Tanzimat* reforms [between 1839 and 1876] had laid the foundations of a secular state, and the Young Turks, even while attempting to preserve the empire, had given a powerful impetus [motivation] to the cause of Turkish nationalism. During the war years [1914–1918], the secularization of education had proceeded and the universities and public positions had been opened to women. Certain of the law courts under the control of the religious authorities had been placed under the Ministry of Justice. A law in 1916 had reformed marriage and divorce....

Source: Peter Mansfield, *A History of the Middle East*, Viking

6 According to Peter Mansfield, what was **one** change that occurred as the Ottoman Empire declined and a new state of Turkey began to take shape? [1]

_____

_____

Score ☐

Document 7

The British Empire and Mandates in the Early 1920s

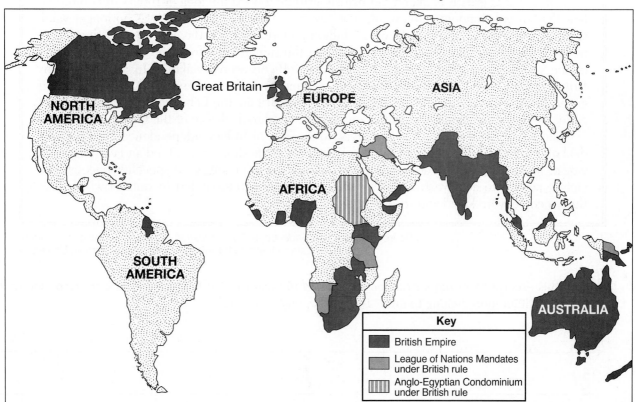

Source: Encyclopedia Britannica Kids (adapted)

7 Based on the information shown on this map, what was a problem the British faced that made it difficult to govern its empire? [1]

_____

_____

Score ☐

Document 8

> ... World War II greatly changed the British attitude toward the idea of India's freedom. The fear that an independent India would not pay its debt to Great Britain was no longer valid. Great Britain actually owed India over a billion pounds. Nor was the concern that there were not enough Indian military officers to take over the Indian army from the British. As a result of the war, more than fifteen thousand Indian officers were available. In addition, many British soldiers who returned home from serving in India realized how unpopular their government was among the Indian people. In Great Britain, the Labour Party under Clement Attlee defeated Winston Churchill's Conservatives and took charge of the government....
>
> The Labour Party, already sympathetic to the idea of India's independence, faced a great deal of unrest in India. The cold winter of 1945–46 made shortages of food and clothing even worse. Many nationalist leaders, recently released from prison, gave speeches encouraging violent actions to achieve freedom. In Calcutta, demonstrations led to riots in which over thirty people were killed and several hundred injured....

Source: *Indian Independence and the Question of Pakistan*, Choices Program, Watson Institute for International Studies, Brown University

8 Based on this excerpt from *Indian Independence and the Question of Pakistan*, what were **two** factors that made Great Britain more willing to grant India independence? [2]

(1)_____

_____

Score ☐

(2)_____

_____

Score ☐

Document 9

> … During the last 60 years [since 1928], the British Empire has broken apart. Most of the nations that were in the empire demanded and got their independence. With the empire gone, Britain lost a major source of wealth. At the same time, it lost industrial advantages it had enjoyed for many years.…

Source: Clare McHugh, *Scholastic World Cultures: Western Europe*, Scholastic, 1988

9 According to Clare McHugh, what was *one* change Great Britain faced with the breakup of its empire? [1]

_____

_____

Score [ ]

Part B
Essay

Directions: Write a well-organized essay that includes an introduction, several paragraphs, and a conclusion. Use evidence from *at least* **four** documents in your essay. Support your response with relevant facts, examples, and details. Include additional outside information.

Historical Context:

Throughout history, empires such as the **Roman**, the **Ottoman**, and the **British** have faced various problems that led to their decline. The decline of these empires has influenced changes in societies and regions.

Task: Using the information from the documents and your knowledge of global history, write an essay in which you

Select *two* empires mentioned in the historical context and for *each*
- Describe problems that led to this empire's decline
- Discuss how this empire's decline influenced change in a society and/or a region

Guidelines:

In your essay, be sure to
- Develop all aspects of the task
- Incorporate information from *at least* **four** documents
- Incorporate relevant outside information
- Support the theme with relevant facts, examples, and details
- Use a logical and clear plan of organization, including an introduction and a conclusion that are beyond a restatement of the theme

DRAFT PROTOTYPES FOR
GLOBAL HISTORY AND GEOGRAPHY II
REGENTS EXAM

DRAFT APRIL 2016

DRAFT April 2016

DRAFT PROTOTYPES FOR
GLOBAL HISTORY AND GEOGRAPHY REGENTS EXAM

PART 1—STIMULUS-BASED MULTIPLE-CHOICE QUESTIONS

MCQ SET #1

> "...Nor is there liberty if the power of judging is not separate from legislative power and from executive power. If it were jointed to legislative power, the power over the life and liberty of the citizens would be arbitrary, for the judge would be the legislator. If it were joined to executive power, the judge could have the force of an oppressor..."

Source: Montesquieu, *The Spirit of the Laws*

1. Which principle is best supported by this excerpt?

    1. <u>Separation of Powers</u>
    2. Divine Right
    3. Universal Suffrage
    4. Self Determination

DRAFT

Task Model	3: Students are given stimuli and asked to identify support for given claim (bound in same timeframe/event/space). Must require student to draw on knowledge rather than the straight comprehension of text.
Framework Reference	10.2a: Enlightenment thinkers developed political philosophies based on natural laws, which included the concepts of social contract, consent of the governed, and the rights of citizens. ➤ Students will examine at least three Enlightenment thinkers, including John Locke, Baron de Montesquieu, and Jean-Jacques Rousseau, and key ideas from their written works.

2. Which group's ideas are best represented by this excerpt?

   1. <u>Enlightenment philosophers</u>
   2. Absolute Monarchs
   3. Communists
   4. Missionaries

Task Model	3: Students are given stimuli and asked to identify support for given claim (bound in same timeframe/event/space). Must require student to draw on knowledge rather than the straight comprehension of text.
Framework Reference	10.2a: Enlightenment thinkers developed political philosophies based on natural laws, which included the concepts of social contract, consent of the governed, and the rights of citizens. ➤ Students will examine at least three Enlightenment thinkers, including John Locke, Baron de Montesquieu, and Jean-Jacques Rousseau, and key ideas from their written works.

DRAFT

3

MCQ SET #2

China—the Cake of Kings and ... of Emperors

China

Source: *The Little Journal*, published in France, January 16, 1898 (Bibliotèque Nationale de France)

DRAFT

3. In this cartoon, the Chinese are reacting to the process of

1. imperialism
2. industrialization
3. collectivization
4. unification

Task Model	6: Students are given a stimulus and asked to identify significance as part of change or part of continuity in history (2a, 1a)
Framework Reference	10.4a: European industrialized states and Japan sought to play a dominant role in the world and to control natural resources for political, economic, and cultural reasons. ➤ Students will trace how imperial powers politically and economically controlled territories and people, including direct and indirect rule in Africa (South Africa, Congo, and one other territory), India, Indochina, and spheres of influence in China.

4

4. Which statement best represents a reason Japan is seated at the table in this cartoon?
   1. <u>The Meiji Restoration industrialized Japan.</u>
   2. The Tokugawa Shogunate centralized Japan's government.
   3. Japan was invited as an ally of China.
   4. Japan had become militarily stronger than most European powers

Task Model	7: Students are given a stimulus and identify a central cause of the described phenomenon (2b, 1c)
Framework Reference	10.3c: Shifts in population from rural to urban areas led to social changes in class structure, family structure, and the daily lives of people. ➤ Students will investigate the social, political, and economic impacts of industrialization in Victorian England and Meiji Japan and compare and contrast them. 10.4a: European industrialized states and Japan sought to play a dominant role in the world and to control natural resources for political, economic, and cultural reasons. ➤ Students will trace how imperial powers politically and economically controlled territories and people, including direct and indirect rule in Africa (South Africa, Congo, and one other territory), India, Indochina, and spheres of influence in China. 10.4b: Those who faced being colonized engaged in varying forms of resistance and adaptation to colonial rule with varying degrees of success. ➤ Students will investigate how Japan reacted to the threat of Western imperialism in Asia.

DRAFT

MCQ SET #3

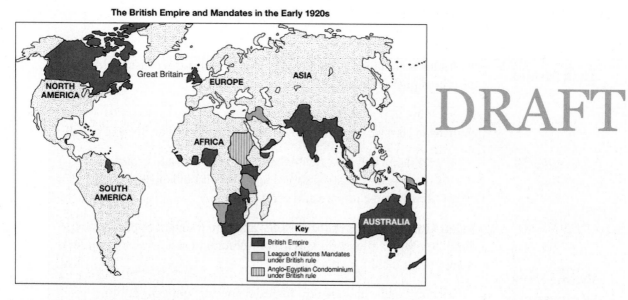

The British Empire and Mandates in the Early 1920s

DRAFT

Source: Encyclopedia Britannica Kids (adapted)

5. A historian could best use this map to study which topic?
   1. <u>imperialism</u>
   2. détente
   3. the transatlantic Slave Trade
   4. United Nations membership

Task Model	1: Students are given stimuli and asked to evaluate and classify (identify) best use
Framework Reference	10.4a: European industrialized states and Japan sought to play a dominant role in the world and to control natural resources for political, economic, and cultural reasons. ➢ Students will trace how imperial powers politically and economically controlled territories and people, including direct and indirect rule in Africa (South Africa, Congo, and one other territory), India, Indochina, and spheres of influence in China.

6. What later development would change a political situation shown on this map?

   1. Augusto Pinochet's human rights abuses
   2. <u>Gandhi's non-violent resistance</u>
   3. Mao Zedong's communist revolution
   4. Ho Chi Minh's nationalist movement

Task Model	6: Students are given a stimuli and asked to identify significance as part of change or part of continuity in history 7: Students are given a stimulus and identifies a central cause of the described phenomenon
Framework Reference	10.7a: Independence movements in India and Indochina developed in response to European control. ➤ Students will explore Gandhi's nonviolent nationalist movement and nationalist efforts led by the Muslim League aimed at the masses that resulted in a British-partitioned subcontinent.

DRAFT

7

MCQ SET #4

Excerpt from a speech by Winston S. Churchill, March 5, 1946 at Westminster College in Fulton, Missouri

> ...From Stettin in the Baltic to Trieste in the Adriatic, an iron curtain has descended across the Continent. Behind that line lie all the capitals of the ancient states of Central and Eastern Europe. Warsaw, Berlin, Prague, Vienna, Budapest, Belgrade, Bucharest and Sofia, all these famous cities and the populations around them lie in what I must call the Soviet sphere, and all are subject in one form or another, not only to Soviet influence but to a very high and, in some cases, increasing measure of control from Moscow. Athens alone—Greece with its immortal glories—is free to decide its future at an election under British, American, and French observation. The Russian-dominated Polish Government has been encouraged to make enormous and wrongful inroads upon Germany, and mass expulsions of millions of Germans on a scale grievous and undreamed-of are now taking place. The Communist parties, which were very small in all these Eastern States of Europe, have been raised to pre-eminence and power far beyond their numbers and are seeking everywhere to obtain totalitarian control. Police governments are prevailing in nearly every case, and so far, except in Czechoslovakia, there is no true democracy....

Source: Winston Churchill, *The Sinews of Peace*," March 5, 1946, The Churchill Centre

7. Which important issue does Winston Churchill discuss in this excerpt?

    1. <u>increasing tension between non-communist and communist nations</u>
    2. buildup of conventional armaments leading up to World War I
    3. rising concerns over the unification of Germany
    4. expanding role of the British Empire in world politics

DRAFT

Task Model	8: Students are given a stimulus and identifies a central effect of the described phenomena
Framework Reference	10.6a: The Cold War originated from tensions near the end of World War II as plans for peace were made and implemented. The Cold War was characterized by competition for power and ideological differences between the United States and the Soviet Union. ➢ Students will compare and contrast how peace was conceived at Yalta and Potsdam with what happened in Europe in the four years after World War II (i.e., Soviet occupation of Eastern Europe, Truman Doctrine, Berlin blockade, NATO).

8. Which organization formed in response to the situation Churchill described in this speech?

    1. <u>North Atlantic Treaty Organization (NATO)</u>
    2. League of Nations
    3. Alliance of Central Powers
    4. European Union (EU)

Task Model	8: Students are given a stimulus and identifies a central effect of the described phenomena
Framework Reference	10.6a: The Cold War originated from tensions near the end of World War II as plans for peace were made and implemented. The Cold War was characterized by competition for power and ideological differences between the United States and the Soviet Union. ➢ Students will compare and contrast how peace was conceived at Yalta and Potsdam with what happened in Europe in the four years after World War II (i.e., Soviet occupation of Eastern Europe, Truman Doctrine, Berlin blockade, NATO).

DRAFT

9

MCQ SET #5

Four Newspaper Headlines from the Twentieth Century:

A. THE BERLIN WALL TORN DOWN
B. TRUMAN DOCTRINE AIDS GREECE AND TURKEY
C. THE U.S.S.R. PLACES NUCLEAR MISSILES IN CUBA
D. NEHRU CALLS FOR INDIA TO BE NON-ALIGNED

9. Which claim is supported by this set of headlines?

1. <u>The Cold War impacted countries other than the Soviet Union and the United States</u>
2. Independence movements developed as a result of Cold War Tensions
3. Globalization is the result of the proliferation of technological and economic networks
4. The Organization of Petroleum Exporting Countries (OPEC) developed as a result of Cold War tensions

Task Model	4: Students are asked to select a plausible claim that logically flows from evidence presented in stimuli
Framework Reference	10.6b: The Cold War was a period of confrontations and attempts at peaceful coexistence.

10. Which of these headlines represents the event that occurred *last*?

1. <u>A</u>
2. B
3. C
4. D

DRAFT

Task Model	N/A
Framework Reference	10.6b: The Cold War was a period of confrontations and attempts at peaceful coexistence.

PART 2—SHORT ANSWER QUESTION SETS

Short Answer Question Set Structure	
Question 1 Historical or Geographic Context (using doc 1)	Historical Context—the historical circumstances surrounding this event/idea/historical development. Using document 1, explain how the historical context affected a historical development in the document. **OR** Geographic Context—where this historical development is taking place, and why it is taking place there. Using document 1, explain the geographic context of the developments shown on the map.
Question 2 Sourcing (using doc 2)	1. Identify bias, point of view, audience, or purpose. 2. Explain how that factor affects the document as a reliable source of evidence.
Question 3 Relationship between documents: • Causation • Turning Point • Comparison (using both docs)	Identify and explain a cause and effect relationship between the events or ideas found in these documents. (Set 1) _____ A turning point is a significant event, idea, or historical event that brings about change. It can be local, regional, national or global. Identify a turning point associated with the events or ideas found in these documents and explain why it is a turning point. (Set 2) _____ Identify and explain a similarity or a difference between the ideas presented in these documents. (Set 3)

DRAFT

11

SHORT ANSWER QUESTION SET #1

Document 1

Select Articles from the Treaty of Versailles

Article 159

The German military forces shall be demobilised and reduced as prescribed hereinafter.

Article 231

The Allied and Associated Governments affirm and Germany accepts the responsibility of Germany and her allies for causing all the loss and damage to which the Allied and Associated Governments and their nationals have been subjected as a consequence of the war imposed upon them by the aggression of Germany and her allies.

Article 232

The Allied and Associated Governments, however, require, and Germany undertakes, that she will make compensation for all damage done to the civilian population of the Allied and Associated Powers and to their property during the period of the belligerency of each as an Allied or Associated Power against Germany by such aggression by land, by sea and from the air, and in general all damage as defined in Annex l hereto.

Source: The Versailles Treaty June 28, 1919

DRAFT

QUESTION 1
Historical Context—the historical circumstances surrounding this event/idea/historical development.

Using Document 1, explain how the historical context affected the development of the Versailles Treaty.

Framework Reference	10.5c: The devastation of the world wars and use of total war led people to explore ways to prevent future world wars. ➤ Students will examine international efforts to work together to build stability and peace, including Wilson's Fourteen Points, the Treaty of Versailles, the League of Nations, and the United Nations.

Document 2

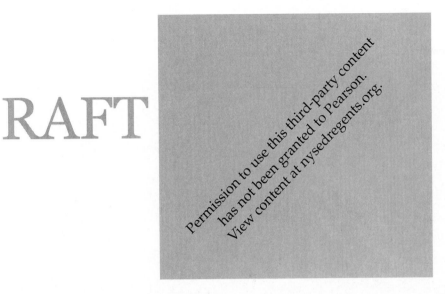

Source: Daniel Fitzpatrick, *St. Louis Post-Dispatch*, October 19, 1930

QUESTION 2

a. **Using document 2, identify Daniel Fitzpatrick's point of view shown in this cartoon.**

b. **Explain how Daniel Fitzpatrick's point of view affects document 2 as a reliable source of evidence.**

------------------------ *Or* ------------------------

a. **Using document 2, identify Daniel Fitzpatrick's purpose for creating this cartoon.**

b. **Explain how Daniel Fitzpatrick's purpose affects document 2 as a reliable source of evidence.**

Framework Reference	10.5d: Nationalism and ideology played a significant role in shaping the period between the world wars. ➤ Students will examine the role of nationalism and the development of the National Socialist state under Hitler in Germany.

QUESTION 3

Identify and explain a cause and effect relationship between the events or ideas found in these documents.

SHORT ANSWER QUESTION SET #2

Document 1

Growth of the Japanese Empire, 1931–41

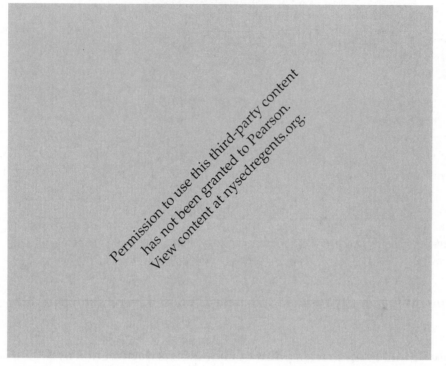

QUESTION 1

Geographic Context—where this historical development is taking place, and why it is taking place there.

Using document 1, explain how the geographic context affected the development of the Japanese Empire.

Framework Reference	10.4 a: European industrialized states and Japan sought to play a dominant role in the world and to control natural resources for political, economic, and cultural reasons. ➢ Students will trace how imperial powers politically and economically controlled territories and people, including direct and indirect rule in Africa (South Africa, Congo, and one other territory), India, Indochina, and spheres of influence in China.

DRAFT

14

Document 2

SOURCE: Dr. Tatsuichiro Akizuki, recalling memories as a physician practicing medicine in Nagasaki, on August 9, 1945, published in his book *Nagasaki 1945*.

There was a blinding white flash of light, and the next moment — *Bang! Crack!* A huge impact like a gigantic blow smote [struck] down upon our bodies, our heads and our hospital. I lay flat— I didn't know whether or not of my own volition [choice]. Then down came piles of debris, slamming into my back....

All the buildings I could see were on fire: large ones and small ones and those with straw-thatched roofs. Further off along the valley, Urakami Church, the largest Catholic church in the east, was ablaze. The technical school, a large two-storeyed wooden building, was on fire, as were many houses and the distant ordnance factory. Electricity poles were wrapped in flame like so many pieces of kindling. Trees on the near-by hills were smoking, as were the leaves of sweet potatoes in the fields. To say that everything burned is not enough. It seemed as if the earth itself emitted fire and smoke, flames that writhed up and erupted from underground. The sky was dark, the ground was scarlet, and in between hung clouds of yellowish smoke. Three kinds of colour – black, yellow, and scarlet loomed ominously over the people, who ran about like so many ants seeking to escape. What had happened? Urakami Hospital had not been bombed—I understood that much. But that ocean of fire, that sky of smoke! It seemed like the end of the world....

Source: Dr. Tatsuichiro Akizuki, *Nagasaki 1945*, Quartet Books

QUESTION 2

    a. **Using document 2, identify Dr. Tatsuichiro Akizuki's purpose for writing this account.**

    b. **Explain how purpose affects document 2 as a reliable source of evidence.**

Framework Reference	10.5 b: Technological developments increased the extent of damage and casualties in both World War I and World War II. ➤ Students will compare and contrast the technologies utilized in both World War I and World War II, noting the human and environmental devastation.

DRAFT

QUESTION 3

A turning point is a significant event, idea, or historical event that brings about change. It can be local, regional, national or global.

Identify a turning point associated with the events or ideas found in these documents and explain why it is a turning point.

15

SHORT ANSWER QUESTION SET #3

Document 1

Macgregor Laird, Scottish explorer and shipbuilder, written after travelling by steamship up the Niger River in West Africa between 1832 and 1834.

We have the power in our hands, moral, physical, and mechanical; the first, based on the Bible; the second, upon the wonderful adaptation of the Anglo-Saxon race to all climates, situations, and circumstances . . . the third, bequeathed [given] to us by the immortal James Watt. By his invention [of the steam engine] every river is laid open to us, time and distance are shortened. If his spirit is allowed to witness the success of his invention here on earth, I can conceive no application of it that would meet his approbation [approval] more than seeing the mighty streams of the Mississippi and the Amazon, the Niger and the Nile, the Indus and the Ganges, stemmed by hundreds of steam-vessels, carrying the glad tidings of "peace and good will towards men" into the dark places of the earth which are now filled with cruelty. This power, which has only been in existence for a quarter of a century, has rendered rivers truly "the highway of nations," and made easy what it would have been difficult if not impossible, to accomplish with out it....

Source: Macgregor Laird and R. A. K. Oldfield, Narrative of an Expedition into the Interior of Africa by the River Niger in the Steam-Vessels Quorra and Alburkah in 1832, 1833, 1834, Volume II, London, Richard Bentley, 1837

QUESTION 1
Historical Context—the historical circumstances surrounding this historical development.

Using the narrative provided in document 1, explain how the historical context affected the development of British imperial attitudes.

------------------------ *Or* ------------------------

Using the narrative provided in document 2, explain how the geographic context affected the development of British imperial attitudes.

Framework Reference	10.4a: European industrialized states and Japan sought to play a dominant role in the world and to control natural resources for political, economic, and cultural reasons.
	➤ Students will trace how imperial powers politically and economically controlled territories and people, including direct and indirect rule in Africa (South Africa, Congo, and one other territory), India, Indochina, and spheres of influence in China.

16

Document 2

Nnamdi Azikiwe, nationalist leader in Nigeria, speech at the British Peace Congress in London, addressing British colonialism in Africa, 1947.

. . . Socially, the ogre [monster] of racial segregation and discrimination makes it extremely difficult for the colonial to develop his personality to the full. Education is obtainable but limited to the privileged. Hospitals are not available to the great number of the people but only to a negligible [small] minority. Public services are lacking in many respects; there are not sufficient water supplies, surfaced roads, postal services and communications systems in most communities of Nigeria. The prisons are medieval, the penal [criminal] code is oppressive, and religious freedom is a pearl of great price.

Source: *Zik: A Selection from the Speeches of Nnamdi Azikiwe*, Cambridge University Press

QUESTION 2

    a. **Using document 2, identify Nnamdi Azikiwe's point of view expressed in this speech.**

    b. **Explain how Nnamdi Azikiwe's point of view affects document 2 as a reliable source of evidence.**

Framework Reference	10.4a: European industrialized states and Japan sought to play a dominant role in the world and to control natural resources for political, economic, and cultural reasons.
	
	  ➤ Students will trace how imperial powers politically and economically controlled territories and people, including direct and indirect rule in Africa (South Africa, Congo, and one other territory), India, Indochina, and spheres of influence in China.
	
	10.7b: African independence movements gained strength as European states struggled economically after World War II. European efforts to limit African nationalist movements were often unsuccessful.
	
	  ➤ Students will explore at least two of these three African independence movements: Ghana, Algeria, Kenya.

QUESTION 3:

Identify and explain a similarity or a difference between the ideas presented in these documents.

17

PART 3—EXTENDED ESSAY

An enduring issue is an issue that exists across time. It is one that many societies have attempted to address with varying degrees of success.

In your essay

- Identify and define an enduring issue raised by this set of documents.
- Using your knowledge of Social Studies and evidence from the documents, argue why the issue you selected is significant and how it has endured across time.

Be sure to

- Identify the issue based on a historically accurate interpretation of three documents.
- Define the issue using evidence from *at least* **three** documents
- Argue that this is a significant issue that has endured by showing:
  - How the issue has affected people or been affected by people
  - How the issue has continued to be an issue or changed over time
- Include outside information from your knowledge of social studies and evidence from the documents.

DRAFT

Guidelines for Part 3 Construction

- Total of five documents

- At least **one** document connected to Framework key ideas 10.1 through 10.6

- At least **two** documents connected to Framework key ideas 10.7 through 10.10

- At least **one** document is a visual (cartoon, map, photograph, chart, timeline, graph)

- More than one enduring issue to be found within each document

- Inclusion of common enduring issues to be found across document set

- Availability of potential outside information considered

DRAFT

PART 3—EXTENDED ESSAY

DOCUMENT SET #1

DOCUMENT 1

Julius Streicher, member of the Nazi Party, March 31, 1933

German national comrades! The ones who are guilty of this insane crime, this malicious atrocity propaganda and incitement to boycott, are the Jews in Germany. They have called on their racial comrades abroad to fight against the German people. They have transmitted the lies and calumnies abroad. Therefore the Reich leadership of the German movement for freedom have decided, in defense against criminal incitement, to impose a boycott of all Jewish shops, department stores, offices, etc., beginning on Saturday, 1 April 1933, at 10 a.m. We are calling on you, German women and men, to comply with this boycott. Do not buy in Jewish shops and department stores, do not go to Jewish lawyers, avoid Jewish physicians. Show the Jews that they cannot besmirch Germany and disparage its honor without punishment. Whoever acts against this appeal proves thereby that he stands on the side of Germany's enemies. Long live the honorable Field Marshal from the Great War, Reich President Paul v. Hindenburg! Long live the Führer and Reich Chancellor Adolf Hitler! Long live the German people and the holy German fatherland!

Source: *Schulthess' europäischer Geschichtskalender. Neue Folge*, ed. by Ulrich Thürauf, Vol. 49 (Munich: Beck, 1933), p. 81

DRAFT

Framework Reference	10.5 d: Nationalism and ideology played a significant role in shaping the period between the world wars. ➤ Students will examine the role of nationalism and the development of the National Socialist state under Hitler in Germany.

DOCUMENT 2

Miron Dolot, eyewitness account of growing up in Ukraine under Stalin's Soviet policy

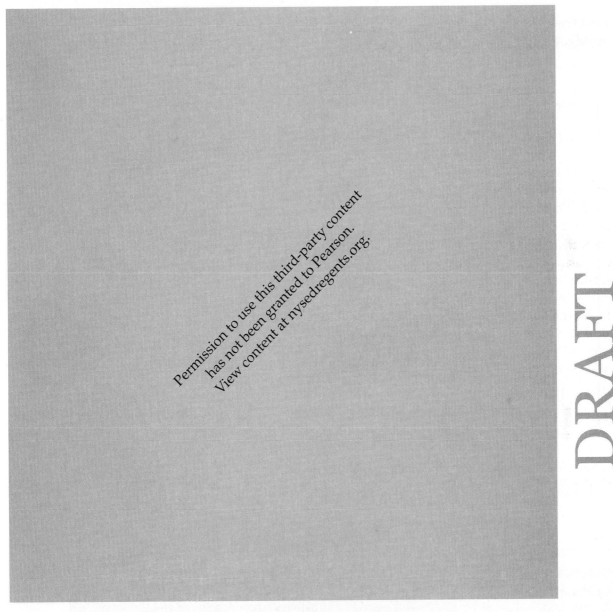

Source: Miron Dolot, *Execution by Hunger: The Hidden Holocaust*, 1985

Framework Reference	10.5 e: Human atrocities and mass murders occurred in this time period.
	➤ Students will examine the atrocities against the Armenians, examine the Ukrainian Holodomor, and examine the Holocaust.

DOCUMENT 3

Excerpt from unanimously adopted Resolution by the United Nations General Assembly, December 9, 1948

Article 1

The Contracting Parties confirm that genocide, whether committed in time of peace or in time of war, is a crime under international law which they undertake to prevent and to punish.

Article 2

In the present Convention, genocide means any of the following acts committed with intent to destroy, in whole or in part, a national, ethnical, racial or religious group, as such:

- (a) Killing members of the group;
- (b) Causing serious bodily or mental harm to members of the group;
- (c) Deliberately inflicting on the group conditions of life calculated to bring about its physical destruction in whole or in part;
- (d) Imposing measures intended to prevent births within the group;
- (e) Forcibly transferring children of the group to another group.

Source: United Nations General Assembly, December 9, 1948, Resolution 260 (III) A.

Framework Reference	10.10 a: Following World War II, the United Nations Universal Declaration of Human Rights (1948) was written. This provides a set of principles to guide efforts to protect threatened groups. ➤ Students will examine the articles contained in the UN Universal Declaration of Human Rights.

DOCUMENT 4

Debbie Wolfe writes about growing up as a white child under apartheid

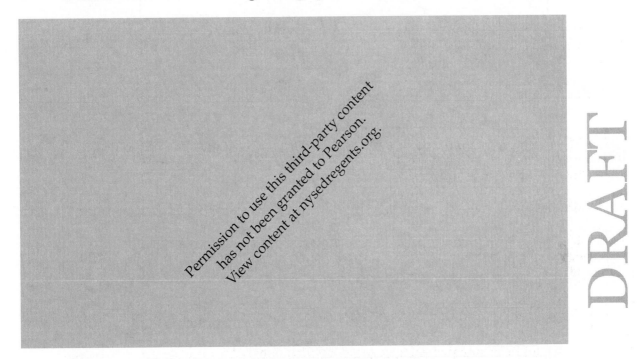

Source: Debbie Wolf, *I Grew Up In South Africa During Apartheid*, Huffington Post, December 6, 2013

Framework Reference	10.10c: Historical and contemporary violations of human rights can be evaluated, using the principles and articles established within the UN Universal Declaration of Human Rights. ➤ Students will examine the policy of apartheid in South Africa and the growth of the anti-apartheid movements, exploring Nelson Mandela's role in these movements and in the post-apartheid period.

DOCUMENT 5

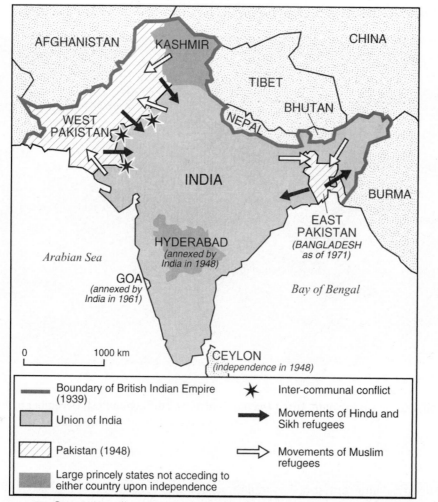

Source: https://en.wikipedia.org/wiki/File:Partition_of_India-en.svg (adapted)

Framework Reference	10.7a: Independence movements in India and Indochina developed in response to European control.